Government Institutes
Internet Series

REF

Environmental

Guide to the
Internet

Fourth Edition

Toni Murphy
Carol Briggs-Erickson

Government Institutes
Rockville, MD

Government Institutes, Inc., 4 Research Place, Rockville, Maryland 20850, USA.

ISBN: 0-86587-643-6

Printed in the United States of America

General Contents

Preface xxxvii

About the Authors. xli

CHAPTER 1 - Introduction to the Internet and the World Wide Web 1

CHAPTER 2 - Environmental Discussion Groups and Mailing Lists. 7

CHAPTER 3 - Environmental Newsgroups 85

CHAPTER 4 - Environmental Newsletters and Journals 103

CHAPTER 5 - Environmental World Wide Web Sites 161

Index 369

Table of Contents

Chapter 1 - Introduction to the Internet and the World Wide Web 1

    Bibliographic References 5

Chapter 2 - Environmental Discussion Groups and Mailing Lists 7

    ACN-L (Aquatic Conservation Network) 9
    AE (Alternative Energy). 9
    AERE-L (Association of Environmental and Resource Economists). 10
    AEROSO-L 10
    AFWATER 10
    AG-IMPACT (Agricultural and Environmental Impact) 11
    AGLAW-L 11
    AGRIC-L 11
    AIRPOLLUTION-BIOLOGY 12
    ALIENS-L 12
    ALT-TRANSP 12
    AMP 13
    AMPHIBIANDECLINE 13
    AR-NEWS (Animal Rights News) 13
    AR-VIEWS (Animal Rights Views) 14
    ASN (Audubon Student Network 14
    AUDUBON 14
    AUDUBON-CHAT 15
    AUDUBON-NEWS 15
    BALLERINA-L 15
    BBLMTAB 16
    BCWATERSHED (Boulder Creek Watershed, Colorado) 16
    BEE-L 17
    BIODIV-L (Biodiversity Information Network/Agenda 21) 17

BIOENERGY 17
BIOGROUP (Bioremediation Group) 18
BIOREGIONAL 18
BIOSPH-L 18
BIRDBAND (Bird Bander's Forum) 19
BIRDCHAT (National Birding Hotline Cooperative) 19
CAREERPRO 19
CARNIVORE-L (Carnivore Research) 20
CA-WATER (California Water) 20
CBCN-L (Canadian Botanical Conservation Network) 20
CCSEA-L (Canadian Coastal Science and Engineering Association) . . . 21
CEAM-USERS (Center for Exposure Assessment
 Modelling Software Users) 21
CECNET (Commission for Environmental Cooperation) 21
CERES-L (Collaborative Environments for Conserving
 Earth Resources) 22
CICHLID-L (Chichlid Systematics) 22
CITES-L (Convention on International Trade in Endangered Species) . 22
CITNET-LIST (Citizens Network for Sustainable Development) 23
CLIM-ECON (Economics of Climate Variability and Global Change) . 23
CMC-OCEANALERT 23
CNIE (Committee for the National Institute for the Environment) 24
COASTNET (Coastal Management Conference) 24
COCE-L (Conference on Communication and our/the Environment) . . 24
COMPOST 25
COMPSY-L (Student Forum for Ecological/Community Psychology) . 25
CONSBIO 25
CONSLINK 26
CORAL-LIST 26
CTB-NEWS (Comprehensive Test Ban News) 26
CTURTLE (Sea Turtle Biology and Conservation) 27
CZM (Coastal Zone Management) 27
DEVEL-L (Technology Transfer in International Development) 27
DIALOG-AGUA-L 28
DIGESTION 28
DIOXIN-L 29
DRIFTERS 29
EARTHNET 29

Earthwatch 30
ECDM (Environmentally Conscious Design and Manufacturing) 30
ECOCITIES 30
ECO-FUND 31
ECOL-AGRIC 31
ECOL-ECON (Ecological Economics) 31
ECOLOG-L (Ecological Society of America) 32
ECOPOLITICS 32
ECOPSYCHOLOGY (Nature-Counseling Community Connection) . . . 32
ECOSYS-L (Ecosystem Theory and Modeling) 33
ECOTALK 33
EE-CAFE 33
EE-INTERNET 34
EGT 34
EIA (Environmental Impact Assessment) 34
EIM (Environmental Interactions of Mariculture) 35
EISG (Environmental Information System Group) 35
ELAN (Environment in Latin America Network) 35
ELI-WETLANDS 36
ENCON-L (Energy Conservation Management Issues
 in Higher Education) 36
ENERGYSTAR 36
eNETDIGEST 37
ENVBEH-L 37
ENVBUS-L (Environment and Business in Central and Eastern Europe) 37
ENVCEE-L (Environmental Issues in Central and Eastern Europe) 38
ENVCONFS-L 38
ENVENG-L 39
ENVEVENTS-L 39
ENVINF-L (Environmental Information Distribution List) 40
ENVIROETHICS 40
ENVIROMINE—ISSUES 40
ENVIROMINE—TECHNICAL 41
ENVIRONB-L (Enviro-Newsbrief) 41
ENVIRO-NEWS 42
ENVIRONEWS 42
ENVIRONMENT-L 42
ENVJOBS-L (Environmental Jobs List) 43

ENVLAWPROFS (Environmental Law Professors) 43
ENVPUBS-L 43
ENVST-L (Environmental Studies Discussion List) 44
ENVTECSOC (Environment Technology and Society) 44
EON (Environment on the Net) 44
EPA- [Federal Register Documents] 45
EPA-GRANTS 45
EPA-PRESS 46
EPA-R2-PRESS 46
ESSA (Earthships and Self Sufficient Architecture) 46
EUROFISH-L 47
EV (Electric Vehicle) 47
EWIRE 47
EW-RADIO 48
Federal Compliance Alert 48
FISHERIES 48
FISHFOLK (Fisheries Social Science Network) 49
FISH-SCI (International Forum for Fishery Science) 49
FOODSAFE 49
FOODSAFETY 50
FOREST 50
FWIM-L (Fish and Wildlife Information Management) 50
FWS-SHOREBIRDS 51
GASIFICATION 51
GENERAL 51
GEO-COMPUTER-MODELS 52
GEO-ENV 52
GEO-GIG 52
GLIN-ANNOUNCE (Great Lakes Information Network) 53
GLIN-EDUCATION (Great Lakes Information Network) 53
GREENSEE 53
GREEN-TRAVEL 54
GRNSCH-L 54
GROUNDWATER 54
GT-ATMDC (Atmospheric Dispersion of Chemicals) 55
GWCAN-L (Canadian Hydrogeology) 55
GWM-L (Groundwater Modelling) 55
H-ASEH (American Society for Environmental History) 56

HealthE 56
Hudson-R 57
Human Dimensions of Global Environmental Change 57
HYDROGEN 57
HYDROLOGY 58
IASEE-L 58
industrial-ecology 58
INFOTERRA 59
IRNES (Interdisciplinary Research Network on the
 Environment and Society) 59
IRRIGATION - L 59
ISEA-L (International Students for Environmental Action) 60
ISO14000 60
ITEX 60
Jam 61
LAKES-L 61
lichens 61
mabnet_america 62
Mangrove 62
marinefish 62
marshbird 63
MEH20-L 63
Michiganbutterflies 63
NACA-GL 64
NATOSCI 64
nc-wq (North Carolina Water Quality) 64
novel-fuels 65
NPSINFO 65
NRLib-L (Natural Resources Librarians List) 65
OILGASLAW-L 66
ONE-L (Organization and the Natural Environment) 66
Ozone 66
Pacific-biosnet 67
PedNet 67
plantpop 67
PONDS-L 68
POPENV-L 68
POPULATION 68

POPULATION-NEWS 69
PPBC-L (Protected Plantscape Biological Control List) 69
prairie 69
Predator_Watch 70
PRINTECH 70
QUEST (Quality, Environment, Safety in Management) 70
RainForest 71
RainForest-M 71
REEL (Resource and Environmental Economics List) 71
RESECON (Land and Resource Economics Network) 72
RE-USE 72
River Network 72
roadsalt 73
rrr-oregon-l 73
SAFETY 73
saf-news 74
seashepherd 74
SENSE-L (Environmental Club) 74
SEWER-LIST 75
SOILS-L 75
solar_utilities 75
SPECIES-ALERT 76
Sylvanet 76
Tenure 76
ToxList 77
TRICKLE-L 77
Tweeters 77
tws-wtwg (Wildlife Toxicology Working Group) 78
URBWLF-L (Urban Wildlife) 78
USIALE-L (International Association of Landscape Ecology) 78
WALL-list 79
WASTE 79
WASTENOT 80
Wastewater-modelling-digest 80
WATER-AND-SANITATION-APPLIED-RESEARCH 80
Water Distribution Systems (WDS) 81
WATER-ON-LINE 81

Water-Quality 81
WDAMAGE (Wildlife Damage Management) 82
WETLAND-NEWS 82
wholesys-l (Whole Systems) 82
wildgarden 83
Wildlife Health 83
Wildnet 83
WLREHAB (Wildlife Rehabilitation Mailing List) 84
Wthydrology 84
x-enews 84

CHAPTER 3 - Environmental Newsgroups **85**
alt.agriculture 87
alt.agriculture.misc 87
alt.animals.whales 87
alt.building.environment 87
alt.building.health-safety 87
alt.building.recycle 88
alt.energy.homepower 88
alt.energy.renewable 88
alt.org.audubon 88
alt.org.earth-first 88
alt.org.sierra-club 88
alt.politics.greens 89
alt.sustainable.agriculture 89
alt.solar.photovoltaic 89
alt.solar.thermal 89
alt.society.sustainable 89
alt.wolves 90
aus.environment.conservation 90
bionet.agroforestry 90
bionet.plants 90
bionet.toxicology 90
ca.environment 91
ca.water 91
clari.tw.environment 91
clari.tw.environment.cbd 91
clari.tw.environment.releases 91

clari.tw.nuclear 92

francom.environnement 92

gov.org.g7.environment 92

gov.us.fed.doc.cbd.solicitations 92

gov.us.fed.doc.noaa.announce 92

gov.us.fed.doe.announce 92

gov.us.fed.doi.announce 93

gov.us.fed.epa.announce 93

gov.us.fed.ferc.announce 93

gov.us.fed.nara.fed-register.contents 93

gov.us.fed.nrc.announce 93

gov.us.fed.nsf.announce 93

gov.us.fed.usda.announce 94

gov.us.topic.agri.farms 94

gov.us.topic.agri.food 94

gov.us.topic.energy.misc 94

gov.us.topic.energy.nuclear 94

gov.us.topic.energy.utilities 95

gov.us.topic.environment.air 95

gov.us.topic.environment.announce 95

gov.us.topic.environment.misc 95

gov.us.topic.environment.toxics 95

gov.us.topic.environment.waste 95

gov.us.topic.environment.water 96

gov.us.topic.gov-jobs.offered.science 96

gov.us.topic.nat-resources.forests 96

gov.us.topic.nat-resources.land 96

gov.us.topic.nat-resources.marine 96

gov.us.topic.nat-resources.minerals 96

gov.us.topic.nat-resources.oil-gas 97

gov.us.topic.nat-resources.parks 97

gov.us.topic.nat-resources.wildlife 97

pa.environment 97

rec.animals.wildlife 97

rec.birds 98

sci.agriculture 98

sci.bio.conservation 98

sci.bio.ecology 98
sci.bio.entomology.homoptera 99
sci.bio.entomology.misc 99
sci.bio.fisheries 99
sci.energy 99
sci.energy.hydrogen 100
sci.environment 100
sci.environment.waste 100
sci.geo.hydrology 100
sci.geo.meteorology 101
sci.geo.oceanography 101
sci.geo.petroleum 101
sci.geo.rivers+lakes 101
scot.environment 101
talk.environment 102
uk.environment 102
uk.environment.conservation 102

CHAPTER 4 - Environmental Journals and Newsletters **103**
Advances in Environmental Research 104
Africa: Environment and Wildlife 104
Alternative Agriculture News 104
Alternatives Journal 105
Amphibian & Reptile Conservation 105
Animal Rights 105
APIS (Apicultural Information and Issues) 105
Aquarius 106
Arid Lands Newsletter 106
Arizona Highways 106
Audubon Advisory 106
Aviation, Space, and Environmental Medicine 107
BEN (Botanical Electronic News) 107
Biolinks (Biodiversity Newsletter) 107
Biological Conservation Newsletter 108
Borderlines 108
Bulletin of the Regional Environmental Center 108
Bushlines (Newsletter of the National Landcare Program) 109
BWZ (Better World Zine) 109

CADDET Energy Efficiency Newsletter 109
Canadian Institute for Environmental Law and Policy Newsletter 109
Canadian Journal of Fisheries and Aquatic Sciences 110
Canadian Journal of Forest Research 110
Carcinogenesis 110
CATF Review 111
Center for Sustainable Agricultural Systems Newsletter 111
Chemistry & Industry 111
Chlorine Monitor 112
Clean Cities Drive Newsletter 112
Clear View, A 112
Climate Variations Bulletin 113
Compliance Online 113
Conscious Choice 113
Consequences: The Nature & Implications of Environmental Change . 113
Conservation Ecology 114
Corporate Watch (News) 114
Dateline Los Alamos 114
Delta (Newsletter of the Canadian Global Change Program) 114
Desert Research Institute Newsletter 115
Developing Ideas Digest 115
e-Amicus 115
E, The Environmental Magazine 115
Earth Action: The Bulletin for Environmental Activists 116
Earth Alert 116
Earth Island Journal 116
Earth Negotiations Bulletin 117
Earth Times 117
ECO (The Climate Action Network Newsletter) 117
Eco-Compass 118
Ecocycle 118
Ecology Law Quarterly 118
EcoNews Africa: Circular on Environment and Development 119
Ecopsychology On-line 119
EcoRegion 119
e design online (Online Journal of the Florida Design Initiative) 120
EDF Letter 120

Electromagnetics Forum 120
Electronic Drummer 121
Electronic Green Journal 121
EM Online (A Magazine for Environmental Managers) 121
Endangered Species & Wetlands Report 122
Endangered Species Bulletin 122
Endangered Species Update 122
Energies 123
Energy Crops Forum 123
Energy Source Builder 123
Environmental Building News 123
Environmental Ethics 124
Environmental Health Monthly 124
Environmental Health Perspectives 124
Environmental Reviews 125
Environmental Values 125
Environment and History 125
Environment Bulletin 126
Environment Business Magazine 126
Environment Matters 126
Environment Writer 126
Envirosense Online 127
EPRI Journal 127
Farm Aid News & Views 127
Forest Voice 127
FROGLOG 128
GEWEX News (Global Energy and Water Cycle Experiment) 128
GHCC Forecast (Global Hydrology and Climate Center) 128
Global Environmental Change Report 129
Global Food Watch 129
GreenBeat!: Profiles & Perspectives in Environmental Endeavors 129
GreenClips 130
GreenDisk Paperless Environmental Journal, The 130
GreeNotes 130
Greenpeace Toxic Trade Updates 131
Green Teacher 131
Habitrends Newsletter 131
High Country News 132

Home Energy Magazine 132
Home Power Magazine 132
HydroWire 133
IALC Online Newsletter (International Arid Lands Consortium) 133
Idaho Rivers United Newsletter 133
IHDP Update (International Human Dimensions Programme) 133
Initiatives in Environmental Technology Investment 134
Inside & Out 134
Intellectual Property & Biodiversity News 134
International Wildlife 135
International Wolf 135
Japan Environment Quarterly 135
Journal of Arboriculture 135
Journal of Industrial Ecology 136
Journal of Political Ecology - JPE 136
Know Your Environment 136
League of Conservation Voters (LCV) - National
  Environmental Scorecard 137
Linkages 137
Living Gently Quarterly 137
Makai 138
Maryland Marine Notes 138
Master Network 138
Michigan Forests Magazine 138
Minnesota Volunteer 139
National Parks 139
National Wildlife 139
NATO Scientific & Environmental Affairs Newsletter 140
Natural Areas Journal 140
Nature Network 140
NETAction Newsletter 141
New Forests News 141
NOAA News 141
Ocean News 142
Oceanography 142
On the Air 142
Open Spaces 142

ORNL Review 143
Our Environment 143
Our Living Oceans Annual Report 143
Our Planet 143
Outdoor Classroom / La Classe en Plein-air 144
PANUPS (Pesticide Action Network North America) 144
People and the Planet 144
Planet, The 144
Prairie Falcon, The 145
Pollution Engineering 145
Project Wildlife Newsletters 145
Rachel's Environment & Health Weekly 146
Raptor Release 146
Recycling World 146
Reef Line 146
Reflections on the Environment 147
Resistant Pest Management Newsletter 147
San Diego Earth Times 147
Scientist 148
Sea Wind 148
Seiche 148
Sierra - The Sierra Club Magazine 149
Silva Fennica 149
Simple Living Newsletter 149
SNAP Shots Newsletter 149
SOS Newsletter (Save Our Seas) 150
Sound Waves 150
Source, The 150
South Florida Environmental Reader 150
Sustainable Agriculture Newsletter 151
Sustainable Developments 151
Sustainable Minnesota 151
SUSTAINABLE Times 152
Terrain: A Journal of the Built & Natural Environments 152
Terra Nova - Nature & Culture 152
Texas On-Site Insights 153
Texas Water Resources 153
Texas Water Savers 153

Tin-Men - The Inquiring Non-Mainstream Environmental News 153
TNW Online (The Neighborhood Works) 154
TOS Newsletter (The Oceanography Society) 154
Toxicology and Ecotoxicology News 154
Tropical Biodiversity 155
Tuna Newsletter 155
U.S. Water News 155
UVB Impacts Reporter 156
Waste Not 156
Watershed Management Council Networker 156
WEF Reporter (Water Environment Federation) 157
Wetlands - The Journal of the Society of Wetland Scientists 157
Whales Alive! 157
Wildlife Notes 158
Wildlife Watch 158
Wild Ohio 158
Windows to Wildlife 158
WMO Antarctic Ozone Bulletins 159
World Climate Report 159
World Rivers Review 159
Worldwide Rainforest/Biodiversity Campaign News Archives 159
Yale Working Papers on Solid Waste Policy 160
Yellowstone Journal 160

CHAPTER 5 - Environmental World Wide Web Sites **161**
The Academy of Natural Sciences 163
Advanced Forest Technologies Program (AFT) 163
Advanced Recovery 163
Advanced Technologies for Commercial Buildings 164
Advanced Technology Environmental Education Center 164
African Environmental Research and Consulting Group 164
Agency for Toxic Substances and Disease Registry (ATSDR) 165
AGRALIN (Agricultural Bibliographic Information
  System of the Netherlands) 165
Agriculture Network Information Center 165
Air & Waste Management Association 166
Air Force Center for Environmental Excellence (AFCEE) 166
Alabama Department of Environmental Management 166

Alaska Department of Environmental Conservation 167
Albany Research Center 167
Alfred Wegener Institute for Polar and Marine Research 167
Alliance for Environmental Technology 167
American Academy of Environmental Engineers 168
American Chemical Society 168
American Council for an Energy-Efficient Economy 168
American Farmland Trust 168
American Forests 169
American Geophysical Union 169
American Hydrogen Association 169
American Rivers 170
American Solar Energy Society 170
The American Water Works Association 170
Ames Laboratory, Environmental Technology Development (ETD) . . 171
Antarctic and Southern Ocean Coalition (ASOC) 171
Appropriate Technology for Community and Environment (APACE) . 171
Arbeitsgemeinschaft ERNEUERBARE ENERGIE (AEE) 172
Argonne National Laboratory 172
Arizona Legislative Information System (ALIS) 172
Arizona Geological Survey 172
Arkansas Natural Heritage Commission 173
ASCE Geotechnical Engineering Seepage/Groundwater Modelling . . 173
Asia-Pacific Centre for Environmental Law 173
Association of Energy Engineers 174
Association of University Leaders for a Sustainable Future 174
Atlantic Salmon Federation 174
Australian Cooperative Research Centres 175
Australian Oceanographic Data Centre 175
Base De Dados Tropical 176
Bat Conservation International 176
Battelle Environmental Systems and Technology Division 176
Battelle Seattle Research Group 177
Bear River Solar Aquatics Wastewater Treatment Facility 177
Bear Watch 177
Bellona Foundation 178
Best Manufacturing Practices Center of Excellence 178
Biocatalysis/Biodegradation Database, University of Minnesota 178

Biodiversity Information Network 21 179
Bioelectromagnetics Society (BEMS) 179
Biology - Careers and Jobs 179
Bird Banding Laboratory 180
Birding on the Web 180
Bonnell Environmental Consulting (BEC) 180
British Atmospheric Data Centre 180
Brookhaven National Laboratory 181
Brown is Green (BIG) 181
Bureau of International Recycling 181
Bureau of Land Management 182
Bureau of Reclamation 182
Bureau of Transportation Statistics 182
Byrd Polar Research Center 183
CADDET (Centre for the Analysis and Dissemination
  of Demonstrated Energy Technologies) 183
California Conservation Corps Home Page 183
California Energy Commission 183
California Environmental Protection Agency 184
California Environmental Resources Evaluation System (CERES) ... 184
California Resources Agency 184
Canada Centre for Inland Waters 185
Canadian Chlorine Coordinating Committee 185
Canadian Council of Ministers of the Environment (CCME) 185
Canadian Environmental Assessment Agency 186
Canadian Institute for Environmental Law and Policy (CIELAP) 186
Canadian Ratite Home Page 186
Carbon Dioxide Information Analysis Center (CDIAC) 187
Carnegie Institute of Technology, Department of Civil and
  Environmental Engineering (Carnegie Mellon University) 187
Catalog of Known and Putative Nuclear Explosions 187
Catalog of Online Vegetation and Plant Distribution Maps 188
Center for Bioenvironmental Research 188
Center for Conservation Biology Network 188
Center for Disease Control (CDC) 189
Center for Environmental Biotechnology 189
Center for Environmental Citizenship 190

Center for Environmental Design Research (CEDR) College of
  Environmental Design, University of California, Berkeley 190
Center for Health Effects of Environmental Contamination 190
Center for International Climate and Environmental Research, Oslo . . 191
Center for International Earth Science Information Network (CIESIN) 191
Center for International Environmental Law (CIEL) 192
Center for Marine Conservation 192
Center for Plant Conservation 192
Center for Renewable Energy and Sustainable Technology (CREST) . 192
Center for Resourceful Building Technology (CRBT) 193
Center for the Study of Environmental Endocrine Effects 193
Central European Environmental Data Request Facility (CEDAR) . . . 193
Centre for Agriculture and Environment, The Netherlands 194
Centre for Alternative Transportation Fuels 194
Centre for Development and Environment 194
Cetacean Society International 195
Chanslor Wetlands Wildlife Project 195
Charles Darwin Research Station 195
Chemcyclopedia 196
Chemical Industry Institute of Toxicology (CIIT) 196
Chicago Wilderness 196
Chilkat Bald Eagle Preserve 197
China Council for International Cooperation on Environment
  and Development (CCICED) 197
Chlorine Chemistry Council 197
Citation Publishing, Inc. 197
City Farmer 198
ClO_2 Water Treatment Resource Center 198
CLU-IN (Hazardous Waste Clean-Up Information) 198
Cochrane Ecological Institute/Cochrane Wildlife Reserve 198
Code of Federal Regulations 199
Colorado Department of Natural Resources 199
Colorado Department of Public Health and Environment 199
Colorado School of Mines 199
Columbia Earth Institute, Columbia University 200
Commission for Environmental Cooperation (CEC) 200
  (Comision para la Cooperacion Ambiental (CCA)
  (Commission de Cooperation Environnementale (CCE)

Committee for the National Institute for the Environment (CNIE) 200
Communications for a Sustainable Future 201
Compost Resource Page 201
Connecticut Department of Environmental Protection 201
Conservation Agency 201
Conservation International 202
Consortium on Green Design and Manufacturing (CGDM) 202
Consultative Group on International Agricultural Research 202
Coral Forest 203
Coral Health and Monitoring Program (CHAMP) 203
Coral Reef Alliance 203
Cornell Center for the Environment 204
Council for Agricultural Science and Technology (CAST) 204
Council on Environmental Quality (CEQ) 204
Coweeta LTER Site 205
Crop Protection Institute 205
Cygnus Group 205
Danube Information System (DANIS) 205
Declining Amphibian Populations Task Force (DAPTF) 206
Defenders of Wildlife 206
Defense Environmental Network & Information eXchange (DENIX) . 206
Defense Environmental Restoration Program (DERP) 207
Defense Technical Information Center 207
Delaware Department of Natural Resources and
    Environmental Control 207
Department of Defense Environmental Cleanup Home Page 207
Department of Energy, U.S. .... / 208
Department of the Environment, Transport and the Regions
    (Great Britain) 208
Department of the Interior, U.S. 209
Desert Research Institute 209
Direct Contact Environmental Toll-Free Directory 209
DiveWeb 210
Earth Council 210
Earth Day Network 210
Earth Island (Institute) 210
Earthlink 211

Earth Observing System Amazon Project (University of Washington) 211
Earth Pledge Foundation 211
Earth Resources Laboratory at MIT 211
Earth's Resources Observation Satellite (EROS) Data Center 212
Earthwatch Institute 212
ECN (Environmental Change Network) 212
Ecologia 213
Ecology Action Centre 213
EcoMall 213
Econet 214
The Ecotourism Society (TES) 214
EcoTradeNet 214
Eco-Village Network 215
Ecovote Online 215
The EcoWeb, University of Virginia 215
EDIE (Environmental Data Interactive Exchange) 215
Edison Electric Institute 216
Edwards Aquifer Research and Data Center (EARDC),
 Southwest Texas State University 216
EE-Link (Environmental Education-Link) 216
Electric Power Research Institute (EPRI) 217
Elsevier Science Tables of Contents 217
Endangered Habitats League 217
Endangered Species Recovery Program 218
ENDS Environmental Data Services 218
Energy & Environmental Research Center (EERC) 218
Energy Ideas Clearinghouse 218
Energy Technology Data Exchange 219
Enviro-Access 219
Envirolink Network 219
ENVIROMINE 220
Environmental Alliance for Senior Involvement (EASI) 220
Environmental and Societal Impacts Group 220
Environmental Assessment Association 220
Environmental Careers Organization 221
Environmental Chemicals Data Information Network 221
Environmental Compliance Assistance Center 221
Environmental Contaminants Encyclopedia 222

Environmental Data Pages 222
Environmental Defense Fund 222
Environmental Industry Web Site 223
Environmental Journalism Home Page 223
Environmental Law Information Center 223
Environmental Measurements Laboratory 224
Environmental News Network 224
Environmental Organization Web Directory 224
Environmental Protection Agency, U. S. 225
Environmental Research Institute of Michigan (ERIM) 225
Environmental Resource Center 226
Environmental Resources Information Network (ERIN)/
 Australian Environment Online 226
Environmental Resources Management 226
Environmental Routenet 227
Environmental Science and Forestry at SUNY 227
Environmental Simulations, Inc. 227
Environmental Treaties and Resource Indicators (ENTRI) 228
Environmental Working Group 228
Environment Canada (The Green Lane) 229
The Environment Council, U. K. 229
Environment in Asia 230
Enviroene 230
EnviroSources 230
EnviroText 231
Essential Information 231
European Centre for Nature Conservation 231
European Environmental Agency 232
European Forest Institute (EFI) 232
Everglades Information Network 232
EXTOXNET (Extension Toxicology Network) 232
Federal Emergency Management Agency (FEMA) 233
Federal Geographic Data Committee 233
Federal Remediation Technologies Roundtable 233
Fedworld Information Network 234
Finnish Forest Research Institute - METLA 234
Fish and Wildlife Information Exchange Homepage 234
Florida Center for Environmental Studies 235

Florida Cooperative Extension Service 235
Florida Department of Environmental Protection 235
Florida Design Initiative 235
Forest History Society 236
Forest Service Ecosystem Management 236
Forest Service Employees for Environmental Ethics 236
Friends of the Earth International 237
The FROGGY Page 237
Gaia Forest Archives 237
Galapagos Coalition 237
GAP (Gap Analysis Program), National 238
General Accounting Office, U. S. 238
GENIE Project 238
Georgia Department of Natural Resources 239
Germinal Project 239
Global Change Master Directory (GCMD) 239
Global Change Research Information Office 239
Global Climate Web Site Research 240
Global Environmental Options (GEO) 240
Global Environment Outlook Project (GEO-1 Report) 240
Global Futures Foundation (GFF) 241
Global Hydrology and Climate Center 241
Global Network of Environment & Technology 241
Global Recycling Network, Inc. 242
Global Research Information Database (GRID) 242
GLOBE Program 242
Government Institutes, Inc. 242
Great Lakes Fishery Commission 243
Great Lakes Information Network (GLIN) 243
Greenbelt Alliance 243
Green Mountain Institute for Environmental Democracy 243
GREEN PAGES 244
Green Parties of North America 244
Greenpeace International 244
Green Seal 245
GREENTIE (Greenhouse Gas Technology Information Exchange) ... 245
Green University Initiative 245
Ground-Water Remediation Technologies Analysis Center 245

Habitats - The Growth of a Forest 246
Harbor Branch Oceanographic Institution 246
Harvard Environmental Resources On-Line 246
Harvard Forest 247
Hawaiian Ecosystems at Risk (HEAR) 247
Hawaii Biological Survey 247
Hawaii National Wildlife Refuges/Marine Sanctuaries 247
Hawaii's Endangered and Threatened Species Page 248
Hawk Mountain Sanctuary 248
HawkWatch International 248
Hazardous Substance Research Centers 249
HazDat - Hazardous Substance Release/Health Effects Database 249
HazWrap 249
Headwaters Forest 250
Headwaters Science Center 250
Heartwood 250
Hiraiso Solar Terrestrial Research Center 250
Holland Island Preservation Foundation 251
Horned Lizard Conservation Society (HLCS) 251
Houston Audubon Society 251
Howl - The PAWS Wildlife Center 251
Hubbard Brook Experimental Forest 252
Hydrographic Survey Data................................... 252
ICLEI - International Council for Local Environmental Initiatives ... 252
Idaho Department of Fish and Game 253
Idaho Wilderness 253
IEEE TAB Environment, Health and Safety Committee 253
IFAW - International Fund for Animal Welfare 254
IISDnet - International Institute for Sustainable Development 254
Illinois Natural Resources Information Network (INRIN) 254
Illinois Recycling Association 254
Indiana Department of Natural Resources 255
Indonesian Mangrove Foundation 255
Information Center for the Environment 255
Inland Seas Education Association 255
Institute for Terrestrial Ecology 256
Institute of Freshwater Ecology (IFE) 256
International Arid Lands Consortium 256

International Bee Research Association (IBRA) 256
International Canopy Network (ICAN) 257
International Center for Living Aquatic Resources Management 257
International Centre for Gas Technology Information 257
International Coral Reef Initiative 257
International Council for the Exploration of the Sea (ICES) 258
International Crane Foundation (ICF) 258
International Energy Agency Solar Heating and Cooling Programme . 258
International Geosphere-Biosphere Programme 258
International Ground Source Heat Pump Association (IGSHPA) 259
International Human Dimension Programme on Global
        Environmental Change 259
International Institute for Industrial Environmental Economics 259
International Marinelife Alliance 260
International Marine Mammal Association 260
International Marine Mammal Project 260
International Oceanographic Foundation 260
International Otter Survival Fund 261
International Primate Protection League (IPPL) 261
International Research Institute for Climate Prediction 261
International Rivers Network 262
International Satellite Land Surface Climatology Project (ISLSCP) . . 262
International Snow Leopard Trust 262
International Society for Ecological Modelling (ISEM) 262
International Society for Environmental Ethics 263
International Society of Arboriculture 263
International Solar Center 263
International Solar Energy Society 264
International Union for the Conservation of Nature 264
International Union of Forestry Research Organizations (IUFRO) 264
International Wildlife Coalition - (IWC) 265
International Wolf Center 265
International Year of the Ocean - 1998 265
Investigating Wind Energy 265
Iowa Department of Natural Resources 266
Iowa Raptor Foundation 266
Iowa's Environment 266
Irish Peatland Conservation Council 266

Island Wildlife Natural Care Centre 267
ISO-14000 Information Center 267
Izaak Walton League of America 267
Jane Goodall Institute 267
Japan Marine Science and Technology Center (JAMSTEC) 268
Jardin Gaia 268
Jefferson Land Trust 268
John M. Judy Environmental Education Consortium 268
John Muir Trust 269
Joint Center for Energy Management (JCEM) 269
Journey North 269
Kansas Environmental Almanac 269
Kentucky Department of Fish and Wildlife Resources 270
Kentucky Water Resources Research Institute 270
Kentucky Water Watch 270
Kola Ecogeochemistry 270
Lake Pontchartrain Basin Foundation 271
Land Conservancy of San Luis Obispo County 271
Land Trust Alliance 271
League of Conservation Voters 271
Leave No Trace 272
LIFE 272
Lincolnshire Trust 272
Living on Earth 273
Lloyd Center for Environmental Studies 273
Louisiana Department of Agriculture & Forestry 273
Louisiana Energy & Environmental Resource &
        Information Center (LEERIC) 274
Lower Rio Grande Ecosystem Initiative 274
LTER (US Long-Term Ecological Research) Network 274
Macaw Landing Foundation 275
Maine Department of Conservation 275
Maine Department of Environmental Protection 275
Maine Department of Inland Fisheries & Wildlife 275
Mangrove Replenishment Initiative 276
Manomet Center for Conservation Science 276
Marine Biological Association 276

Marine Conservation Society 276
Marine Environmental Research Institute 277
Marine Mammal Center 277
Marine Mammal Stranding Center 277
Maryland Department of Natural Resources 277
Maryland Forests Association 278
Massachusetts Department of Fisheries, Wildlife and
        Environmental Law Enforcement 278
Matheson Wetlands Preserve 278
Mediterranean Oceanic Data Base 279
Medomak Valley Land Trust 279
Mendocino County Ecology Web 279
Messinger Woods Wildlife Care and Education Center 279
Michigan Department of Environmental Quality 280
Michigan Department of Natural Resources 280
Michigan Environmental Science Board 280
Michigan Forest Association 280
Michigan Pulp and Paper Pollution Prevention Program 281
Michigan United Conservation Clubs 281
Midwest Renewable Energy Association (MREA) 281
Milton Keynes Wildlife Hospital 281
Mineral Policy Center 282
Minnesota Department of Natural Resources 282
Minnesotans for An Energy-Efficient Economy (ME3) 282
Minnesota Pollution Control Agency 282
Missouri Audubon Council 283
Missouri Coalition for the Environment 283
Missouri Department of Conservation 283
Missouri Prairie Foundation 283
Mmarie 284
Monarch Watch 284
Montana Natural Resource Information System 284
Montanas Verdes 285
Monterey Bay Aquarium-At the CoRE 285
Morris Parks and Land Conservancy 285
Mote Marine Laboratory 285
Mountain Institute 286
Mountain Lion Foundation 286

Mr. Solar Home Page 286
Namibia Animal Rehabilitation Research and Education Centre 286
Napa County Resource Conservation District 287
NAPEnet - National Association of Physicians for the Environment . . 287
National Agricultural Pest Information System (NAPIS) 287
National Arborist Association 288
The National Association of Environmental Professionals 288
National Association of State Foresters 288
National Audubon Society 289
National Center for Atmospheric Research 289
National Center for Ecological Analysis and Synthesis 289
National Councils for Sustainable Development 289
National Drought Mitigation Center 290
National Energy Foundation 290
National Estuary Program 290
National Ground Water Association 291
National Institute for Environmental Studies 291
National Institute of Environmental Health Sciences (NIEHS) 291
National Outdoor Leadership School 292
National Parks & Conservation Association 292
National Pollutant Release Inventory 292
National Pollution Prevention Center for Higher Education (NPPC) . . 292
National Renewable Energy Laboratory (NREL) 293
National Resources Defense Council 293
National Sea Grant Depository 293
National Sea Grant Program 294
National Seal Sanctuary 294
National Society for Clean Air 294
National Watchable Wildlife Program 294
National Wildlife Health Center 295
National Wildlife Refuge System 295
National Wildlife Rehabilitators Association 295
Native Americans and the Environment 295
Native Forest Council 296
Native Forest Network 296
NATO SACLANT Undersea Research Centre 296
Natural Energy Laboratory of Hawaii 297
Natural Environment Research Council 297

Natural Heritage Programs 297
Natural Resource Directory 298
Natural Resources Services 298
Nature Conservancy 298
Nature Conservancy of Texas 299
NatureNet 299
Nature Saskatchewan 299
Nebraska Wildlife Resources 299
NEMO - Oceanographic Data Server 300
New England Wild Flower Society 300
New England Wildlife Center 300
New Forests Project 301
New Hampshire Department of Environmental Services (DES) 301
New Hampshire Fish and Game Department 301
New Jersey Department of Environmental Protection 302
New Jersey Division of Fish, Game and Wildlife 302
New Mexico Wilderness Alliance 302
The New Mexico Wildlife Association 302
New York State Association for Reduction, Reuse and Recycling 303
New York State Department of Environmental Conservation 303
NHBS (Natural History Book Service) 303
NIREX 303
NOAA (National Oceanic and Atmospheric Administration) 304
North Carolina Coastal Federation 304
North Carolina Department of Environment and Natural Resources . . 304
North Cascades Conservation Council 305
North Dakota Atmospheric Resource Board 305
Northeast Alternative Vehicle Consortium (NAVC) 305
Northeast Sustainable Energy Association (NESEA) 305
Northern Lights (Nordlicht) 306
Northern Michigan Wildlife Rehabilitation 306
Northern Prairie Wildlife Research Center 306
North Island Wildlife Recovery Association 307
Nova Scotia Bird Society 307
Oceania Project 307
Oceanic 307
Oceanic Planetary Boundary Layer (OPBL) Laboratory 308
Oceanic Resource Foundation 308

Ocean Process Analysis Laboratory 308
Ocean Voice International 308
Office of Energy Efficiency 309
Office of Protected Resources 309
Ohio Department of Natural Resources 309
Ohio Environmental Protection Agency 309
Ohio Wildlife Center 310
Okefenokee Swamp Natural Education Center 310
Oklahoma Department of Wildlife Conservation 310
Ontario Environment Network 310
Ontario Ministry of the Environment 311
Open University Ecology and Conservation Research Group (ECRG) 311
Operation Wildlife 311
Oregon Department of Fish and Wildlife 312
Oregon Department of Forestry 312
Organization for Tropical Studies 312
ORNL (Oak Ridge National Laboratories) 313
Orphaned Wildlife Rehabilitation Society 313
Otter Habitat and Wildlife Rehab Center 313
Oxford Forestry Institute 313
Ozone Action 314
Pacific Forestry Center - Canadian Forest Service 314
Pacific Northwest Pollution Prevention Resource Center 314
Pacific Rim Consortium in Energy, Combustion, and the Environment 315
Palos Verdes Peninsula Land Conservancy 315
ParkNet - The National Park Service 315
Patuxent Wildlife Research Center 315
Penn State University Weather Pages 316
Pennsylvania Department of Environmental Protection 316
Pennsylvania Resources Council 316
Peregrine Falcons at the University of Calgary 316
Peregrine Fund 317
Pesticide Action Network North America - PANNA 317
Pew Center on Global Climate Change 317
Pinecrest: An Adventure Living Off The Utility Grid 317
Piping Plover Guardian Program 318
PlanetKeepers 318

PLANT-IT 2000 318
Pollution Probe 318
Potomac Conservancy 319
Prairie Ecosystem Study Project 319
Preserve the Dunes, Inc. 319
Primate Info Net 319
Princeton University's Center for Energy & Environmental Studies . . . 320
Project WILD 320
Project Wildlife 320
Protected Areas Virtual Library 320
Protected Marine Species 321
Puget Sound Green Pages 321
Puget Sound On Line 321
Raincoast Conservation Society 321
Rainforest Action Network (RAN) 322
Rainforest Foundation International 322
Rainforest Workshop 322
Raptor Center at the University of Minnesota 323
Raptor Rehabilitation of Kentucky 323
Raptor Resource Project 323
Recycled Pulp and Paper Coalition 323
Reef Relief 324
Refuge Net 324
Regional Air Quality Council 324
Regional Environmental Center for Central and Eastern Europe 325
Renewable Energy Association of Central Texas (REACT) 325
Resource Renewal Institute (RRI) 325
Restore America's Estuaries 326
RotWeb 326
Royal Forestry Society of England 326
St. Catherines Sea Turtle Conservation Program 326
The Salmon Page 327
The Salt and the Earth Wetlands Nursery 327
San Francisco Estuary Institute 327
San Gorgonio Volunteer Association 327
Santa Barbara County Air Pollution Control District 328
Sarvey Wildlife Center 328
Savannah River Site 328

Save Our Everglades 328
Save Our Seas 329
Save the Manatee Club 329
Save-the-Redwoods League 329
Save the Rhino International 329
Scottish Environment Protection Agency 330
Scripps Institution of Oceanography 330
SEACC (Southeast Alaska Conservation Council) ... 330
Sea Shepherd Conservation Society 330
Sea Turtle Restoration Project (STRP) 331
SeaWorld 331
Second Nature 331
Sefton Coast Life Project 331
Sempervirens Fund 332
Sierra Club Home Page 332
Sierra Solar Systems 332
Silva Forest Foundation 332
Simple Living Network 333
Skies Above Foundation 333
Skogforsk 333
Skye Environmental Centre 333
Smithsonian Institution's Conservation and Research Center 334
Society for Ecological Restoration 334
Society of American Foresters 334
Society of Municipal Arborists 334
Society of Wetland Scientists 335
Solar Cooking Archive 335
Solar Energy Network 335
Solar Energy Society of Canada Inc. 336
Solid Waste Association of North America 336
South Carolina Department of Natural Resources ... 336
South Dakota Parks & Wildlife Foundation 337
Southeastern Raptor Rehabilitation Center 337
Southern Africa Environment Page 337
Southern Florida Wildlife Rehabilitation Center ... 338
South West Florida Wildlife Rehabilitation and Conservation Center . 338
Southwestern Riparian Expertise Directory 338

State and Territorial Air Pollution Program Administrators - STAPPA 338
Students for Environmental and Ecological Development (SEED) . . . 339
Surfrider Foundation USA 339
Sustainable Ecosystems Institute 339
Sustainable Forestry Directory 339
Sustainable Sources 340
Taiga Rescue Network 340
Tallgrass Prairie in Illinois 340
Tall Timbers Research Station 340
Tarkine: Wilderness for Heritage 341
Tata Energy Research Institute 341
Teaming with Wildlife 341
Terrene Institute 342
Texas A&M University Oceanography 342
Texas Environmental Center (TEC) 342
Texas Marine Mammal Stranding Network 343
Texas Natural Resource Conservation Commission (TNRCC) 343
Threatened Species Network 343
Tiempo Climate Cyberlibrary 343
Tiger Information Center 344
Timber Wolf Information Network 344
Toxics Release Inventory 344
Tree Canada Foundation 345
Trees for the Future 345
Tropical Rain Forest in Suriname 345
Trouble With Manatees, The 345
Trumbull Land Trust 346
The Trust for Public Land (TPL) 346
Turtle Trax 346
Tusk Force 346
UCLA Center for Clean Technology 347
UnCover 347
Union of Concerned Scientists 347
United Nations Environment Programme (UNEP) 348
University of Florida's Range Science Program 348
University of Maine - Department of Wildlife Ecology 348
Urban Forest Ecosystems Institute 348
USACHPPM Hazardous and Medical Waste Program 349

U.S. Army Corps of Engineers - Sacramento District 349
U.S. Code 349
U.S. Code - Title 16 Conservation 350
USDA Forest Service 350
U.S. FWS Division of Habitat Conservation - National
       Wetlands Inventory 350
U.S. Geological Survey Earth and Environmental Science 351
Utah Department of Environmental Quality 351
Utah Department of Wildlife Resources 351
Utah Public Lands 352
Vancouver Island Marmot Pages 352
Vegan Action 352
Vegan Outreach 352
Verde River Watershed 353
Vermont Agency of Natural Resources 353
Vermont Land Trust 353
Virginia Coast Reserve LTER 353
Virginia Department of Forestry 354
Virginia Natural Heritage Program 354
Walk in the Woods 354
Washington State Environmental Resources 354
Waste Prevention Association 355
Water Environment Web 355
Waterfront 355
Water Management Research Laboratory (WMRL) 356
Watershed Management Council 356
WATERSHEDSS Water Quality Decision Support System 356
WaterWorld 357
Weather and Global Monitoring 357
Whale and Dolphin Conservation Society 357
Whale Conservation Institute 357
WhaleNet 358
WhaleTimes SeaBed 358
Wild Animal Rescue Foundation of Thailand (WAR) 358
Wild Bird Rehabilitation Center 358
Wildlands League 359
Wildlands Project 359
Wildlife at Risk-Canada 359

Wildlife Center of Silicon Valley 359
Wildlife Preservation Trust International 360
Wildlife Rescue Association of B.C. 360
Wildlife Rescue Center of Napa County 360
Wildlife Society 360
Wildlife Trusts 361
WildNet Africa 361
Wild Rockies Slate 361
Windstar Wildlife Institute 361
Wisconsin Wildlife Federation 362
Wolf Haven International 362
World Business Council for Sustainable Development (WBCSD) 362
World Climate Research Programme 363
World Conservation Monitoring Centre 363
World Conservation Society 363
World Energy Efficiency Association (WEEA) 364
World Forum for Acoustic Ecology 364
World Meteorologic Organization 364
World Resource Foundation 364
World Resources Institute 365
World Society for the Protection of Animals (WSPA) 365
World Wide Fund Global Network 365
World Wide Water 365
World Wildlife Fund 366
Wright's PestLaw 366
Yellow Mountain Institute for Sustainable Living 366
Yellowstone Grizzly Foundation 367
Zero Emissions Research Initiative 367
Zero Waste America 367
The Zoe Foundation 367

Index 369

Preface

Statistics on the growth of the Internet continue to multiply at an astounding pace and the World Wide Web is the fastest growing segment of the Internet. Newspapers, television programs, schools, libraries, businesses, and most government departments now have their own Web sites. Any individual with access to a computer or a public library can have a personal homepage without charge. Environmental resources are no exception to this phenomenal growth rate. Environmental education and awareness sites, professional environmental society sites, commercial sites, single and multiple endangered species sites, sites concerned with biodiversity, aquaculture sites, sustainable development sites, wildlife rescue and rehabilitation sites, and land trust sites all seem to be making their presence known.

The objective of this book continues to be providing access to the best sites dealing with the preservation and protection of the environment, ecology, and conservation that are available to environmental researchers, information professionals, and all individuals and groups who have a genuine interest in the future of our biosphere. We have arranged this edition in the same chapter divisions that we used in the previous editions. Chapter One is an update on the history of the Internet and the World Wide Web and contains some information on subject indexes and search engines.

Chapter Two provides an introduction to email discussion groups and the most usual types of discussion group software that you are likely to encounter. This introduction is followed by an alphabetical listing of email groups that we found most pertinent to environmental topics and that had a reasonable amount of traffic flow. Lists that looked interesting but did not receive any messages in the time we devoted to monitoring them were not used. Each list description contains information on how to subscribe to the list and a frequency indicator to give you an idea of how many messages you might expect to receive. The number of new discussion lists follows the growth trend of the rest of the Internet and the new lists in this edition mirror the trends in environmental research topics. Part of the growth in the number of lists is also due to the use of mailing lists to distribute information on a one-way basis. That is, timely news, press releases, and action alerts are sent to the members; however, members do not respond or discuss any of the information being sent to the list. These "read-only" lists are quick and efficient ways to disseminate information to a large number of people.

Chapter Three contains a description of the Usenet newsgroup service and a list of environment and conservation related newsgroups that we were able to access from our

Internet providers. Newsgroups tend to be more informal than email discussion groups, and this casual nature makes them more appealing to the general public than to professionals. This quality also makes them more prone to "flame wars" than email discussion lists of a professional nature, particularly moderated lists. There are many more newsgroups than we have listed in this chapter and this is for two reasons. The first is that Internet providers may choose which newsgroups they will allow their customers to access and the second is that many university-sponsored and professional society newsgroups are only open to the students, faculty, or members of the sponsoring institution. This clearly limits the ability of reviewers to participate in and observe the discussion that takes place on these newsgroups. In this edition, there are 45 new newsgroups. Thirty of these are from the newly created government hierarchy. The U.S. government has taken advantage of the simplicity of the newsgroup medium to quickly disseminate a large portion of its daily reports.

We have combined newsletters and electronic journals into one chapter. The newsletters and journals in Chapter Four may be distributed by commercial publishers or may be published by professional societies, government agencies, international organizations, independent groups, or volunteer associations. They may be full-text online and include illustrations, there may be excerpts or abstracts, or you may only be able to retrieve the table of contents. Some sites offer the full text of only the current issue, while others have archives from the first issue to the most recent copy. Their growth is due primarily to the growing number of producers of information who have the ability to offer their materials on the Internet. The 75 newly added electronic journals and newsletters cover a broad spectrum of topics and are published by a variety of governmental and non-governmental organizations.

Chapter Five covers all the sites that are accessible using Uniform Resource Locators, or URLs, other than electronic journals, which are covered by Chapter Four. These sites may be gopher sites, telnet sites, ftp sites or World Wide Web sites, although Web sites are the fastest growing portion of all Internet sites. Nearly 200 new Web sites have been added in this edition and more than 50 percent of the entries for the sites from the previous edition have been revised due to changes and additions at the sites. With this edition, there are more Web sites that offer global databases. Many of these databases have been established and are being maintained by groups from several countries and sectors. The joint effort and expertise among academia, governments, and industry from different regions of the world has created some valuable global database systems. Chapter Five also contains some information on HyperText Mark-up Language, known as HTML, which is used to code Web pages. There is a brief description of some of the new additions to HTML tagging and some of the new World Wide Web innovations plus a small example of a tagged document and what it would look like using a graphical browser.

Just as the number of new Internet sites has increased since the previous edition of this book, we expect the number of sites to continue to grow exponentially. Joining electronic discussion groups on topics you find relevant is still a good way to keep up with new resources, because the URLs of new Web sites are often posted to discussion lists by members who often provide detailed descriptions and reviews. Another profitable way to keep up with the deluge of new sites is to join the listserv, Net-Happenings, by sending an email message to listserv@cs.wisc.edu To subscribe to Net-Happenings, leave the subject line blank and in the body of the message type: subscribe Net-Happenings firstname lastname. Net-Happenings announces new sites, events, publications, training, and miscellaneous information about things happening on the Internet. You will receive between forty and sixty messages in digest format each day if you join this list. The messages sent to this list are also posted to the Net-Happenings newsgroup. You may prefer to read the news at their newsgroup address: comp.internet.net-happenings. An archive of messages and more information on subscribing may be found at http://scout.cs.wisc.edu/scout/net-hap/index.html. There are also some good mailing lists in Chapter Two that alert users to new environmental sites and resources on the Internet. (ENVINF-L, EnetDigest, and ENVPUBS-L)

It is our hope that you will find this book useful in your pursuit of Internet information on themes relating to the environmental and ecological state of our earth, regardless of which aspects of these topics are the most significant to you and your work.

Toni Murphy
Carol Briggs-Erickson

About the Authors

Toni Murphy is a technical services librarian at the Parke-Davis Pharmaceutical Research Division of Warner-Lambert in Ann Arbor, Michigan where she is responsible for most of the monograph copy cataloging and all of the original cataloging of the book collection. She is involved in team teaching on Internet searching and browsing skills and is a member of the Research Library webmaster team. Before receiving her MILS from the University of Michigan in 1995, she co-authored *A Guide to Environmental Resources on the Internet* and was one of the founders of the Internet Public Library.

Carol Briggs-Erickson is an electronic services/reference librarian at Muskegon Community College in Muskegon, Michigan. She received her Master's degree in Information and Library Studies from the University of Michigan where she contributed to the Clearinghouse for Subject-Oriented Resource Guides by co-authoring *A Guide to Environmental Resources on the Internet*. That document was the first environmental resource guide on the Internet. She continues to monitor the activity of the environmental discussion groups and databases on the Internet to remain current. She also has taught several Internet classes, workshops, and seminars on searching and using the Internet for research.

To Katie Hubbard and Connor Christie.
--Toni

To my husband, Leif, and my daughter, Christine.
--Carol

Chapter 1

Introduction to the Internet
and the World Wide Web

Since our previous edition of the *Environmental Guide to the Internet*, the size of the Internet has grown exponentially every year. There are dozens of free email sites and anyone with access to a networked computer can have a free personal home page. Internet providers are becoming better and faster and are available for less money than ever before. If you don't have a computer or an Internet provider, you can log on at your public library for free or a small fee. The World Wide Web is getting so big and so commercial that scientists and universities are considering creating a second Internet just for science and education. We would like to begin this guide to environmental Internet resources with a brief history of the Internet and the World Wide Web for those who may be interested and especially for those who are new to the Internet.

The Internet is a global network of networks that allows anyone with a computer, a modem, and an Internet service provider to access information stored at host computer servers around the globe. Internet service providers come in all shapes and sizes. Some are plain vanilla, offering only email and text browsing, although this is becoming rare. Other providers offer unique services that are only available to their customers. Local telephone companies may provide Internet access, or you may purchase your network service from a company that is dedicated to providing connections to the Internet and the World Wide Web. New innovations include systems that provide access via your television screen.

The Internet began as a project of the Pentagon's Advanced Research Projects Agency (ARPA) and was designed to send packets of information from one supercomputer node to another over high speed transmission lines, without a predetermined route. That is, two packets of data that were sent from the same node could, and probably would, take widely divergent routes and yet arrive at the same place. The first U.S. network, called ARPANET, was designed this way in order to keep communication lines open in the event that nuclear war would result in the destruction of many of the network nodes. If the information that was being sent could change its route, bypassing damaged lines, it could still reach its destination, hopefully outwitting the enemy, as long as there were operating nodes still in existence. From the first four ARPANET nodes that were in place in 1969, the network grew to fifteen nodes in 1971 and to thirty-seven nodes in 1972. Soon scientists and researchers were using the ARPANET to send information about their work to each other.

And before long they were using the network not only to discuss research, but also to talk to each other about all sorts of topics unrelated to their work. As more and more people began using the network, mailing lists were born. Mailing lists were used to send one message to many interested subscribers. Within a short time, these email discussion group lists were being created to exchange ideas on all sorts of subjects, from pets to religion to children's literature, not just scientific topics. Although this was viewed by employers as a misuse of the ARPANET, mailing lists running listserv and other list software have become as diverse as the interests of the individuals comprising the Internet community.

As the ARPANET grew, its communication standard, the "Network Control Protocol," or NCP, was replaced by the faster, more-efficient standard called the "Transmission Control Protocol" or TCP. The transmission control protocol over Internet Protocol or TCP/IP allows the sending of messages to the specified Internet address across many nodes and networks. TCP/IP was the common protocol that linked other networks with ARPANET. TCP/IP is frequently used as a catch-all term for the suite of protocols, which include telnet and ftp (file transfer protocol). Telnet is a tool that allows a user to access locations containing such things as bulletin boards, freenets, and online library catalogs, although many libraries now have World Wide Web access available for their patrons as well. Ftp is another tool that connects the user to a host computer server capable of storing and serving both documents and software (freeware or shareware). Documents may be retrieved in ASCII text format and software in binary format from the host server to your hard drive. If you are importing software from an ftp site, always remember to scan it for viruses.

In the late 1970s, USENET began as a way to send information between Duke University and the University of North Carolina. This was the beginning of the utilization of newsgroups. At the present time there are large numbers of newsgroups, some private but also many public, which are used as forums for discussion on an immense number of distinct subjects. Some of these newsgroups are professional forums, but many exist for the recreational Internet user. Discussions on public newsgroups tend to be much more casual than those on mailing lists.

By the 1980s, networks were springing up all over the country. In New York, the City University of New York began BITNET (Because It's Time Network), which uses email and listserv servers to dispense information, primarily in academic institutions. And in 1986 the National Science Foundation created the NSFNET, which was to become the backbone of the Internet. At the same time, the number of connections to the Internet began its phenomenal growth, starting in universities. In 1989, the number of Internet hosts surpassed 100,000.

With NSFNET providing the Internet backbone, in cooperation with IBM, MCI, and the Merit Network, ARPANET finally went out of existence. The 1990s produced many new network technologies, including the University of Minnesota's Gopher, with its analogies of burrowing through the Internet and getting lost in gopher holes. Gopher is a menu driven system that allows the user to choose a numbered menu item. This menu item connects to another menu or to a document. Gopher has several search engines, including Jughead and Veronica, for the keyword searching of menu items and document titles.

While many of us were still gophering; the World Wide Web, a hypermedia data retrieval system, was released to the Internet world and hypertext/hypermedia became the watchwords of Internet growth. This introduction of the World Wide Web gave rise to an explosion of click and go sites created for and by educational institutions, research facilities, government agencies and every individual who wanted a graphical presence on the Internet. As a result, many gopher and telnet sites have disappeared or been transformed into World Wide Web sites. Many online library catalogs that once could only be accessed by means of telnet are now using the easier graphical user interface of the Web.

The World Wide Web was created at CERN as an internal project whose objective was the exchange of ideas and research among its members located in several European countries. The first WWW software allowed the viewing of hypertext documents by people connected to the Internet. Hypertext is text that links to other text. It may link to another place in the same document, to another page of document on the same server, or to another document that physically lives at a site on the other side of the world. Hypertext allows you to connect to that place in the document or to the other site transparently. You just click on the highlighted text or graphic and the browser takes you to the link. Hypermedia is any medium that links to an image, sound, animation, or video file. Web browsers are the vehicles through which you view the hypertext/hypermedia link. World Wide Web pages are made up of combinations of text and graphics that are marked with Hypertext Mark-up Language (HTML) tags that tell the browser how to display the text and graphics. The graphical elements may be images, video, audio clips, or one of several new applications that are beginning to show up—like tables, frames, and Java applets.

Within a short time of the World Wide Web's inception, the ability to view animated graphics and video and to listen to audio clips gave rise to Web browser design and development. This became the focus of a number of people who put their browsers out on the Internet, usually in anonymous ftp files, as shareware. Soon the commercial world stepped in, hiring programmers to turn out more stable products that could be licensed and sold. This resulted in commercial versions of Mosaic, the development of Netscape Navigator, and many other, similar products.

Because all of the unique Web browsers have diverse capabilities and since computers have differing graphical resolution capabilities, what you see or hear when you navigate the World Wide Web can be very different from what someone else using another browser may see or hear. But the text and active links should be the same, even though the formatting is different. Some sites have text-only pages for slower browsers and you may see a warning message to the effect that the page is best viewed with a certain version of a browser. Many commercial Internet providers such as America Online, CompuServe, and

Netcom have their own browsers and each one has distinct capabilities. Other providers may offer you a choice between Netscape and Internet Explorer as part of their service.

The Internet and WWW are the closest thing we have to a universal database of information available internationally. Each piece of information, software package, database, or Web site resides at a unique address called a Uniform Resource Locator or URL. If you have the URL for a site or document, you can go straight to it without browsing around for it. The following are examples of URLs:

http://www.yahoo.com/
gopher://marvel.loc.gov:70/11/services/cataloging/weekly
ftp://una.hh.lib.umich.edu

There has never been one comprehensive catalog of the Internet as it stands, although there have been some very good endeavors at organizing the available sites, documents, and locations by subject content. Some of the better indexes exist on the World Wide Web at Yahoo (http://yahoo.com), TradeWave Galaxy (http://www.einet.net/galaxy.html) and the oldest and possibly the most exhaustive index, the World Wide Web Virtual Library (http://www.w3.org/hypertext/DataSources/bySubject/Overview.html). Many search engines have added subject indexes to their search pages. These include Infoseek, WebCrawler, and Lycos. There are also many subject guides to the Internet, both in text and hypertext formats. Many of them exist or have links from the Clearinghouse for Subject-Oriented Internet Resource Guides (http://www.clearinghouse.net/). One of the beauties of the World Wide Web is that it can represent nearly anything on the Internet. You can access gopher sites, documents at ftp locations, USENET newsgroups, anything served by a WAIS server, anything on telnet, and numerous hypertext documents.

The types of information available through the World Wide Web vary widely. There are documents on every imaginable subject, which can be found by browsing, using subject indexes, or using search engines. There are finger and whois servers for locating people on the Internet, Archie and Archieplex servers for locating software and documents, and many sites with multiple search engines that are specific to the kind of search you want to do. Some search engines do simple keyword searches, while others do more complex boolean, proximity, and nested searches. You no longer need to do searches on several search engines to get the results you need. Now there are metasearch engines that send your search to seven or more search engines simultaneously, sort the matches, discard duplicates and tell you which search engines returned the results. Two of these parallel search engines are MetaCrawler (http://www.muw.edu/ search.html) and Highway 61 (http://www.highway61.com/). Many World Wide Web subject catalogs and search engines provide only the name or URL of the sites they find, so you won't know what you'll be retrieving until you click on the link, while others offer relevancy ranking, short descriptions, and/or abstracts about the site or document. Tools for finding people may need only a name, while others require a lot more information.

The Internet and World Wide Web are growing at a phenomenal rate. The number of Internet host computers in January of 1993 was around 1,300,000. In July 1995 the number had grown to 6,500,000 and by July 1996 the figure had nearly doubled to 12,881,000 hosts. In the time period from 1993 to 1995, the number of Internet domains had increased from 21,000 to 120,000 and by 1996 the number of Internet domains had quadrupled to 488,000. By January of 1998 there were more than 1,000,000 Internet domains and 29,670,000 Internet hosts. The World Wide Web is still the fastest growing segment of the Internet. There seems to be no slowing it down. Just as tables, frames, pop-up menus and Java applets are seen at many sites now, newer applications are being created from the next wave of ideas including Javascript and cascading style sheets.

Bibliographic References

Boutell, Thomas. *What are WWW, hypertext and hypermedia?*
URL: http://sunsite.unc.edu/boutell/faq/htext.htm

Hughes, Kevin. *Entering the World Wide Web: A Guide to Cyberspace.*
URL: http://www.hcc.hawaii.edu/guide/www.guide.html

Krol, Ed. *FYI What Is the Internet?*
URL: http://www.hcc.hawaii.edu/iss/macdos/support/fyi_20.htm

Leiner, Barry M. *A Brief History of the Internet.*
URL: http://www.isoc.org/internet-history/brief.html

Sterling, Bruce. *Short History of the Internet.*
URL: http://w3.aces.uiuc.edu/AIM/scale/nethistory.html

Zakon,Robert H'obbes'. *Hobbes Internet Timeline.* v3.3
URL: http://info.isoc.org/guest/zakon/Internet/History/HIT.html/Growth

Chapter 2

Environmental Discussion Groups and Mailing Lists

Electronic discussion groups are meant to bring together those who share a common interest so that members of the group may benefit from the diverse knowledge and contributions of one another. Within the environmental community, there are many of these discussion groups. Their memberships range from small groups within universities or research centers to massive associations with worldwide membership. But the purpose of these groups, regardless of their size, remains the same: to share knowledge and discussion as outlined by the mission, focus, and intent of the group.

There are a tremendous number of electronic discussion groups having the environment—or some aspect of it—as their focus. We could not list them all here. Listed here are the groups that have the potential to be of interest to scientists, researchers, students, and professionals within the environmental community. In addition, all groups listed in this section have been monitored for their relevance and deemed to have merit to a large number of people.

In addition to being a means to carry out discussion by group members, these lists are used for announcements of meetings or conferences, advertisements for job openings, notices, calls for papers, dissemination of pertinent, newsworthy information including government regulations, queries asking for the members' expertise, and announcements of new books, articles, and Internet sites pertaining to environmental issues.

Many of the groups listed in this chapter are designated as "read only." This means that there is no input from the members of the group. These are also called "one-way groups." These "read only" or "one-way groups" are created so that information such as news bulletins, press releases, or reports may be disseminated quickly to all group members.

Although several different types of software are used to disseminate the discussion and information to subscribers on the electronic lists, they all generally follow the same format. That is, messages to subscribe and unsubscribe to the list are sent to the mail server software (listserv, listproc, mailbase, majordomo, etc.); and, messages intended for the group are sent to the group address (audubon, biodiv, bioenergy). As people subscribe to the list, their email addresses are automatically added by the computer program to its membership directory. Consequently, every message that is sent to the list is received by all persons on the membership list.

For example, the first electronic discussion group is ACN-L (Aquatic Conservation Network). The group's address is acn-l@acn.ca. To subscribe to this list, a message is sent to majordomo@acn.ca, with the message: subscribe acn-l. You do not need to include a subject. Also, you do not need any additional information in the message. Therefore, if you have set up your email software so that a signature is added to your messages, this should be turned off.

Usually, when the "subscribe" message is received by the list software, the subscriber is automatically added to the discussion list. However, many discussion groups require a reply to the automated message acknowledging acceptance into the group. Usually, when this is the case, one need only reply to the message with the text "ok." Some of the lists require human intervention to accept new members. When this is the case, the subscribe message is automatically forwarded to the person (a moderator or owner of the list) who is responsible for approving membership into the group. When that person adds new members, the new members receive a confirmation that they have been added to the list.

Regardless of how the subscribe message is handled by the list software or the moderator, the message that is ultimately sent to the new member indicating that that person has been added to the list generally includes several guidelines pertaining to effective and appropriate use of the list. At minimum, it should show the computer commands that may be used to retrieve information about the list. Those commands may include how to retrieve files from the mailing list software, how to get a list of subscribers to the list, or how to receive a digest of the messages. In addition, it may tell if the messages sent to the group are automatically archived. These archives may be publicly available to anyone regardless of membership; or, they may be accessible only to members of the group.

Some groups may have a "moderator" who screens messages that arrive for the list. The moderator determines if the messages fit the criteria established for the group. The benefit of a moderator is that neither "spam" (unsolicited, bulk junk mail) nor any irrelevant or off-topic messages will be received by the group. On the other hand, many people feel that a moderator may stifle creative dialog and want their group managed more freely and openly with no moderator intervention.

Many discussion groups also maintain a file of frequently asked questions (FAQs). These have been established so that persons may consult the FAQs before asking questions of the group. Check to see if a FAQ file exists before you ask a question. Very often, the FAQ file contains a wealth of information; therefore it is a good starting point for quick answers. (If no FAQ file exists, check to see if the group's messages are archived.)

Very often, when replying to a message sent by a member of the group, it is not appropriate to send your reply to the entire group. If your reply will be of peripheral interest to the group, send it only to the individual who requested the information. This is one of the most common discussion group errors and the Internet and mail servers are slower because of these breaches in "netiquette" (Internet etiquette). Lastly, if you send a question to a group, it is also good netiquette to summarize the individual responses that you received from your query and send that summary to the list members. For more on discussion group netiquette, see Arlene Rinaldi's site at: http://www.fau.edu/~rinaldi/netiquette.html. This site covers the proper use of discussion groups as well the proper use of other tools of the Internet and World Wide Web.

When new environment-related discussion groups are created, the list managers usually send out alerts to the relevant mailing lists in this chapter. Another way of learning about new discussion groups that may have been created since the publication of this book, is to use one of the discussion group search engines such as Lists.com (http://www.lists.com) or Reference.com (http://www.reference.com).

ACN-L (Aquatic Conservation Network)

Email address	majordomo@acn.ca
To subscribe:	subscribe acn-l

Description: This list is provided for the members of the Aquatic Conservation Network, which is based in Ottawa, Canada, but is open to non-members as well. It was established to encourage "discussion pertaining to aquatic biodiversity and conservation" and to disseminate announcements and other information pertaining to the activities of the ACN.

Likely users:	Aquarists, conservationists, and scientists.
Frequency:	Low to moderate activity.
Contact:	owner-acn-l@acn.ca

AE (Alternative Energy)

Email address:	listproc@listproc.sjsu.edu
To subscribe:	subscribe ae firstname lastname

Description: This list serves as a vehicle to discuss the variety of forms and applications of alternative energy. Topics cover new and emerging alternative energy sources and innovative ways to use solar, wind, and other power sources. This is a very interesting and down-to-earth group.

Likely users:	Conservationists, educators, scientists, and home hobbyists will all find something of interest on this list.
Frequency:	Low to moderate activity.
Contact:	Clyde Visser: cvisser@cyberg8T.com

AERE-L (Association of Environmental and Resource Economists)

Email address: listserv@lsv.uky.edu
To subscribe: subscribe aere-l firstname lastname

Description: This is the mailing list for the Association. It is used primarily to disseminate information about the activities and events pertaining to the Association. Those who wish to discuss topics related to land management are encouraged to use the RESECON list, which is sponsored by AERE.

Likely users: Members of the Association, those interested in environmental economics.
Frequency: Low to moderate activity.
Contact: Glenn Blomquist: gcblom@pop.uky.edu

AEROSO-L

Email address: listserv@nic.surfnet.nl
To subscribe: subscribe aeroso-l

Description: This list was established for those whose interests are in the health effects "associated with exposure to various concentrations and classes of particulate matter (PM) in ambient air." This list was established for discussion about topics such as "generation and characterization methods of aerosols, biological effect parameters (e.g. biochemical, immunological) and respiratory tract dosimetry models." Pure medical or ecological aspects are not in the group's focus.

Likely users: Environmental health workers, environmental engineers, scientists, researchers.
Frequency: Low to moderate activity.
Contact: Flemming Cassee: fr.cassee@rivm.nl

AFWATER

Email address: majordomo@aqua.ccwr.ac.za
To subscribe: subscribe afwater

Description: This discussion group was formed to encourage discussion of water in Southern Africa. Topics may range from water quality, the environment, people, programs, or policies.

Likely users: Environmental engineers, civil engineers, hydrologists.
Frequency: Low activity.
Contact: John Carter: john@dwaf-hri.pwv.gov.za

AG-IMPACT (Agricultural and Environmental Impact)

Email address:	listproc@mtn.org
To subscribe:	subscribe ag-impact firstname lastname

Description:	This group was formed to enable discussion regarding the assessment of the impact of agriculture on the environment and is administered by the Institute for Agriculture and Trade Policy in Minneapolis, Minnesota. Postings also include conference announcements and information.

Likely users:	Agriculturalists, environmentalists, horticulturalists, extensionists.
Frequency:	Low activity.
Contact:	owner-ag-impact@mtn.org
	John Vickery: jvickery@iatp.org

AGLAW-L

Email address:	listproc@lawlib.wuacc.edu
To subscribe:	subscribe aglaw-1 firstname lastname

Description:	This list was created for the exchange of ideas, opinions, and information regarding laws, legislation, policies, and rulings pertaining to agriculture.

Likely users:	Agriculturalists, academicians, law students, legal professionals.
Frequency:	Low activity.
Contact:	Paul Arrigo: zzarri@acc.wuacc.edu

AGRIC-L

Email address:	listserv@listserv.uga.edu
To subscribe:	subscribe agric-1 firstname lastname

Description:	Discussion pertaining to agriculture. Information received upon subscribing lists several relevant topics including grassland husbandry, crop science, ecological modeling, water resource management, soil science, and plant propagation. Sustainable agriculture is also discussed.

Likely users:	Extensionists, researchers, educators.
Frequency:	Low to moderate activity.
Contact:	lsvmaint@uga.cc.uga.edu

AIRPOLLUTION-BIOLOGY

Email address: mailbase@mailbase.ac.uk
To subscribe: join airpollution-biology firstname lastname

Description: This list was established to allow discussion among scientists whose interests are centered on the impact of air pollution on the environment. Topics include ecology, genetics, physiology, and biochemistry; however, the effects that air pollution has on human health are not discussed here.

Likely users: Scientists, environmental engineers, educators.
Frequency: Low activity.
Contact: airpollution-biology-request@mailbase.ac.uk
Emma.Clamp@ncl.ac.uk

ALIENS-L

Email address: ssc-mgr@indaba.iucn.org
To subscribe: subscribe aliens-l

Description: This discussion group was formed by the Invasive Species Specialist Group (ISSG) under the auspices of the IUCN Species Survival Commission. They are interested in reducing "the threats posed by invasive species to natural ecosystems and their native species, through increasing awareness of invasive species and means of controlling or eradicating them." Discussion covers all aspects of invasive species. Nonmembers are welcome to join in the discussion.

Likely users: Conservationists, ecologists, IUCN members.
Frequency: Moderate to high activity.
Contact: aliens-l-owner@indaba.iucn.org

ALT-TRANSP

Email address: majordomo@flora.org
To subscribe: subscribe alt-transp

Description: This list was created to further the discussion of alternative means of transportation. Discussion may cover a range of issues including public transit systems, bicycling, air pollution, alternative energies, and environmental and economic issues. Postings include methods, theories, and practical solutions to the growing problem of the sole-passenger-automobile as our main means of transportation.

Frequency: Moderate activity.
Likely users: Public works personnel, civil engineers, environmentalists.
Contact: owner-alt-transp@flora.org

AMP

Email address:	listproc@rana.im.nbs.gov
To subscribe:	subscribe amp firstname lastname

Description: This group was formed to discuss "aspects of the development and implementation of extensive programs for amphibian monitoring." Recognizing the need for information on the distribution of amphibians, they focus on monitoring programs. Though intended for coverage in North America, discussion may cover other areas of the world. They do not cover the specific topics related to the decline of amphibians.

Likely users:	Herpetologists, biologists, ecologists, conservationists.
Frequency:	Low to moderate activity.
Contact:	frog@nbs.gov *or* Brett.Hoover@nbs.gov

AMPHIBIANDECLINE

Email address:	listproc@ucdavis.edu
To subscribe:	subscribe amphibiandecline firstname lastname

Description: This group was formed to provide for discussion of the conservation of the declining amphibian population. Discussion involves environmental concerns including pollution and other threats. In the welcome message, relevant topics also include the discussion of measuring techniques.

Likely users:	Ecologists, biologists, herpetologists, conservationists.
Frequency:	Low activity.
Contact:	Gary M. Fellers: gmfellers@ucdavis.edu

AR-NEWS (Animal Rights News)

Email address:	listproc@envirolink.org
To subscribe:	subscribe ar-news your@emailaddress firstname lastname

Description: This list was formed for the dissemination of information pertaining to animal rights. Postings include news items, program announcements, and requests for news information.

Likely users:	Animal rights activists, consumers, educators, entrepreneurs.
Frequency:	High activity.
Contact:	ar-admin@envirolink.org

AR-VIEWS (Animal Rights Views)

Email address: listproc@envirolink.org
To subscribe: subscribe ar-views your@emailaddress firstname lastname

Description: This list was formed for the discussion of issues pertaining to animal rights. This
                  may cover a broad area including animal rights pertaining to dissection, laboratory
                  use, research, testing, hunting, farming, education, entertainment, and use in
                  consumer products. Discussion may also be on ethical, social, or religious theories
                  as they relate to animal rights.

Likely users: Animal rights activists, consumers, educators, entrepreneurs.
Frequency: High activity.
Contact: cassi@cybernetica.de

ASN (Audubon Student Network)

Email address: majordomo@list.audubon.org
To subscribe: subscribe asn

Description: This discussion group, sponsored by the National Audubon Society, was created
                  to support environmentally active students. The goal is to foster communication
                  and enhance the environmental awareness of the student membership.

Likely users: College students and their advisors
Frequency: Low activity.
Contact: ASN Coordinator: asn@audubon.org

AUDUBON

Email address: autoshare@rip.physics.unk.edu
To subscribe: sub audubon firstname lastname

Description: This is an unmoderated list formed for National Audubon Society chapter
                  members; however anyone interested in the conservation and use of the
                  environment is welcome to join the group. Discussion centers on wildlife,
                  conservation efforts, and distribution of information.

Likely users: Educators, students, naturalists.
Frequency: Low to moderate activity.
Contact: Robert Price: price@rip.physics.unk.edu

AUDUBON-CHAT

Email address:	listserv@list.audubon.org
To subscribe:	subscribe audubon-chat

Description: This group was formed to discuss the variety of issues surrounding the environment. Members of the group also receive information about the National Audubon Society's programs and current activities. You need not be a member of the National Audubon Society to join this group.

Likely users: Audubon Society members, students, conservationists, activists, anyone interested in the environment.

Frequency: Moderate to high activity.

Contact: audubon-chat-request@audubon.org

AUDUBON-NEWS

Email address:	listserv@list.audubon.org
To subscribe:	subscribe audubon-news

Description: Members of this group receive news and information from the National Audubon Society. This information may be about their programs, their activities, current events, or any other information pertaining to the environment that the list owners feel would be important to the list members. This is a read-only group. (Messages may not be posted by members.)

Likely users: Members of the Audubon Society, naturalists, conservationists.

Frequency: Moderate activity.

Contact: audubon-news-request@list.audubon.org

BALLERINA-L

Email address:	lists@lists.grida.no
To subscribe:	subscribe ballerina-l

Description: This list was created to enable discussion among those "concerned with issues related to environment, natural resources, and sustainable development in the Baltic Sea Region." It serves as an avenue for dissemination of information, discussion, and inquiries in support of the BALLERINA Initiative. This initiative aims "to contribute to the sustainable development of the Baltic Sea Region environment, by improving the availability and accessibility of relevant information on the Internet for decision-making at all levels."

Likely users: Environmentalists, conservationists, natural resource personnel, anyone interested in the environmental health of the Baltic Sea Region.

Frequency: Low to moderate activity.

Contact: ballerina-l-owner@lists.grida.no

BBLMTAB

Email address:	listproc@rana.im.nbs.gov
To subscribe:	subscribe bblmtab firstname lastname

Description: This list was created under the auspices of the North American Bird Banding Program and its Bird Banding Laboratory (BBL) so that information, official BBL memos, and other banding information may be disseminated and shared. Discussion of the role of the Bird Banding Laboratory in avian research is encouraged.

Likely users:	Bird banders, conservationists, avian researchers.
Frequency:	Very low activity.
Contact:	Mary Gustafson: mary_gustafson@usgs.gov

BCWATERSHED (Boulder Creek Watershed, Colorado)

Email address:	listproc@csf.colorado.edu
To subscribe:	subscribe bcwatershed firstname lastname

Description: This group was established to discuss issues surrounding the Boulder Creek Basin. The boundaries of this area are "the Continental Divide from Navajo, [Colorado] to James Peak and then east to the confluence of Boulder Creek with the St. Vrain watershed east of Longmont." Several tributaries and 12 immediate communities in Colorado are involved. Though developed to encourage discussion about the water quality and use and management efforts among the residents of the communities, this list is open to those outside the area. Nonresidents may find the projects of interest.

Likely users:	Residents of Colorado, nonresidents with interests in watershed management, environmentalists, policy makers, planners.
Frequency:	Very low activity.
Contact:	Mark McCaffrey: mccaffrm@csf.colorado.edu

BEE-L

Email address:	listserv@cnsibm.albany.edu
To subscribe:	subscribe bee-l

Description: This list was created to enable discussion regarding research and information concerning the biology of bees. Discussion may cover "sociobiology, behavior, ecology, adaptation/evolution, genetics, taxonomy, physiology, pollination, and flower nectar and pollen production of bees." Posts to this list have covered all aspects of beekeeping, air pollution, pesticides, parasites of bees, weather and bee behavior.

Likely users: Biologists, ecologists, beekeepers, extensionists, those involved in sustainable agriculture.
Frequency: High to very high activity.
Contact: bee-l-request@cnsibm.albany.edu

BIODIV-L (Biodiversity Information Network/Agenda 21)

Email address:	listserv@bdt.org.br
To subscribe:	subscribe biodiv-l firstname lastname

Description: This list is sponsored by the Base de Dados Tropical (BDT) in Brazil and was designed to discuss the establishment of a network for use in disseminating biodiversity information. It serves as a vehicle to alert members of issues pertaining to environmental and biological threats.

Likely users: Conservationists, ecologists, biologists.
Frequency: Low to moderate activity.
Contact: manager@bdt.org.br

BIOENERGY

Email address:	majordomo@crest.org
To subscribe:	subscribe bioenergy

Description: Discussion of biomass as a sustainable energy resource. The welcome message that is sent to group members indicates that relevant discussion would include: combustion, gasification and power generation, biomass energy resources, biofuel conversion, and anaerobic digestion. Also covered are news releases regarding research and development, funding, and programs related to bioenergy. Discussion covers a broad spectrum, including energy efficiency and sustainable energy.

Likely users: Scientists, educators, researchers, government officials, and those involved in research or production of biomass and its conversion to energy.
Frequency: Moderate activity.
Contact: owner-bioenergy@crest.org

BIOGROUP (Bioremediation Group)

Email address:	bioremediation-request@bio.gzea.com
To subscribe:	subscribe your@emailaddress biogroup
	(Or, join via the BioGroup home page at http://biogroup.gzea.com)

Description: The Bioremediation group is made available by GZA GeoEnvironmental, Inc. to enable discussion among those interested in bioremediation. Topics may include standards, protocols, innovative approaches, testing, and news regarding bioremediation efforts.

Likely users:	Environmental engineers, hydogeologists, soil scientists.
Frequency:	Moderate activity.
Contact:	I. Richard Schaffner, Jr.: rschaffner@gzea.com

BIOREGIONAL

Email address:	listproc@csf.colorado.edu
To subscribe:	subscribe bioregional firstname lastname

Description: This list was created to enhance the exchange of information, ideas, and discussion relating to "bioregionalism across bioregional boundaries." The list owners encourage discussion on the "design and evolution of healthy, interdependent, and self-reliant communities."

Likely users:	Community planners, civic leaders, ecopsychologists, environmentalists.
Frequency:	Low to moderate activity.
Contact:	Fred Cagle: cagle1@mail.sdsu.edu
	Dan Earle: EarleLa@aol.com
	Phil Ferraro: Pferraro@cycor.ca
	Ed Self: SelfE@csf.colorado.edu

BIOSPH-L

Email address:	listserv@listserv.aol.com
To subscribe:	subscribe biosph-l

Description: A biosphere and ecology discussion list created to allow dialogue among persons interested in the biosphere and ecological concerns. The topics are biologically oriented.

Likely users:	Researchers, biologists, ecologists.
Frequency:	Low to moderate activity.
Contact:	biosph-l-request@listserv.aol.com *or*
	Dave Phillips: davep@niagaracyber.com

BIRDBAND (Bird Bander's Forum)

Email address:	listserv@listserv.arizona.edu
To subscribe:	subscribe birdband firstname lastname

Description: List devoted to discussion surrounding banding of birds. Discussion has covered problems and procedures related to banding.

Likely users:	Bird watchers, naturalists, and conservationists.
Frequency:	Low activity.
Contact:	Jean Bickal: jbickal@pluto.njcc.com
	Lyndon Kearsley: kearsley@club.innet.be

BIRDCHAT (National Birding Hotline Cooperative)

Email address:	listserv@listserv.arizona.edu
To subscribe:	subscribe birdchat

Description: This group was created for discussion of "birds, birding, and birders." This covers a very broad area including: taxonomy, identification, populations, conservation, sitings, and equipment. The list owner discourages any postings regarding birds as pets or bird feeding.

Likely users:	Bird watchers, naturalists, conservationists, biologists.
Frequency:	High to very high activity.
Contact:	Chuck Williamson: CWilliamson@PimaCC.Pima.EDU
	birdchat-request@listserv.arizona.edu

CAREERPRO

Email address:	majordomo@igc.org
To subscribe:	subscribe careerpro

Description: This group was created under the auspices of the California Economic Recovery and Environmental Restoration Project (Career/Pro) at the Urban Institute (San Francisco State University). This group fosters communication dealing with military base closure, cleanup, and conversion. They are very interested in the environment and the problems, activities, and legislation surrounding military base closure.

Likely users:	Environmentalists, activists, California residents.
Frequency:	Low activity.
Contact:	owner-careerpro@igc.org or
	Aimee Houghton: aimeeh@igc.org

CARNIVORE-L (Carnivore Research)

Email address: listserv@freeside.nrm.se
To subscribe: subscribe carnivore-l

Description: This list was developed for the professional whose interests are in the evolution, systematics, behavior, ecology, or conservation of mammalian carnivores. Topics dealing with living as well as fossil are encouraged. Topics dealing with domestic animals are discouraged. Discussion may relate to research projects, publications, conferences, meetings, or other activities.

Likely users: Taxonomists, paleontologists, ecologists, conservationists, environmentalists.
Frequency: Low activity.
Contact: carnivore-l-request@freeside.nrm.se *or* werdelin@nrm.se

CA-WATER (California Water)

Email address: majordomo@list.dcn.davis.ca.us
To subscribe: subscribe ca-water

Description: A discussion group established to share information relating to California's water issues.

Likely users: Hydrologists, environmentalists, California residents.
Frequency: Low activity.
Contact: kjwolf@wheel.dcn.davis.ca.us

CBCN-L (Canadian Botanical Conservation Network)

Email address: listproc@listserv.cis.mcmaster.ca
To subscribe: subscribe cbcn-l firstname lastname

Description: The Canadian Botanical Conservation Network is comprised of organizations and individuals including the Department of Biology at McMaster University and the Royal Botanical Gardens. This group was created to discuss botanical conservation, restoration ecology, and other topics important to botanical ecology.

Likely users: Botanists, conservationists, ecologists.
Frequency: Low to moderate activity.
Contact: David Galbraith: davidg@mcmail.cis.mcmaster.ca

CCSEA-L (Canadian Coastal Science and Engineering Association)

Email address: majordomo@csx.cciw.ca
To subscribe: subscribe ccsea-l

Description: This group was formed so that communication and discussion regarding Canadian coasts may be facilitated. Any issues relevant to the coastal areas of the Atlantic Ocean, Pacific Ocean, Great Lakes or the Arctic Ocean may be covered.

Likely users: Scientists, engineers, natural resource managers, environmentalists.
Frequency: Low activity.
Contact: Michael Skafel: michael.skafel@cciw.ca

CEAM-USERS (Center for Exposure Assessment Modelling Software Users)

Email address: listserver@unixmail.rtpnc.epa.gov
To subscribe: subscribe ceam-users

Description: Members of this group receive information about the Center for Exposure Assessment Modelling's software products and their use, the Center's activities and events. Members of the group may also share and discuss their experiences with CEAM software.

Likely users: Users of CEAM software.
Frequency: Low activity.
Contact: disney.dave@epamail.epa.gov

CECNET (Commission for Environmental Cooperation)

Email address: listserv@listserv.arizona.edu
To subscribe: subscribe cecnet

Description: The CEC is a group formed by Canada, Mexico, and the United States with headquarters in Montreal. This list serves as their communication vehicle for discussion and to disseminate announcements and reports of studies and events pertaining to NAFTA. The list owners intentions are to stimulate debate and to provide information about issues pertaining to the objectives and impact of the CEC. For further information on the mission of CEC, see their Web site at: http://www.cec.org.

Likely users: Members of The Commission, North American entrepreneurs, those with interests in environmental laws.
Frequency: Low activity.
Contact: cecnet-request@listserv.arizona.edu

CERES-L (Collaborative Environments for Conserving Earth Resources)

Email address:	listserv@wvnvm.wvnet.edu
To subscribe:	subscribe ceres-l firstname lastname

Description: This list was created to enhance the dissemination of information related to recyclability, disposability, and the regulatory statutes surrounding those topics. Their goal is to elicit changes in manufacturing that will conserve our natural resources.

Likely users: Engineers, natural resource researchers, manufacturing concerns, and policy makers.

Frequency: Low activity.

Contact: ceres-l-request@wvnvm.wvnet.edu

CICHLID-L (Cichlid Systematics)

Email address:	listserv@nrm.se
To subscribe:	subscribe cichlid-l

Description: This group's focus is on "all issues related to the field of cichlid documentation, with emphasis on systematics, ecology, behavior, and conservation."

Likely users: Scientists, conservationists, ecologists.

Frequency: Low to moderate activity.

Contact: CICHLID-L-Request@NRM.SE

CITES-L (Convention on International Trade in Endangered Species)

Email address:	majordomo@wcmc.org.uk
To subscribe:	subscribe cites-l firstname lastname

Description: Sponsored by the World Conservation Monitoring Centre. This list was established for the discussion of wildlife trade and issues related to the Convention on International Trade in Endangered Species.

Likely users: Wildlife service workers, persons involved in natural resources management, legislators, educators, and conservationists.

Frequency: Moderate activity.

Contact: owner-cites-l@petra.wcmc.org.uk or
J. R. Caldwell: john.caldwell@wcmc.org.uk

CITNET-LIST (Citizens Network for Sustainable Development)

Email address: majordomo@igc.org
To subscribe: subscribe citnet-list

Description: This list was developed to enable discussion among citizens whose interests are in sustainable development. News releases and information pertaining to the environment and sustainable development are disseminated and discussed.

Likely users: Activists, environmental journalists.
Frequency: Moderate activity.
Contact: owner-citnet-list@igc.org

CLIM-ECON (Economics of climate variability and global change)

Email address: listproc@csf.colorado.edu
To subscribe: subscribe clim-econ firstname lastname

Description: This list is intended to bridge the gap between the social and the natural sciences and to discuss the economic issues surrounding climate change. This list is one of many sponsored by the Communications for a Sustainable Future.

Likely users: Economists, students of economics, educators, researchers, and environmentalists.
Frequency: Moderate activity.
Contact: kathleen@vorlon.esig.ucar.edu
    parkin@csf.colorado.edu

CMC-OCEANALERT

Email address: majordomo@igc.org
To subscribe: subscribe cmc-oceanalert

Description: This list was established by the Center for Marine Conservation. It is a read-only list, which distributes information to activists regarding marine conservation issues. The information may be in the form of press releases, fact sheets, and recent legislation and rulings.

Likely users: Activists, conservationists, environmentalists.
Frequency: Low activity.
Contact: owner-cmc-oceanalert@igc.org

CNIE (Committee for the National Institute for the Environment)

Email address: listproc@csf.colorado.edu
To subscribe: subscribe cnie firstname lastname

Description: The Committee for the National Institute for the Environment created this group to facilitate discussion pertaining to the creation of the National Institute for the Environment. The NIE and other environmental research and development projects may be discussed.

Likely users: Environmentalists, business leaders, scientists.
Frequency: Low activity.
Contact: khutton@cnie.org or cnie@cnie.org

COASTNET (Coastal Management Conference)

Email address: listserv@uriacc.uri.edu
To subscribe: subscribe coastnet firstname lastname

Description: This group was formed by the Coastal Resources Center and the Department of Marine Affairs at the University of Rhode Island. Discussion centers on national and international coastal management issues. Topics include ecosystem management strategies, theories and philosophies, conservation, and ongoing research. Postings also include tables of contents from coastal journals.

Likely users: Marine biologists, conservationists, decision makers, planners.
Frequency: Low activity.
Contact: Coastnet-request@uriacc.uri.edu

COCE-L (Conference on Communication and our/the Environment)

Email address: listserv@yorku.ca
To subscribe: subscribe coce-l

Description: This group was formed to communicate about the biennial Conference on Communication and Environment and to discuss issues relating to environmental communication. Communication may be mass media, speech communication, rhetorical, linguistic, and cultural studies. Postings may include job announcements, publication announcements, news releases, and general information relating to communication and the environment. The periodical, *Ecologue*, may also be distributed to list members.

Likely users: Educators and scholars from a variety of disciplines, especially environmental science professors.
Frequency: Moderate activity.
Contact: Mark Meisner: mesiner@yorku.ca

COMPOST

Email address:	listproc@listproc.wsu.edu
To subscribe:	sub compost firstname lastname

Description:	A list created for discussion of composting. Problems, solutions, and practical applications are discussed.

Likely users:	Composters, agriculturalists, gardeners, home extensionists, ecologists.
Frequency:	Moderate activity.
Contact:	wright@wsu.edu
	mattsen@coopext.cahe.wsu.edu
	cbmac@wsu.edu

COMPSY-L (Student forum for ecological/community psychology)

Email address:	listserv@postoffice.cso.uiuc.edu
To subscribe:	sub compsy-l firstname lastname

Description:	This discussion group was formed to enable communication between students of ecological and community psychology. Their primary focus is on ecological aspects as they relate to psychology. Though some messages pertain to specific, local issues, much of the discussion is relevant to students and educators all over.

Likely users:	Graduate and undergraduate students, educators.
Frequency:	Very low activity.
Contact:	compsy-l-request@postoffice.cso.uiuc.edu

CONSBIO

Email address:	listproc@u.washington.edu
To subscribe:	sub consbio firstname lastname

Description:	This group was created to discuss issues relating to conservation biology.

Likely users:	Biologists, educators, researchers, conservationists.
Frequency:	Low activity.
Contact:	pdh@u.washington.edu

CONSLINK

Email address:	listserv@sivm.si.edu
To subscribe:	subscribe conslink firstname lastname

Description: Conslink was established by the Conservation and Research Center of the Smithsonian Institution to enable discussion on biological conservation. Postings include news releases and summaries of bills and legislation pertinent to the environment.

Likely users:	Biologists, conservationists, educators.
Frequency:	Low activity.
Contact:	Michael Stuewe: nzpem001@sivm.si.edu

CORAL-LIST

Email address:	majordomo@coral.aoml.noaa.gov
To subscribe:	subscribe coral-list

Description: This list was created to enable discussion on the health and conservation of coral reefs. Issues discussed focus on environmental, biological, and ecological topics and their relationship to the sustainability of coral reefs.

Likely users:	Biologists, conservationists, marine biologists, ecologists.
Frequency:	Moderate to high activity.
Contact:	owner-coral-list@coral.aoml.noaa.gov

CTB-NEWS (Comprehensive Test Ban News)

Email address:	majordomo@igc.org
To subscribe:	subscribe ctb-news

Description: This list was established by the Comprehensive Test Ban Clearinghouse (CTBC) to serve as a vehicle to quickly disseminate information regarding nuclear testing, disarmament, and the Comprehensive Test Ban Treaty. Members of CTBC are Greenpeace, Peace Action, Physicians for Social Responsibility, and Plutonium Challenge.

Likely users:	Activists, environmentalists, educators, environmental journalists.
Frequency:	Very low activity from the CTBC. Low activity from members.
Contact:	owner-ctb-news@igc.org

CTURTLE (Sea Turtle Biology and Conservation)

Email address:	listserv@lists.ufl.edu
To subscribe:	subscribe cturtle firstname lastname

Description: Discussion surrounding the conservation of sea turtles. Topics include breeding, species' habits, environmental threats, and current issues in the news pertaining to the sea turtle population.

Likely users:	Marine biologists, conservationists.
Frequency:	Moderate to high activity.
Contact:	cturtle-request@lists.ufl.edu

CZM (Coastal Zone Management)

Email address:	majordomo@ecology.bio.dfo.ca
To subscribe:	subscribe czm

Description: This discussion group was created to exchange, share and discuss information about coastal zone management. Members are encouraged to share and discuss scientific applications.

Likely users:	Natural resource managers, conservationists.
Frequency:	Low activity.
Contact:	owner-czm@ecology.bio.dfo.ca

DEVEL-L (Technology Transfer in International Development)

Email address:	listserv@american.edu
To subscribe:	subscribe devel-l firstname lastname

Description: This list is sponsored by Volunteers in Technical Assistance and was created to enable discussion relating to international development and the transfer of technology. The discussion ranges from theoretical to practical issues, and from technical to very broad issues.

Likely users:	Activists, environmentalists, policy makers, social scientists, public service officials, anyone with an interest in developing countries and international development.
Frequency:	Moderate activity.
Contact:	devel-l-request@american.edu

DIALOG-AGUA-L

Email address:	listserv@centauri.ces.fau.edu
To subscribe:	subscribe dialog-agua-l firstname lastname
	(Or, use the site at http://www.ces.fau.edu/online/dialogagual/ subscription.html)

Description: This list is sponsored by the Inter-American Dialogue on Water Management (IADWM) and the Water Research Network (IWRN). It was established by the Florida Center for Environmental Studies to share information on water technologies among the countries of the Western Hemisphere.

Likely users:	Marine biologists, aquaculturists, ecologists.
Frequency:	Moderate activity.
Contact:	dialog-agua-L-request@centauri.ces.fau.edu

DIGESTION

Email address:	majordomo@crest.org
To subscribe:	subscribe digestion your@emailaddress

Description: This list, sponsored by the Center for Renewable Energy and Sustainable Technology (CREST), was created to enable discussion of anaerobic digestion as a sustainable energy resource. Discussion may cover practical applications and barriers to the use of AD technology. The list managers created this group to provide a means for sharing "lessons learned" from past experiences and to "provide reliable information on the cost effectiveness of AD, markets for biogas and other co-products, advanced technologies for biogas utilization, environmental benefits, and institutional barriers."

Likely users:	Waste managers, scientists, researchers, educators.
Frequency:	Low to moderate activity.
Contact:	Philip Lusk: plusk@usa.pipeline.com
	Richard Nelson: rnelson@oz.oznet.ksu.edu
	David Stephenson: cdstephenson@tva.gov
	Patrick Wheeler: patrick.wheeler@aeat.co.uk

DIOXIN-L

Email address:	listproc@essential.org
To subscribe:	subscribe dioxin-l firstname lastname

Description: This discussion group was created by the Citizen's Clearinghouse for Hazardous Waste (CCHW). Members of this group receive bulletins and news releases on issues involving dioxin.

Likely users: Persons involved in policy making and decision making, persons who want to keep abreast of the decisions, laws, and research surrounding dioxin.

Frequency: Low to moderate activity.

Contact: dioxin-l-owner@essential.org

DRIFTERS

Email address:	majordomo@reeusda.gov
To subscribe:	subscribe drifters

Description: This group was formed "to share information, data, and training activities on managing pesticide drift." It is intended to coordinate the efforts of those involved in drift management by allowing them to share and discuss the advantages and disadvantages of various techniques.

Likely users: Educators, researchers, trainers, government, and industry regulators.

Frequency: Low to moderate activity.

Contact: John W. Impson: jimpson@reesusda.gov

EARTHNET

Email address:	majordomo@igc.org
To subscribe:	subscribe earthnet

Description: EarthNet was created so that discussion about environmental issues could continue between students and interested scholars after the Campus Earth Summit in 1994. It is sponsored by Campus Green Vote and serves as a vehicle to share environmental news, activities, and projects pertaining to the environment.

Likely users: Students, academicians, environmentalists, campus officials.

Frequency: EarthNet news bulletins have been sent on a weekly or monthly basis.

Contact: cgv@igc.apc.org

Earthwatch

Email address: listproc@envirolink.org
To subscribe: subscribe earthwatch firstname lastname

Description: Earthwatch is a nonprofit organization that focuses on all aspects of the health of
                   our environment. Members participate in a wide variety of scientific research. This
                   list was established to enable discussion between the Earthwatch volunteers and
                   researchers.

Likely users: Earthwatch volunteers, researchers, students and those interested in the
                   activities of Earthwatch and its research.
Frequency: Low to moderate activity.
Contact: network_manager@earthwatch.org
                   dmoy@earthwatch.org

ECDM (Environmentally Conscious Design and Manufacturing)

Email address: listserv@pdomain.uwindsor.ca
To subscribe: subscribe ecdm firstname lastname

Description: This discussion group focuses on environmentally conscious manufacturing,
                   including designing for recycling, costs involved, and a variety of other issues. In
                   the informational material received upon subscription to the list, possible topics for
                   inclusion in discussion are life-cycle analysis, disassembly, material recovery,
                   testing, quality, reliability, designing for product reuse, and establishing markets.

Likely users: Industry, government, engineers, entrepreneurs.
Frequency: Low to moderate activity.
Contact: ecdm-request@pdomain.uwindsor.ca

ECOCITIES

Email address: majordomo@oneworld.org
To subscribe: subscribe ecocities

Description: This list was established to foster discussion involving sustainable urban
                   development. Discussion may cover, but is not limited to, population issues,
                   environmental ethics, and pollution.

Likely users: Urban planners and managers, ecologists, ecopsychologists, sociologists and
                   environmentalists.
Frequency: Low activity.
Contact: owner-ecocities@oneworld.org

ECO-FUND

Email address:	listserv@umdd.umd.edu
To subscribe:	subscribe eco-fund firstname lastname

Description: This list was formed to discuss environmental finance issues. Sponsored by the Environmental Finance Center of the Coastal and Environmental Policy Program and the Maryland Sea Grant College, the focus is on issues pertaining to environmental finance as it relates to all aspects of environmental planning. The stated mission of the group is to explore new ways to: (1) take into consideration finance as part of the strategic management process, and (2) help communities in their search for creative approaches to funding environmental projects.

Likely users:	Decision makers, environmental engineers, educators.
Frequency:	Low activity.
Contact:	eco-fund-request@umdd.umd.edu

ECOL-AGRIC

Email address:	mailbase@mailbase.ac.uk
To subscribe:	join ecol-agric firstname lastname

Description: This list is for discussion focusing on agriculture and its relationship to biological and organic ecology.

Likely users:	Researchers, academics, and persons in ecological and sustainable agriculture.
Frequency:	Low to moderate activity.
Contact:	ecol-agric-request@mailbase.ac.uk

ECOL-ECON (Ecological Economics)

Email address:	listproc@csf.colorado.edu
To subscribe:	subscribe ecol-econ firstname lastname

Description: This list is sponsored by Communications for a Sustainable Future and was created to elicit innovative ideas pertaining to economic theories and their relationship to ecology and the environment. (The archives of this list are available at the CSF web address: http://csf.colorado.edu/ecolecon).

Likely users:	Students of economics, educators, economists, decision makers, and legislators.
Frequency:	Moderate activity.
Contact:	roper@csf.colorado.edu or 70412.3303@compuserve.com

ECOLOG-L (Ecological Society of America)

Email address: listserv@umdd.umd.edu
To subscribe: subscribe ecolog-l firstname lastname

Description: This is a moderated list for members of the Ecological Society of America, but nonmembers may also subscribe. A majority of the discussion focuses on job and fellowship announcements, conferences, and publications. Theoretical and applied ecological issues are also discussed.

Likely users: Persons who wish to stay informed about job postings and conferences relating to ecology. In addition, educators, students, professional ecologists, and biologists would find the discussion of interest.
Frequency: Moderate activity.
Contact: David Inouye: di5@umail.umd.edu

ECOPOLITICS

Email address: listproc@efn.org
To subscribe: subscribe ecopolitics firstname lastname

Description: This group was formed to facilitate discussion of politics in the "Age of Ecology." This list welcomes discussion of all facets of ecological politics. This would include, but not be limited to, topics involving the relationships that "local communities have with both their immediate ecosystem and the broader forces of political economy." For example, this may include government regulations, policies, global warming, and pollution.

Likely users: Urban planners, environmentalists, educators, anthropologists, geographers, and political scientists whose interests are in the environment.
Frequency: Moderate activity.
Contact: Milton Takei: miltont@efn.org

ECOPSYCHOLOGY (Nature-Counseling Community Connection)

Email address: listserv@maelstrom.stjohns.edu
To subscribe: subscribe ecopsychology firstname lastname

Description: This discussion group was created to share "artful, spirited and scientific discussion on a wide range of topics" surrounding the field of ecopsychology. This group conducts some very lively, positive, invigorating discussion.

Likely users: Ecopsychologists, social ecologists, social psychologists, ecologists.
Frequency: Moderate to high activity.
Contact: ecopsychology-request@maelstrom.stjohns.edu

ECOSYS-L (Ecosystem Theory and Modelling)

Email address:	listserv@listserv.gmd.de
To subscribe:	subscribe ecosys-l firstname lastname

Description:	This group was created to foster discussion on ecosystem theory and modelling. Discussion includes mathematical models and theories.

Likely users:	Researchers, educators, ecologists.
Frequency:	Low activity.
Contact:	Joachim Benz: Benz@wiz.uni-kassel.de

ECOTALK

Email address:	ecotalk-request@earthsystems.org
To subscribe:	Send message to above address with SUBSCRIBE as the subject.

Description:	EcoTalk is sponsored by Earth Systems, a non-profit organization at http://earthsystems.org. The list group was formed to facilitate discussion on issues "related to the operation of an environmental non-profit organization. Topics include problems non-profits face, how non-profits receive funding for their cause, and how best to get the message of a particular non-profit to the public."

Likely users:	Those involved in environmental, nonprofit organizations.
Frequency:	Low activity.
Contact:	www@earthsystems.org

EE-CAFÉ

Email address:	listserv@csf.colorado.edu
To subscribe:	subscribe ee-café firstname lastname

Description:	This is an unmoderated list sponsored by Communications for a Sustainable Future. A major goal of CSF is to foster positive communications regarding environmental topics. To help meet this end, this list was created to elicit innovative ideas pertaining to economic theories and their relationship to ecology and the environment.

Likely users:	Students of environmental economics, educators, economists, decision makers, and legislators.
Frequency:	High activity.
Contact:	roper@csf.colorado.edu

EE-INTERNET

Email address:	ee-internet-subscribe@eelink.net
To subscribe:	Send a blank message to above address. You will need to respond to the automated message that you will then receive.
Description:	This discussion group was established to help identify and share environmental education resources located on the Internet.
Likely users:	Teachers of environmental education.
Frequency:	Moderate activity.
Contact:	p-nowak@eelink.net

EGT

Email address:	listproc@csf.colorado.edu
To subscribe:	sub egt firstname lastname
Description:	This group was designed for the study and discussion of game theory as it relates to environmental issues. Topics may include compliance to environmental laws, issues dealing with trading, and modelling applications.
Likely users:	Graduate students who wish to discuss their anticipated topics of dissertations. Also educators, lawyers, and environmentalists.
Frequency:	Low activity.
Contact:	Mark Cronshaw: cronshaw@magellan.colorado.edu

EIA (Environmental Impact Assessment)

Email address:	majordomo@cedar.univie.ac.at
To subscribe:	subscribe eia your@emailaddress
Description:	This list was designed to be used by those in all venues of professional employ whether governmental, nongovernmental, academic, or research institutions. Discussion relates to environmental impact issues such as site assessment, laws and regulations, and economics.
Likely users:	Policy makers, engineers, environmental researchers and anyone interested in the international scope of environmental impact assessment.
Frequency:	Low to moderate activity.
Contact:	Bernhard Lorenz: bernhard.lorenz@cedar.univie.ac.at

EIM (Environmental Interactions of Mariculture)

Email address:	majordomo@biome.bio.dfo.ca
To subscribe:	subscribe eim your email address

Description: This group was created to discuss monitoring and modelling the environmental interactions of mariculture.

Likely users:	Ecologists, researchers, and marine biologists.
Frequency:	Low activity.
Contact:	owner-eim@ecology.bio.dfo.ca

EISG (Environmental Information System Group)

Email address:	majordomo@enviro.arcs.ac.at
To subscribe:	subscribe eisg

Description: This group was formed to enhance the discussion of techniques, developments, and issues relating to environmental information systems. Discussion may include software design, conferences, and informatic technologies.

Likely users:	Software developers, systems personnel, researchers, and those involved in the field of informatics technology.
Frequency:	Low activity.
Contact:	majordomo@enviro.arcs.ac.at

ELAN (Environment in Latin America Network)

Email address:	listproc@csf.colorado.edu
To subscribe:	subscribe elan firstname lastname

Description: This unmoderated list was created by the Environment and Natural Resources Working Group of the Latin American Studies Association to foster communication between researchers, educators, activists, and any other persons with an interest in the issues that are facing the Latin American countries today. Many of the postings are in Spanish, many are in English, and a few are posted in both languages.

Likely users:	Those with an interest in Latin America and the problems relating to its natural resources.
Frequency:	Low to moderate activity.
Contact:	David Barkin: barkin@servidor.dgsca.unam.mx

ELI-WETLANDS

Email address:	majordomo@igc.org
To subscribe:	subscribe eli-wetlands

Description: This discussion group was created under the auspices of the Environmental Law Institute (ELI). Its purpose is to foster communication regarding legal, scientific, and managerial concerns of wetlands, floodplains, and coastal water resources. ELI, a nonprofit organization, is very active in providing environmental information to professionals.

Likely users: Environmentalists, wetlands professionals, educators, conservationists, members of the legal profession, scientists, and natural resource managers.

Frequency: Low to moderate activity.

Contact: owner-eli-wetlands@igc.org

ENCON-L (Energy Conservation Management Issues in Higher Education)

Email address:	listserv@listserv.syr.edu
To subscribe:	subscribe encon-l

Description: This list was created for exchange of discussion among persons interested in applying conservation procedures and measures in their institutions.

Likely users: College and university facilities maintenance and management personnel, conservationists, educators, researchers, scientists.

Frequency: Very low activity.

Contact: emducey@summon.syr.edu

ENERGYSTAR

Email address:	listserver@unixmail.rtpnc.epa.gov
To subscribe:	subscribe energystar firstname lastname

Description: This is the mailing list for the Green Lights and Energy Star Buildings programs of the Environmental Protection Agency. This is a read-only list where a newsletter containing information about events and activities is issued.

Likely users: Those interested in energy conservation, energy-efficient lighting or in the Green Lights or other Energy Star Buildings programs.

Frequency: Approximately two issues per month.

Contact: Christie Smith: smith.christie@epamail.epa.gov

eNetDigest

Email address:	subscribe@enetdigest.com
To subscribe:	subscribe eNetDigest your@email address
	(The subject of the message should be: subscribe)
	The body of the message should include your title and affiliation.
	You may also subscribe at: http://www.enetdigest.com/subscribe.html

Description: EnetDigest is a guide to environmental, agricultural, and natural resources sites on the Internet. Resources include Web sites and discussion lists. The resources are rated for their content and usability. This is a read-only list.

Likely users:	Students, researchers, educators, environmental science professors.
Frequency:	Issued bi-monthly.
Contact:	Kathy E. Gill: kegill@enetdigest.com

ENVBEH-L

Email address:	listproc@duke.poly.edu
To subscribe:	subscribe envbeh-l firstname lastname

Description: Discussion focusing on human behavior. Issues relating to the effects of human behavior on the environment as well as environmental effects on human behavior.

Likely users:	Sociologists, biologists, ecologists, social psychologists, social ecologists.
Frequency:	Low to moderate activity.
Contact:	root@duke.poly.edu or
	rwener@duke.poly.edu

ENVBUS-L (Environment and Business in Central and Eastern Europe)

Email address:	listserv@rec.org
To subscribe:	subscribe envbus-l firstname lastname

Description: This list was established by the Regional Environmental Center for Central and Eastern Europe (REC) to elicit communication and collaboration among persons who are interested in the business and environmental issues that are facing Central and Eastern Europe today. The geographic, topical coverage includes Albania, Bulgaria, Croatia, Czech Republic, Hungary, Poland, Romania, Slovak Republic, Slovenia, and the former Yugoslav Republic of Macedonia. Topics include regulations and standards, financing, pollution, environmental jobs, conferences, and news releases.

Likely users:	Educators, environmentalists, decision makers, international business owners.
Frequency:	Low to moderate.
Contact:	rossen@rec.hu or emil@fs2.bp.rec.hu

ENVCEE-L (Environmental Issues in Central and Eastern Europe)

Email address: listserv@rec.org
To subscribe: subscribe envcee-l firstname lastname

Description: This list was established by the Regional Environmental Center (REC) for Central and Eastern Europe to elicit communication and collaboration among persons who are interested in the environmental issues that are facing Central and Eastern Europe today. The geographic, topical coverage includes Albania, Bulgaria, Croatia, Czech Republic, Hungary, Poland, Romania, Slovak Republic, Slovenia, and the former Yugoslav Republic of Macedonia. The mission of this list is to "promote cooperation among diverse environmental groups and interests in Central and Eastern Europe; to act as a catalyst for developing solutions to environmental problems in this region; and to promote the development of a civil society." Sharing of a variety of environmental information regarding the region is done via this list.

Likely users: Central and Eastern European environmental scientists, educators, legislators.
Frequency: Moderate activity.
Contact: Ivelin Roussev: ivo@rec.org or ivo@fs2.bp.rec.hu

ENVCONFS-L

Email address: listproc@environment.harvard.edu
To subscribe: subscribe envconfs-l firstname lastname

Description: The EnvConfs mailing list disseminates information regarding conferences, workshops, symposiums, and seminars pertaining to the environment. This list is also used to announce publication opportunities.

Likely users: Environmental science professors, natural, or physical sciences professors.
Frequency: Low to moderate activity.
Contact: Tom Parris: tparris@fas.harvard.edu

ENVENG-L

Email address: majordomo@drexel.edu
To subscribe: subscribe enveng-l

Description: This list was created "for the discussion of environmental engineering practice, education, and research." Topics may cover waste treatment and management, water supply, air pollution control, noise and radiation protection, and related issues. There is much technical discussion on this list with a substantial sharing of expertise.

Likely users: Environmental engineers, environmental science professors, researchers, and scientists.
Frequency: Moderate activity.
Contact: HAASCN@Dunx1.ocs.drexel.edu
HAASCN@duvm.ocs.drexel.edu

ENVEVENTS-L

Email address: listserv@rec.org
To subscribe: subscribe envevents-l

Description: This list was established under the auspices of the Regional Environmental Center (REC) for Central and Eastern Europe to disseminate information regarding environmental events taking place in Central and Eastern Europe. The geographic, topical coverage includes Albania, Bulgaria, Croatia, Czech Republic, Hungary, Poland, Romania, Slovak Republic, Slovenia, and the former Yugoslav Republic of Macedonia.

Likely users: Environmentalists, conservationists, scientists, and members of Central and Eastern Europe with interests in the environment.
Frequency: Low to moderate activity.
Contact: Ivelin Roussev: ivo@rec.org or ivo@fs2.bp.rec.hu

ENVINF-L (Environmental Information Distribution List)

Email address: listserv@nic.surfnet.nl
To subscribe: subscribe envinf-l firstname lastname

Description: This list was established to share information about publications and educational materials relating to the environment. Activity on the list therefore is focused more on disseminating recent information about the environment rather than being a place for discussion. However, teaching strategies for various environmental topics may be discussed.

Likely users: Environmental scientists, researchers, students, and anyone involved in teaching about the environment.
Frequency: Moderate activity.
Contact: Jos Boelens: jos.boelens@ivm.vu.nl
                 Peter Maarleveld: maarleveld@vsnu.nl

ENVIROETHICS

Email address: mailbase@mailbase.ac.uk
To subscribe: join enviroethics firstname lastname

Description: This list was established to provide for discussion and exchange of ideas relating to environmental ethics. Discussion covers a wide range of ethical topics surrounding the environment: conservation, wetlands, wildlife, and pollution. There are messages pertaining to practical applications of theories as well.

Likely users: Decision makers, legislators, educators, conservationists, ecologists.
Frequency: Low to moderate activity.
Contact: enviroethics-request@mailbase.ac.uk
                 Clare Palmer: C.A.Palmer@greenwich.ac.uk
                 Ian Tilsed: I.J.Tilsed@exeter.ac.uk

ENVIROMINE-ISSUES

Email address: listproc@info-mine.com
To subscribe: subscribe enviromine-issues firstname lastname

Description: Created for the non-technical discussion of mining-related environmental issues. Topics may cover issues such as qualitative impacts, socio-economic considerations, cultural aspects, political items, or rulings and regulations. This group has several *mentors* on its membership list to enable discussion.

Likely users: Policy makers, decision makers, researchers, persons in the mining industry.
Frequency: Low to moderate activity.
Contact: mailinglists@info-mine.com

ENVIROMINE-TECHNICAL

Email address:	listproc@info-mine.com
To subscribe:	subscribe enviromine-technical firstname lastname

Description: Created for the discussion of mining-related environmental issues that are technical in nature. Topics cover issues related to environmental technology and management. These may include reclamation, pollution prevention, design, waste management practices and requirements, case histories, acid rock drainage, and environmental monitoring. This group has several *mentors* on its membership list to enable discussion.

Likely users:	Environmental engineers, researchers, persons in the mining industry.
Frequency:	Low activity.
Contact:	enviroman@info-mine.com

ENVIRONB-L (Enviro-Newsbrief)

Email address:	listserver@unixmail.rtpnc.epa.gov
To subscribe:	subscribe environb-l firstname lastname

Description: This list was established to disseminate news regarding EPA activities by sending the daily update, *Enviro-Newsbrief*, to list members. News items cover EPA appointments, changes in processes, environmental legislation, and reauthorization of key legislation. This is a read-only list. A searchable archive of past Enviro-Newsbriefs are located at this EPA address: http://www.epa.gov/natlibra/hqirc/enb.htm

Frequency:	Once daily.
Likely users:	Policy makers, environmentalists, conservationists.
Contact:	library-hq@epamail.epa.gov

ENVIRO-NEWS

Email address:	majordomo@nal.usda.gov
To subscribe:	subscribe enviro-news

Description: This list was created to distribute timely environmental news. The news, information, and announcements posted here cover the broad area of the natural environment. In addition to press releases from environmental agencies and organizations, postings may include information on conferences, seminars, congressional briefings, employment opportunities, and new Internet resources. Members may post information to the list, but may not ask for information or discuss any of the issues reported on.

Likely users: Scientists, information specialists, administrators, librarians, and other professionals of the U.S. Department of Agriculture's Agricultural Research Service and National Agricultural Library.

Frequency: Moderate.

Contact: John Makuch: jmakuch@nal.usda.gov

ENVIRONEWS

Email address:	listproc@envirolink.org
To subscribe:	subscribe environews firstname lastname

Description: This is a moderated, environmental news service. News may be about pending laws and regulations, environmental monitoring efforts, or other issues that need to be made public and are international in scope. Members may submit environmental news to the contact address below.

Likely users: Anyone interested in keeping up with current happenings regarding the environment.

Frequency: Low to moderate activity.

Contact: newsdesk@envirolink.org

ENVIRONMENT-L

Email address:	listproc@cornell.edu
To subscribe:	subscribe environment-l firstname lastname

Description: This list was formed to discuss environmental issues in and around New York State; however, much of their discussion, news releases, and topics of concern are of national and international interest. The list is maintained under the auspices of the Center for the Environment at Cornell University.

Likely users: Students, environmental journalists, researchers, educators, and decision makers.

Frequency: Moderate activity.

Contact: cmc39@cornell.edu or cs10@cornell.edu

ENVJOBS-L (Environmental Jobs List)

Email address:	listproc@environment.harvard.edu
To subscribe:	subscribe envjobs-l firstname lastname

Description: This list was formed to publicize job openings, fellowships, and other employment opportunities in the environmental sciences. Governmental, academic, nonprofit and commercial sectors are all represented here.

Likely users: In addition to employers and employees, students of the sciences should find this valuable as an aid in class selection for job focus.

Frequency: Approximately two digest issues per week.

Contact: Tom Parris: tparris@fas.harvard.edu

ENVLAWPROFS (Environmental Law Professors)

Email address:	majordomo@lists.uoregon.edu
To subscribe:	subscribe envlawprofs

Description: This list was created to enable discussion among Environmental Law Professors. Conference information, news, legislation, and research interests may be discussed.

Likely users: Environmenal law professors, law professors.

Frequency: Low to moderate activity.

Contact: owner-envlawprofs@lists.uoregon.edu

ENVPUBS-L

Email address:	listproc@environment.harvard.edu
To subscribe:	subscribe envpubs-l firstname lastname

Description: This list was created to disseminate and share information about the many environmental publications and resources that are made available on the Internet. Sources are from all sectors of the environmental community: government agencies, commercial concerns, nonprofit organizations, researchers, and practitioners.

Likely users: Students, researchers, environmentalists, and librarians.

Frequency: Weekly digests.

Contact: Tom Parris: tparris@fas.harvard.edu

ENVST-L (Environmental Studies Discussion List)

Email address: listserv@brownvm.brown.edu
To subscribe: subscribe envst-l firstname lastname

Description: This group was created to facilitate discussion between educators who are involved
                  in teaching about the environment. Topics discussed include strategies and software
                  used for teaching specific environmental topics, evaluation of textbooks, and basic,
                  theoretical concepts of environmental studies. Information regarding conferences,
                  symposia, and issues affecting the environment are also discussed here.

Likely users: Environmental science professors, others teaching in the natural sciences, students,
                  researchers.
Frequency: Moderate activity.
Contact: Envst-l-request@brownvm.brown.edu

ENVTECSOC (Environment Technology and Society)

Email address: listproc@csf.colorado.edu
To subscribe: subscribe envtecsoc firstname lastname

Description: The Environment Technology and Society group was founded by the American
                  Sociology Association. Discussion focuses on social ecology with topics including
                  social theories and their applications to the ecology of our planet, environmental
                  applications, legal issues, and ecopsychology.

Likely users: Sociologists and students of sociology, educators, decision makers, lawyers, and
                  planners.
Frequency: Low to moderate activity.
Contact: Timmons Roberts: timmons@mailhost.tcs.tulane.edu

EON (Environment on the Net)

Email address: majordomo@world.std.com
To subscribe: subscribe eon

Description: This group is focused on the use of the Internet and intranets for environmental
                  applications. Their goal is to find and share effective and innovative ways to use
                  the Internet for the betterment of our environment.

Likely users: Environmentalists, environmental studies academicians, activists, governmental
                  employees, and persons in industry.
Frequency: Low to moderate activity.
Contact: owner-eon@world.std.com

EPA- (Environmental Protection Agency)

Email address: listserver@unixmail.rtpnc.epa.gov
To subscribe: subscribe epa- firstname lastname
(You must send a separate email message for each list that you wish to join, for example, subscribe epa-air John Doe)

Description: The U.S. Environmental Protection Agency currently has twelve read-only lists to help distribute environmental information as it is added to the *Federal Register* from the various offices. These are very often large textual files. Each of the twelve lists is devoted to a topic, format, or office:

EPA-AIR	Office of Air and Radiation
EPAFR-CONTENTS	Complete table of contents of the *Federal Register*
EPA-GENERAL	General EPA and non-program specific documents; presidential documents
EPA-IMPACT	Environmental impact statements
EPA-MEETINGS	Meeting notices
EPA-PEST	Office of Pesticide Programs
EPA-SAB	Science Advisory Board documents
EPA-SPECIES	Endangered species documents
EPA-TOX	Office of Pollution Prevention and Toxic Substances documents
EPA-TRI	Community-Right-To-Know documents (Toxic Release Inventory)
EPA-WASTE	Hazardous and Solid Waste documents
EPA-WATER	Office of Water documents

Likely users: Environmentalists, conservationists, environmental studies academicians, industrial officers, activists.
Frequency: The number (and size) of documents sent varies.
Contact: envsubset@epamail.epa.gov

EPA-GRANTS

Email address: listserver@unixmail.rtpnc.epa.gov
To subscribe: subscribe epa-grants firstname lastname

Description: This discussion group was formed to "promote the interactive exchange of news and information within the environmental grants community." It is managed by the Grants Administration Division of EPA.

Likely users: Researchers, educators, students, anyone with an interest in environmental grant information.
Frequency: Low activity.
Contact: garner.donald@epamail.epa.gov

EPA-PRESS

Email address:	listserver@unixmail.rtpnc.epa.gov
To subscribe:	subscribe epa-press firstname lastname

Description: This read-only list was created to distribute information to the news media and others with interest in the activities of the EPA. The material sent via this list are official EPA press releases.

Likely users: Environmental journalists, environmentalists, conservationists, environmental science academicians.

Frequency: Moderate to high volume of releases.

Contact: press@epamail.epa.gov

EPA-R2-PRESS

Email address:	listserver@unixmail.rtpnc.epa.gov
To subscribe:	subscribe epa-r2-press firstname lastname

Description: This is the press release mailing list for EPA Region 2. This region covers New York, New Jersey, Puerto Rico, and the Virgin Islands. Distributed here in addition to press releases may be advisories and related fact sheets.

Likely users: Environmental journalists, environmentalists, conservationists, environmental science academicians.

Frequency: Moderate.

Contact: stapleton.richard@epamail.epa.gov

ESSA (Earthships and Self Sufficient Architecture)

Email address:	listproc@csf.colorado.edu
To subscribe:	subscribe essa firstname lastname

Description: This list was created to provide for the exchange of communication and information regarding self-sufficient architecture. Members of Earthship Global Operations and Solar Survival Architecture provide "a knowledge base for all subscribed." The discussion covers technical aspects, materials, design, and environmental considerations.

Likely users: The environmentally-conscious, engineers, activists, and those interested in building or maintaining an earthship.

Frequency: Moderate to high activity.

Contact: donal@nm.net or
roper@csf.colorado.edu

EUROFISH-L

Email address:	listserv@nrm.se
To subscribe:	subscribe eurofish-l firstname lastname

Description: This European Ichthyology Conference List "is maintained primarily for the academic community and a major objective is to further international communication among individual scientists and research institutions in Europe, in particular to assist in forming networks and to help locate human and material resources within the European Community." This group was not designed for discussion of particular research topics.

Likely users:	European ichthyologists and others interested in European ichthyology.
Frequency:	Low activity.
Contact:	EUROFISH-L-request@grundoon.nrm.se

EV (Electric Vehicle)

Email address:	listproc@listproc.sjsu.edu
To subscribe:	subscribe ev firstname lastname

Description: This group was formed to facilitate discussion pertaining to electric vehicles. Many areas are covered including practical, technical, environmental, social, or theoretical issues.

Likely users:	Environmental engineers, those in industry, scientists, anyone interested in building or maintaining their own electric vehicle.
Frequency:	High to very high activity.
Contact:	Clyde Visser: cvisser@cyberg8T.com

EWIRE

Email address:	ewire@igc.apc.org
To subscribe:	subscribe e-wire

Description: This list was established to distribute environmental press releases. News items cover topics such as environmental health and safety, hazardous waste cases and decisions, alternative energy, industrial developments, and endangered species.

Likely users:	Environmentalists, conservationists, policy makers.
Frequency:	Low to moderate.
Contact:	Jim Crabtree: ewire@igc.apc.org

EW-RADIO

Email address:	listserver@relay.doit.wisc.edu
To subscribe:	subscribe EW-RADIO firstname lastname

Description: Earthwatch Radio is sponsored by the Sea Grant Institute and the Institute for Environmental Studies at the University of Wisconsin-Madison. Earthwatch Radio broadcasts cover a variety of topics related to science and the environment. Special attention is given to the Great Lakes region, the oceans, and the climate. Members of this list receive the script of each broadcast. This is a "read only" list; no messages are accepted from subscribers.

Likely users:	Researchers, ecologists, academicians.
Frequency:	Five scripts per week.
Contact:	owners-ew-radio@relay.doit.wisc.edu

Federal Compliance Alert

URL:	http://elsevier.enviroinfo.com/frame3.shtml
To subscribe:	Fill out form at above Web site.

Description: This free mailing service is provided by Elsevier Science to keep users up-to-date on the latest U.S. regulatory developments. Based on a user-interest profile, email is issued when a regulatory action of interest is published in the *Federal Register*. The message sent contains the date of the action, the *Federal Register* page numbers, affected part of the *Code of Federal Regulations* and a brief summary of the action.

Likely users:	Anyone interested in environmental regulations.
Frequency:	Varies with personal profile.
Contact:	elsevier@elsevier-hr.com

FISHERIES

Email address:	majordomo@ecology.bio.dfo.ca
To subscribe:	subscribe fisheries

Description: This list was created for the discussion of fish-related topics. Issues covered include the broad area of fisheries management: laws and regulations, stock dynamics, pollution, breeding, and management issues.

Likely users:	Persons involved in aquaculture, the fishing industry, research, or education relating to fish and fishes.
Frequency:	Low activity.
Contact:	Bill Silvert: bill@biome.bio.dfo.ca

FISHFOLK (Fisheries Social Science Network)

Email address:	listserv@mitvma.mit.edu
To subscribe:	subscribe fishfolk firstname lastname

Description: This list was created by a group of social scientists with an interest in fisheries. The founders of the group met at the National Maritime Fisheries Aquarium in Woods Hole, Massachusetts and their shared conversations there led to the establishment of the group. Topics include sustainability, laws and legislation, and any issues relating to the fishing industry.

Likely users: Persons involved in the fisheries industry, biologists, social scientists, conservationists, and academicians.

Frequency: Moderate to high activity.

Contact: fishfolk-request@mitvma.mit.edu

FISH-SCI (International Forum for Fishery Science)

Email address:	listserv@segate.sunet.se
To subscribe:	subscribe fish-sci fristname lastname

Description: This list was created for the discussion of fish and fisheries. The list owners welcome topics related to fishery science which may include the "relevant aspects of biology, oceanography, ecology, limnology, economics, mathematics, sociology and any other scientific disciplines contributing to current understanding of fish, shellfish, and their fisheries." This replaces the former fish-ecology discussion group.

Likely users: Fishery scientists, resource managers, educators.

Frequency: Moderate to high activity.

Contact: fish-sci-request@segate.sunet.se

FOODSAFE

Email address:	majordomo@nal.usda.gov
To subscribe:	subscribe foodsafe firstname lastname <your@email address>
	(Be sure to include the < > around your email address.)

Description: Though this discussion group is sponsored by units within the U.S. Department of Agriculture and the Food and Drug Administration, the discussion may not necessarily reflect the opinions and policies of the USDA or FDA. And, though much of the discussion covers safe food preparation, postings periodically include issues related to the environment such as pesticides, organic farming, and food contamination and safety issues.

Likely users: Environmental health and safety officials.

Frequency: High activity.

Contact: croberts@nal.usda.gov

FOODSAFETY

Email address:	majordomo@igc.org
To subscribe:	subscribe foodsafety your@emailaddress

Description: This group was previously the CHLORINE-NEWS discussion group. They continue to focus on the use of non-toxic alternatives to chlorine. It was created by the Institute for Agriculture and Trade Policy. Discussion is focused on alternatives to chlorine use in industry, agriculture, and water treatment. They also are interested in discussing the effects of organochlorines on human health, on our wildlife, and on the environment. The Institute's bulletin, *Chlorine Monitor*, is posted here.

Likely users:	Agriculturalists, environmentalists, conservationists, water quality personnel.
Frequency:	Low activity.
Contact:	owner-foodsafety@igc.org or
	Jackie Hunt Christensen: iatp@igc.apc.org

FOREST

Email address:	listserv@nic.funet.fi
To subscribe:	subscribe forest firstname lastname

Description: This group was formed to enable discussion on forest research. Topics cover conservation, sustainable forestry, and research issues.

Likely users:	Natural resources professionals, forest scientists, researchers, educators, biologists.
Frequency:	Moderate to high activity.
Contact:	forest-request@listserv.funet.fi

FWIM-L (Fish and Wildlife Information Management)

Email address:	listserv@listserv.vt.edu
To subscribe:	subscribe fwim-l firstname lastname

Description: This discussion group was formed by the Organization of Fish and Wildlife Information Management, The Wildlife Society Remote Sensing Working Group, the American Fisheries Society Computer User's Group, and the Information Management Committee of the International Association of Fish and Wildlife Agencies. It was created to serve as a vehicle for exchange of information and expertise on issues regarding fish and wildlife management. Topics may include specific software applications, technologies, training issues, and data collection.

Likely users:	Professional information managers in the fields of wildlife, fisheries, and land management, biologists, natural resources officials.
Frequency:	Low to moderate activity.
Contact:	fwim-l-request@listserv.vt.edu

FWS-SHOREBIRDS

Email address: majordomo@listserv.fws.gov
To subscribe: subscribe fws-shorebirds

Description: This discussion group, established by the U.S. Fish and Wildlife Service, was created so that students, teachers, parents and shorebird enthusiasts could share information during the spring migration of Arctic nesting shorebirds. Information exchanged may cover field trip sightings, the shorebirds' behavior, habitats, or ecology, or questions and answers.

Likely users: Students, educators, bird enthusiasts, conservationists.
Frequency: During the "off-season", activity is very low; however during the spring migration, this group does get quite lively.
Contact: Heather Johnson: heather_johnson@mail.fws.gov

GASIFICATION

Email address: majordomo@crest.org
To subscribe: subscribe gasification

Description: This list was created to enable discussion of gasification of biomass as a form of sustainable energy. Discussion may cover all aspects of "gasification and related chemical processes such as pyrolysis."

Likely users: Environmental engineers, energy personnel.
Frequency: Low to moderate activity.
Contact: owner-gasification@crest.org

GENERAL

Email address: General-Subscribe@lists.holisticmanagement.org
To subscribe: Send blank message with no subject to above address.

Description: This discussion group is hosted by the Center for Holistic Resource Management and was created to enhance discussion involving the practice of "holistic resource management." They encourage discussion pertaining to the use of ecological, economical and social considerations in land management and community development.

Likely users: Natural resources officials, urban planners and managers, environmentalists.
Frequency: Low activity.
Contact: center@holisticmanagement.org

GEO-COMPUTER-MODELS

Email address: mailbase@mailbase.ac.uk
To subscribe: join geo-computer-models firstname lastname

Description: The geo-computer-models list was established to share information on the growing
                   use of computer models in the fields of geology, geography, hydrogeology,
                   geochemistry, and engineering. Any issue or topic, including conference
                   announcements, relating to computer modelling in the geosciences is welcome.

Likely users: Geologists, environmental engineers.
Frequency: Low activity.
Contact: geo-computer-models-request@mailbase.ac.uk

GEO-ENV

Email address: mailbase@mailbase.ac.uk
To subscribe: join geo-env firstname lastname

Description: This list was created to distribute information from the Geological Society's (UK)
                   Environment Group and to discuss and share information regarding "environmental
                   issues that interface with geology." Any aspect of the geosciences in relation to the
                   environment is welcome discussion. May include postings of conferences, events,
                   programs, and publications.

Likely users: Members of the Geological Society and its Environment Group, geologists,
                   environmental scientists.
Frequency: Low to moderate activity.
Contact: geo-env-request@mailbase.ac.uk

GEO-GIG

Email address: mailbase@mailbase.ac.uk
To subscribe: join geo-gig firstname lastname

Description: This list was created by the Geoscience Information Group (GIG) of The
                   Geological Society to distribute, exchange, and discuss geological information. The
                   geographical information may include numeric, non-numeric, bibliographic, or
                   computer applications.

Likely users: Geological Society members, geologists, environmentalists, researchers,
                   academicians, geoscientists.
Frequency: Low activity.
Contact: Paul Browning: Paul.Browning@bris.ac.uk

GLIN-ANNOUNCE (Great Lakes Information Network)

Email address:	majordomo@great-lakes.net
To subscribe:	subscribe glin-announce

Description: This read-only list was established to distribute information regarding the Great Lakes region. Information may be announcements about events, legislation, or news releases.

Likely users:	Environmentalists, conservationists, hydrologists, ecologists, educators.
Frequency:	Low to moderate activity.
Contact:	Christine Manninen: manninen@glc.org

GLIN-EDUCATION (Great Lakes Information Network)

Email address:	majordomo@great-lakes.net
To subscribe:	subscribe glin-education

Description: This list was created to enable discussion among educators regarding the Great Lakes Region. Discussion covers a wide variety of environmental information pertaining to the Great Lakes Region. They welcome input from educators on teaching strategies and instructional theories that have been effective.

Likely users:	Educators, students, scientists, natural resource managers, policy makers and governmental employees.
Frequency:	Low activity.
Contact:	Christine Manninen: manninen@glc.org

GREENSEE

Email address:	listserv@plearn.edu.pl
To subscribe:	subscribe greensee

Description: This list was established to facilitate discussion among and about Greens in Central and Eastern Europe.

Likely users:	Students, academicians, activists.
Frequency:	Low activity.
Contact:	GREENSEE-request@plearn.edu.pl

GREEN-TRAVEL

Email address:	majordomo@igc.org
To subscribe:	subscribe green-travel

Description: This is a moderated list designed to share information about environmentally conscious travel and tourism. Postings include state department travel information and environmentally conscious travel guidelines. Discussion involves holistic tourism, ecotourism, and the promotion of tourism with a minimal impact on the environment.

Likely users:	Travelers, persons involved in hospitality and tourism, department of state officials, environmentalists, conservationists.
Frequency:	Moderate activity.
Contact:	owner-green-travel@igc.org or
	Marcus Endicott: Mendicott@igc.apc.org

GRNSCH-L

Email address:	listserv@brownvm.brown.edu
To subscribe:	subscribe grnsch-l

Description: Discussion of practical recycling programs and use of recycling materials on college campuses. Ideas are shared on how to manage and maintain recycling efforts, the problems involved in initiating campus-wide recycling programs, and effective uses of student involvement.

Likely users:	College and university facility managers.
Frequency:	Low to moderate activity.
Contact:	GRNSCH-L-Request@brownvm.brown.edu

GROUNDWATER

Email address:	majordomo@ias.champlain.edu
To subscribe:	subscribe groundwater

Description: The groundwater list was created to enable discussion and facilitate the distribution of information "pertaining to groundwater science and its related disciplines." Relevant postings may cover technologies, conferences, seminars, workshops, or publications.

Likely users:	Hydrogeologists, geoscientists, natural resources managers, policy makers.
Frequency:	Moderate activity.
Contact:	Ken Bannister: kenbannister@groundwater.com

GT-ATMDC (Atmospheric Dispersion of Chemicals)

Email address:	listserv@nic.surfnet.nl
To subscribe:	subscribe GT-ATMDC firstname lastname

Description: This is a group formed under the auspices of the Global Research Network on Sustainable Development for those with a professional interest in atmospheric dispersion of chemicals. It was formed to study and share findings on the sources, actions and effects of chemicals on the atmosphere, and the consequent atmospheric effects on land and water.

Likely users:	Scientists, geochemists.
Frequency:	Low activity.
Contact:	Ivo Bouwmans: Bouwmans@Interduct.tudelft.nl

GWCAN-L (Canadian Hydrogeology)

Email address:	majordomo@gw2.cciw.ca
To subscribe:	subscribe gwcan-l

Description: Discussion group pertaining to groundwater in Canada.

Likely users:	Natural resource personnel, conservationists, environmental engineers, educators, and researchers.
Frequency:	Low activity.
Contact:	gwcan-l-approval@gwrp.cciw.ca or Pat.Lapcevic@cciw.ca

GWM-L (Groundwater Modelling)

Email address:	majordomo@gwrp.cciw.ca
To subscribe:	subscribe gwm-l

Description: This list was created for the discussion of all aspects of groundwater modelling. Its intended emphasis is on research and practical aspects, methods, and applications of groundwater modelling. Discussion may cover tools and techniques and ongoing research. Conference, workshop, and seminar announcements may also be posted here.

Likely users:	Researchers, those involved in groundwater modelling.
Frequency:	Low to moderate activity.
Contact:	gwm-l-approval@gwrp.cciw.ca

H-ASEH (American Society for Environmental History)

Email address:	listserv@h-net.msu.edu
To subscribe:	subscribe H-ASEH firstname lastname:

Description: Environmental history deals with the past interactions of human beings with their physical environment. This list encourages scholarly discussion and exchange of information and research on interaction of humans with the environment since early times. Many of the leading professionals in the field participate in the discussion here.

Frequency:	Moderate activity.
Likely users:	Environmental historians and those who wish to trace the effect human beings have had on the earth's environment.
Contact:	Dennis Williams: DWILLIAM@SNU.EDU

HealthE

Email address:	listserv@home.ease.lsoft.com
To subscribe:	subscribe HealthE firstname lastname

Description: This moderated list was established to "educate the general public about potential environmental threats to physical, emotional, and psychological health and well-being." They also aim to develop strategies to aid in the reduction of health risks and to work "towards finding solutions to prevent environmentally caused health problems." The welcome message received upon subscription to this list gives more details about the goals and appropriate discussion topics. Topics may cover water, air, soil, radiant energy, food safety, noise, consumer products, or the workplace.

Likely users:	Health professionals, environmentalists, policy makers, sociologists.
Frequency:	High activity.
Contact:	Andrea "Andi" DesJardins: healtheadmin@juno.com or enviroknow@aol.com

Hudson-R

Email address:	majordomo@matrix.newpaltz.edu
To subscribe:	subscribe hudson-r

Description: The Hudson-R list has been established to encourage the exchange of ideas on all aspects of the Hudson River and its surrounding regions. Some topics discussed here include environmental conservation, regional planning and development, ecology, riparian rights, transportation issues, and jurisdictional aspects.

Likely users: Professional environmentalists and those living in areas affected by the ecology of the Hudson River.

Frequency: Low activity.

Contact: Robert Chasan: Chasan73@matrix.newpaltz.edu

Human Dimensions of Global Environmental Change

Email address:	majordomo@listhost.ciesin.org
To subscribe:	subscribe hdgec

Description: CIESIN and the International Human Dimensions of Global Change Programme (IHDP) sponsor the HDGEC list. The intention of this list is to provide a platform for the exchange of ideas on the human dimensions of global environmental change. The list archives exist at http://listhost.ciesin.org/lists/public/hdgec/.

Likely users: Scientists, scholars, policy makers, journalists, students, and any others interested in the human dimensions of global environmental change.

Frequency: Moderate activity.

Contact: ciesin.info@ciesin.org

HYDROGEN

Email address:	listserv@uriacc.uri.edu
To subscribe:	subscribe HYDROGEN firstname lastname

Description: The purpose of the Hydrogen list is to exchange information and ideas about the production, storage, and use of hydrogen as an alternative fuel. Some of the topics discussed pertain to terminology, processes, and environmental fuel issues. Information on seminars and conferences, products, services, pertinent news, and questions for discussion may be posted to this list.

Likely users: Researchers from universities, governments, and industry and all who are interested in the environmental aspects of alternative fuels.

Frequency: Moderate to high activity.

Contact: hydrogen-request@uriacc.uri.edu

HYDROLOGY

Email address:	MAJORDOMO@eng.monash.edu.au
To subscribe:	subscribe hydrology

Description:	This list was created for the exchange of information and ideas about the science of water in the environment. The focus is Australian, but membership is open to all who are interested in scientific research in hydrology.

Likely users:	Persons outside the traditional field of engineering hydrology.
Frequency:	Low activity.
Contact:	Andrew Haines: andrew.haines@eng.monsh.edu.au

IASEE-L

Email address:	listserv@vm.gmd.de
To subscribe:	subscribe IASEE-L firstname lastname

Description:	The IASEE-L list is a discussion list for solar energy education and encourages the exchange of ideas and information on solar energy as an alterative to other depletable energy sources. Current postings have concerned solar energy powered personal computers.

Likely users:	Educators, researchers, students and others with ideas about solar energy.
Frequency:	Low activity.
Contact:	kblum@prehp.physik.uni-oldenburg.de

industrial-ecology

Email address:	mailbase@mailbase.ac.uk
To subscribe:	join industrial-ecology firstname lastname

Description:	Industrial-ecology welcomes dialogue on industrial environmental issues including enviro/economics, tools, implications of new legislation, clean technology/ industrial ecology, EIA/sustainable planning, and commercial environmental policy.

Likely users:	Industrial environmentalists and those who want to keep up with new environmental legislation issues.
Frequency:	Low activity.
Contact:	mailbase@mailbase.ac.uk

INFOTERRA

Email address:	majordomo@cedar.univie.ac.at
To subscribe:	subscribe infoterra your@email.address

Description: Infoterra is an international list whose purpose is to encourage the exchange of ideas on general environmental topics. Questions and responses are welcome as well as postings on conferences, seminars, and reviews of new books on environmental issues.

Likely users:	Those interested in the environment in general.
Frequency:	Moderate to high activity.
Contact:	majordomo@cedar.univie.ac.at

IRNES (Interdisciplinary Research Network on the Environment and Society)

Email address:	mailbase@mailbase.ac.uk
To subscribe:	join IRNES firstname lastname

Description: IRNES is a discussion list for those interested in the relationship between humans and their environment and the impact that each has on the other. Other topics include the interrelationship between ecosystems and the earth's biodiversity. This list includes news about conferences, meetings, publications, jobs, and discussions on collaborative work within the Network.

Likely users:	Members of the Interdisciplinary Research Network on the Environment and Society and others concerned with human impact on the environment.
Frequency:	Very low activity.
Contact:	irnes-request@mailbase.ac.uk

IRRIGATION-L

Email address:	listserv@listserv.gmd.de
To subscribe:	subscribe IRRIGATION-L firstname lastname

Description: The primary purpose of IRRIGATION-L is to share information on irrigation, soil, drainage, irrigation technology, and problems related to these and other topics. Any type of irrigation system, product, theory or project may be discussed here. New subscribers are asked to submit a short posting about themselves, why they are interested in this list, and how the discussion topics pertain to their work.

Likely users:	People involved in any type of irrigation project, researchers, farmers, persons interested in soil and water conservation.
Frequency:	Moderate activity.
Contact:	Thomas-M. Stein: stein@wiz.uni-kassel.de

ISEA-L (International Students for Environmental Action)

Email address:	listserv@nic.surfnet.nl
To subscribe:	subscribe ISEA-L firstname lastname

Description: The International Students for Environmental Action list contains discussions of students and student groups lobbying for sustainable development at universities around the world. Topics include respecting nature, environmental care, greening the curricula, and environmental action.

Likely users:	Students involved with environmental lobbying.
Frequency:	Moderate activity.
Contact:	ISEA-L-Request@NIC.SURFNET.NL

ISO14000

Email address:	majordomo@quality.org
To subscribe:	subscribe iso14000

Description: This list was created to enable discussion concerning the ISO 14000 certification guidelines for environmental and related industries. Discussion may cover specific cases, implementations, training, and standards. Discussion has also been on the ISO 14001 EMS.

Likely users:	Environmental industries, water treatment facilities, and waste facilities professionals.
Frequency:	Moderate to high activity.
Contact:	iso14000-approval@quality.org

ITEX

Email address:	listproc@lists.Colorado.EDU
To subscribe:	subscribe ITEX firstname lastname

Description: List for the dissemination of information on the International Tundra Experiment. Topics include but are not limited to genetics, populations, and species-ecosystems interactions.

Likely users:	Members of ITEX and others interested in tundra research.
Frequency:	Low activity.
Contact:	mwalker@taimyr.colorado.edu

Jam

Email address:	majordomo@ufsia.ac.be
To subscribe:	subscribe jam

Description: JAM is a discussion list for anyone interested in oceanography and earth science. The goal of this list is to help members with theoretical and administrative oceanography problems, to relay information about jobs, conferences and workshops, and to establish contacts.

Likely users:	Oceanographers and anyone interested in oceanography and earth science.
Frequency:	Low activity.
Contact:	michel.daulie@ufsia.ac.be

LAKES-L

Email address:	majordomo@badger.state.wi.us
To subscribe:	subscribe lakes-l

Description: This list encourages the discussion of lakes and their watersheds, lake management ideas, lake ecology, and the technology to assess their management. All lake-related, bio-geo-scientific topics, particularly behavioral, evolutionary, paleo-theoretical and community ecology, are welcome to be discussed here.

Likely users:	Lake dwellers and professional lake environment managers.
Frequency:	Low activity.
Contact:	James Vennie: LAKEBB@dnr.state.wi.us

lichens

Email address:	majordomo@sun.simmons.edu
To subscribe:	subscribe lichens

Description: The lichens list looks at lichen growth as a bioindicator of air quality. Lichen growth in rural, suburban, and urban areas are compared and contrasted.

Likely users:	Ecologists and others interested in air quality.
Frequency:	Low activity.
Contact:	owner-lichens@sun.simmons.edu

mabnet_america

Email address:	listproc@ucdavis.edu
To subscribe:	subscribe mabnet_america firstname lastname

Description: Mabnet_America is the electronic networking list for MAB Biosphere Reserves in the United States. This list promotes discussion on issues relating to man and the biosphere. Mabnet_America is part of the UNESCO Mabnet Programme.

Likely users: Members of MABnet and persons interested in the MAB reserves in the United States.

Frequency: Low activity.

Contact: listproc@ucdavis.edu

Mangrove

Email address:	majordomo@essun1.murdoch.edu.au
To subscribe:	subscribe mangrove your email-address

Description: The purpose of MANGROVE (Mangrove Research Discussion List) is to provide a global forum for the discussion of all aspects of mangrove biology, including the ecology and management of mangrove ecosystems.

Likely users: Ecologists interested in mangrove ecosystems management.

Frequency: High activity.

Contact: Eric I. Paling: paling@essun1.murdoch.edu.au

marinefish

Email address:	majordomo@netsteps.com
To subscribe:	subscribe marinefish

Description: Marinefish is an open discussion list for marine (saltwater) fish enthusiasts. All topics related to marine fish are welcome including habitat, sightings, workshops and conferences.

Likely users: Saltwater fish enthusiasts, researchers.

Frequency: Low to moderate frequency.

Contact: Majordomo@netsteps.com

marshbird

Email address:	listproc@rana.im.nbs.gov
To subscribe:	subscribe marshbird firstname lastname

Description: Marshbird is open for discussion of all aspects of marshbird topics and issues, including sightings, habitat destruction, calendars of events, workshops, and conferences.

Likely users:	Researchers, marshbird devotees, birders.
Frequency:	Low activity.
Contact:	frogs@usgs.gov *or* Brett_Hoover@nbs.gov

MEH20-L

Email address:	listserv@vm.tau.ac.il
To subscribe:	subscribe MEH2O-L

Description: The Middle East Water list is sponsored by Israel's Natural Center for Mariculture. It welcomes the exchange of ideas on limnology, oceanography, marine biotechnology aquaculture, conservation, reclamation, ecology, shared resource management, and other related topics.

Likely users: This list is directed toward the academic and research communities but all who are interested are welcome.

Frequency:	Low activity.
Contact:	Robert Chasan: hrowner@MATRIX.NEWPALTZ.EDU

Michiganbutterflies

Email address:	michiganbutterflies@onelist.com
To subscribe:	You must join ONElist at http://www.onelist.com/home.html. Subscription is free.

Description: Anyone who lives in Michigan is encouraged to use this list to share information about butterflies or moths that they observe in their gardens, yards, parks, wild areas, and fields.

Likely users: Michigan butterfly enthusiasts and ecologists interested in lepidoptera conservation and habitat.

Frequency:	Moderate activity.
Contact:	michiganbutterflies@onelist.com

NACA-GL

Email address:	listserv@ulkyvm.louisville.edu
To subscribe:	subscribe NACA-GL firstname lastname

Description: This is the discussion forum of the National Association of Campus Activities - Great Lakes Region. Its members are on campuses in Kentucky, Michigan, Ohio, Pennsylvania, and West Virginia.

Frequency:	Low activity.
Contact:	David Baugh: d.baugh@louisville.edu

NATOSCI

Email address:	listserv@cc1.kuleuven.ac.be
To subscribe:	subscribe NATOSCI firstname lastname

Description: This list provides information on the NATO Science and Environment Programmes. The data comes in the form of publication papers concerning particular issues.

Likely users:	International environmentalists, researchers, environmental law professionals.
Frequency:	Varies. Issued when available.
Contact:	scheurwe@stc.nato.int

nc-wq (North Carolina Water Quality)

Email address:	listserv@listserv.ncsu.edu
To subscribe:	subscribe nc-wq firstname lastname

Description: The North Carolina Water Quality list promotes the exchange of water quality information in North Carolina. Seminar announcements, meetings, quality workshops, job announcements, articles on water quality issues, grant announcements, and questions are all welcome on this list.

Likely users:	Persons interested in North Carolina water quality, environmentalists, researchers.
Frequency:	Low activity.
Contact:	John Parsons: john_parsons@ncsu.edu or
	Greg Jennings: greg_jennings@ncsu.edu

novel-fuels

Email address:	listserver@ic.ac.uk
To subscribe:	subscribe novel-fuels firstname lastname

Description: Novel-fuels is a list dedicated to the exchange of ideas and information on research into fuel cells and new energy techniques. Discussion on alternative energy sources is welcome here.

Likely users:	Alternative energy researchers, those interested in solar power.
Frequency:	Moderate activity.
Contact:	b.barker@ic.ac.uk

NPSINFO

Email address:	listserver@valley.rtpnc.epa.gov
To subscribe:	subscribe NPSINFO firstname lastname

Description: Nonpoint source pollution (NPS) is caused by runoff from rain, irrigation, and snowmelt moving over and through the land, collecting natural and human-made pollutants as it goes. The NPSINFO list is a medium for discussion of NPS issues and is sponsored by the EPA's Office of Wetlands, Oceans, and Watersheds. Some topics for discussion are urban runoff, coastal NPS, forest management, hydrological modification, and aquatic habitat modification.

Likely users:	Environmentalists and all concerned with water pollution.
Frequency:	Very high activity.
Contact:	forshee.carol@epamail.epa.gov

NRLib-L (Natural Resources Librarians List)

Email address:	maiser@library.lib.usu.edu
To subscribe:	subscribe NRLib-L

Description: The primary purpose of this list is to encourage the discussion and exchange of ideas between natural resources librarians and information specialists. All topics relating to natural resources librarianship are welcomed. This list replaces NatResLib-L.

Likely users:	Natural resources librarians and information specialists.
Frequency:	Low activity.
Contact:	Anne Hedrich: annhed@cc.usu.edu or Kevin: kevbre@cc.usu.edu

OILGASLAW-L

Email address:	listserv@lawlib.wuacc.edu.
To subscribe:	subscribe OILGASLAW-L firstname lastname

Description: OILGASLAW-L provides a platform for the exchange of ideas, opinions, and information about legislation in the oil and gas industries. These concepts may include the impacts of these legal issues on the environment.

Frequency:	Low activity.
Contact:	server@acc.wuacc.edu

ONE-L (Organization and the Natural Environment)

Email address:	listserv@clvm.clarkson.edu
To subscribe:	subscribe ONE-L firstname lastname

Description: One-L is a forum for discussion on the connection between different organizations and the natural environment. Topics of discussion range from ISO standards to environmental products and services.

Likely users:	Environmentalists involved in ISO standards.
Frequency:	Low activity.
Contact:	Gary Throop: throop@clvm.clarkson.edu

Ozone

Email address:	majordomo@sun.simmons.edu
To subscribe:	subscribe ozone

Description: List for data entry and discussion of tropospheric (ground level) ozone.

Likely users:	Professionals involved in ground level ozone research.
Frequency:	Low activity.
Contact:	owner-ozone@sun.simmons.edu

Pacific-biosnet

Email address:	listproc@listproc.wsu.edu
To subscribe:	subscribe pacific-biosnet firstname lastname

Description: Pacific-Biosnet is a free, moderated mailing list serving as a forum for information on native plants, weeds, ecological restoration, wetland science, conservation, and biological resource regulation and management, with emphasis on Pacific Northwest issues. The exchange of ideas on related topics is welcome.

Frequency:	Moderately active.
Contact:	Clayton J. Antieau: antieau@coopext.cahe.wsu.edu

PedNet

Email address:	majordomo@flora.org
To subscribe:	subscribe pednet

Description: This list was created to discuss issues surrounding pedestrians with the focus on promoting pedestrian activity. Issues have covered safety, pollution, motorist behaviors, pedestrian problems, and traffic laws and regulations.

Likely users:	Urban planners, public transit personnel, anyone with an interest in pedestrians or being a pedestrian.
Frequency:	Moderate to high activity.
Contact:	owner-pednet@flora.org

plantpop

Email address:	majordomo@SDSC.EDU
To subscribe:	subscribe plantpop your@email address

Description: Plantpop is a list for the exchange and dissemination of ideas and information about plant population ecology around the world. It is sponsored by the Ecological Society of America for those doing research in plant population ecology.

Likely users:	Plant population ecologists and researchers.
Frequency:	Low activity.
Contact:	Gordon A. Fox: gfox@ucsd.edu

PONDS-L

Email address:	listserv@lists.execpc.com
To subscribe:	subscribe ponds-l

Description:	Ponds-l is a group for the exchange of ideas about pond and lake management. Some of the areas addressed are the construction of small lakes and ponds, the management of fisheries, weed and algae control, and management of nutrients in lakes and ponds. This is a moderated list and is primarily for the lay person who owns or lives on a pond or small lake.

Likely users:	Persons who own or live on small lakes or ponds, state fishery personnel, anyone interested in the management or clean-up of small bodies of water.
Frequency:	Moderately active. Four or five messages most days.
Contact:	Scott Seymour: aqsys@execpc.com

POPENV-L

Email address:	listproc@info.usaid.gov
To subscribe:	subscribe popenv-l firstname lastname

Description:	This group was created for the "discussion and dissemination of information related to the interactions between Earth's environment and aspects of human population density, distribution, growth, and activity."

Likely users:	Conservationists, urban planners, sociologists, researchers.
Frequency:	Low activity.
Contact:	rcincotta@usaid.gov

POPULATION

Email address:	listserv@list.audubon.org
To subscribe:	subscribe population

Description:	This group was formed by the Human Population and Resource Use Department of the National Audubon Society. Its focus is on issues involving the growth of the human population. Its stated purpose is for the members of the group to "share timely information about local, state, regional, national, and international population and habitat issues, legislation, and policy..." You do not need to be a member of NAS to join this group.

Likely users:	Members of the Audubon Society, naturalists, environmentalists, sociologists, conservationists.
Frequency:	Moderate activity.
Contact:	Lise Rousseau: Lrousseau@audubon.org

POPULATION-NEWS

Email address:	majordomo@npg.org
To subscribe:	subscribe population-news

Description: This list is sponsored by Negative Population Growth whose mission is to "educate Americans about overpopulation's effect on our environment." News publications and other media sources are monitored for population-related stories and the articles are sent to list members. Topics cover immigration, population, and the environment. This is a read-only list; however, members may send relevant news articles and information to the address below.

Likely users: Naturalists, environmentalists, sociologists, conservationists, urban planners, sociologists, researchers.

Frequency: Moderate to high activity.

Contact: population-news@npg.org

PPBC-L (Protected Plantscape Biological Control List)

Email address:	listserv@tamvm1.tamu.edu
To subscribe:	subscribe PPBC-L firstname lastname

Description: The purpose of this list is to promote communication between those who work in public gardens, horticultural related business and research institutions. Some of the topics addressed are pest control, selecting plant species, watering, fertilization and its effect on the environment, and biological pest management.

Likely users: Gardeners, professional horticulturists, plant researchers, and persons interested in alternatives to chemical pest control.

Frequency: Low activity.

Contact: Steve Stauffer: rss2987@acs.tamu.edu

prairie

Email address:	majordomo@mallorn.com
To subscribe:	subscribe prairie

Description: This list is dedicated to the discussion of all prairie-related topics, including restoration, management, botany, and ecology.

Likely users: Prairie ecologists and those concerned with prairie habitats.

Frequency: Moderate activity.

Contact: Christopher Lindsey: lindsey@mallorn.com

Predator_Watch

Email address:	listserv@home.ease.lsoft.com
To subscribe:	subscribe Predator_Watch firstname lastname

Description: This list serves as a forum for the discussion of predator reintroduction and recovery programs, predator threats to livestock and agribusiness, and environmentally advantageous coexistence solutions.

Likely users:	The agricultural community, wildlife advocates, and environmentalists.
Frequency:	Low frequency. Comes as a digest.
Contact:	Predator_Watch-request@home.ease.lsoft.com

PRINTECH

Email address:	majordomo@cedar.cic.net
To subscribe:	subscribe printech

Description: PRINTECH is focused on technical aspects of environmental compliance issues faced by printers. Special attention is given to providing practical information on materials, practices, and technologies that can prevent wastes and emissions at their source.

Likely users: Professionals at trade associations or state/university pollution prevention technical assistance providers who help printers address compliance or waste reduction issues.

Frequency:	Low activity.
Contact:	owner-printech@cedar.cic.net

QUEST (Quality, Environment, Safety in Management)

Email address:	listserv@vm1.nodak.edu
To subscribe:	sub QUEST firstname lastname

Description: QUEST is a moderated list that endeavors to provide a venue for the discussion and dissemination of information about the relationship of quality, environment and safety to the body of national standards, which include ISO 9000, ISO 14000 and EPA and OSHA regulations.

Likely users:	Those involved in international trade.
Frequency:	Traffic on this list is moderate, usually 10 to 15 messages per day.
Contact:	Nancy Jennejohn: Jennejohn@uwstout.edu

RainForest

Email address:	listserv@gdarwin.cox.miami.edu
To subscribe:	subscribe RainForest firstname lastname

Description:	RainForest is an unmoderated list committed to the interchange of ideas about such topics as rain forest ecology, wildlife of the rain forest, rain forest management, fundraising, and indigenous cultures.
Likely users:	Both professional environmentalists and the lay person are welcome to enter the discussions on this list. Those who are interested in saving the rainforest and its inhabitants from the ravages of encroaching civilization will find this list informative.
Frequency:	A low to moderate number of postings occur daily on this list.
Contact:	administrator@gdarwin.cox.miami.edu

RainForest-M

Email address:	listserv@gdarwin.cox.miami.edu
To subscribe:	subscribe RainForest-M firstname lastname

Description:	RainForest-M is a moderated list whose purpose is to promote discussion among professional environmental scientists and researchers on rainforest issues. This list is confined to scientific discussion only. Subscribers may have membership on this list or on the unmoderated RainForest list, but not on both simultaneously.
Likely users:	Professional rainforest researchers and scientists.
Frequency:	Moderate to high activity.
Contact:	administrator@gdarwin.cox.miami.edu

REEL - Resource and Environmental Economics List

Email address:	listserv@latrobe.edu.au
To subscribe:	subscribe reel firstname lastname

Description:	REEL is an unmoderated list that concentrates on all aspects of the environment including but not limited to air, water, wildlife, energy, fish ecology, and forestry resources and their economic impact on the Australia-New Zealand area. Information that is exchanged may also consist of book reviews on relevant topics, announcements of seminars, and calls for papers.
Likely users:	Persons interested in economic environmental issues, especially ecologists living in Australia or New Zealand. The topics encountered are broad enough that environmentalists world-wide may find topics of concern on this list.
Frequency:	The number of messages on REEL is fairly low, perhaps 10-15 messages per week.
Contact:	Andrew K. Dragun: a.dragun@latrobe.edu.au

RESECON (Land and Resource Economics Network)

Email address:	listserv@lsv.uky.edu
To subscribe:	subscribe RESECON firstname lastname

Description: This group's focus is on the management of public resources. They are affiliated with the Association of Environmental and Resource Economists. Discussion covers the wide range of issues surrounding land and natural resource management.

Likely users: Natural resource managers, researchers, educators, and others with an interest in the economics of natural resources.

Frequency: Moderate to high activity.

Contact: RESECON-l-request@lsv.uky.edu

RE-USE

Email address:	reuse@onelist.com
To subscribe:	You must join ONElist at http://www.onelist.com/home.html. Subscription is free.

Description: Re-Use Centre serves not only as a waste management initiative but through their Supported Work Adjustment Training (S.W.A.T.) as an employment training program, providing related skills, experience, and work habits. This list is a forum for the dissemination of information on the growing field of municipal initiatives in waste reduction.

Likely users: Professionals participating in and others interested in municipal waste reduction programs.

Frequency: Low activity.

Contact: jkinnear@pianoguy.com

River Network

Email address:	majordomo@igc.org
To subscribe:	subscribe rivernet-info

Description: Rivernet-info is the mailing list for River Network and is intended to promote communication, discussion, and information exchange on topics relating to watershed conservation. River Network is a nonprofit organization that helps people organize to protect and restore rivers and watersheds.

Likely users: Watershed and river managers, conservationists.

Frequency: Moderate activity.

Contact: rivernet-info@igc.org

roadsalt

Email address:	majordomo@whale.simmons.edu
To subscribe:	subscribe roadsalt

Description: Roadsalt promotes the understanding of watershed components, surface and groundwater movement in watersheds, and the potential effects of sodium chloride on soil and estuarine systems.

Likely users: Researchers and ecologists concerned with the issue of road salt damage to rivers and streams.

Frequency: Moderate activity.

Contact: Majordomo-owner@sun.simmons.edu

rrr-oregon-l

Email address:	majordomo@teleport.com
To subscribe:	subscribe rrr-oregon-l

Description: Rrr-oregon-l is a discussion list for people who live in Oregon and want to exchange information and recommendations about reducing waste, reusing resources, and recycling. Those interested in serious discussion are welcome, advertising and flaming are not.

Likely users: Professional and amateurs interesting in recycling and reducing waste of natural resources.

Frequency: Very low activity.

Contact: Michal Angus: michala@teleport.com

SAFETY

Email address:	listserv@uvmvm.uvm.edu
To subscribe:	subscribe SAFETY firstname lastname

Description: This list discusses all aspects of environmental safety. Topics include safe disposal of hazardous waste, laboratory chemical hazards, biohazards, and disaster recovery. Much of the discussion is aimed at academic laboratory safety personnel. Other topics of interest are books on the safe disposal of toxic products and announcements of safety conferences.

Likely users: Academic safety officers, laboratory research scientists, and persons interested in safe laboratory practices.

Frequency: Very active list. There may be as many as forty messages per day.

Contact: Ralph Stuart: rstuart@zoo.uvm.edu

saf-news

Email address:	majordomo@igc.org
To subscribe:	subscribe saf-news

Description: Saf-news is the discussion list of the Society of American Foresters. It is intended for SAF members and others who are interested in forestry issues. Information, ideas, and questions relevant to forestry issues are welcomed.

Likely users:	Foresters and others interested in forestry issues.
Frequency:	Moderate activity.
Contact:	Jennifer Plyler: plylerj@safnet.org

seashepherd

Email address:	requests@lists.estreet.com
To subscribe:	subscribe seashepherd firstname lastname

Description: The Sea Shepherd Conservation Society has been protecting endangered marine wildlife for nearly 20 years. This list was created to collect and distribute information for the society to use in direct action conservation, documentation, and enforcement of international marine laws and treaties.

Likely users:	Those intent on protecting marine wildlife.
Frequency:	Low activity.
Contact:	Nick Voth: nvoth@estreet.com

SENSE-L (Environmental club)

Email address:	listserv@american.edu
To subscribe:	subscribe SENSE-L firstname lastname

Description: This list is for members and others interested in or who participate in the American University Eco-SENSE environmental club.

Likely users:	Club members and others interested in the Eco-Sense environmental club.
Frequency:	Low activity.
Contact:	Jeremy Woodrum: jw1970a@american.edu

SEWER-LIST

Email address:	listproc@mcfeeley.cc.utexas.edu
To subscribe:	subscribe SEWER-LIST firstname lastname

Description: The SEWER-LIST is unmoderated and strives to encourage discussions about the design, installation, operation, and maintenance of sewers. It includes ideas about sanitary, storm and combined system sewers, detention basins, and treatment plants. Dialogue from personal experiences of participants is welcome and encouraged.

Frequency:	Moderate number of messages.
Contact:	Miles Abernathy: miles@mail.utexas.edu

SOILS-L

Email address:	LISTSERV@CRCVMS.UNL.EDU
To subscribe:	sub SOILS-L firstname lastname

Description: Soils-l is an unmoderated list that was created to encourage the interchange of soil science information by both the professional and the layman. This list is recognized by the Soil Science Society of America and is open to all persons interested in the environmental aspects of the soil.

Likely users:	Soil science professionals, anyone interested in soil and soil nutrient conservation.
Frequency:	Moderate activity.
Contact:	Jerome Pier: jp@UNL.EDU

solar_utilities

Email address:	majordomo@world.std.com
To subscribe:	subscribe solar_utilities

Description: The Solar Energy Deployment and Utilization List is a forum for the exchange and discussion of topics relating to solar energy and other renewable energy sources.

Likely users:	Energy professionals and others interested in renewable energy sources.
Frequency:	Low activity.
Contact:	solar_utilities@world.std.com

SPECIES-ALERT

Email address:	majordomo@panda.org
To subscribe:	subscribe species-alert

Description: Endangered Species Alert Network is the World Wide Fund for Nature's mailing list for those concerned with issues regarding the conservation and preservation of endangered species.

Likely users:	All concerned with preserving endangered species.
Frequency:	Low activity.
Contact:	owner-species-alert@panda.org

Sylvanet

Email address:	listserv@listserv.ncsu.edu.
To subscribe:	subscribe sylvanet firstname lastname

Description: This list is the electronic version of the hard-copy newsletter begun in 1986. Sylvanet recounts the progress in international forestry and related subjects and relies on communications from members for information on issues associated with tropical forestry, agroforestry, conservation, deforestation and biodiversity.

Likely users:	Professional foresters and those concerned with environmental and ecological forest issues.
Frequency:	Low activity.
Contact:	kewightm@unity.ncsu.edu

Tenure

Email address:	listserver@relay.doit.wisc.edu
To subscribe:	subscribe TENURE

Description: Tenure is an unmoderated list which provides a medium for discussion of land use, poverty, natural-resource management and sustainable management. The list is sponsored by the Land Tenure center.

Likely users:	Land managers and those involved with environmental ethics and sustainable development.
Frequency:	Low activity.
Contact:	Steve Smith: owners-tenure@relay.doit.wisc.edu

ToxList

Email address:	listserv@esc.syrres.com
To subscribe:	subscribe ToxList firstname lastname

Description: ToxList correspondents provide information and ideas related to toxicology. Some of the topics covered in the discussions include pesticides, hazardous wastes, pharmaceutical toxicology, and immunotoxicology. Communications on environmental toxins and their implications for humans are welcome on the list.

Likely users: Toxicologists in any pertinent profession, those who have an interest in the effects of hazardous wastes, the consequences of pesticide use, and lay persons who wish to discuss these and other issues concerning poisons in the environment.

Frequency: Low activity.

Contact: Toxlist-request@esc.syrres.com

TRICKLE-L

Email address:	listserv@unl.edu
To subscribe:	subscribe TRICKLE-L firstname lastname

Description: The TRICKLE-L list deals with trickle/drip irrigation of crops or plants and related topics such as conservation of water resources and control of rodent damage to crops when using this system of irrigation.

Frequency: Moderate activity.

Contact: RMEAD@agrilink-int.com

Tweeters

Email address:	listproc@u.washington.edu
To subscribe:	subscribe tweeters firstname lastname

Description: Tweeters is a forum for Northwest birding information and serves birders in Washington State, and parts of Oregon, Idaho, and British Columbia. Tweeters was founded by Dan Victor of the Washington Ornithological Society and Seattle Audubon. Discussion topics include unique field trip reports, interesting sightings, unusual bird anecdotes, and questions for the experts. Archives may be accessed at http://weber.u.washington/ ~dvictor.

Likely users: Serious birders.

Frequency: High activity.

Contact: Dan Victor: dvictor@u.washington.edu

tws-wtwg (Wildlife Toxicology Working Group)

Email address: listserv@mail.orst.edu
To subscribe: subscribe tws-wtwg firstname lastname

Description: This is the mailing list for The Wildlife Society's Wildlife Toxicology Working Group. Suitable discussion topics involve the activities of TWS-WTWG and toxicology and contaminant issues influencing wildlife.

Likely users: Members of TWS and others interested in wildlife toxicology.
Frequency: Low activity.
Contact: tws-wtwg-request@mail.orst.edu

URBWLF-L (Urban Wildlife)

Email address: listserv@uriacc.uri.edu
To subscribe: subscribe URBWLF-L

Description: The Urban Wildlife list encourages the exchange of ideas and experiences related to wildlife habitats, urban ecosystems, and the quality of life. This network is the initiative of members from The Wildlife Society (TWS). Anyone with an interest in urban wildlife problems is welcome to take part in the discussions.

Likely users: Researchers, wildlife managers, planners, and educators involved with wildlife habitats and/or urban ecosystems.
Frequency: Moderate activity.
Contact: Mark C. Wallace: c7wmc@ttacs.ttu.edu or
                  Peter August: pete@edcserv.edc.uri.edu

USIALE-L (International Association of Landscape Ecology)

Email address: listserv@uriacc.uri.edu
To subscribe: subscribe USIALE-L firstname lastname

Description: This is the International Association of Landscape Ecology List. Topics discussed on this list include but are not limited to ecology, landscape, conservation, animal wildlife, plant wildlife, and plant ecology.

Likely users: Landscape ecologists and those concerned with plant and wildlife ecology.
Frequency: Low activity.
Contact: Peter August: pete@edcserv.edc.uri.edu

WALL-list

Email address:	majordomo@igc.org
To subscribe:	subscribe wall-list

Description: WALL stands for Witness Against Lawless Logging. The rescissions rider passed by Congress in August 1995, and signed by President Clinton allows public timber to be sold without considering environmental laws. The WALL mailing list will inform you of upcoming protests and other events of resistance to lawless logging occurring in the Northwest and elsewhere.

Likely users:	Everyone concerned with environmental law and lawless logging.
Frequency:	Moderate to high activity.
Contact:	majordomo@igc.org

WASTE

Email address:	majordomo@cedar.univie.ac.at
To subscribe:	subscribe waste your@email address

Description: This group was created to provide a means for the discussion of collecting, fractioning, conditioning, dumping, and recycling of waste. Acknowledging that there is a vast amount of information on each of the techniques of these activities, it is hoped that this forum may act as an exchange of world-wide information regarding those techniques. Topics may cover types of wastes and their effects on the environment, hazardous wastes, underground sites, recycling and reusing wastes, waste combustion, energy production, or waste transportation issues. List archives may be accessed at http://www.cedar.univie.ac.at/archives/waste/

Likely users:	Environmentalists, scientists, policy makers, urban planners.
Frequency:	Moderate to high activity.
Contact:	Wolfgang Bujatti: wolfgang.bujatti@bmu.gv.at

WASTENOT

Email address:	listserv@MAELSTROM.STJOHNS.EDU
To subscribe:	subscribe wastenot

Description: Wastenot was designed for the professional interchange of information on usage of organic wastes and the compostable materials whether from industrial, commercial, municipal, or agricultural sources.

Likely users: Professionals in charge of waste disposal and others interested in recycling of waste products.
Frequency: Low frequency.
Contact: Phil Fredericks: pjff@nwark.com
Bob Zenhausern: drz@sjuvm.stjohns.edu

Wastewater-modelling-digest

Email address:	majordomo@hydromantis.com
To subscribe:	subscribe wastewater-modelling-digest

Description: Any topics related to wastewater modelling, simulation, and control will be allowed on this list. The Wastewater Modelling Mailing List is hosted by Hydromantis, Inc.

Likely users: Professionals involved in wastewater modelling.
Frequency: Low frequency.
Contact: owner-wastewater-modelling@hydromantis.com

WATER-AND-SANITATION-APPLIED-RESEARCH

Email address:	mailbase@mailbase.ac.uk
To subscribe:	join water-and-san-applied-research firstname lastname

Description: This moderated list is committed to the exchange of information and ideas about research in the area of water supply and sanitation. It is primarily aimed at researchers in the United Kingdom and emerging nations with backgrounds in technical engineering and public health.

Likely users: Water scientists, hydrologists, public health officials.
Frequency: Low activity.
Contact: d.l.saywell@lut.ac.uk

Water Distribution Systems (WDS)

Email address:	mailbase@mailbase.ac.uk
To subscribe:	join water-distrib-systems firstname lastname

Description: WDS is dedicated to the interchange of information and concepts regarding water distribution systems research. Discussion topics may include water quality, quantity and reliability modelling, management and decision systems, and optimization techniques.

Likely users:	Water quality researchers, environmental and civil engineers.
Frequency:	Moderate activity.
Contact:	Dragan Savic: D.Savic@exeter.ac.uk

WATER-ON-LINE

Email address:	listproc@ucdavis.edu
To subscribe:	subscribe WATER-ON-LINE firstname lastname

Description: This listserv is dedicated to the discussion of California's water problems. It is related to the Website of the same name at http://www.ceres.ca.gov/ceres/WOL/home.html.

Likely users:	California residents and others interested in the state's water situation.
Frequency:	Low activity.
Contact:	kjwolf@wheel.dcn.davis.ca.us

Water-Quality

Email address:	majordomo@sun.simmons.edu
To subscribe:	subscribe water-quality

Description: List for issues related to water quality and water monitoring activities.

Likely users:	Water quality professionals.
Frequency:	Low activity.
Contact:	owner-water-quality@sun.simmons.edu

WDAMAGE (Wildlife Damage Management)

Email address:	listserv@vm1.nodak.edu
To subscribe:	subscribe WDAMAGE firstname lastname

Description: WDAMAGE is concerned with managing wildlife damage. Some topics discussed are rabid bats, coyote traps, and squirrel damage to human habitation. Meeting announcements, discussion of research projects, and requests for assistance or information are also appropriate communications for this list.

Likely users: Those who are concerned about wildlife damage to homes, gardens, and other wildlife, including government agencies that handle such problems. Other interested persons might be those involved in the prevention of destruction of telephone lines, public health personnel, and farmers.

Frequency: Low to moderate activity.

Contact: Robert H. Schmidt: rschmidt@cc.usu.edu

WETLAND-NEWS

Email address:	listserv@list.audubon.org
To subscribe:	subscribe wetland-news

Description: This group was formed by the National Audubon Society's Wetlands Campaign to encourage discussion and disseminate information pertaining to wetland policies, issues, laws, and legislation. List members receive "updates and action alerts on timely issues affecting the state of our nation's wetlands as well as notices about upcoming National Audubon Society wetlands related events."

Likely users: Environmentalists, conservationists, ecologists, policy makers.

Frequency: Low activity.

Contact: wetland-news-request@list.audubon.org or
                Mac Blewer: mblewer@audubon.org

wholesys-l (Whole Systems)

Email address:	majordomo@netcom.com
To subscribe:	subscribe wholesys-l

Description: This is an unmoderated list whose purpose is to talk about a positive vision for the future of the Earth. The concept of the earth as a whole system is integral to the discussion on this list.

Likely users: Environmental researchers interested in preserving the resources of the earth as a whole, conservationists.

Frequency: Low activity.

Contact: Flemming Funch: ffunch@netcom.com

wildgarden

Email address:	wildgarden-request@userhome.com
To subscribe:	subscribe

Description: The wildgarden list is a forum for discussion on attracting birds, bees, butterflies, bats, frogs, toads, and other wildlife through the use of plant life.

Likely users: Environmentalists and those interested in maintaining an ecological balance in wildlife habitats.

Frequency: High volume.

Contact: owner-wildgarden@userhome.com

Wildlife Health

Email address:	listserver@relay.doit.wisc.edu
To subscribe:	subscribe WildlifeHealth firstname lastname

Description: This list is a platform for the discussion of national and international wildlife health issues. It was developed to serve environmental professionals working with free-ranging and captive wildlife by facilitating the exchange of information and ideas among a diverse group working in the wildlife health field.

Likely users: Environmental professionals and others working in the field of wildlife health.

Frequency: Low activity.

Contact: Joshua Dein: fjdein@facstaff.wisc.edu

Wildnet

Email address:	wildnet-request@tribune.usask.ca
To subscribe:	subscribe Wildnet firstname lastname

Description: Wildnet's objective is to promote discussion about statistical issues in wildlife and fishery research and management. Included in the exchange of ideas are ecological modelling, G.I.S., and biological research. Conference announcements and calls for papers are welcome.

Likely users: Wildlife researchers, professionals in fishery management.

Frequency: Low activity.

Contact: Eric Woodsworth: wildnet-request@tribune.usask.ca

WLREHAB - Wildlife Rehabilitation Mailing List

Email address: listserv@listserv.nodak.edu
To subscribe: subscribe WLREHAB firstname lastname

Description: This list is dedicated to the discussion of all aspects of the rehabilitation of injured and orphaned wildlife and the release into the wild of fauna which have been restored to health. WLREHAB also has a newsletter exchange and an animal placement service.

Likely users: Wildlife rehabilitators and those interested in wildlife and the rescue and restoration of injured animals and birds in the wild.
Frequency: Very low activity.
Contact: Ronda DeVold: devold@badlands.nodak.edu

Wthydrology

Email address: Wtlists@uwin.siu.edu
To subscribe: subscribe Wthydrology

Discussion: The WThydrology discussion group is devoted to all issues related to the science of water in the environment.

Likely users: Anyone whose work is related to hydrology or who is interested in hydrology issues would benefit from the interaction on this list.
Frequency: Moderate activity.
Contact: Wtlists-Owner@uwin.siu.edu

x-enews

Email address: listserv@fem.unicamp.br
To subscribe: subscribe x-enews firstname lastname

Description: It is the goal of ENEWS to develop an exchange of ideas and information on energy-related issues, especially on topics of diffusion energy and renewable energy technologies in developing countries.

Likely users: Researchers and people in developing countries interested in renewable energy resources.
Frequency: Low to moderate activity.
Contact: ENEWS@FEM.UNICAMP.BR

Chapter 3

Environmental Newsgroups

Newsgroups are very similar to the electronic discussion groups covered in Chapter Two. They are similar in that messages pertaining to a particular, shared interest are sent to an address that has been established to receive messages for the newsgroup. However, these messages are handled, stored, read, and deleted in an entirely different manner than the personal email messages that are received from a discussion group.

The structure, organization, and messaging within the various newsgroups are comparable to electronic bulletin boards where messages are posted (or sent) and read at the users' convenience. Users cannot delete messages that have been posted. Instead, older messages are deleted by the software based on an established time frame as determined by the newsgroup administrator. This time frame may be anywhere from a few days to several weeks.

To read messages from a newsgroup, you must have access to a newsreader. You may have access to Usenet news as part of your Internet service. Look for areas that mention "news," "newsgroups," "newsreader," or "Usenet News." Ask your system administrator or Internet provider if you are unsure.

Your system administrator must decide which of the thousands of newsgroups will be made available to you. From the newsgroups made available to you by your Internet provider, you may choose those you want to read. When you access your newsreader, the newsgroups you have chosen are presented.

If you do not have a newsreader configured or if your Internet provider does not provide access to newsgroups, you may still read the messages posted to many of the newsgroups. There are several sites where the postings to these newsgroups may be read. One of these sites is DejaNews (http://www.dejanews.com), another is Supernews (http://wren.supernews.com).

Covered in this chapter are Usenet News with the exception of four newsgroups from the ClariNet News service. The ClariNet newsgroups included here may not be available on all systems.

Traditionally, Usenet News has had a hierarchical naming structure for newsgroup classification. For environmental researchers, the Usenet News categories of interest have been:

sci.	**(science)**	This is where the best newsgroups for environmental information can be found
bionet	**(biology)**	There are also some good environmental newsgroups in this hierarchy. These will deal with biological or ecological aspects.
rec.	**(recreation)**	Generally, hobbyists who share common interests.
talk.	**(discussion)**	Created for general discussion.
alt.	**(alternative)**	Alternative groups are usually less serious. These very often are designed for lay persons.

Country and U.S. state designations are becoming more common as newsgroups are formed that pertain to specific areas around the world. In this chapter, the following areas of the world are represented:

aus.	**Australia**
ca.	**California, U.S.**
francom.	**France**
pa.	**Pennsylvania, U.S.**
scot.	**Scotland**
uk.	**United Kingdom**

A governmental hierarchical structure was recently established to disseminate information from and about national and international governmental organizations. The structure is in place for the hierarchy to also include state government organizations as well, though no state government newsgroups have been established as of this writing. For more information on the government newsgroups, visit: http://www.govnews.org.

There are many different newsgroups under the new national government realm. Those newsgroups that would be of interest to environmental researchers contain the following structure:

gov.org	**International government/public activities**
gov.us.fed.	**From or about a U.S. Federal agency**
gov.us.topic	**U.S. newsgroups on topics of national interest**

Like the electronic discussion groups, one of the nice features of newsgroups is that they usually have a frequently asked question file (FAQ). They establish these files as a means to answer the most frequently-asked-questions posed to the group, and thus avoid having the same questions posed over and over to a group.

If you are interested in finding additional newsgroups or searching for contents of messages, use DejaNews (http://www.dejanews.com). DejaNews offers a nice, user-friendly interface.

alt.agriculture

Summary: Newsgroup created for informal discussion of topics relating to agriculture. Postings to this newsgroup cover all aspects of agriculture including equipment, methods, diseases, weather, and herbicides.

alt.agriculture.misc

Summary: Postings to this newsgroup cover a variety of aspects pertaining to agriculture. Messages have been on population, job announcements, agricultural equipment, and farm production statistics.

alt.animals.whales

Summary: This newsgroup covers "everything from harbour porpoises to blue whales." Postings have covered sightings, population statistics, and commercial ventures.

alt.building.environment

Summary: The alt.building.environment newsgroup was created to discuss issues pertaining to building and the environment. Postings here may cover the effects of construction on the environment, business information, publication notices, laws, legislation and rulings, compliance to laws, pollution, and green products.

alt.building.health-safety

Summary: This newsgroup was created to discuss health and safety issues as they pertain to the building industry. Postings have covered materials, information sources, and work environments.

alt.building.recycle

Summary: This newsgroup was created to discuss issues and events pertaining to recycling within the building industry. Postings to this group include queries for parts and materials, methods and processes for removing or separating materials, and uses of recycled materials.

alt.energy.homepower

Summary: Deals with consumer created home power (for "Off-Grid Living"). Postings have included questions on portable generators, wind generators, thermoelectrics for power generation, and sensitive electronic equipment.

alt.energy.renewable

Summary: This newsgroup enjoys discussion regarding renewable energy. Included in the messages are discussions of hydropower, wind energy, and solar energy and their uses and applications. They are a very vocal group with an underlying concern with saving our natural resources. Their postings have also delved into the works of Einstein, Tesla, and other scientists. News releases also may be posted here.

alt.org.audubon

Summary: This newsgroup is used to discuss activities and interests of the National Audubon Society. Postings include announcements, bird sightings, and conservation issues.

alt.org.earth-first

Summary: Earth First's interests are in the conservation and restoration of our planet. Topics discussed here have been about technology, evolution, corporations, pollution, and population. News releases are also posted here.

alt.org.sierra-club

Summary: This newsgroup was created to discuss issues pertaining to the Sierra Club and to the environment in general. Postings may include chapter events and meeting notices, and job and employment information. The Sierra Club action newsletter *Defending the Environmental Agenda* is also issued here.

alt.politics.greens

Summary: This newsgroup is dedicated to the discussion of Green party politics and activities. Discussion covers politicians and their views and voting records on environmental issues. Some recent topics of discussion concern politicians changing parties and redistributing environmental votes, the problems of our current government, rerouting of waterways for profit and the link between earthquakes and nuclear testing. Postings to this group range from professional opinion to anti-environmental rantings.

alt.society.sustainable

Summary: This newsgroup was created to allow networking for the development and maintenance of sustainable communities. Postings include materials, projects, legal and political issues, manufacturing, and architecture.

alt.solar.photovoltaic

Summary: This group's focus is on the generation of voltage from the sun. Postings have included methods, procedures, plans, batteries, regulators, and alternators.

alt.solar.thermal

Summary: Discussion on this newsgroup is focused on practical solar thermal energy use. Postings have included solar water heating systems, solar pool heaters, and solar cookers and stoves.

alt.sustainable.agriculture

Summary: Alt.sustainable.agriculture promotes the exchange of ideas on all forms of organic growing techniques and technology including growing and milling your own flour to bake bread, pesticides and the environment, and cotton pest problems. Recent postings have covered home-grown fish, compost heating, pesticides, and uses for peanut shells. Conference announcements and book review appear on this newsgroup at times. There are also some strange topics occasionally introduced.

alt.wolves

Summary: The alt.wolves newsgroup promotes discussion about wolves, their habitat, reintroduction of wolves into their historical ranges, and the impact on humans who now inhabit those ranges as ranchers and farmers. Postings have covered legal issues, management plans, and safety issues. There are also postings about hybrid wolves, both pro and con on this group.

aus.environment.conservation

Summary: This newsgroup is centered around conservation of the Australian environment and its natural resources. Postings may occasionally cover international issues as well. Topics cover anything from broad environmental protection issues to home composting. Recent postings have been on alternative energy, sustainable forestry, the ozone, and wildlife conservation. Conference, seminar, and environmental news may also appear here.

bionet.agroforestry

Summary: Bionet.agroforestry has an international flavor. The discussion ranges from reforestation practices to the correct types of soil for growing conifers. Legal and political issues have also been posted here. In addition, there are book discussions, conference announcements, calls for papers, requests for educational information, and job announcements posted to this newsgroup.

bionet.plants

Summary: A newsgroup formed to discuss all aspects of plant biology. There frequently are postings pertaining to sustainable agriculture, soil, organic fertilization, herbicides, and toxic substances on this newsgroup that may be of interest to environmental researchers. Relevant environmental postings are from researchers, biologists, and biochemists.

bionet.toxicology

Summary: This newsgroup deals with biological toxicology issues. Some postings have covered the biological dangers of (prescribed and nonprescribed) medications, pollution, contaminants, use of recycled solvents, and pesticides. News regarding seminars and conferences may also appear here.

ca.environment

Summary: The ca.environment newsgroup was created to enable discussion pertaining to California's environment. Postings have dealt with California's natural disasters, flood protection, the natural environment and conservation issues, recycling, legislation, electronic vehicles, and political issues that relate to the environment. Postings may also alert subscribers to events, seminars, and conferences.

ca.water

Summary: This newsgroup was created for discussion of California's water. Issues such as conservation and use, water quality, flooding, and agriculture may be covered.

clari.tw.environment

Summary: This is a news service offered by ClariNet. Posts consist of environmental news articles that have been issued by United Press International, Agence France-Presse, and the Associated Press. This is not the typical newsgroup where messages may be posted by readers. Postings cover the state of the environment worldwide.

clari.tw.environment.cbd

Summary: One of ClariNet's newsgroups, this was created to disseminate the environment-related postings from *Commerce Business Daily* (CBD). The environmental CBD postings are from several arms of the government and include notices of governmental employment contracts pertaining to the environment—for example, for the removal and disposal of hazardous waste, for tree planting, or for natural resources studies.

clari.tw.environment.releases

Summary: This ClariNet newsgroup posts environmental news releases from Business Wire. Postings deal with companies that are using environmentally-friendly manufacturing processes, unique environmental applications and technologies from industry, and Environmental Protection Agency news releases.

clari.tw.nuclear

Summary: This ClariNet newsgroup covers issues and news pertaining to nuclear activities. Postings are from Reuters, Agence France-Presse, Associated Press, and United Press International. These news postings cover nuclear testing, national and international political issues, human health endangerment, and effects on the environment.

francom.environnement

Summary: This newsgroup focuses on the environment of France. Recent postings have covered water pollution, and forestry.

gov.org.g7.environment

Summary: A newsgroup to enable discussion and to distribute news and information relating to the G7 Environment and Natural Resources Management Project. The ENRM Project strives to provide access to "global information relating to the state of our planet and its ecosystems."

gov.us.fed.doc.cbd.solicitations

Summary: This newsgroup distributes postings from *The Commerce Business Daily*, which is published by the U.S. Department of Commerce. The CBD is used to publicize proposed Government procurements over $50,000, and all contract awards over $50,000 when subcontracting is likely. This is useful to environmental engineers and environmental businesses.

gov.us.fed.doc.noaa.announce

Summary: U.S. National Oceanic and Atmospheric Administration announcements are posted to this newsgroup. These postings include announcements regarding programs, public meetings, issuance of research permits, and restrictions and regulations. Most postings are from the *Federal Register*.

gov.us.fed.doe.announce

Summary: Announcements from the U.S. Department of Energy are sent to this newsgroup. These include announcements from the Office of Fossil Energy, the Office of Energy Efficiency and Renewable Energy, the Energy Information Administration, and other offices operating under the DOE. The postings cover programs, proposals, meetings, and other activities. Most postings are from the *Federal Register*.

gov.us.fed.doi.announce

Summary: Announcements from the U.S. Department of the Interior are sent to this newsgroup. These postings cover notices from the different sectors of the DOI such as the Fish and Wildlife Service, Bureau of Land Management, and Minerals Management Service. Most postings are from the *Federal Register*.

gov.us.fed.epa.announce

Summary: This newsgroup receives notices and announcements of proposed rulings, policies, settlements and other information dispatched from the Environmental Protection Agency. Most postings are from the *Federal Register*.

gov.us.fed.ferc.announce

Summary: Announcements from the Federal Energy Regulatory Commission are posted to this newsgroup. These announcements may cover tariffs, refunds, permit actions, settlements, and other activities that are controlled by the FERC. Most postings are from the *Federal Register*.

gov.us.fed.nara.fed-register.contents

Summary: This newsgroup receives the tables of contents and the indexes of the *Federal Register*. In addition, a listing on the areas of the *Code of Federal Regulations* affected by the entries is included.

gov.us.fed.nrc.announce

Summary: The Nuclear Regulatory Commission announcements are posted here. These include announcements on findings, rulings, applications, actions, and other activities that are carried out by the NRC. Most postings are from the *Federal Register*.

gov.us.fed.nsf.announce

Summary: This newsgroup receives announcements on meetings and other activities surrounding the National Science Foundation.

gov.us.fed.usda.announce

Summary: The U.S. Department of Agriculture uses this newsgoup to issue announcements from the Forest Service, Rural Utilities Service, Animal and Plant Health Inspection Service, Foreign Agricultural Service, Natural Resources Conservation Service, and other services within the Department. Most postings are from the *Federal Register*.

gov.us.topic.agri.farms

Summary: This newsgroup is focused on agriculture with emphasis on farms. Postings are from the many departments and services of the U.S. government that affect farms and farming. These departments may include the Environmental Protection Agency or the Department of Agriculture. This moderated group also allows postings from individuals.

gov.us.topic.agri.food

Summary: This newsgroup is focused on agriculture with an emphasis on food production and distribution and nutrition. This moderated group has postings mainly from the Food and Drug Administration, although other postings are also made by the Bureau of Alcohol, Tobacco and Firearms, as well as individuals. Postings include actions taken on food labeling and health claims, food additives, and other activities related to the Administration. Most postings are from the *Federal Register*.

gov.us.topic.energy.misc

Summary: This newsgroup was created to disseminate information on the generation and delivery of energy. Postings are from the various Department of Energy offices and cover rate formulas, importation and exportation rulings, and meeting announcements.

gov.us.topic.energy.nuclear

Summary: Nuclear energy is the focus of this newsgroup. The majority of the postings are issued by the Nuclear Regulatory Commission; however, there are also postings from the Environmental Protection Agency. The articles and documents cover rulings, meetings, operating license modifications, and other actions taken. These are mainly documents from the *Federal Register*.

gov.us.topic.energy.utilities

Summary: This newsgroup was formed to disseminate information on regulated utilities that provide gas and electricity. Announcements from the Federal Energy Regulatory Commission are posted to this newsgroup. These announcements may cover tariffs, refunds, permit actions, settlements, and other activities that are controlled by the FERC. Most postings are from the *Federal Register.*

gov.us.topic.environment.air

Summary: Air quality, ozone, greenhouse gases, and noise are all the focus of this moderated newsgroup. Government postings from the Environmental Protection Agency have included proposed and final rulings, notices, and meeting announcements.

gov.us.topic.environment.announce

Summary: This newsgroup was formed to distribute announcements on environmental protection. Most postings are from the Environmental Protection Agency though individuals may post to this moderated group.

gov.us.topic.environment.misc

Summary: This moderated newsgroup covers general topics relating to environmental protection. Postings from the Environmental Protection Agency appear here as well as postings from individuals. Messages have covered good Internet sites for environmental information, laws and legislation, oil spills, and environmental rights.

gov.us.topic.environment.toxics

Summary: Environmental toxics are the focus of this moderated newsgroup. Topics cover hazardous material use, disposal, and cleanup. Messages from the Environmental Protection Agency cover rulings on land disposal restrictions, listing of CERCLA hazardous substances, identification and listing of hazardous waste and other mandates.

gov.us.topic.environment.waste

Summary: This moderated newsgroup was created to disseminate information on waste disposal and recycling of waste. Messages cover good Internet sites for waste recycling, announcements of conferences, and contaminated sites. Environmental Protection Agency rulings are also posted here.

gov.us.topic.environment.water

Summary: This moderated newsgroup covers water issues including drinking, irrigation, and sewage. Environmental Protection Agency rulings are posted here as well as messages from individuals. Messages have covered testing for water quality, stabilizing water, and locating Internet resources dealing with water. Environmental Protection Agency rulings are also posted here.

gov.us.topic.gov-jobs.offered.science

Summary: Physical sciences job opportunities in government are posted to this moderated newsgroup. These positions are from many sectors of the government. These cover a range of positions including Natural Resources Biologists, Fish and Wildlife Biologists, Fire Management Specialists, Foresters, and Soil Scientists.

gov.us.topic.nat-resources.forests

Summary: This moderated newsgroup focuses on forestry, logging, and wood production. Many of the postings are from the U.S. Department of Agriculture Forest Service. Individual messages cover a range of topics from national parks to wood processing.

gov.us.topic.nat-resources.land

Summary: This moderated newsgroup was created to distribute and discuss information on other uses of public land, e.g., grazing, wetlands, watershed.

gov.us.topic.nat-resources.marine

Summary: Fishing, aquaculture, and marine sanctuaries are the focus of this moderated newsgroup. Many of the postings are from the National Oceanic and Atmospheric Administration.

gov.us.topic.nat-resources.minerals

Summary: This moderated newsgroup covers the extraction and transportation of minerals. Postings may be from governmental offices, such as the Office of Surface Mining Reclamation and Enforcement, or from individuals.

gov.us.topic.nat-resources.oil-gas

Summary: This moderated newsgroup was created to distribute information on the extraction and transportation of oil and gas. Topics generated by individuals have covered refineries and gas to liquid conversion. Regular postings from governmental offices have been from the Department of the Interior and the Department of Transportation covering regulatory actions.

gov.us.topic.nat-resources.parks

Summary: This moderated newsgroup focuses on public land for recreation, tourism, and museums. Regular postings from the Department of the Interior include rulings and other announcements.

gov.us.topic.nat-resources.wildlife

Summary: Wildlife management and hunting are the focus of this moderated newsgroup. Rulings and announcements are regularly posted here from the Fish and Wildlife Service. Postings include information on endangered and threatened wildlife and plants, hunting regulations, and management regulations.

pa.environment

Summary: Pa.environment is a forum for the discussion of environmental issues in Pennsylvania. The current postings exchange ideas on papermill waste runoff, global warming, endangered species, state environmental bills, and bioremediation monitors. This group also talks about environmental discussion lists to join and employment opportunities in environmental fields.

rec.animals.wildlife

Summary: Rec.animals.wildlife was created in response to the posting of animal ecology and conservation questions to other inappropriate newsgroups to generate a forum for answering queries about injured animals, wildlife pests, recognizing diseased wildlife and other related topics. Some recent postings have been about the effects of mountain biking on wildlife, commercial overfishing and its effects on both fish and birds.

rec.birds

Summary: This newsgroup contains postings about every type of bird, bird watching, bird raising and problems such as keeping squirrels away from bird feeders. Some topics that have been discussed are returning orphaned birds to the wild, how to care for an injured purple martin, questions on attracting bluebirds, and discouraging woodpeckers from damaging trees.

sci.agriculture

Summary: Though many of the messages pertain to farm-related topics, some of the messages do cover topics that would be of interest to environmentalists. These postings pertain to pollution, global warming, hydrology, organic fertilization, ethanol as an alternative fuel and pesticide toxicity. There are also employment postings and information on environmental courses and workshops on this newsgroup.

sci.bio.conservation

Summary: Sci.bio.conservation is a moderated newsgroup whose mission is to promote the general interchange of ideas on conservation biology. Some of the subjects that are encouraged are general conservation biology issues and basic and applied research. This newsgroup aspires to advance greater communication between professional biologists and the general public who have an environmental interest. Current postings have included such topics as job announcements, legislative issues, workshops, symposia, and environmental course work. There has also been some discussion of political and philosophical effects on conservation.

sci.bio.ecology

Summary: As a medium for discussion for members of the Ecological Society of America, this newsgroup contains postings on all aspects of ecology. It encompasses such topics as ozone depletion, the greenhouse effect, fire ecology, wildlife rehabilitation, deforestation, world population growth, diatoms as water quality indicators, and sustainable agriculture. Reports of the Society's activities, new Internet sites, job postings, conference announcements, funding possibilities, and book reviews also appear here. Some recent topics of discussion have been ecology vs. economy, biotech weapons, and wildlife banding.

sci.bio.entomology.homoptera

Summary: Homoptera is one of three sections of the sci.bio.entomology newsgroup and is concerned with the discussion of sap-sucking insects such as aphids, whiteflies, leafhoppers, and planthoppers and research about them. Some of the topics discussed include beneficial insects, leaf cutting insects, and referrals to other insect sites and resources.

sci.bio.entomology.misc

Summary: The sci.bio.entomology.misc newsgroup discusses all types of insects. Some of the talk concerns environmental issues such as damage to trees by wood-eating insects, plant pests and how to attract beneficial insects. There are also job postings and discussions about published entomology literature on this group.

sci.bio.fisheries

Summary: The sci.bio.fisheries newsgroup is an unmoderated discussion group that was created for the exchange of new ideas on fish systematics, fisheries management, fish early life history, and aquaculture. Topics may include postings on all aspects of fish and fisheries. The general public is encouraged to post to the group, as well as students and professionals in fish and fishery related fields. Some current topics on this list include starting your own fish farm, sea lice treatments and shrimp breeding. This list also includes postings of employment opportunities and pointers to fishery sites and newsletters.

sci.energy

Summary: The sci.energy newsgroup is comprised of discussions on electric vehicle lead emissions, radiation safety, wind energy, recycling, solar energy, oil usage and other energy-related topics. Conference announcements, book reviews, job postings, and energy society's news messages are also posted to this newsgroup. Topics which have been discussed recently are solar energy, global warming, aquafuels, nuclear power, biological impact of carbon dioxide and converting organic hydrocarbons to methane.

sci.energy.hydrogen

Summary: Sci.energy.hydrogen was originated to advance the understanding of hydrogen as an alternative fuel. All issues relating to this concept are welcome. This newsgroup is directed toward university, government, and industry researchers. In addition, announcements of conferences, calls for papers, new findings, current events, service announcements, product information, book reviews, and general discussion of hydrogen related topics are encouraged. Recent discussion topics have been turbines in cars, lifting gas for fuel, and Raman spectroscopy for checking hydrogen concentration.

sci.environment

Summary: Sci.environment includes postings on all features of the earth's environment including fluorocarbons in the ozone, global warming, recycling, lead paint, eating meat, solar energy, and the Endangered Species Act. Book reviews, conference announcements, calls for papers, and position announcements are also discussed on this list. Some topics currently under discussion include the health effects of aircraft noise, global warming: fact or fiction?, and the effects of chemical treatment of water on mines.

sci.environment.waste

Summary: This newsgroup was formulated to discuss the impact of wastes on the environment and waste management methods. Discussion topics include types of wastes and their effects on the environment, greenhouse gases, waste reduction, reuse and recycling of waste products, collection systems, fractioning of wastes, impacts of waste treatment plants, waste incineration, wastewater, sludge digestors, waste dumping, and composting of sludges.

sci.geo.hydrology

Summary: This moderated newsgroup contains discussion on hydrology, water quality, and water resource management. It covers both surface and groundwater hydrology issues. Recent postings have included such topics as water contamination, nuclear waste deposits, geochemistry and the environment, and heat transfer in groundwater flows. There are many employment postings on this group for geohydrologists and related jobs as well as discussion on newly published geological hydrology literature.

sci.geo.meteorology

Summary: Although this newsgroup's focus is on weather and climate, the periodic posts on the ozone, pollution, solar observations and variability, water quality, and the earth's atmosphere should be of interest to environmental researchers.

sci.geo.oceanography

Summary: This is an unmoderated newsgroup. Sci.geo.oceanography contributors discuss marine issues such as water and sediment quality, deep water seismic surveys, tsunami, paleomagnetic maps, bathymetry, and paleomagnetic data sources. There are also announcements of position openings, book reviews, notices of new Internet sites, conference announcements, and calls for papers on marine issues on this newsgroup. Recent postings have addressed issues on global warming, la Niña, nearshore turbidity, and sea microorganisms.

sci.geo.petroleum

Summary: The purpose of sci.geo.petroleum is to offer a forum for informal discussion of petroleum research, exploration, and use by professionals involved in petroleum research, environmental organizations, and the general public in order to exchange ideas and opinions on global energy planning. Topics for discussion include the efficient recovery and use of hydrocarbons, downhole wellbore diagrams, Canadian junior oil companies, sonic logging tools, crude oil characteristics, measuring gases from compost and new pipeline circuit technology. Seminar and course work announcements, discussion of related software and systems, and job opportunities are also shared on this newsgroup.

sci.geo.rivers+lakes

Summary: The sci.geo.rivers+lakes newsgroup is a forum for the discussion of geological issues concerning rivers and lakes. Some of the topics talked about on this group are riverbank erosion from wake waves of river traffic, water level measurement by the USGS, and the use of hovercraft to study water wildlife without environmental damage.

scot.environment

Summary: This newsgroup is concerned with the discussion of environmental issues in Scotland. Recent postings have been about global warming, renewable energy studies, and water conservation.

talk.environment

Summary: This newsgroup is very informal and includes postings on all aspects of the environment, ecology, and conservation. Recent topics include global warming, people fighting toxic contamination in their neighborhoods, overpopulation, and Australian sharks frenzy feeding near beaches. Courses, calls for papers, and conference announcements are also posted to this newsgroup.

uk.environment

Summary: Uk.environment covers environmental issues in the United Kingdom. Recent postings include information on English wild flowers, water conservation, and pointers to environmental sites in the United Kingdom.

uk.environment.conservation

Summary: This newsgroup contains discussions on such topics as controlling algae in ponds, waste water filtration systems, saving the rainforests, the reduction in the butterfly population and water conservation. There are also announcements of seminars and workshops posted to this group.

Chapter 4

Environmental Journals and Newsletters

Electronic journals and newsletters continue to be a very efficient, cost-effective way to disseminate timely information. They are easy to establish, costs are considerably lower than the print version, there are no wasted, unread issues, and they can be electronically searched by the user. Like print versions of serial publications, there is a wide range of missions, topics, and depth of coverage among the electronic versions. This chapter includes that wide variety.

Many of these journals and newsletters are published by institutions and associations that perform research. Their publications include timely reports on research activities and are a good way to keep up on the research that is being conducted around the world. Some of them are refereed and have several contributors.

Electronic journals and newsletters can be distributed in different ways. Some are subscribed to in the same manner as subscribing to a discussion group. Issues are then distributed by way of email. Often the entire electronic publication is sent; however, with some, only the table of contents or abstracts of articles are received. When this is the case, the reader can determine if he or she should retrieve the entire issue. Usually, those issues that are sent via email are also archived at an Internet site for user access. Most of the publications in this chapter are only available via the Web and are not available via email. When this is the case, the reader must make a connection to the site and download, open or print the file. Some of these publications have no print counterpart—the electronic version is the only means of distribution. However, many of the electronic publications listed here are copies of the print version. A popular format for these is Portable Document Format (PDF). Many government documents are made available in PDF. The Adobe Acrobat Reader may be used to view these documents. The Acrobat Reader is available for free at the Adobe site (http://www.adobe.com) and at many of the Web sites that offer their publications in the PDF format.

For the researcher, the most valuable online journals are those where the full text of the articles are available. There are many of those included in this chapter. However, there are some excellent journals included in this chapter that offer only the abstracts of the articles. These, too, can be very valuable as one may quickly scan these abstracts to learn about the research being presented. Very often the text of the abstracts is searchable so that researchers may enter a journals's Web site and search through several issues for keywords. Finally, we have included some journals whose tables of contents only appear. Though not as valuable as the full text or abstracts, the tables of contents of journals can be useful in tracking down the research one needs.

We could not include all environmentally-oriented publications in this chapter. What we have included are the ones that should appeal to a broad audience, are published by an established group or organization, or have some research value.

Advances in Environmental Research (1093-7927)

URL: http://www.sfo.com/~aer/

Summary: This timely, peer-reviewed journal focuses on "original research in the fields of environmental science, engineering and technology." The full text of the first two issues are available at this site. The text and titles are searchable online.

Contact::   aer@sfo.com

Africa: Environment and Wildlife

URL: http://www.exinet.co.za/publish/aew/aew_main.html

Summary: *Africa: Environment and Wildlife* is an independent bi-monthly magazine sponsored by WWF South Africa and the National Parks Board of South Africa. The scope is on Africa's environmental and conservation challenges and efforts. Abstracts of the articles appear here along with striking pictures of the flora and fauna.

Alternative Agriculture News

URL: http://envirolink.org/seel/aanews

Summary: This monthly newsletter is a publication of the Henry A. Wallace Institute for Alternative Agriculture and is one of the electronic publications made available by the Sustainable Earth Electronic Library (SEEL) through the Envirolink Network. Past issues contain articles on pesticides, composting, and sustainable agriculture. Also included in each issue is a bibliography of recent publications of interest, job postings, and a calendar of events.

Contact: hawiaa@access.digex.net

Alternatives Journal

URL:	http://www.fes.uwaterloo.ca/alternatives
Summary:	This is "a quarterly magazine of news and analysis on environmental thought, policy and action." It is the journal of the Environmental Studies Association of Canada and has been in publication for 25 years. This site contains abstracts of the articles published in the print version, some fulltext articles, and subscription information.
Contact:	alternat@fes.uwaterloo.ca

Amphibian & Reptile Conservation

URL:	http://www.biopark.org/arc/
Summary:	This journal is subtitled "The International Journal Devoted to the Worldwide Preservation and Management of Amphibian and Reptilian Diversity." This site includes articles and subscription information.
Contact:	arc@byu.edu

Animal Rights

URL:	http://arrs.envirolink.org/AnimaLife/
Summary:	This is published two times per year by Cornell Students for the Ethical Treatment of Animals (CSETA). Articles provide information on issues surrounding animal rights and liberation. Submissions for the magazine may come from Cornell students and anyone with an interest in animal rights. Articles have covered environmental damage, vegetarian diets, laboratory animals, and hunting. This is also available in print for a modest fee.
Contact:	bp26@cornell.edu

APIS (Apicultural Information and Issues) (0889-3764)

URL:	http://www.ifas.ufl.edu/~mts/apishtm/apis.htm
Summary:	This monthly newsletter covers all aspects of the art and science of beekeeping. It is comprehensive both in time (issues available from 1984 to present) and scope. Articles have covered honey quality, organic honey developments, transgenic plants, honey prices, pollination, and diseases.
Contact:	mts@gnv.ifas.ufl.edu

Aquarius

URL: http://129.123.9.100/aquarius.html

Summary: This is a publication of the Utah Center for Water Resources Research and the Utah Water Research Laboratory. It covers a wide range of water issues including bioremediation, technologies, water quality, and testing.

Arid Lands Newsletter

URL: http://ag.arizona.edu/OALS/ALN/ALNHome.html

Summary: This semiannual newsletter is published at the University of Arizona by the Office of Arid Lands Studies and is printed in a paper format as well as being available via this Web address. Each issue is devoted to a specific topic in arid lands research. Issues have centered on the conservation of biodiversity in arid lands and building and architecture implications in arid lands.

Contact: kwaser@ag.arizona.edu

Arizona Highways

URL: http://www.arizhwys.com/

Summary: *Arizona Highways*, published by the State of Arizona's Department of Transportation, reports on the natural resources, environment, and wildlife of Arizona. The pictures are exceptional. The print version of this magazine has 400,000 readers from the U.S. and 120 countries around the world. Included at this site are a historical display of selected covers dating from 1937 to 1983.

Contact: webwrangler@arizhwys.com

Audubon Advisory

URL: http://www.audubon.org/campaign/aa/index.html

Summary: The *Audubon Advisory* is published by the Campaigns department of the National Audubon Society on a weekly basis. It is also issued on the audubon-news mailing list. It contains reports and summary articles on all aspects of the environment: wildlife and wildlife conservation issues, sustainable agriculture, wetlands research, laws and legislation, and forestry.

Aviation, Space, and Environmental Medicine (ISSN 0095-6562)

URL: http://www.dciem.dnd.ca:80/ASEM/

Summary: This peer-reviewed monthly journal is a publication of the Aerospace Medical Association. Searchable abstracts are made available by the Defence and Civil Institute of Environmental Medicine, which is part of Canada's Department of National Defence Research and Development Branch. There are some interesting articles in this journal that pertain to environmental topics. Recent articles have covered toxicity, effects of noise, cancer, and laser exposure to the eye.

Contact: grichardh@aol.com

BEN (Botanical Electronic News) (1188-603X)

URL: http://www.ou.edu/cas/botany-micro/ben
Subscribe by sending an email message to aceska@victoria.tc.ca

Summary: This publication covers botany, biodiversity, conservation, and ecology. Many of the articles deal with the northwestern portion of North America. Articles may cover people, events, research reports, or news items.

Contact: aceska@victoria.tc.ca

Biolinks (Biodiversity Newsletter) (1073-4434)

URL: http://www.erin.gov.au/life/general_info/biolinks/biolinks.html

Summary: This Australian newsletter is published by the Biodiversity Unit of the Department of the Environment, Sport and Territories in Canberra and is part of the Biodiversity Series. Issues contain research, news releases, and reports about conservation efforts in Australia. The issues are comprehensive and contain scholarly articles.

Biological Conservation Newsletter

URL: http://nmnhgoph.si.edu/botany/newslet.html

Summary: This is published by the Department of Botany, National Museum of Natural History at the Smithsonian Institution. Published both in print and in electronic format, this newsletter covers all issues related to conservation, wildlife, biodiversity, and world geography. In addition, job postings, conferences, meetings and new publications are included. Also included in each issue are bibliographies of current resources pertaining to conservation and biodiversity.

Contact: villa-lobos@nmnh.si.edu

Borderlines

URL: http://www.zianet.com/irc1/bordline/

Summary: *Borderlines* is published monthly by the Interhemispheric Resource Center (IRC). The IRC publishes books and educational materials about U. S. foreign relations. The articles in *Borderlines* cover the issues of management of transboundary water resources, sustainable development, ecosystems, and geographic considerations between Mexico and the U. S. It is available in Spanish. Print and email copies are available by paid subscription.

Contact: resourcectr@igc.apc.org

The Bulletin (of the Regional Environmental Center)

URL: http://www.rec.org/REC/Bulletin/RECBull.html

Summary: *The Bulletin* is the quarterly publication of the Regional Environmental Center for Central and Eastern Europe. It covers all issues pertaining to Central and Eastern Europe. Articles are comprehensive and have covered environmental management in specific countries, teaching environmental health, and sustainability. Also included are reports on events, symposia, studies, and news about the Regional Environmental Center's activities and publications.

Contact: editor@rec.org

Bushlines (Newsletter of the National Landcare Program)

URL: http://www.anca.gov.au/conserva/communit/intro.htm

Summary: This monthly newsletter covers all aspects of nature conservation and the land programs of Australia. Topics include rainforests, fires, and grant information.

Contact: webmaster@anca.gov.au

BWZ (Better World Zine)

URL: http://www.betterworld.com

Summary: *BWZ* covers environmentally-conscious products, companies and ideas that are making a "better world." The quarterly issues contain feature articles and regular columns. Past issues have dealt with sustainability, alternative technologies, and social responsibility. Issues contain practical ideas for conservation of our natural resources and book reviews.

Contact: webmaster@betterworld.com

CADDET Energy Efficiency Newsletter

URL: http://www.caddet-ee.org/home.htm

Summary: The *CADDET Energy Efficiency Newsletter* is a quarterly magazine published by the Centre for the Analysis and Dissemination of Demonstrated Energy Technologies. It contains informative articles on energy-saving technologies from all over the world. Issues also report on news, new publications, and events. Included at this site is the most recent issue and a searchable archival file of citations arranged by topic.

Contact: caddet@caddet.org

Canadian Institute for Environmental Law and Policy Newsletter

URL: http://www.web.apc.org/cielap/newslett.htm

Summary: The print version of this quarterly newsletter is sent to members of CIELP and to paid subscribers. This online site contains abstracts of the articles and subscription information. Articles cover policies, opinions, proposals, regulations, and initiatives. It is a great way to stay informed about the evolving environmental situation in Canada.

Contact: cielap@web.net

Canadian Journal of Fisheries and Aquatic Sciences

URL: http://www.nrc.ca/cisti/journals/cjfas.html

Summary: Published by the National Research Council (NRC) Research Press, this journal publishes scholarly, "original research, critical reviews, perspectives (essays of opinion or hypothesis), and comments." Published monthly, the tables of contents, abstracts in English and French, and ordering information for the online and print full text is available at this site.

Contact: research.journals@nrc.ca

Canadian Journal of Forest Research

URL: http://www.nrc.ca/cisti/journals/tocfor.html

Summary: This monthly journal has been ranked as one of the top three journals in its field for the past decade by the Institute for Scientific Information, Inc. Articles are from international and Canadian sources and cover "silviculture, ecophysiology, forest ecology, biotechnology, forest genetics and tree improvement, tree physiology, forest entomology and pathology, land management and classification, harvesting, wood processing, pollution effects, forest economics, and other forest-related topics." The tables of contents, abstracts in English and French, and ordering information for the online and print full text is available at this site.

Contact: research.journals@nrc.ca

Carcinogenesis

URL: http://www.oup.co.uk/carcin

Summary: This journal focuses on research "will ultimately lead to the prevention of cancer in man." Topics may cover viral, physical and chemical carcinogenesis and mutagenesis, as well as the factors that affect these including the "formation, detection, identification, and quantification of environmental carcinogens." Tables of contents and extensive abstracts are available at this site. There is a search form that may search through all past issues.

Contact: www-admin@oup.co.uk

CATF Review

URL: http://www.bcr.bc.ca/catf/review/

Summary: This quarterly publication is published by BC Research Incorporated's Centre for Alternative Transportation Fuels. Topics cover the research involved with alternative transportation fuels such as natural gas, propane, and hydrogen. There are two years of this quarterly publication at the Web site.

Contact: ainglis@bcr.bc.ca

Center for Sustainable Agricultural Systems Newsletter

URL: http://ianrwww.unl.edu/ianr/csas/newsletr/sustnews.htm

Summary: This bimonthly newsletter is published under the auspices of the Institute of Agriculture and Natural Resources at the University of Nebraska-Lincoln. The Center for Sustainable Agricultural Systems at UNL promotes "agriculture that is efficient, competitive, profitable, and environmentally and socially sustainable..." Articles cover government policies, bills, resources, reports, strategies, conferences, meetings, and other events.

Contact: csas003@unlvm.unl.edu

Chemistry & Industry (0009-3068)

URL: http://ci.mond.org

Summary: This international magazine is published twice a month by the Society of Chemical Industry. It reports on chemistry and the natural sciences and the commercial, industrial and political aspects of these sciences. Articles pertaining to the environment may cover "waste minimisation, treatment and disposal, industrial pollution, global warming, acid rain, release of genetically engineered organisms and environmental protection technology." Located at this site are the current issue, searchable archived contents, and news.

Contact: webmaster@chemind.demon.co.uk

Chlorine Monitor

URL: http://host.envirolink.org/publications/IATP/chlorine/

Summary: This monthly periodical is published by the Institute for Agriculture and Trade Policy. It covers world-wide aspects of chlorine and the environment. Articles cover testing, chlorine alternatives, pollution, effects on wildlife, news releases, reports, research, and events.

Contact: jchristensen@iatp.org
                iatp@iatp.org

Clean Cities Drive Newsletter

URL: http://www.ccities.doe.gov/ccnews

Summary: Published quarterly by the Alternative Fuels Division of the National Renewable Energy Laboratories, U.S. Department of Energy, this newsletter includes articles pertaining to the efforts of the Clean Cities Drive. Articles are on the cities and their experiences with pollution.

Contact: ccities@afdc.nrel.gov

A Clear View

URL: http://www.ewg.org/pub/home/clear/view/view.html

Summary: Published two times per month, this periodical disseminates information on the activities of the anti-environmental "Wise Use" movement. The site contains the full text of the current and past newsletters. Brief articles cover activities, organizational profiles, and resources. *A Clear View* is sponsored by the Environmental Working Group.

Contact: clear@ewg.org

Climate Variations Bulletin

URL: http://www.ncdc.noaa.gov/publications/cvb/cvb.html or
ftp://ftp.ncdc.noaa.gov/pub/data/cvb

Summary: This monthly publication is published by the National Climatic Data Center (NCDC). It presents monthly climate anomalies as reported by the National Weather Service's Climate Prediction Center and National Severe Storms Forecast Center for the purpose of historical analyses. The issues are available in PostScript or WordPerfect.

Contact: webmaster@ncdc.noaa.gov

Compliance Online

URL: http://www.ieti.com/taylor/compliance.html

Summary: *Compliance Online* is a monthly publication sponsored by Taylor Engineering. Its purpose is to help its readers keep up-to-date on environmental regulations from the U.S. EPA, DOT, and OSHA offices.

Contact: woodshow@interpath.com

Conscious Choice

URL: http://www.consciouschoice.com/

Summary: *Conscious Choice* reports bimonthly on environmental issues and on natural, alternative health care. The fully searchable articles are written for the lay person.

Contact: ccwebmaster@consciouschoice.com

Consequences: The Nature & Implications of Environmental Change

URL: http://www.gcrio.org/CONSEQUENCES/introCON.html

Summary: This online publication was created to "provide reliable assessments of practical concerns related to the national and international consequences of changes in the global environment." It is published with funding provided by NOAA, NASA, and the National Science Foundation.

Contact: jeddy@tardis.svsu.edu

Conservation Ecology (1195-5449)

URL: http://www.consecol.org/Journal/

Summary: This is a refereed journal published two times per year—on an ongoing basis—by
                    the Ecological Society of America. The scholarly articles are from both applied and
                    theoretical perspectives. Though geared toward the biological, the content includes
                    topics surrounding the conservation of ecosystems, landscapes, and populations;
                    hence, this publication should be of interest to environmental researchers. There are
                    mirror sites in Australia, Brazil, and South Africa.

Contact: questions@consecol.org

Corporate Watch (News)

URL: http://www.corpwatch.org/corner/hotnews.html

Summary: This publication contains news pertaining to companies that have adverse effects
                    on the environment and society. Articles deal with health effects on workers,
                    current news, and alerts.

Contact: corpwatch@igc.org

Dateline Los Alamos

URL: http://lib-www.lanl.gov/pubs/dateline.htm

Summary: *Dateline Los Alamos* is published monthly by the Public Affairs Office of Los
                    Alamos National Laboratory. The purpose of the periodical is to distribute
                    information to the Los Alamos funding sources about the research activities that are
                    taking place. The articles cover the many advances in science and technology that
                    are ongoing at the Laboratory.

Contact: library@lanl.gov

Delta (Newsletter of the Canadian Global Change Program)

URL: http://datalib.library.ualberta.ca/~cgcp/publications/delta/menu.html

Summary: This newsletter is published quarterly by the Royal Society of Canada. The articles,
                    written by scholars, cover issues pertaining to global warming, pollution, and
                    sustainable development. Also covered are conventions, activities, fellowships,
                    grants, and recent publications.

Contact: cgcp@rsc.ca

Desert Research Institute Newsletter

URL: http://www.dri.edu/General/Newsletter/NewsletterMenu.html

Summary: The Desert Research Institute is a nonprofit organization of the University and Community College System of Nevada. This newsletter reports quarterly on the research activities and results of research conducted by the DRI scientists.

Developing Ideas Digest

URL: http://iisd1.iisd.ca/didigest/

Summary: This is a bimonthly publication that is published by the International Institute for Sustainable Development. The goal of the publishers is to "provide a snapshot of the most influential ideas shaping the international sustainable development dialogue..." Each issue is devoted to a specific topic. Issues have covered social capital, flooding, ethics and sustainable development, and the rights of sustainability.

Contact: didigest@iisd.ca

e-Amicus

URL: http://www.igc.apc.org/nrdc/eamicus/home.html

Summary: *e-Amicus* is the online version of *The Amicus Journal* and is published by the Natural Resources Defense Council. Sections include past articles from *The Amicus Journal*, recommended books, and recommended (Web) browsing. The past articles include thoughtful essays on a range of topics such as pollution, biodiversity, population, and health.

Contact: amicus@nrdc.org

E, The Environmental Magazine

URL: http://www.emagazine.com

Summary: This bimonthly publication was designed to relay important environmental information to interested people. Articles cover national and international issues. There is an archive of past articles and a current issue available at this site. The print publication is available by subscription and rates are available online.

Contact: webmaster@emagazine.com

Earth Action: The Bulletin for Environmental Activists

URL: http://www.nrdc.org/nrdc/field/acti.html

Summary: This twice-monthly publication from the National Resources Defense Council contains alerts to new and ongoing threats to natural resources and the environment. Editions have covered standards and regulations, national parks, public land, rain forests, environmentally threatening construction projects, and putting an end to the waste that unwanted mail is responsible for. Each article contains actions to take, who to contact, and links to background information.

Contact: nrdcinfo@nrdc.org

Earth Alert

URL: http://www.discovery.com/news/earthalert/earthalert.html

Summary: This previously was *Earth Week: A Diary of the Planet*. Now hosted by The Discovery Channel, it continues posting reports on news pertaining to the earth and the earth's environment. Daily reports are in the form of brief summaries and cover natural disasters, weather, pollution, wildfires, floods, etc. The presentation uses a world map with symbols at various geographic locations to signify the type of news event and the location of the news event. News summaries also include links to background information.

Earth Island Journal

URL: http://www.earthisland.org/ei/journal/journal.html

Summary: This is the journal of the Earth Island Institute (EII). EII was created to aid in the support and development of projects pertaining to "the conservation, preservation, and restoration of the global environment." Articles have covered world-wide conservation efforts, legislation, and actions of corporations.

Contact: earthisland@earthisland.org

Earth Negotiations Bulletin

URL: http://www.iisd.ca/linkages/voltoc.html

Summary: This bulletin is published daily during selected United Nations conferences by the International Institute for Sustainable Development and covers UN activities and speeches made during the conferences. Earth Negotiation Bulletins are available for the United Nations Conference on Environment and Development (UNCED), the Convention to Combat Desertification and Drought, the United Nations Commission on Sustainable Development, the Convention on Biological Diversity, the Convention on Climate Change, and several others.

Contact: enb@iisd.org

Earth Times

URL: http://earthtimes.org

Summary: This biweekly publication is published by The Earth Times Foundation. It focuses on environmental issues and economic development and draws from a wide variety of worldwide political interests in its opinion articles. Includes a searchable archive. Annual subscriptions vary from $10.00 (student) to $36.00 (foreign).

Contact: editor@earthtimes.org

ECO (The Climate Action Network Newsletter)

URL: http://www.igc.apc.org/climate/Eco.html

Summary: This publication covers the UN Climate talks. Included here are the Subsidiary Bodies Meetings, from Bonn in June, 1998; the AGBM8 and Kyoto meetings; and the Ministerial Meeting in Tokyo.

Contact: larris@igc.apc.org

Eco-Compass (1083-8546)

URL:	http://www.islandpress.org/index.ssi or, send the following message to majordomo@igc.apc.org: subscribe islandpress-L
Summary:	This newsletter was created to publicize new and useful environmental sites on the Internet. It is a public service of Island Press, a nonprofit publisher of environmental books. It is intended for anyone who wants to be kept current on the environmental resources that are available. Entries include summaries of the contents of the site.
Contact:	info@islandpress.com

Ecocycle

URL:	http://www.ec.gc.ca/ecocycle
Summary:	This newsletter deals with information, policies, and technical issues pertaining to life-cycle management. It is published under the auspices of the Hazardous Waste Branch of the Waste Prevention Division of Environment Canada in both English and French. Articles cover life-cycle assessment, life-cycle tools, management, policies, and applications of the life-cycle management approach. The scope is international.
Contact:	ecocycle@ec.gc.ca

Ecology Law Quarterly

URL:	http://www.law.berkeley.edu/~elq/
Summary:	This honored journal focuses on issues pertaining to environmental law and policies. Articles cover environmental affairs from the legal and technical perspective. The journal is published by students at the University of California at Berkeley's Boalt Hall School of Law. In June, 1990 the journal was awarded the Global 500 award from the United Nations Environmental Programme (UNEP). Tables of contents, some full text, and past issues appear here.
Contact:	elq@www.law.berkeley.edu

EcoNews Africa: Circular on Environment and Development

URL: http://www.web.apc.org/~econews/

Summary: This newsletter is sponsored by the Humanistic Institute for Cooperation with Developing Countries (HIVOS) and NGONET based in Montevideo, Uruguay. Its mission is to report on activities that enhance global development. Includes a searchable index. Recent articles cover climate change and sustainable development.

Contact: econews@web.net

Ecopsychology On-line

URL: http://www.csuhayward.edu/alss/ECO/

Summary: This quarterly journal is supported with a grant from Goldman Environmental Foundation and is edited by Theodore Roszak. Regular sections include *Why Ecology Needs Psychology, Why Psychology Needs Ecology, Essays in Ecopsychology,* and *Research in Ecopsychology.* This online journal is a valuable addition to the field of ecopsychology.

Contact: ecopsy@csuhayward.edu

EcoRegion

URL: http://www.cec.org/english/resources/ecoregion/

Summary: This is the newsletter of the Secretariat of the Commission for Environmental Cooperation (CEC). *EcoRegion* was created to inform readers of the activities, projects, and membership of the CEC. It covers North American environmental issues as they impact the three NAFTA countries of Canada, Mexico, and the United States. Readers may be alerted when a new issue of *EcoRegion* is available by submitting their email address at this site. It is available in French, English, and Spanish.

Contact: Marcos Silva: msilva@ccemtl.org

e design online (Online Journal of the Florida Design Initiative)

URL: http://fcn.state.fl.us./fdi/e-design/online/edo.htm

Summary: This monthly online journal is published by the School of Architecture at Florida A & M University. Full text articles cover sustainability, green building materials, and global climate change. It also contains interviews, listings of books and conference materials.

Contact: fdi@famu.edu

EDF Letter

URL: http://www.edf.org/pubs/edf-letter/

Summary: The *EDF Letter* is the newsletter of the Environmental Defense Fund. This site contains the full text of issues from 1970 to present. Recorded here are endangered species legislation, pesticide litigation, superfund information, and a history of environmental actions.

Contact: webmaster@edf.org

Electromagnetics Forum

URL: http://www.tassie.net.au/emfacts/

Summary: This is a quarterly publication dealing with "environmental impacts of non-ionising electromagnetic energy (EME) and health and safety issues relating to: the siting of cellular phone towers and powerlines, the use of mobile phone handsets, computer monitors and associated technologies and the setting of appropriate safety standards." Articles have dealt with breast cancer, melatonin, EMF guidelines, litigation, and international concerns.

Contact: emfacts@tassie.net.au

Electronic Drummer

URL: http://www.teleport.com/~rot/

Summary: This newsletter is published by the Thoreau Institute, which strives to preserve the environment while keeping governmental control at a minimum. The most recent edition of the newsletter resides at this electronic site and is updated at the beginning of each month. Also included are reports and articles from the *Different Drummer*, which is also published by the Thoreau Institute.

Contact: rot@ti.org

Electronic Green Journal (1076-7975)

URL: http://www.lib.uidaho.edu:70/docs/egj.html
                Subscribe by sending email to majordomo@uidaho.edu with the following text: subscribe egj your_email_address

Summary: Sponsored by the University of Idaho Library, this is a refereed journal with editorial advisors from universities and research laboratories all over the world. The intent is to provide solid environmental information and resources to academics and professionals worldwide. This is must reading for anyone who is overwhelmed by the amount of information available on the Internet.

Contact: majanko@uidaho.edu *or* mikep@neill-lib.org

EM Online

URL: http://online.awma.org/em/Default.htm

Summary: *EM Online* is published monthly by the Air & Waste Management Association. Its print counterpart is *EM, a Magazine for Environmental Managers*. EM Online contains articles and news about environmental issues and the impact the issues have on environmental managers.

Contact: emonline@awma.org

Endangered Species & Wetlands Report

URL: http://www.eswr.com/

Summary: This is a nonpartisan, monthly newsletter covering regulations, laws, political activities, and other events pertaining to the Endangered Species Act and wetlands. It also covers private property rights issues. Information for the newsletter is culled from a variety of sources including Congress, the courts—federal circuit and district courts, and the Supreme Court—and federal agencies.

Contact: poplar@crosslink.net

Endangered Species Bulletin

URL: http://www.fws.gov/r9endspp/bulinfo.html

Summary: Published bimonthly by the U.S. Fish and Wildlife Service's Division of Endangered Species, this bulletin was created to disseminate "information on rulemakings (listings, reclassifications, and delistings), recovery plans and activities, regulatory changes, interagency consultations, changes in species' status, research developments, new ecological threats, and a variety of other issues."

Contact: r9fwe_des.bim@fws.gov

Endangered Species Update

URL: http://www.umich.edu/~esupdate

Summary: This update is published bimonthly by the University of Michigan's School of Natural Resources. It acts as a vehicle to disseminate news and information on the science and politics of the discipline of conservation biology. Each issue contains featured articles, the *Endangered Species Bulletin* from the U. S. Fish and Wildlife, and *News from the Zoos*. An additional section, *Marine Matters*, will be added in future issues.

Contact: esupdate@umich.edu

Energies

URL: http://www.nrglink.com

Summary: Published weekly by Green Energy News, this newsletter reports on clean, efficient, and renewable energy. Focus is on uses in transportation, industry, and home use of renewable energy. Brief articles have covered advances in electric vehicles, fuel cells, solar energy, wind power, wood power, and biomass.

Contact: bmulliken@nrglink.com

Energy Crops Forum

URL: http://www.esd.ornl.gov/bfdp/forum/ecftoc.html

Summary: *Energy Crops Forum* is published quarterly by the Biofuels Feedstock Development Program of the Environmental Sciences Division of Oak Ridge National Laboratory. It contains information about research efforts and programs. Research has covered such areas as breeding, diseases, sampling, genetic applications, and cloning.

Contact: are@ornl.gov

Energy Source Builder

URL: http://www.oikos.com/esb

Summary: Sponsored by Iris Communications, Inc., Oikos and Infiltec, this is a bimonthly newsletter for energy-conscious builders. Articles cover activities, tools, and techniques for making buildings more energy efficient. Past articles have covered solar energy and site waste. This newsletter is nicely presented and the archives are searchable.

Contact: iris@oikos.com

Environmental Building News

URL: http://www.ebuild.com

Summary: This monthly newsletter covers all aspects of and promotes environmentally sustainable design and construction. Articles have covered green building products and technologies. The site includes some full text articles and subscription information to the print version.

Contact: spider@ebuild.com

Environmental Ethics

URL: http://www.cep.unt.edu/enethics.html

Summary: This journal is published by the Center for Environmental Philosophy and the University of North Texas. It is "an interdisciplinary journal dedicated to the philosophical aspects of environmental problems." The tables of contents are available as well as a cumulative index to the past 19 years.

Contact: cep@unt.edu

Environmental Health Monthly

URL: http://host.envirolink.org/publications/CCHW/ehm/

Summary: This publication was established "to provide a forum to educate and inform health professionals and community leaders on current scientific knowledge on environmental health issues." It is a publication of the Citizen's Clearinghouse for Hazardous Waste. Informative abstracts from back issues are presented at this site. Past issues have covered landfill gases, dioxin and cancer, neurotoxicity and exposure to chlordane, and gasoline additives.

Environmental Health Perspectives

URL: http://ehpnet1.niehs.nih.gov/docs/journals.html

Summary: This periodical is published by the National Institutes of Health's Environmental Health Sciences Division. Issues contain scientific articles, discussion, and news on the environment and its affect on human health. Also includes legislative and regulatory developments, information about the National Toxicology Program and other important programs. The site contains some full text and the articles are searchable online.

Contact: webmaster@ehis.niehs.nih.gov

Environmental Reviews

URL: http://www.nrc.ca/cisti/journals/envep.html

Summary: Published by the National Research Council (NRC) Research Press, this journal publishes "authoritative and readable reviews on a wide range of topics in the environmental sciences." International in scope, the focus is on the "effects on and responses of both natural and man-made ecosystems to anthropogenic stress." Published quarterly, the tables of contents, abstracts in English and French, and ordering information for the online and print full text is available at this site.

Contact: research.journals@nrc.ca

Environmental Values (0963-2719)

URL: http://www.erica.demon.co.uk/EV.html

Summary: This is a quarterly publication of White Horse Press. The Bioline site (http://www.bdt.org.br/bioline/ev) contains informative, searchable abstracts of the publication. The articles deal with environmental philosophy, economics, and environmental policy.

Contact: bio@biostrat.demon.co.uk or A.Holland@lancaster.ac.uk

Environment and History (0967-3407)

URL: http://www.erica.demon.co.uk/EH.html

Summary: This is an interdisciplinary journal from White Horse Press that "aims to bring scholars in the humanities and biological sciences closer together, with the deliberate intention of constructing long and well-founded perspectives on present day environmental problems." Published three times per year, scholarly articles have covered historical perspectives of land use, gender and environmental history, and historical perspectives on pollution. The abstracts are available at this site.

Contact: aj@erica.demon.co.uk

Environment Bulletin

URL:	http://www-esd.worldbank.org/html/esd/env/publicat/publicat.htm
Summary:	Published quarterly by the Environment Department of the World Bank, this publication disseminates information on environmental activities. Articles have covered conservation, investment decisions, global water concerns, ozone, and environmental assessment.
Contact:	asnyder@worldbank.org

Environment Business Magazine

URL:	http://www.ifi.co.uk/ebm.htm
Summary:	*Environment Business Magazine* is the result of the merging of *Incorporating Environment Today* and *Integrated Environmental Management* and is published monthly. This is a paid subscription of an environmental business magazine that is currently in print; however, some excerpts and articles appear at this Web address. Topics covered are management, pollution monitoring, technology, recycling, environmental software, contaminated land, energy management, and environmental management systems.

Environment Matters

URL:	http://www-esd.worldbank.org/envmat/
Summary:	*Environment Matters* is published three times per year by the World Bank. Articles cover "biodiversity, water resource management, pollution management, new indicators of progress, climate change and ozone, partnerships and others." Also includes links to significant environmental resources at the World Bank Web site.
Contact:	kbannon@worldbank.org

Environment Writer

URL:	http://www.nsc.org/ehc/ewtoppg.htm
Summary:	*Environment Writer* is published ten times per year by the Environmental Health Center of the National Safety Council. Free to environmental journalists, it focuses on issues of interest to environmental journalists. Regular features are Chemical Backgrounder, Reading Rack, and Webs of Interest. Subscriptions are available to nonjournalists. Back issues are available.
Contact:	ehc@nsc.org

Envirosense Online

URL: http://www.envirosense.org

Summary: *Envirosense Online* is sponsored by the Envirosense Consortium. A nonprofit organization, the Envirosense Consortium is comprised of companies with interests in the quality of indoor air. Their goals are to "address poor indoor air quality and related environmental issues," to "monitor legislative and regulatory activity relating to indoor air quality and related environmental issues," and to provide information on indoor air quality.

Contact: iaq@envirosense.org

EPRI JOURNAL

URL: http://www.epri.com/EPRI_Journal/index.html

Summary: This journal is issued by the Electric Power Research Institute (EPRI). EPRI is a research consortium with 700 members. Articles in their bimonthly journal have been on biodiversity, water regulations, assessments, superconductivity, biomass, fire-resistant cables, fuel cells, and pollution.

Farm Aid News & Views

URL: http://host.envirolink.org/publications/IATP/farmaid/

Summary: *Farm Aid News & Views* is published by the Institute for Agriculture and Trade Policy for Farm Aid. Older monthly issues are located at this site. Articles cover topics such as weather, drought, financial issues, land ownership, and the marketplace.

Contact: farmaid1@aol.com

Forest Voice

URL: http://www.efn.org/~savtrees/forestvoice.html

Summary: *Forest Voice* is quarterly publication of the Native Forest Council. The NFC is an active voice in protecting the forests from logging activities. Articles cover government actions and regulations, policies, and laws pertaining to forests and the timber industry.

Contact: savtrees@efn.org

FROGLOG

URL: http://acs-info.open.ac.uk/info/newsletters/FROGLOG.html

Summary: *Froglog* is the newsletter of the Declining Amphibian Populations Task Force that was established by the Species Survival Commission of the World Conservation Union. It is published under the auspices of the Ecology and Conservation Research Group at The Open University in the United Kingdom. This quarterly newsletter contains information on conservation efforts and endangered species worldwide.

Contact: DAPTF@open.ac.uk

GEWEX News

URL: http://www.cais.com/gewex/gewex_nwsltr.html

Summary: *GEWEX News* is a publication of the International Global Energy and Water Cycle Experiment project. This project was initiated by the World Climate Research Programme. The project focuses on radiation, hydrometeorology, and modeling and prediction. Their newsletter contains reports on the research activities and available data.

Contact: gewex@cais.com

GHCC Forecast

URL: http://wwwghcc.msfc.nasa.gov/Newsletter/

Summary: This is the newsletter of the Global Hydrology and Climate Center. It disseminates information on projects, seminars, publications, and research performed at the GHCC.

Contact: diane.samuelson@msfc.nasa.gov

Global Environmental Change Report

URL: http://www.cutter.com/gecr

Summary: Cutter Information Corporation publishes this periodical twice a month. Its objective is to deliver "concise, objective, comprehensive information on policy trends, scientific research, and industrial developments concerning global warming, stratospheric ozone depletion, deforestation, sustainable development, and related topics." The tables of contents are available to guests at this site; subscription is required for full text.

Contact: gecr@igc.apc.org

Global Food Watch

URL: http://host.envirolink.org/publications/IATP/farmbill/

Summary: Formerly the *Farm Bill Review*, this periodical is published by the Institute for Agriculture and Trade Policy. Past articles are posted here. It was established to cover international agricultural policy, production, prices, trade and food security. Topics covered have been on prices and stocks, consumer market, taxes on exports, food consumption, and congressional activity.

Contact: gdigiacomo@iatp.org

GreenBeat!: Profiles & Perspectives in Environmental Endeavors

URL: http://www.tec.org/greenbeat

Summary: *Greenbeat!*, a monthly publication of the Texas Environmental Center, covers a variety of environmental topics. Past topical issues have covered green building and construction, wastewater, bioregionalism, earth day, air quality, drought, and water quality.

Contact: greenbeat@earth.tec.org

GreenClips

URL: http://solstice.crest.org/sustainable/greenclips/info.html

Summary: *GreenClips* is published every two weeks. It is available at this site or via email. Summaries of recent articles from press sources involve environmentally conscious design of buildings, legislature surrounding green architecture, and business activities that may affect sustainable architecture. Articles have covered conservation of energy, use of recycled materials, urban planning, and population.

Contact: Chris Hammer: greenclips@aol.com

The GreenDisk Paperless Environmental Journal

URL: http://www.igc.apc.org/greendisk

Summary: *GreenDisk* is published bimonthly and covers a very wide range of environmental issues from input by several established and well-recognized environmental organizations. Each issue (disk) focuses on a specific topic; and, for each topic, an extensive bibliography is given. Also included in each issue are action alerts, press releases, news from associations, and listings of new publications.

Contact: greendisk@igc.apc.org

GreeNotes

URL: http://www.ala.org/alaorg/rtables/srrt/greenotes/greenotes.html

Summary: This is a publication of the American Library Association's Task Force on the Environment. It contains news from the Task Force, the U.S. Environmental Protection Agency, and the National Institute for the Environment. Also included are articles about environmental resources that may be found on the Internet.

Contact: fstoss@acsu.buffalo.edu

Greenpeace Toxic Trade Updates

URL: gopher://gopher.igc.apc.org:70/11/pubs/gptox

Summary: Published by the Greenpeace Toxic Trade Campaign of Greenpeace International, this publication was created to help stop the trade of toxic substances. Articles describe the various activities surrounding global trading and shipments of pesticides, waste, fertilizers, and chlorine. Contained in each quarterly edition are many articles pertaining to the international trade in toxic wastes and toxic products. Though no longer being added to, the archived issues at this site may be useful to researchers.

Green Teacher

URL: http://www.web.net/~greentea/

Summary: This quarterly magazine was created "to enhance environmental and global education across the curriculum at all grade levels." Issues contain perspective articles, practical articles, activities, news and announcements, and information on resources. Some of the articles are available online. The site contains a searchable interface which allows searching by author, title, article description, type of article, focus of article, and issue number.

Contact: greentea@web.net

Habitrends Newsletter

URL: http://eelink.umich.edu/wild/habmenu.html

Summary: *Habitrends* contains information on many environmental topics including threatened wildlife, oceans, wildlife migration, and environmental organizations. It is a periodic publication of Project Wild.

Contact: natpwild@igc.apc.org

High Country News

URL: http://www.hcn.org/

Summary: *High Country News* is for people who care about the West. This paper contains information on current environmental topics such as nuclear power, pollution, and toxics. It also includes data on meetings, a calendar of events, and letters from subscribers. There is a searchable archive of past issues as far back as 1993.

Contact: lindab@hcn.org

Home Energy Magazine

URL: http://www.homeenergy.org/

Summary: *Home Energy Magazine* provides energy professionals with dependable, easy-to-read reporting on the latest energy-efficient technologies for the home. This online magazine contains information on insulation, lighting, solar water heating, window energy efficiency and a myriad of other topics to help the public make decisions about energy conservation. Issues may be searched or there is a convenient topic and table of contents index search available.

Contact: homeenergy@anl.org

Home Power Magazine

URL: http://www.homepower.com/hp/

Summary: *Home Power Magazine* was created to assist users of home-made electricity. Each issue contains at least one "system article" complete with charts, spreadsheets, and system schematics. The magazine is published every other month. This site contains information on subscribing, an index of back issues, and data on writing articles for the *Home Power Magazine*.

Contact: Richard.Perez@homepower.org

HydroWire

URL:	http://www.hydrowire.org/
Summary:	*HydroWire* bills itself as the "Online weekly for aquatic science." This site contains a calendar of meetings of the American Geophysical Union, the Estuarine Research Federation and the American Society of Limnology and Oceanography. There are also articles of interest to oceanographers, job postings, international news, and a directory of professionals in ocean science.
Contact:	Webmistress@marine.usf.edu

IALC Online Newsletter

URL:	http://ag.arizona.edu/OALS/IALC/NL/News-top.html
Summary:	The *IALC Online Newsletter* is a monthly publication of The International Arid Lands Consortium. It contains information on conferences, jobs, publications, courses, and requests for proposals. The archive goes back to 1995.
Contact:	Katherine Waser: kwaser@ag.arizona.edu

Idaho Rivers United Newsletter

URL:	http://www.desktop.org/iru/newsletter.htm
Summary:	The *IRU Newsletter* deals with issues of endangered rivers and fish in the state of Idaho. This quarterly newsletter of the Idaho Rivers United nonprofit conservation group contains information on flooding, river damming, salmon fishing, conservation meetings and conferences, and other environmental topics.
Contact:	iru@desktop.org

IHDP Update

URL:	http://www.uni-bonn.de/IHDP/public.htm
Summary:	*IHDP Update* is the quarterly newsletter of The International Human Dimensions Programme on Global Environmental Change. It contains meeting and conference news and environmental articles.
Contact:	Use form at Web site: http://www.uni-bonn.de/IHDP/cgi.htm

Initiatives in Environmental Technology Investment

URL: http://www.wpi.org/Initiatives/

Summary: *Initiatives in Environmental Technology Investment* is published four times a year by the Waste Policy Institute and contains articles on energy and transportation issues within the Department of Energy. Its purpose is to foster the interchange of information on technology and development opportunities. The archive contains all issues from the newsletter's inception in 1994 and includes a search form.

Contact: editor@wpi.org

Inside & Out

URL: http://come.to/insideandout/

Summary: *Inside & Out* is a monthly syndicated column about personal health and the environment. Its objective is to enlighten you about new findings on your health and its relationship to things you do everyday, without undue alarm, making you aware of how to evaluate the health risks for yourself. This site contains articles from several current issues plus health and environment tips.

Contact: cgerena@earthlink.net

Intellectual Property & Biodiversity News

URL: http://envirolink.org/seel/IATP/biodiv

Summary: This publication is published by the Institute for Agriculture and Trade Policy and formerly was entitled Bio/Technology/Diversity News. Articles have covered areas such as ethics and genetic research, genetic applications in agricultural science, environmental actions, and events. The information on this has not been updated since 1996.

Contact: seel@envirolink.org

International Wildlife

URL: http://www.nwf.org/intlwild/

Summary: *International Wildlife* is one of several wildlife journals published by the National Wildlife Federation. Its focus is on global wildlife conservation. This site contains selected articles from the last six issues, subscription information, and data on awards given to NWF publications.

Contact: pubs@nwf.org

International Wolf

URL: http://www.wolf.org/GH/Preview/Magazine.html

Summary: *International Wolf* is the quarterly publication of the International Wolf Center. It contains feature articles, national news, updates from the Center and a "Wolves of the World" section. Issues are available from 1997 to the present.

Contact: wolfinfo@wolf.org

Japan Environment Quarterly

URL: http://www.eic.or.jp/eanet/e/jeq/

Summary: *Japan Environment Quarterly* is published by the Global Environment Department, Environment Agency in Tokyo, Japan. It contains information on meetings, legislation, publications, and events, plus articles of environmental interest. Issues are available from 1996 to the present.

Contact: globe.dep@eanet.go.jp

Journal of Arboriculture

URL   http://www.ag.uiuc.edu/%7Eisa/JofA/abstracts/abstracts.html

Summary: This is the journal of the International Society of Arboriculture. It covers a variety of tree care topics ranging from fungicide sprays to tree-caused electric outages. Information on how to subscribe and other ISA data resides at this site.

Contact: isa@isa-arbor.com

Journal of Industrial Ecology

URL: http://mitpress.mit.edu/journal-home.tcl?issn=10881980

Summary: This quarterly journal is an international, multi-disciplinary quarterly designed to foster both understanding and practice in the emerging field of industrial ecology. The *Journal of Industrial Ecology* addresses topics of material and energy flow studies, eco-industrial parks, product-oriented environmental policy, and eco-efficiency. The journal is peer reviewed and submission guidelines are found at this site.

Contact: Reid Lifset: indecol@yale.edu

Journal of Political Ecology - JPE

URL: http://www.library.arizona.edu/ej/jpe/jpeweb.html

Summary: This peer-reviewed journal strives to foster an interdisciplinary exchange of ideas and research by professionals on the connection between political economy and ecosystems. Articles from the *Journal of Political Ecology* are available in ASCII or postscript for the 1994 through 1996 issues.

Contact: Jgreenber@ccit.arizona.edu

Know Your Environment

URL: http://www.acnatsci.org/erd/ea/KYE_mainpage.html

Summary: *Know Your Environment* is a series of environmental bulletins published by the Environmental Group of the Academy of Natural Sciences. This site provides an index of articles containing unbiased factual information and the full text of those articles.

Contact: garth@say.acnatsci.org

League of Conservation Voters (LCV) - National Environmental Scorecard

URL: http://www.lcv.org/scorecards/index.htm/

Summary: The League of Conservation Voters publishes a yearly *National Environmental Scorecard*, which shows how your government leaders voted on environmental issues. This site displays a list of vote descriptions and the voting score of government officials by state from 1993 to 1997.

Contact: lcv@lcv.org

Linkages

URL: http://kaos.erin.gov.au/newsletter/newsletter.html

Summary: Formerly *ERINYES*, this is the newsletter of the Environmental Resources Information Network (ERIN) in Australia. It covers research reports and environmental activities in Australia. Also included in the newsletter are helpful, informative articles on the structure and data of the ERIN network.

Contact: Use form at Web site.

Living Gently Quarterly

URL: http://www.islandnet.com/~see/living.htm

Summary: *Living Gently Quarterly* is a journal for sharing ways to live a good life that is environmentally gentle and inexpensive. Its outlook is to reduce consumption, waste, energy, and water use, while maintaining the quality of life. The seasonal reports cover issues of importance to urban and rural dwellers who seek a simpler lifestyle. This site includes guidelines for submitting articles to the journal.

Contact: see@islandnet.com

Makai

URL:	http://www.soest.hawaii.edu/SEAGRANT/sgcpcomm.html
Summary:	*Makai* is the monthly publication of the Hawaii Sea Grant College Program. It contains articles on aquaculture and marine environment. Information on grants, education programs, events, and marine environmentalists appear in several issues.
Contact:	dianen@soest.hawaii.edu

Maryland Marine Notes

URL:	http://www.mdsg.umd.edu/MDSG/Communications/MarineNotes/index.html
Summary:	*Maryland Marine Notes* is published by the Maryland Sea Grant College for and about the marine research, education, and outreach community around the state. Issues are available back to 1994 and contain historical information, articles on current marine projects, data on educational programs, and information about awards.
Contact:	mdsg@umbi.umd.edu

Master Network

URL:	http://www.lnt.org/Newsletter/LNTNewsltrHome
Summary:	*Master Network* is the newsletter of Leave No Trace. This site contains articles on LNT research, LNT in education, international wilderness ethics, wilderness recreation areas, and an LNT executive report.
Contact:	lnt@nols.edu

Michigan Forests Magazine

URL:	http://www.spring-board.com/two/mfa/mfamag.htm
Summary:	This journal is published by the Michigan Forest Association and includes articles on such topics as the number of trees in Michigan and woodland wildlife. Stewardship reports, interviews of forest conservation officers, and data on Michigan timberland growth are other themes found in this quarterly magazine.
Contact:	lrudel@i-star.com

Minnesota Volunteer

URL   http://www.dnr.state.mn.us/information_and_education/publications/volunteer/index.html

Summary: *Minnesota Volunteer* is devoted specifically to wildlife and conservation issues in Minnesota. It is published by the Minnesota DNR and contains articles on such diverse topics as white pine restoration, strategies of pollinators, and teaming with wildlife. Sample articles and an index of past issues back to 1973 are available at this site.

Contact: info@dnr.state.mn.us

National Parks

URL: http://www.npca.org/newsstand.html

Summary: *National Parks* is the magazine of the National Parks and Conservation Association. It contains information on saving our national parks and reports from the regional offices of NPCA. There is only a current issue online. Subscription is free with your membership in NPCA.

Contact: npca@npca.org

National Wildlife

URL: http://www.nwf.org/natlwild/

Summary: *National Wildlife* is one of a number of magazines published by the National Wildlife Federation. The focus of this journal is on wildlife in the United States. This site contains selected articles from the past six issues, information on the mission of NWF, and subscription and membership data. Its purpose is to inform readers about current conservation issues and to examine the latest discoveries affecting the natural world.

Contact: pubs@nwf.org

NATO Scientific & Environmental Affairs Newsletter

URL: http://www.vm.ee/nato/science/news.htm

Summary: This NATO newsletter contains articles on international environmental issues including such topics as the problems of cleaning up chemically contaminated sites, workshop topics, and environmental security. There are also articles covering environmental award recipients, conferences, and cooperative environmental efforts between nations.

Contact: science@hq.nato.int

Natural Areas Journal

URL: http://www.natareas.org/

Summary: The *Natural Areas Journal* is one of the leading voices in natural areas management and protection of natural diversity. This journal furnishes a medium for the exchange of ideas about the identification, preservation, protection, and management of natural areas and elements of natural diversity. The NAJ site contains tables of contents and abstracts for recent issues, guidelines for authors for information about submissions, subscription information, and Natural Areas Conference information.

Contact: cottermanj@aol.com

Nature Network

URL: http://www.defenders.org/nnabout.html

Summary: *Nature Network* is the quarterly newsletter of the National Watchable Wildlife Program and is published by Defenders of Wildlife, a national, non-profit organization whose purpose is protecting and restoring wildlife to their natural habitat. This site also includes conference information and Watchable Wildlife's mission and goals statement.

Contact: defender@teleport.com

NETAction Newsletter

URL: http://data.envirotrust.com/envirotrust/netaction.qry
            (Also available via email subscription.)

Summary: This is a publication of the National Environmental Trust (formerly EICAction Newsletter of the Environmental Information Center). The NET strives to disseminate timely news about important environmental events.

Contact: info@list.envirotrust.com

New Forests News

URL: http://www.newforestsproject.com/nfpnws.html

Summary: The *New Forests News* is the newsletter of the New Forests Project. It contains articles on agroforestry and reforestation in developing countries as well as program and membership news. The archive contains several issues from 1993 to the present.

Contact: icnfp@erols.com

NOAA News

URL: http://www.nmfs.gov

Summary: *NOAA News* is the newsletter of the National Oceanic and Atmospheric Administration. It contains information on weather, tides, and climate. There are also reports of NOAA legislative affairs and international weather data in this newsletter.

Contact: help@esdim.noaa.gov

Ocean News

URL: http://www.elsevier.nl/homepage/browse.htt

Summary: This free marine science newsletter is of interest to all oceanographers and contains discussion of contents of Elsevier science journals and topical items by experts in the field. To sign up for your free subscription see the contact below.

Contact: Hans Zilstra: h.zijlstra@elsevier.nl

Oceanography

URL: http://www.tos.org/tos/tos_magazine_menu.html

Summary: This journal of The Oceanography Society is published three times a year by The Oceanography Society. This site contains tables of contents for selected issues back to 1988, style guidelines for contributors, schedules, deadlines, and planned contents for future issues.

Contact: atkinson@ccpo.odu.edu

On the Air

URL: http://www.silcom.com/~apcd/ota/otaindex.htm

Summary: *On the Air* is the bimonthly newsletter of the Planning and Community Assistance Section of the Santa Barbara County Air Pollution Control District. It contains articles on air pollution in Santa Barbara County, meeting announcements, events listings, awards, and legislation. Articles are available from issues back to 1996.

Contact: Bobbie Bratz: bbratz@apcd.santa-barbara.ca.us

Open Spaces

URL: http://www.pvplc.org/pvplc_news.htm

Summary: *Open Spaces* is the quarterly newsletter of the Palos Verdes Peninsula Land Conservancy. It contains full-text articles on all aspects of ecology and conservation and includes information on meetings, educational programs, and projects.

Contact: pvplc@aol.com

ORNL Review

URL: http://www.ornl.gov/ORNLReview/

Summary: Published quarterly by the Oak Ridge National Laboratory, the *ORNL Review* site contains tables of contents, full-text articles and some hypertext articles, many of which relate to environmental issues. Archives include issues from 1992 to the present. Subscription: Free to ORNL employees and interested parties in government, industry, academia, and others.

Contact: http://www.ornl.gov/ORNLReview/rev26-2/text/email.html

Our Environment

URL: http://www.maui.net/~jstark/ournvmag.html

Summary: This is an online environmental journal that contains articles on current environmental issues. Topics include renewable energy sources, extinction of wildlife species, and global warming.

Contact: jstark@maui.net

Our Living Oceans Annual Report

URL: http://kingfish.ssp.nmfs.gov/olo.html

Summary: This is an annual report of the National Marine Fisheries Services of NOAA. It includes many reports on national fisheries and fish species such as salmon, rainbow trout, and marine mammals.

Contact: Thomas.McIntyre@noaa.gov

Our Planet

URL: http://www.ourplanet.com/imgversn/planethme.html

Summary: *Our Planet* is the United Nations Environmental Programme's bimonthly magazine for sustainable development and the environment. Each issue centers around a single theme and contains information on conferences, issues, and events dealing with that theme. Articles are written by UN officials, international government leaders, experts, and opinion leaders.

Contact: banson@ourplanet.com

Outdoor Classroom / La Classe en Plein-air

URL: http://www.evergreen.ca/oc2cover.html

Summary: *Outdoor Classroom* is a Canadian Newsletter on school ground naturalization. Topics in this newsletter include pesticide concerns at schools, a pond project, a butterfly book bibliography, Metro Toronto Zoo's Adopt-a-Pond Program, native plants, and integrating school curriculum with the environment. The latest online issue is 1995. The next expected issue will be online in 1999.

Contact: info@evergreen.ca

PANUPS

URL: http://www.panna.org/panna/panups/subscribe_panups.html

Summary: *PANUPS* is a free online news service of the Pesticide Action Network North America. It contains weekly news articles on pesticide use and sustainable agriculture, as well as action alerts and conference reports from around the world.

Contact: panna@panna.org

People and the Planet

URL: http://www.oneworld.org/patp/

Summary: *People and the Planet* is a quarterly international publication that focuses on people, their consumption, their technologies, and their numbers and how they interact with the environment of the earth. It contains articles on all aspects of the environment, with a special focus on the effects of human population. Issues are available from 1996 to the present.

The Planet

URL: http://www.insideout.com/e_news/s_club/planet25.htm

Summary: *The Planet* is the newsletter of the Sierra Club. Some articles are available in full text at this site. Topics include all general environmental subjects.

Contact: planet@sierraclub.org

The Prairie Falcon

URL:	http://www.ksu.edu/audubon/falcon.html
Summary:	*The Prairie Falcon* is the monthly (except August) newsletter of the Northern Flint Hills Audubon Society. The current issue is available online. There are no archives. It contains information on prairie birds, plants, and other wildlife and includes news of events and meetings. This newsletter site also contains many links to other wildlife sites.
Contact:	audubon@ksu.edu

Pollution Engineering

URL:	http://www.manufacturing.net/magazine/polleng/
Summary:	This monthly publication is published by Cahners Business Information, which is a division of Reed Elsevier, Inc. It covers technical news, features, and product information to meet the information needs of environmental professionals with pollution control responsibilities in air, water, solid and hazardous waste.
Contact:	c.hodson@cahners.com

Project Wildlife Newsletters

URL:	http://www.projectwildlife.org/newsletters.html
Summary:	The *Project Wildlife Newsletters* contain information on all aspects of wildlife rehabilitation and includes environmental calendars of events, what to do about injured wildlife, and bird counts. Issues are available from 1996 to the present.
Contact:	Jazmyn Concolor: jazmyn@firstlight.net

Rachel's Environment & Health Weekly

URL:	http://www.envirolink.org/pubs/rachel/contents.htm
Summary:	This site contains full text articles on the environment and the impact of its misuse on human health. The goal of this newsletter is to put a weapon into the hands of environmentalists to use in local fights to maintain or better the earth's natural resources for the health of the world.
Contact:	Info@rachel.clark.net

Raptor Release

URL:	http://www.raptor.cvm.umn.edu/raptor/nletter.html
Summary:	*Raptor Release* is the newsletter of the Raptor Center. The site contains selected articles from current and back issues along with images of peregrine falcons.
Contact:	raptor@umn.edu

Recycling World

URL:	http://www.tecweb.com/recycle/rwcont.htm
Summary:	*Recycling World* is a regularly published online newsletter. Each issue contains this month's view of what's going on in recycling, the latest news from the recycling industry, and detailed articles on current topics affecting the UK. There are no archives.
Contact:	recycle@tecweb.com

Reef Line

URL:	http://www.reefrelief.org/news.html
Summary:	*Reef Line* is the twice a year publication of Reef Relief. Issues provide information on Reef Relief's educational programs, grants, coral reef legislation, and other environmental topics related to coral reefs. Issues from 1997 to the present are available online.
Contact:	reef@bellsouth.net

Reflections on the Environment

URL: http://www.anr.state.vt.us/reflect.htm

Summary: *Reflections on the Environment* is the monthly newsletter of the Vermont ANR. The articles are primarily written by the Vermont Agency of Natural Resources staff. Topics include news of the State ANR, pollution prevention, air and water quality, habitat conservation, wildlife and individual species, forestry, state parks, and land conservation.

Contact: johnd@anrimsgis.anr.state.vt.us

Resistant Pest Management Newsletter

URL: http://www.msstate.edu/Entomology/EntHome.html

Summary: Several issues of this newsletter from Mississippi State University are available full-text for downloading to your computer. Topics include monitoring insecticide resistance of diamondback moth larvae and mechanisms in monitoring the tobacco budworm for resistance to insecticides.

Contact: Mike Caprio: mcaprio@entomology.msstate.edu

San Diego Earth Times

URL: http://www.sdearthtimes.com/

Summary: *SDET On-Line* is a monthly publication that encompasses a wide variety of local, national, and international environmental topics. This site provides access to the complete contents of every issue published since 1993 and offers a monthly *Calendar of Earth Friendly Events*, the Marketplace providing access to organic and eco-friendly products, Eco-puzzles, and links to other environmental sites.

Contact: sdet@sdearthtimes.com

Scientist

URL:	http://www.the-scientist.library.upenn.edu/
Summary:	This is a free bi-weekly online journal for and by scientists. Articles cover all scientific topics including the environmental sciences. Issues of *The Scientist* at this site go back to 1995. There are many scientific job opportunities listed in this journal.
Contact:	editorial@the-scientist.com

Sea Wind

URL:	http://www.conveyor.com/ovi/seawind.html
Summary:	*Sea Wind* is the quarterly bulletin of Ocean Voice International and is provided to its owners, members, and subscribers. It contains articles and information on the biology, conservation, biodiversity, and sustainable use of marine life. This site contains the tables of contents for a number of issues and submission guidelines for authors.
Contact:	mcall@superaje.com

Seiche

URL:	http://www.d.umn.edu/seagr/seiche.html
Summary:	*Seiche* is the newsletter of the Minnesota Sea Grant and is published four times a year, on a slightly irregular schedule. The purpose of the newsletter is to provide a flow of information about Lake Superior and Minnesota's inland waters. Articles cover legislation, aquaculture, new publications, marine genetics, and more. Available issues go back to 1995 and subscriptions are free.
Contact:	Marie Sales: msales@d.umn.edu

Sierra - The Sierra Club Magazine

URL: http://www.sierraclub.org/sierra/

Summary: *Sierra* is the official bimonthly magazine of the Sierra Club. It covers all environmental topics including endangered species, water conservation, rainforests, clean energy, organic farming, air pollution, and toxic waste. Guidelines for article authors and photographers can be found at this site.

Contact: sierra.magazine@sierraclub.org

Silva Fennica

URL: http://www.metla.fi/silvafennica

Summary: *Silva Fennica* is a quarterly, refereed journal that is distributed internationally and published by the Finnish Society of Forest Science. Topics include forest environment issues, ecology, soil science, and forest management. Abstracts of articles from some recent issues are available at this site.

Contact: tommi.salonen@metla.fi

Simple Living Newsletter

URL: http://www.slnet.com/free/newsletter/archivesdefault.htm

Summary: The *Simple Living Newsletter* is a bimonthly publication of the Simple Living Network. It contains articles on voluntary simplicity resources, consumerism and the environment, and other earth friendly topics. The archive contains only issues from 1998 at present, but back issues will soon be available.

Contact: slnet@slnet.com

SNAP Shots Newsletter

URL: http://www.stolaf.edu/other/snap/newsletter.html

Summary: *SNAP Shots* is the School Nature Area Projects newsletter from St. Olaf College, Northfield, Minnesota. It contains articles, bibliographies, reviews, information about environmental grants, and data on SNAP partnership projects. Issues are available from 1994 to the present.

Contact: Bill Lindquist: lindquis@stolaf.edu

SOS Newsletter

URL: http://planet-hawaii.com/sos/sosnewsletters.html

Summary: The *SOS Newsletter* is a quarterly publication of Save Our Seas and focuses on articles concerning protecting the oceans and sea life. Issues contain a message from the president, meeting news, and membership information. Newsletters are available from 1995 to the present.

Contact: sos@aloha.net

Sound Waves

URL: http://www.wa.gov/puget_sound/psnews/sw_spring_98/

Summary: *Sound Waves* is the bimonthly newsletter about of the Puget Sound Water Quality Action Team and contains articles on water quality protection. Team news, conference announcements, and water quality legislation are discussed at this site. Issues are available back to 1996.

Contact: shindle@psat.wa.gov

Source, The

URL: http://www.igshpa.okstate.edu/Publications/source/SrcFrame.htm

Summary: *The Source* is the bimonthly publication of the International Ground Source Heat Pump Association. It contains articles, conference and meeting reports, information about training, and other news of interest to IGSHPA members.

Contact: Helen Robertson: cheetah@master.ceat.okstate.edu

South Florida Environmental Reader

URL: http://envirolink.org/florida

Summary: *The South Florida Environmental Reader* is an electronic newsletter that encompasses environmental issues pertaining to South Florida. SFER welcomes articles from readers on wetlands, oil pollution, recycling, water conservation, marine and freshwater habitats, and other relevant themes.

Contact: Andrew Mossberg: aem@symcor.com

Sustainable Agriculture Newsletter

URL: http://www.extension.umn.edu/Documents/titles.html?supercat=F&cat=D

Summary: This newsletter of the University of Minnesota Extension Service provides sustainable agriculture information including organic methods to save honey bees from mites, the use of pesticides and organic farming methods. Online issues are available from 1995 to the present and each issue includes a calendar of events and information on submitting articles.

Contact: jsperbeck@extension.umn.edu.

Sustainable Developments

URL: http://www.iisd.ca/sd/

Summary: *Sustainable Developments* contains summaries of international conferences, workshops, symposia and regional meetings addressing issues of sustainable development. It is published by the International Institute for Sustainable Development.

Contact: enb@iisd.org

Sustainable Minnesota

URL: http://www.me3.org/newsletters/

Summary: *Sustainable Minnesota* is the quarterly newsletter of Minnesotans for An Energy-Efficient Economy. It contains feature articles, meeting announcements, environmental legislative information, reports, a calendar of events, conservation updates, and ME3 project reports. The archive contains issues from 1995 to the present.

Contact: bailey@ilsr.org

SUSTAINABLE Times

URL: http://www.ccn.cs.dal.ca/CommunitySupport/CUSO/home2.html

Summary: This quarterly journal focuses on international success stories and articles on environmental sustainability to let Canadians understand that there are alternative ways to live and do business. Some of the topics include, green jobs, eco-tourism, saving Africa's elephants, butterfly farming and natural sewage treatment.

Contact: ip-cuso@chebucto.ns.ca

Terrain: A Journal of the Built & Natural Environments

URL: http://www.bod.net/terrain

Summary: This is a new quarterly journal whose editorial board is comprised of literature, planning, environmental, graphics, technical, and editorial experts from the U.S. It will contain poetry, essays, fiction, technical and journalistic articles, artwork, and case studies, primarily from submissions. Focus will be "on the environments around us—the built and natural environments—that both affect and are affected by the human species." Forthcoming theme-based issues at this writing are to cover The Urban Neighborhood, Patterns of Mobility, The River's Turn, and The Suburban Frontier.

Contact: buntin@bod.net

Terra Nova - Nature & Culture

URL: http://mitpress.mit.edu/journal-home.tcl?issn=10810749

Summary: *Terra Nova* is a quarterly journal whose mission is to attempt to understand the ethical, metaphysical, and aesthetic aspects of the relationship between people and nature. The table of contents and abstracts of some articles are viewable online.

Contact: rothenberg@admin.njit.edu

Texas On-Site Insights

URL: http://twri.tamu.edu/twripubs/Insights/

Summary: *Texas On-Site Insights* is concerned with issues pertaining to on-site wastewater systems, their performance, new technologies, and the environmental impact of failing systems. Issues are available from 1992 to the present.

Contact: twri@tamu.edu

Texas Water Resources

URL: http://twri.tamu.edu/twripubs/WtrResrc/

Summary: *Texas Water Resources* is a quarterly publication of the Texas Water Resources Institute. It contains in-depth articles on critical Texas water issues. The issue archive contains volumes from 1974 to the present.

Contact: Jonathan Jones: jej@tamu.edu

Texas Water Savers

URL: http://twri.tamu.edu/twripubs/WtrSavrs/

Summary: *Texas Water Savers* is the quarterly publication of the Texas Water Resources Institute which provides details on water conservation, recycling, and reuse. The archive contains issues from 1994 to the present.

Contact: jan@twri.tamu.edu

Tin-Men - The Inquiring Non-Mainstream Environmental News

URL: http://tinmen.org/index.html

Summary: *Tin-Men* is a Canadian online environmental newsletter that contains articles on all environmental issues in Canada. Some of the current topics include wildlife destruction and environmental legislation. This site contains an archive of letters and an email form to let your politicians know what you're thinking about environmental issues.

Contact: webmaster@tinmen.org

TNW Online (The Neighborhood Works)

URL: http://www.cnt.org/tnw/tnwhome.htm

Summary: *TNW Online* is the bimonthly, non-profit magazine published by the Center for Neighborhood Technology in Chicago. It is dedicated to the employment of a practical approach to energy use, job creation, housing, development, food production, and the materials used to develop a healthier neighborhood environment, a sustainable economy, and more viable neighborhoods.

Contact: tnwedit@cnt.org

TOS Newsletter

URL: http://www.tos.org/newsletter_menu.html

Summary: *TOS* is the newsletter of The Oceanography Society and is published a few times a year, not on a schedule. It contains information about the Society activities.

Contact: webmaster@tos.org

Toxicology and Ecotoxicology News

URL: http://www.bdt.org.br/bioline/te

Summary: Several issues of this journal's tables of contents are available to browse and the site provides a search engine to search the available issues. Some articles provide abstracts. Topics covered range from dioxins to toxic drinking water. *Toxicology and Ecotoxicology News* is published quarterly by Taylor & Francis in the UK.

Contact: bio@biostrat.demon.co.uk

Tropical Biodiversity

URL: http://www.bdt.org.br/bioline/tb

Summary: This journal is a publication of Indonesian Foundation for the Advancement of Biological Sciences. The table of contents and abstracts of articles are available to scan online. Sample articles range in topic from lists of amphibians and reptiles in Java and Bali to forest conservation in the tropics and primates as a human food source. A search engine is available at this journal site to search the contents and abstracts.

Contact: bio@biostrat.demon.co.uk

Tuna Newsletter

URL: http://swfsc.ucsd.edu/tunanews.html

Summary: This newsletter is published quarterly by NOAA, National Marine Fisheries Service (NMFS), and the Southwest Fisheries Science Center to inform the fishing industries and the general public about the status of U.S. tuna fisheries and research. Issues from 1995 to the present are available in full text at this site.

Contact: Alan Jackson: ajackson@ucsd.edu

U.S. Water News

URL: http://www.uswaternews.com/

Summary: *U.S. Water News'* topics include water supply, water quality, policy and legislation, litigation and water rights, conservation, climate, and international water news. This site contains an archive of past issues, meeting and conference announcements, and reviews of books published by *U.S. Water News* plus purchasing information.

Contact: uswatrnews@aol.com

UVB Impacts Reporter

URL:	http://www.islandnet.com/~see/uvb.htm
Summary:	The *UVB Impacts Reporter* contains information and research on the ozone layer and solar ultraviolet radiation impacts on human health and the environment. This site contains a sample issue and subscription information. Some of the article topics relate to UVB and amphibian population decline, freshwater ecosystems and UVB, and the Antarctic Ozone Hole.
Contact:	see@islandnet.com

Waste Not

URL:	http://it.stlawu.edu:80/~wastenot/index.html
Summary:	*Waste Not* is a one-page newsletter which furnishes data on waste issues that the waste industry prefers to keep hidden. The topics it covers include dangers posed by incineration of solid, hazardous and medical waste, health threats to plant workers, financial risks to the local economy and political dangers to the local democracy. Issues at this site go back to September 1994.
Contact:	Ellen and Paul Connett, 82 Judson St., Canton, NY

Watershed Management Council Networker

URL:	http://watershed.org/wmc/news/wmcnews.html
Summary:	*Watershed Management Council Networker* is the quarterly newsletter of WMC. It covers all aspects of watershed management including watershed ecology, riparian systems, environmental education, water quality monitoring, watershed tools, and watershed ecosystems. Issues are available from 1990 to the present.
Contact:	Mike Furniss: furniss@watershed.org

WEF Reporter

URL: http://www.wef.org/docs/wefreporter/

Summary: The *WEF Reporter* is the weekly newsletter of the Water Environment Federation. It is published on Wednesdays. The newsletter reports on international water quality, wetlands, and other environmental legislation that has been proposed or enacted.

Contact: webfeedback@wef.org

Wetlands - The Journal of the Society of Wetland Scientists

URL: http://www.sws.org/wetlands.html

Summary: *Wetlands* is a quarterly journal whose goal is to centralize the publication of pioneering wetlands work. It deals with such topics as wetlands biology, ecology, hydrology, water chemistry, wetlands management, law and regulations. This site contains submission guidelines, text of past issues, and author and keyword indexes, which can be either searched or browsed.

Contact: Douglas A. Wilcox: douglas_wilcox@usgs.gov

Whales Alive!

URL: http://elfnet1a.elfi.com/csihome.html

Summary: *Whales Alive!* is the newsletter of the Cetacean Society International. It contains articles about whales, whaling, and dolphins. Some of the topics covered include banning commercial whaling, dolphin and whale releases in Japan, and information on joining CSI. Issues go back to 1995.

Contact: Brent Hall: bshall@snet.net

Wildlife Notes

URL: http://www.dnr.state.oh.us/odnr/wildlife/publications/wildnotes/wildnote.html

Summary: *Wildlife Notes* is a publication of the Ohio DNR. It is free online and may also be ordered in hard copy without charge. It contains information on Ohio's animal wildlife, including description, habits, habitats, reproduction, rearing of young, and viewing opportunities. There are also facts at a glance and a bibliography in some of the *Notes*.

Contact: Ohio Division of Wildlife, 1840 Belcher Dr., Columbus, OH 43224-1329

Wildlife Watch

URL: http://iwc.org/Newsletters/newsletters.html

Summary: *Wildlife Watch* is the quarterly newsletter of the International Wildlife Coalition. Each issue targets one or more endangered species. There are several issues at this site from 1995, 1996, and 1998 concerning koalas, kangaroos, seals, manatees, and whales.

Contact: iwcadopt@capeonramp.com

Wild Ohio

URL   http://www.dnr.state.oh.us/odnr/wildlife/publications/wildohio/wildohio.html

Summary: *Wild Ohio Magazine* is a free publication of the Ohio Department of Natural Resources. There are several issues available online and paper copies may be ordered free of charge from the Ohio DNR. It covers all aspects of Ohio wildlife.

Contact: Ohio Division of Wildlife, 1840 Belcher Dr., Columbus, OH 43224-1329

Windows to Wildlife

URL: http://www2.state.id.us/fishgame/publicat.htm

Summary: *Windows to Wildlife* is a quarterly newsletter dedicated to Idaho's nongame wildlife and watchable wildlife. Issues are available in .pdf format for 1996 to the present.

Contact: papeters@idfg.state.id.us

WMO ANTARCTIC OZONE BULLETINS

URL: http://www.wmo.ch/web/arep/ozobull.html

Summary: The Secretariat of the World Meteorological Organization distributes bulletins annually on data gathered from August through November on the state of the ozone layer in Antarctica. The bulletin data is provided by WMO member countries that operate ozone satellites and stations in the southern polar region.

Contact: gorre-dale_e@gateway.wmo.ch

World Climate Report

URL: http://www.nhes.com/

Summary: *World Climate Report* is a bimonthly publication covering the breaking news concerning the science and political science of global climate change. Archives contain issues back to 1997.

Contact: wcr@nhes.com.

World Rivers Review

URL: http://www.irn.org/pubs/wrr/index.html

Summary: *World Rivers Review* is the bimonthy publication of the International Rivers Network. It focuses on river issues and appropriate freshwater management. The archives contain the text of issues from 1994 to the present.

Contact: irnweb@irn.org

Worldwide Rainforest/Biodiversity Campaign News Archives

URL: http://forests.org/worldfor.html

Summary: This site contains the text of a large number of up-to-date reports on biodiversity and rainforest destruction from all parts of the world. An alphabetical listing of countries and topics, with the date they were updated, is included.

Contact: Glen Barry: grbarry@students.wisc.edu

Yale Working Papers on Solid Waste Policy

URL: http://www.yale.edu/pswp/

Summary: This site contains the abstracts of papers by experts in the field of solid waste that have been commissioned by the Yale School of Forestry and Environmental Studies Program on Solid Waste Policy to address neglected topics in solid waste policy. Full articles may be ordered from this site.

Contact: pswp@yale.edu

Yellowstone Journal

URL: http://www.yellowstonepark.com/

Summary: The *Yellowstone Journal* is a publication of Yellowstone National Park. It is produced five times a year and covers information on such themes as wolves, grizzly bears, bison and wildfires. The current issue is online and, as each new issue comes out, there will be an archive of older issues. The online site contains information on subscribing to the hard copy journal and access to a chat room.

Contact: yelpaper@wyoming.com

Chapter 5

Environmental World Wide Web Sites

The World Wide Web or WWW, as we have said in the first chapter, is a hypermedia data retrieval system which encompasses the global network of networks which is the Internet. It can retrieve anything that can be retrieved using gopher, telnet, ftp, or WAIS and many documents that exist only on the World Wide Web. To view the World Wide Web, you will need a TCP/IP connection and a web browser or a commercial Internet provider whose service includes a web browser. There are numerous different providers and browsers. Some look only at text, while others view the Web with graphics, quick-time movies, Java applets, tables, and frames.

World Wide Web pages are created in a subset of Standard Generalized Mark-up Language (SGML) called Hypertext Mark-up Language, or HTML. Hypertext Mark-up Language is a tagging language. The page creator writes the text that he or she wants to be seen and then tags it so that the browser will display it in a certain way. He or she may add whatever type of graphics are most likely to catch your attention. This is a small sample of an HTML tagged page:

```
<HTML>
<HEAD><TITLE>Sample HTML Page</TITLE></HEAD>
<BODY>
<H1>Sample HTML Page</H1>
<P>This is a sample HTML page. All of the tags are enclosed in left and right arrows. The
opening and closing HTML tags tell the browser where to begin reading the HTML tagging. The
HEAD tags enclose the TITLE tags. These are displayed in the title bar of the browser. The BODY
tags tell the browser where to begin and end the page display. The H1 tags are heading tags and they
tell the browser how large to make the heading. There are six heading tags, H1 being the biggest.
Space means nothing to the browser, so HTML is able to force a space between paragraphs with the
P tag. </P>

</BODY>
</HTML>
```

Your browser would display this HTML page something like this:

Sample HTML Page

This is a sample HTML page. All of the tags are enclosed in left and right arrows. The opening and closing HTML tags tell the browser where to begin reading the HTML tagging. The HEAD tags enclose the TITLE tags. These are displayed in the title bar of the browser. The BODY tags tell the browser where to begin and end the page display. The H1 tags are heading tags and they tell the browser how large to make the heading. There are six heading tags, H1 being the biggest. Space means nothing to the browser, so HTML is able to force a space between paragraphs with the P tag.

There are a number of HTML editors available as shareware on the Internet. Some of them are at ftp sites and are downloadable to your hard drive using your WWW browser. Many of them will let you use their editor for a trial period before you decide if you would like to purchase it. You can find them using archieplex at (http://www.lerc.nasa.gov/archieplex/).

The number of environmental sites on the WWW has increased dramatically in the last several years. Some of these sites and pages are produced by professionals in the various environmental fields. Others are created by students who are preparing to enter one of those fields. Still others are developed by individuals who would like to make an impact on cleaning up the earth and its atmosphere, save endangered species, protect forests and wildlife habitats, and make people aware of what is happening to our world, its inhabitants, and those who will come after us. We will never be able to collect every environmental site that is on the WWW at any particular time, partly because trying to gather everything on the Internet on any subject is an impossible task—even the search engines claim 90% or less coverage of the Internet, and partly because there are many new sites and home pages being created daily. Our intention is to give you a collection of good sites, on a wide range of environmental topics, so that you might have a starting place to begin collecting a group of sites in your own area of interest.

The Academy of Natural Sciences

URL: http://www.acnatsci.org

Summary: The Academy of Natural Sciences is a nonprofit organization that was founded in 1812. The Environmental Associates of The Academy publish electronic "Know Your Environment" bulletins and make them available at this site. "Know Your Environment" bulletins provide unbiased, factual information on a variety of topics. The interesting articles have covered butterflies, chlorine, wetlands, water, and waste. There is an index to other publications of The Environmental Associates.

Contact: webmaster@www.acnatsci.org

Advanced Forest Technologies Program (AFT)

URL: http://www.aft.pfc.forestry.ca/

Summary: Some of the information offered at this Canadian forestry site includes the SEIDAM (System of Experts for Intelligent Data Management) project and documentation, multimedia systems, forest fuel characterization by remote sensing, remote sensing of foliar chemistry, and the earth observation for sustainable development of forests. Includes abstracts and images.

Contact: pbhogal@Banyan.PFC.Forestry.CA

Advanced Recovery

URL: http://www.AdvancedRecovery.com

Summary: Advanced Recovery, based in New Jersey, is involved in the recycling industry. They promote the proper disposal of all scrap, but are particularly interested in the disposal of electronic equipment, such as computer monitors consisting of lead.

Contact: visitus@AdvancedRecovery.com

Advanced Technologies for Commercial Buildings

URL: http://www.advancedbuildings.org

Summary: This database is directed at the building professional. It contains information on more than 60 environmentally-appropriate technologies and is dedicated to "improving the energy and resource efficiency of commercial, industrial, and multi-unit residential buildings." The design and construction areas include: indoor air quality, daylighting, non-toxic materials, waste management, electricity production, water conservation, energy efficiency, and recycled materials. This database is provided by Enermodal Engineering, Ltd., Gas Technology Canada, and the Canadian Centre for Mineral and Energy Technology.

Contact: scarpenter@enermodal.com

Advanced Technology Environmental Education Center

URL: http://www.ateec.org/

Summary: ATEEC's mission is to foster the advancement of environmental technology education through "curriculum development, professional development, and program improvement in the nation's community colleges and high schools." Included are curriculum aids, program descriptions, a directory of environmental programs in schools and colleges, the publication, *Defining Environmental Technology*, program assessment materials, professional development resources, and links to pertinent Web sites.

Contact: dgere@eiccd.cc.ia.us

African Environmental Research and Consulting Group

URL: http://www.africaenviro.org/

Summary: The AERCG is a U.S. nonprofit organization with offices in African and Western countries. The group focuses on "improving the quality of life, mitigating environmental hazards, and protection of human health in Africa." They are involved in promoting sustainable development in African communities and their site contains information about their efforts.

Contact: isuberu@aol.com

Agency for Toxic Substances and Disease Registry (ATSDR)

URL: http://atsdr1.atsdr.cdc.gov:8080/atsdrhome.html

Summary: The ATSDR operates under the auspices of the U.S. Department of Public Health's
              Center for Disease Control. This site includes HazDat (ATSDR's Hazardous
              Substance Release/Health Effects Database), ToxFAQs, searchable Public Health
              Statements, the guidance manual, *Environmental Data Needed for Public Health
              Assessments, A Primer on Health Risk Communication Principles and Practices,*
              CERCLA Priority List of Hazardous Substances, Congressional testimony of the
              ATSDR staff, and a glossary of terms. The ToxFAQs (http://atsdr1.atsdr. cdc.
              gov:8080 /toxfaq.html) is a series of summaries developed by the ATSDR Division
              of Toxicology about hazardous substances. Information for this series is excerpted
              from the ATSDR Toxicological Profiles and Public Health Statements. Answers
              are provided to the most frequently asked questions about exposure to hazardous
              substances. Also found here is CLUSTER version 3.1, a DOS program designed
              to help the researcher determine if there is statistical significance that a disease
              cluster occurred other than by random phenomena.

Contact: Mike Perry: lmp1@cdc.gov

AGRALIN (Agricultural Bibliographic Information System of the Netherlands)

URL: http://www.bib.wau.nl/agralin/src-agr1.html

Summary: This system is made possible by the combined efforts of the Wageningen
              Agricultural University (WAU) Library and the Dutch Ministry of Agriculture,
              Nature Conservation and Fisheries. The information contained here is from over
              70 Dutch libraries with substantial agricultural holdings. Topics include plant
              breeding, environmental sciences, nature conservation, and many others. This is a
              large database with published books and papers from the countries all over the
              world including the Netherlands, the U.S., Finland, Germany, the United Kingdom,
              and Belgium.

Contact: de.helpdesk@pd.bib.wau.nl

Agriculture Network Information Center

URL: www.agnic.org

Summary: AgNIC is a network of resources pertaining to agricultural information. Of interest
              to the environmental researcher would be the *Data Base of the Occurrence and
              Distribution of Pesticides in Chesapeake Bay,* renewable natural resources,
              pollution, and forestry information.

Contact: agnic@agnic.org

Air & Waste Management Association

URL: http://www.awma.org

Summary: This site contains information pertaining to the activities and research of the AWMA. Materials include information on staff and membership, meetings, employment, news, educational opportunities, and a listing and brief summary of their publications. Their online magazine for environmental managers, *EM Online,* is also available at this site.

Contact: jdougherty@awma.org

Air Force Center for Environmental Excellence (AFCEE)

URL: http://www.afcee.brooks.af.mil

Summary: This site contains publications and materials from its various directorates. Of particular interest are the pollution program guides and other materials created by the Pollution Prevention Directorate. This directorate "identifies pollution/ compliance opportunities, develops and executes strategic initiatives to identify and implement solutions to common Air Force pollution prevention and compliance problems, and crossfeeds information on successful programs, good ideas, and "best technologies" from throughout the Air Force and other federal agencies."

Contact: kathy.rice@hqafcee.brooks.af.mil or william.kivela@hqafcee.brooks.af.mil

Alabama Department of Environmental Management

URL: http://www.adem.state.al.us/

Summary: This site contains information related to the organization and activities of the Department and news releases. Downloadable reports and forms are also available. Includes a daily ozone forecast and Uniform Air Quality Index for sections of Alabama.

Contact: Dcp@adem.state.al.us

Alaska Department of Environmental Conservation

URL: http://www.state.ak.us/local/akpages/ENV.CONSERV/home.htm

Summary: The mission of this agency is to strengthen "families and job opportunities through a cooperative stewardship with the citizens of Alaska that ensures protection of public health and the environment." Materials supporting this mission include newsletters and brochures. Information about the programs from the divisions is available. Divisions of interest to environmentalists are: air and water quality, facility construction and operation, environmental health, and spill prevention and response.

Contact: WebSite@envircon.state.ak.us

Albany Research Center

URL: http://www.alrc.doe.gov

Summary: The Albany Research Center, established under the auspices of the Department of Energy, is devoted to the research of materials conservation of energy resources. This site contains information regarding their research activities. Research endeavors have been in the area of reactive metal technology, casting and melting technologies, refractories, and aluminum recycling.

Contact: palmer@alrc.doe.gov

Alfred Wegener Institute for Polar and Marine Research

URL: http://www.awi-bremerhaven.de

Summary: This German site has a large amount of data related to global change research. Included are real time ozone soundings and a hydrographic atlas of the Southern Ocean.

Contact: cdahm@awi-bremerhaven.de or webmaster@AWI-Bremerhaven.de

Alliance for Environmental Technology

URL: http://aet.org

Summary: This is an international association of chemical manufacturers and forest products companies "dedicated to improving the environmental performance of the pulp and paper industry." Members are chemical manufacturers as well as companies using those chemicals for papermaking. Their site contains press releases, reports, and their newsletter, *News Splash*.

Contact: info@aet.org

American Academy of Environmental Engineers

URL: http://www.enviro-engrs.org

Summary: This group is "dedicated to excellence in the practice of environmental engineering to ensure the public health, safety, and welfare to enable humankind to co-exist in harmony with nature." Their site contains brief abstracts from the quarterly publication, *Environmental Engineer,* a bookstore, an events calendar, and other pertinent information for members.

Contact: Use form at Web site.

American Chemical Society

URL: http://www.acs.org

Summary: This site has much to offer the environmental researcher. Included are sections on education, government affairs, and publications. Some of the publications have searchable tables of contents by title and author, including *Energy & Fuels, Environmental Science & Technology, Environmental Science & Technology News & Research Notes, Journal of Agricultural and Food Chemistry*, and *Journal of the American Chemical Society.*

Contact: webmaster@acs.org

American Council for an Energy-Efficient Economy

URL: http://www.aceee.org

Summary: This site contains information pertaining to the activities of the ACEEE and its publications, proceedings, books, and reports. Abstracts of research reports from several areas including energy policy, economic development, utilities, industrial energy efficiency, and transportation are included. Also included here is the *Green Guide to Cars and Trucks,* which rates new vehicles.

Contact: info@aceee.org

American Farmland Trust

URL: http://www.farmland.org/

Summary: The mission of this group is "to stop the loss of productive farmland and to promote farming practices that lead to a healthy environment." Their site contains information about farmland protection activities by state, a comprehensive farmland information library, news, top 20 threatened farming regions, and much more.

Contact: info@farmland.org

American Forests

URL: http://www.amfor.org

Summary: American Forests was established in 1875. They are focused on creating a
                sustainable forest system throughout the U.S. and have several programs to assist
                in this goal. Their Global ReLeaf program was created to plant trees at specific
                sites in the U.S. where environmental damage has occurred. The site contains
                information from their Forest Policy Center, Urban Forestry Center, Citizen
                Forestry Support System, and their *National Register of Big Trees.*

Contact: member@amfor.org

American Geophysical Union

URL: http://earth.agu.org

Summary: The American Geophysical Union is an international society. The members of
                AGU are dedicated to "advancing the understanding of Earth and its environment
                in space and making the results available to the public." This site contains news and
                a nice portion of their research and publications. Users may sign up to receive AGU
                Science Legislative Alerts via email.

Contact: webmaster@kosmos.agu.org

American Hydrogen Association

URL: http://www.clean-air.org

Summary: This is a nonprofit association with interests in "the advancement of inexpensive,
                clean, and safe hydrogen energy systems." Their interests are on "hydrogen, solar,
                wind, hydro, ocean and biomass resource materials, energy conversion,
                wealth-addition economics, and the environment." Materials available include
                hydrogen facts, fuel cell facts, and a link to the newsletter, *Hydrogen & Fuel Cell
                Letter.* There is also a link to the Arcosanti project, which AHA supports.

Contact: aha@getnet.com

American Rivers

URL: http://www.amrivers.org

Summary: American Rivers is an organization dedicated to the conservation, protection, and restoration of America's rivers and to "fostering a river stewardship ethic." To meet this goal, they support a number of programs and research involving floodplains, hydropower, river campaigns, endangered rivers, wild salmon, and urban rivers. They also provide news releases on laws and legislation affecting river systems and other pertinent information.

Contact: amrivers@amrivers.org

American Solar Energy Society

URL: http://www.sni.net/solar

Summary: The American Solar Energy Society (ASES) is a "national organization dedicated to advancing the use of solar energy for the benefit of U.S. citizens and the global environment." Included at this site is information about the annual Solar Energy Conference, publications, and events and awards. This site also contains the full text of the *Education Division Newsletter,* subscription information, and citations to articles in *Solar Today Magazine,* position papers, and alerts.

Contact: ases@ases.org

The American Water Works Association

URL: http://www.awwa.org

Summary: The American Water Works Association (AWWA) is an international nonprofit society whose mission is to improve the quality and supply of drinking water. This site contains conference information, indexes of companies, products and services, and information on its publications and publications of the Research Foundation of AWWA (http://www.awwarf.com), educational information, regulations, policies, reports, and job listings.

Contact: cberberi@awwa.org

Ames Laboratory, Environmental Technology Development (ETD)

URL: http://www.etd.ameslab.gov or http://www.external.ameslab.gov

Summary: Ames Laboratory, Environmental Technology Development is part of the Department of Energy and is operated by Iowa State University. One of its goals is to solve the problems encountered by hazardous waste and facilitate the cleanup process. This site includes information on the Ames' scientists and their research activities and press releases. The site also includes links to environmental Internet resources.

Contact: etdwebkeeper@ameslab.gov or webmaster@ameslab.gov

Antarctic and Southern Ocean Coalition (ASOC)

URL: http://www.asoc.org

Summary: This coalition contains more than 200 organizations in 50 countries. The Antarctica Project focuses on the protection of the biological diversity and wilderness of Antarctica and its surrounding oceans and marine life. They work closely with the scientists, tourists, and governments who use Antarctica to ensure minimal environmental impact. The site contains their newsletter, project information, and listing of their publications.

Contact: antarctica@igc.org

Appropriate Technology for Community and Environment (APACE)

URL: http://www.pactok.net.au/docs/apace/home.htm

Summary: APACE is an organization that works with villagers in the Pacific and South East Asian regions in designing and installing micro-hydro electricity systems. This site contains information and pictures on their many renewable energy programs and projects.

Contact: apace@uts.edu.au

Arbeitsgemeinschaft ERNEUERBARE ENERGIE (AEE)
(Society for Renewable Energy)

URL: http://www.datenwerk.at/arge_ee/

Summary: The AEE is an independent association whose goal is to "promote and support the meaningful use of renewable sources of energy and the efficient durable use of energy." Presented in both German and English, materials include research and reports on thermal solar plants, transparent insulation, solar electricity from the roof, biomass, and natural sewage purification.

Contact: arge-ee-gl@sime.com or walter_kathan@blackbox.at

Argonne National Laboratory

URL: http://www.anl.gov/

Summary: This laboratory operates under direction of the U.S. Department of Energy and is involved in many areas of scientific research. Both the Environmental Research Division and the Energy Systems Division have information located at this site. Research includes alternative energy and environmental assessments.

Contact: webmaster@anl.gov

Arizona Legislative Information System (ALIS)

URL: http://www.azleg.state.az.us/ars/ars.htm

Summary: This site contains a form that allows searching of the full text of the Arizona Revised Statutes using keywords. Also allows browsing by individual statutes. Of interest to environmental researchers would be Title 49 (The Environment), Title 27 (Minerals, Oil and Gas), Title 37 (Public Lands), and Title 45 (Waters).

Contact: webmaster@azleg.state.az.us

Arizona Geological Survey

URL: http://www.state.az.us/gs/index.htm

Summary: The mission of the Arizona Geological Survey is to provide "unbiased earth-science information to the public, businesses, and governmental agencies to facilitate development of relevant policies and courses of action for prudently managing and using Arizona's land, water, mineral, and energy resources." Includes a searchable listing of the many publications that are available from this office.

Contact: Harris_Ray@pop.state.az.us

Arkansas Natural Heritage Commission

URL: http://www.heritage.state.ar.us/nhc/index.html

Summary: The Arkansas Natural Heritage Commission was created in 1973 to "construct a system of natural areas to be under its protection; to conduct research and publish information on natural areas; and to perform other duties relating to the use, management, and preservation of Arkansas's outstanding natural features." Included here is the Baker Prairie Wildflower Collection, which contains watercolor paintings of plants found at the Baker Prairie Natural Area at Harrison, Arkansas.

Contact: info@dah.state.ar.us

ASCE Geotechnical Engineering Seepage/Groundwater Modelling

URL: http://www.ecgl.byu.edu/faculty/jonesn/asce/geotech/software/

Summary: This site contains information on a large variety of software used in seepage and groundwater modelling. Each entry includes a description of the software, the responsible agency, and contact person. Some entries also include system requirements and additional information.

Contact: Dr. Norman L. Jones: njones@et.byu.edu.

Asia-Pacific Centre for Environmental Law

URL: http://sunsite.nus.sg/apcel/

Summary: APCEL was created by the Faculty of Law, National University of Singapore, on the initiative of the Faculty of Law and the Commission on Environmental Law of the World Conservation Union, in collaboration with the United Nations Environment Programme. This site contains the full text of major global environmental treaties and selected regional and national legislation from the ASEAN nations in their Database of Environmental Instruments.

Contact: lawapcel@nus.sg

Association of Energy Engineers

URL: http://www.aeecenter.org

Summary: This association creates, collects, and distributes information on "energy efficiency, energy services, deregulation, facility management, plant engineering, and environmental compliance." Information at this site is in the form of abstracts of technical reports, information about seminars and conferences, and information about its books. The site also contains news reports, a virtual trade show, and a place to chat with others.

Contact: webmaster@AEEcenter.org

Association of University Leaders for a Sustainable Future

URL: http://www.ulsf.org

Summary: The mission of this association is to provide "leadership for global environmental literacy." Included at their site is information about their mission and history, their environmental literacy programs, services and support, related institutes, news, publications, and employment opportunities.

Contact: ULSF@aol.com

Atlantic Salmon Federation

URL: http://www.asf.ca

Summary: The Atlantic Salmon Federation is an international nonprofit organization created to conserve and maintain the Atlantic Salmon and its environment. Included at this site is information pertaining to the Federation and its research, which involves breeding, diseases, and genetic factors.

Contact: asfedu@nbnet.nb.ca

Australian Cooperative Research Centres

URL: http://www.dist.gov.au/crc/

Summary: These Research Centers are created and maintained with the joint support of the Australian Government and its universities and industries with the goal of facilitating the development and commercialization of technology through cooperative arrangements between the three sectors. There is a wealth of information from the many research centers at this site. Research fields included are Manufacturing Technology, Mining and Energy, Agriculture and Rural Based Manufacturing, and Environment. The Mining and Energy field includes a link to the Australian Cooperative Research Centre for Renewable Energy (http://ee.unsw.edu.au/~std_mon/). This group is responsible for ACRE Project 5.31, which involves the testing and development of standards methodology and protocols. There is information about each of the CRCs with links to many of their respective home pages. Some of the relevant CRCs include:

CRC for Antarctica and the Southern Ocean
CRC for Biological Control of Vertebrate Pest Populations
CRC for Catchment Hydrology
CRC for Conservation and Management of Marsupials
CRC for Ecologically Sustainable Development of the Great Barrier Reef
CRC for Freshwater Ecology
CRC for Soil and Land Management
CRC for Southern Hemisphere Meteorology
CRC for Sustainable Cotton Production
CRC for Sustainable Sugar Production
CRC for Sustainable Tourism
CRC for the Sustainable Development of Tropical Savannas
CRC for Tropical Rainforest Ecology and Management
CRC for Waste Management and Pollution Control
CRC for Water Quality and Treatment
CRC for Weed Management Systems

Contact: crc@dist.gov.au

Australian Oceanographic Data Centre

URL: http://www.aodc.gov.au/AODC.html

Summary: The AODC participates in several national and international research projects. This site contains some of the data, research, and information produced by the AODC. Included here is real time access to climatic data and a searchable interface to the *Marine Climatic Atlas of the World* and the *World Ocean Atlas* for searching for sea surface temperatures. Another searchable database is the Australian Marine & Coastal Directory. This site also offers several research publications and a newsletter.

Contact: webmaster@AODC.gov.au

Base De Dados Tropical

URL: http://www.bdt.org.br/bdt

Summary: The Base de Dados Tropical is a Brazilian nonprofit foundation located in São
                Paulo. This award-winning site provides access to several databases and a great
                amount of information. It includes biodiversity at species level, biological control,
                Brazilian ecosystems (including Caatinga, Brazilian Savanna, Amazon, Atlantic
                Rain Forest and Marine Continental Platform.) This is one of the BIN 21 nodes (see
                Biodiversity Information Network 21).

Contact: webmaster@bdt.org.br

Bat Conservation International

URL: http://www.batcon.org

Summary: This site contains educational resources, information about the organization's
                activities and conservation efforts, publications (including *Bat Magazine*), and a
                link to the North American Bat Conservation Partnership site, which contains a
                searchable bibliography of over 6,000 citations to information on bats in the form
                of reprints, books, dissertations, and popular journal articles.

Contact: vrc@batcon.org

Battelle Environmental Systems and Technology Division

URL: http://www.estd.battelle.org/

Summary: This site contains information regarding the research efforts of this Battelle
                Division, which operates under the auspices of the Battelle Memorial Institute.
                Covered are life cycle management systems, chemical process safety,
                environmental restoration, waste management, pollution prevention,
                decontamination, and ocean sciences.

Contact: webmaster@www.estd.battelle.org

Battelle Seattle Research Group

URL: http://www.seattle.battelle.org/

Summary: This site operates under the auspices of the Battelle Memorial Institute. BMI is an independent contract research organization. Included here is the full text of *Laboratory Waste Minimization and Pollution Prevention: A Guide for Teachers.* This guide explains how hazardous wastes and other chemical pollution generated by experiments that are performed in classroom laboratories may be minimized. Another full text publication is *The Population-Environment Connection: What Does Is Mean for Environmental Policy?* This site includes pollution information.

Contact: johnsons@battelle.org,

Bear River Solar Aquatics Wastewater Treatment Facility

URL: http://clan.tartannet.ns.ca/~munofann/solaraqu.htm

Summary: This site contains information about Canada's first solar aquatics wastewater treatment facility. Located in Annapolis Valley, Nova Scotia and engineered by Applied Environment Systems, this facility uses no chemicals in its processing. Included at this site are pictures and information on its operation.

Contact: pworks@annapoliscounty.ns.ca or edm@fox.nstn.ca
                (Pubic Works Department) (Applied Environment Systems)

Bear Watch

URL: http://users.imag.net/~sry.bearwtch/

Summary: Bear Watch is a loose association of people opposed to killing of the black bear. Their emphasis is in Canada and especially in British Columbia. Its purpose is to educate people about the threats to the black bear's survival. Information about their public campaign and news releases are available at this site.

Contact: bears@bearwatch.org

Bellona Foundation

URL: http://www.bellona.no

Summary: This foundation is also known as the Environmental Foundation Bellona. It was
                  created by environmentalists Frederic Hauge, Rune Haaland, and others shortly
                  after the Tchernobyl accident in 1986. It is in Russian, English, and Norwegian and
                  contains news, nuclear power plant information, records of nuclear incidents, and
                  a listing of its publications.

Contact: bellona@bellona.no

Best Manufacturing Practices Center of Excellence

URL: http://www.bmpcoe.org

Summary: This organization is sponsored by the Office of Naval Research. It was created to
                  collect, analyze, and share methods, procedures, and policies that exemplify "best
                  manufacturing practices." Included here are completed surveys from industries and
                  downloadable software to measure technical risk management.

Contact: biruta@bmpcoe.org

Biocatalysis/Biodegradation Database, University of Minnesota

URL: http://www.labmed.umn.edu/umbbd/index.html

Summary: This is a database of microbial biocatalytic reactions and biodegradation pathways
                  primarily for xenobiotic, chemical compounds that would be of interest to
                  environmentalists involved in bioremediation or chemical manufacturers.
                  "Individual reactions and metabolic pathways are presented with information on
                  the starting and intermediate chemical compounds, the organisms that transform
                  the compounds, the enzymes, and the genes." The database is searchable by
                  compound, CAS registry number, formula, enzyme, or microorganism and
                  browsable by compounds, reactions, enzymes, pathways, graphics, or
                  microorganisms.

Contact: lynda@email.labmed.umn.edu or wackett@biosci.cbs.umn.edu

Biodiversity Information Network 21

URL: http://www.bdt.org.br/bin21/bin21.html

Summary: BIN21 was created to carry out the goals of Agenda 21 following the Earth Summit in 1992. BIN was established to help produce, organize, and disseminate the wealth of information available. There are BIN21 nodes around the world where the same criteria and goals are followed in information storage and delivery. Country nodes that have relevant local data are the:

Australian National Botanic Gardens
http://155.187.10.12/index.html

Base de Dados Tropical
http://www.bdt.org.br/bdt/index/binbr/

Biodiversity and Ecosystems Network (BENE)
http://straylight.tamu.edu/bene/bene.html

Canadian Biodiversity Information Network
http://www.cbin.ec.gc.ca

Environmental Resource Information Network
http://www.erin.gov.au/life/life.html

Finnish Biodiversity Information Network
http://www.metla.fi/biodiversity/finbin/

The Bioelectromagnetics Society (BEMS)

URL: http://biomed.ucr.edu/bems.htm

Summary: BEMS is an independent organization of scientists, physicians, and engineers whose focus is on the interactions of nonionizing radiation with biological systems. Their publications and newsletter are available as well as past tables of contents and ordering information for their peer-reviewed journal, *Bioelectromagnetics.*

Contact: richard.luben@ucr.edu or 75230.1222@compuserve.com

Biology - Careers and Jobs

URL: http://ublib.buffalo.edu/libraries/units/sel/bio/careers.html

Summary: This site is made possible by librarians at the Science & Engineering Library at the University of Buffalo. It is a "comprehensive inventory of career and job-finding sources." Though aimed at the broad scope of biology, there are many environmental areas found here.

Contact: fstoss@acsu.buffalo.edu

Bird Banding Laboratory

URL: http://www.im.nbs.gov/bbl/bbl.html

Summary: This laboratory, in Laurel, Maryland, operates under the auspices of the National
                    Biological Service's Office of Inventory and Monitoring. They are responsible for
                    the U.S. activities of the North American Bird Banding Program. Included here is
                    information about their Mapping Avian Productivity and Survivorship Program and
                    a link to their banding data and software site.

Contact: BBL@nbs.gov

Birding on the Web

URL: http://www.birder.com

Summary: This site points to a variety of resources pertaining to birds. These resources
                    include bird discussion archives, newsletters, birding sites, societies, and clubs
                    from around the world, a listing of books, videos and CD-ROMs, and links to other
                    bird sites.

Contact: ornithologist@birder.com

Bonnell Environmental Consulting (BEC)

URL: http://infoweb.magi.com/~tauceti/

Summary: BEC is a Canadian company with expertise in assessing the chemical effects on the
                    environment. Specializing in assessments and quality guideline development, they
                    also provide information on projects, publications, and reports.

Contact: tauceti@magi.com

British Atmospheric Data Centre

URL: http://www.badc.rl.ac.uk/

Summary: The BADC is the Natural Environment Research Council's designated data center
                    for the atmospheric sciences. It serves as a depository of atmospheric datasets for
                    researchers, governmental officials, and professionals. Coverage includes pollution,
                    radiation, temperature, and chemicals. They are searchable by method or collection
                    or by area of study.

Contact: BADC@rl.ac.uk

Brookhaven National Laboratory

URL: http://www.bnl.gov

Summary: This laboratory operates under direction of the Department of Energy and is involved in a wide variety of scientific research including environmental research. Included at their site are news releases, bulletins, and a radio series. This site maintains a searchable catalog of its publications. The search interface allows access by free-text searching, by date, and by division or department within the Brookhaven National Laboratory. There are some full-text reports here in pdf (Adobe's Portable Document Format) format.

Contact: pubaf@bnl.gov

Brown Is Green (BIG)

URL: http://www.brown.edu/Departments/Brown_Is_Green/

Summary: This is an area that was developed by the faculty, staff, and students at Brown University. There are reports and information on their unique conservation and recycling efforts.

Contact: BIG_Web@Brown.edu

Bureau of International Recycling

URL: http://www.bir.org/

Summary: This bureau is the international federation of the world's recycling industries. More than 50 countries are represented through companies and national associations. The site contains information on recycling of ferrous and non-ferrous metals, stainless and special alloys, paper, textiles, plastics, rubber, and glass. It also contains press releases, newsletters, and publications. The site is in French, German, and English.

Contact: bir.sec@skynet.be

Bureau of Land Management

URL: http://www.blm.gov/

Summary: The mission of the Bureau of Land Management is "to sustain the health, diversity, and productivity of the public lands for the use and enjoyment of present and future generations." Information available at this site includes environmental education, news about the activities of the Bureau, events, and regulations. In addition, there is information about ALMRS (Automated Land and Mineral Record System). This is an information system that contains more than one billion land and mineral records that the Bureau has maintained over the past 200 years.

Contact: woinfo@wo.blm.gov or woweb@wo.blm.gov
                (General information) (Website information)

Bureau of Reclamation

URL: http://www.usbr.gov

Summary: The Bureau of Reclamation was formed to protect and manage water resources of the Western states of the U.S. Projects include storage dams and reservoirs, hydroelectric power plants, and canals. This site includes information on power resources, water conservation, the Bureau's reclamation activities, and press releases.

Contact: http://www.usbr.gov/main/comments.html or dschwarz@usbr.gov

Bureau of Transportation Statistics

URL: http://www.bts.gov

Summary: One of BTS's roles is to share in the administration of the National Transportation Library. The National Transportation Library contains documents and databases provided from public and private organizations throughout the transportation community. The full text of documents is available. The database is searchable and contains research and reports on runoff, soils, erosion, and wetlands loss. The database is also browsable by subjects, which include air quality, alternative fuels, environmental impacts, hazardous materials transportation and aviation, maritime, rail and transit energies and environments.

Contact: webmaster@bts.gov

Byrd Polar Research Center

URL: http://www-bprc.mps.ohio-state.edu/BPRC.html

Summary: The Byrd Polar Research Center, at Ohio State University, contains research reports and images, *Ice Sheets Newsletter*, and a list of "Polar Pointers" to Internet resources pertaining to the Arctic Regions.

Contact: mehta@polarmet1.mps.ohio-state.edu

CADDET (Centre for the Analysis and Dissemination of Demonstrated Energy Technologies)

URL: http://www.caddet.org

Summary: CADDET is comprised of two organizations: CADDET Energy Efficiency (www.caddet-ee.org) and CADDET Renewable Energy (www.caddet-re.org). CADDET-EE is a nonprofit organization in the Netherlands whose mission is to disseminate the myriad of information on the use of energy-efficient technologies used in manufacturing, construction, transportation, utilities, and agriculture. CADDET provides a searchable database of reports related to energy-efficient and renewable energy applications from its 12 member countries. The reports are searchable by location, industry, and type of application (such as wind energy, biomass fuel, cogeneration, etc.)

California Conservation Corps Home Page

URL: http://www.ccc.ca.gov

Summary: This state agency was created for two purposes: to protect the natural environment and to enhance youth's development by offering them satisfying employment. The information contained at this site is primarily about the work and emergency response efforts of the Corps.

Contact: webmaster@ccc.ca.gov or info@ccc.ca.gov

California Energy Commission

URL: http://www.energy.ca.gov

Summary: Though this site includes a lot of information specific to the state of California, it is a nice site for basic information on alternative and renewable energy, solar energy, and education programs.

Contact: energia@energy.ca.gov

California Environmental Protection Agency

URL: http://www.calepa.cahwnet.gov/

Summary: This agency has several boards, offices, and departments to assist in its
                environmental protection efforts. Links to those entities are at this site; they are the
                Air Resources Board, Department of Pesticide Regulation, Department of Toxic
                Substances Control, Integrated Waste Management Board, the Office of
                Environmental Health Hazard Assessment, and the State Water Resources Control
                Board. This site also contains legislation, press releases, and information on their
                programs. Some of the publications available here include newsletters, speeches,
                and fact sheets.

Contact: cepacomm@calepa.ca.gov

California Environmental Resources Evaluation System (CERES)

URL: http://ceres.ca.gov

Summary: CERES was created by the California Resources Agency to help disseminate
                environmental information regarding the state. This site has links to several
                departments of the California Resources Agency, including the Departments of
                Conservation, Fish, and Game, Forestry and Fire Protection, Parks and Recreation,
                and Water Resources. Also included are links to many of the environmental
                councils and commissions. Resources include images, datasets, and text. The
                wealth of data is made more accessible via a search interface that allows searching
                by geographic area, by subject area, or by keyword.

Contact: http://ceres.ca.gov/cgi-bin/referer.pl?/comment.html
                (Access to this form on the home page.)

California Resources Agency

URL: http://www.ceres.ca.gov/CRA

Summary: This agency is responsible for the conservation, enhancement, and management of
                California's environmental resources. Included under the direction of this agency
                are the California Environmental Resources Evaluation System (CERES), the
                California Conservation Corps, and a variety of programs, committees, and
                commissions. Links to these other programs are also available at this location.
                Included at this site are press releases regarding the agency's activities and
                newsletters.

Contact: http://ceres.ca.gov/cgi-bin/referer.pl?/comment.html
                (Access to this form on the home page.)

Canada Centre for Inland Waters

URL: http://www.cciw.ca/

Summary: The National Water Research Institute and the Canada Centre for Inland Waters are involved in research that focuses on sustainable, freshwater ecosystems. They publish the quarterly NWRI Digest and make it available at this site. Under the auspices of the above agencies are aquatic conservation, protection, and restoration divisions. The Aquatic Ecosystem Restoration Branch was created to restore aquatic systems in the Great Lakes Region. This Branch is devoted to the Groundwater Remediation Project (http://gwrp.cciw.ca/index_e.html). The site includes software used in modelling and analysis, groundwater information, and publications. Research and activity reports are available. These research project reports would be of value to anyone involved in environmental research.

Contact: http://www.cciw.ca/tell-us-nwri.html *or* Stu.Beal@cciw.ca

Canadian Chlorine Coordinating Committee

URL: http://www.cfour.org

Summary: This group's focus is on the responsible use of chlorine chemistry. Comprised of associations and companies, their stated mission is to "facilitate and promote coordinated dialogue and action in Canada among key stakeholders in order to provide a balanced view of chlorine chemistry to enable society to make informed, science-based decisions on issues involving chlorine." This site contains information about their projects and case studies.

Contact: info@cfour.org

Canadian Council of Ministers of the Environment (CCME)

URL: http://www.mbnet.mb.ca/ccme/

Summary: The CCME are very active in the promotion of a more healthy environment. Their proposals and recommendations regarding waste management, air pollution, and toxic chemicals help ensure a cleaner and safer environment. Some of their publications are made available at this site. Information about their federal, provincial, and territorial databases for environmental analysis is also available.

Contact: info@ccme.ca
            http://www.mbnet.mb.ca/ccme/feedback.html

Canadian Environmental Assessment Agency

URL: http://www.ceaa.gc.ca/

Summary: This site won the 1995 Canadian Internet Award for the Best Law Resource Site. The CEAA is a national organization that administers Canadian environmental assessment policies. There is a large amount of information here covering environmental assessment, laws, and regulations.

Contact: http://www.ceaa.gc.ca/contact_e.htm

Canadian Institute for Environmental Law and Policy (CIELAP)

URL: http://www.web.net/cielap

Summary: CIELAP was founded in 1970. It is an independent nonprofit organization that was created to "provide leadership in the development of environmental law and policy that promotes the public interest and the principles of sustainability, including the protection of the health and well-being of present and future generations, and of the natural environment." Pertinent information at this site includes abstracts of articles from their newsletter, research notes, and news releases.

Contact: cielap@web.net

Canadian Ratite Home Page

URL: http://duke.usask.ca/~ladd/ratfram.htm

Summary: The Canadian Ratite Home Page contains a large selection of information on ostriches, rheas, emus, and cassowaries. It includes several searchable bibliographies, which include publications from the veterinary, research, and industry sectors. It also includes a listing of Canadian ostrich and emu organizations. Instructions for logging into the ratite bibliography database using telnet are also available at this site.

Contact: Ken Ladd: ladd@sklib.usask.ca

Carbon Dioxide Information Analysis Center (CDIAC)

URL: http://cdiac.esd.ornl.gov

Summary: CDIAC, which is located at the Oak Ridge National Laboratory, provides
               information on carbon dioxide and climatic changes. The CDIAC site includes
               portions of the publication, *Trends: A Compendium of Data on Global Change*,
               their newsletter, *CDIAC Communications,* and a listing of the top 10 most
               requested publications available at this site.

Contact: cdiac@ornl.gov

Carnegie Institute of Technology, Department of Civil and Environmental Engineering

URL: http://www.ce.cmu.edu

Summary: Carnegie Mellon University promotes environmentally conscious engineering,
               product design, manufacturing, and architecture. To support this goal, they began
               the Green Design Initiative (GDI). This site provides information regarding their
               research, their publications, and their program.

Contact: nc0y@andrew.cmu.edu

Catalog of Known and Putative Nuclear Explosions

URL: gopher://wealaka.okgeosurvey1.gov/11/nuke.cat

Summary: This large file, compiled by James Lawson from unclassified sources, contains
               information on over 1,900 atmospheric and underground nuclear explosions. These
               explosions have occurred all over the world and have been conducted by a variety
               of governments including the United States, the United Kingdom, Russia, France,
               India, China, Israel, and Pakistan. Data includes the means of dispersal, device
               type, the longitude and latitude of the site, wave magnitudes, and other detailed
               information. For underground tests, the type of rock at the site is also given.
               Explosions date from 1945 to the present.

Contact: Jim Lawson: jimlawson@okgeosurvey1.gov

Catalog of Online Vegetation and Plant Distribution Maps

URL: http://www-sul.stanford.edu/depts/branner/vegmaps.htm

Summary: This large collection of links to maps is made available by Branner Earth Sciences Library and Map Collections at Stanford University. Included here are maps displaying forestry, vegetation, and plant distribution. The maps are arranged by geographic coverage, which includes world, country, and regional or state maps.

Contact: phoehn@sulmail.stanford.edu

Center for Bioenvironmental Research

URL: http://www.tmc.tulane.edu/cbr/

Summary: This site is operated under Tulane University and Xavier University. The researchers are "dedicated to investigating the causes and effects of environmental problems and devising practical solutions for them." Included here are numerous full text research reports on topics relating to health and the environment such as the Bioenvironmental Hazards Research Program, the Hazardous Materials Management and Emergency Response (HaMMER) project, and Hazardous Material in Aquatic Environments of the Mississippi River Basin. This site also includes a section entitled *Environmental Concepts Made Easy* and a link to the Consortium for Environmental Risk Evaluation (CERE), also a Tulane/Xavier program.

Contact: flawles@mailhost.tcs.tulane.edu

Center for Conservation Biology Network

URL: http://conbio.rice.edu/ (Rice University)
                http://conbio.bio.uci.edu/ (University of California, Irvine)

Summary: This network was formed "to help develop the technical means for the protection, maintenance, and restoration of life on this planet—its species, its ecological and evolutionary processes, and its particular and total environment..." The site contains information about Native Americans and the environment, academic programs in conservation biology, biogeochemical research in wetlands, and a database of orchid data. Also included is a searchable database of Internet resources pertaining to biodiversity, ecology, and the environment. This network also hosts information and resources pertaining to the Society for Conservation Biology.

Contact: about@conbio.rice.edu or conbio@uci.edu

Center for Disease Control (CDC)

URL: http://www.cdc.gov

Summary: The CDC is an agency of the Public Health Service of the U.S. Their site includes information on diseases, travel tips including food, water, and vaccine guidelines. Information regarding the eleven offices included in the CDC is also available. Of interest may be the National Center for Environmental Health (http://www.cdc.gov /nceh/ncehhome.htm) or the National Institute for Occupational Safety and Health (http://www.cdc.gov/niosh/homepage.html), which are located here. CDC also makes available *The Prevention Guidelines Database,* which includes all of the official guidelines and recommendations published by the CDC for the prevention of diseases, injuries, and disabilities. The publication, *Medical Management Guidelines for Acute Chemical Exposure* is available here. In addition, the CDC site includes educational reports and research from the Agency for Toxic Substances and Disease Registry (ATSDR) on environmental health risks, contact centers, and a wealth of topics regarding exposure to toxic substances. The ATSDR was established to assess and prevent exposure to hazardous substances found in the environment and at waste sites. The ATSDR site is available at http://atsdr1.atsdr. cdc. gov: 8080/atsdrhome.html.

Contact: netinfo@cdc.gov

Center for Environmental Biotechnology

URL: http://deep13.ra.utk.edu/ceb/home.htm

Summary: This Center operates under the auspices of the University of Tennessee, Knoxville. Members of the research teams are involved in investigating the application of biotechnological approaches for environmental bioremediation. This site contains research project summaries, which includes bioremediation of polychlorinated biphenyls (PCBs) from contaminated soils and the use of genetically engineered bacteria for bioremediation.

Contact: agoslen@utkvx.utk.edu

Center for Environmental Citizenship

URL: http://www.igc.org/cgv

Summary: CEC is a nonprofit organization that promotes and supports college student activities pertaining to environmental policies. Information about the many programs the CEC supports is available here. The Campus Green Vote section contains information for college and university campus leaders who are interested in helping students gain a better understanding of environmental issues and to provide a means for the students to actively voice their ideas and opinions. Materials include information on how to run a "Campus Green Vote Drive." In addition, EarthNet and Shadow Congress information is included. The text of *Blueprint for a Green Campus* and *Campus Green Pages* ("a directory of 1700 environmental contacts at 750 campuses") is also available.

Contact: cgv@igc.apc.org

Center for Environmental Design Research (CEDR), College of Environmental Design

URL: http://www.ced.berkeley.edu/cedr

Summary: This center at the University of California, Berkeley, assists the research efforts of faculty, students, and other researchers in the area of the design and planning of the built environment. Includes information on GIS applications of the Applied Environmental Geographic Information Science Research Lab (AEGIS) (http://www.ced.berkeley.edu/aegis/) and the Research Program in Environmental Planning and Geographic Information Systems (REGIS) (http://www.regis. berkeley.edu/) and the Building Science Group.

Contact: earens@ced.berkeley.edu

Center for Health Effects of Environmental Contamination

URL: http://tango.cheec.uiowa.edu/

Summary: CHEEC is operated by the University of Iowa. It was created to "determine the levels of environmental contamination that can be specifically associated with human health effects." Summaries of the research being conducted at this center are available at this site.

Contact: webmaster@www.cheec.uiowa.edu

Center for International Climate and Environmental Research, Oslo (CICERO)

URL: http://www.cicero.uio.no/

Summary: This nonprofit research organization was established by the Norwegian government in association with the University of Oslo. Their many research projects are outlined here. Just a few of them include research on the effect that aircraft emissions have on ozone in the upper troposphere and lower stratosphere, air quality in China, and climate change in Africa. Many complete publications and abstracts are available. Content is in Norwegian and English.

Contact: admin@cicero.uio.no

Center for International Earth Science Information Network (CIESIN)

(Formerly the Consortium for International Earth Science Information)

URL: http://www.ciesin.org

Summary: CIESIN, which now operates under the auspices of Columbia Earth Institute at Columbia University, is a nonprofit, nongovernmental organization created to allow "the interdisciplinary study of global environmental change." To meet this end, they have established a wealth of environmental information including projects, resources, treaties, global change unpublished papers, user services support, and guides to datasets available via their Gateway. CIESIN and the U.S. EPA reached an agreement whereby CIESIN would develop a catalog of EPA materials for improved public access to EPA information. The Toxic Release Inventory database and the Comprehensive Environmental Response, Compensation, and Liability Information System (CERCLIS) for the Great Lakes Region is available here for searching. CERCLIS allows the user to search by state and county for Superfund sites. The Great Lakes Regional Environmental Information System offers a wealth of information regarding the Great Lakes Region. CIESIN is the World Data Center A (WDC-A) for Human Interactions in the Environment. This site also contains a great deal of information regarding population.

Contact: ciesin.info@ciesin.org

Center for International Environmental Law (CIEL)

URL: http://www.igc.org/ciel

Summary: This is one of the many resources available from the Institute for Global
                Communications. In addition to legal resources, this site contains information about
                CIEL and its activities and publications.

Contact: cielus@igc.apc.org

Center for Marine Conservation

URL: http://www.cmc-ocean.org/

Summary: The CMC informs citizens on issues pertaining to the marine environment. This
                site contains information about the Center's programs and activities. They are
                involved in the protection of marine ecosystems with projects in marine reserves
                and sanctuaries, clean oceans, marine wildlife and fisheries conservation, and
                conservation of biological diversity. Includes some educational materials.

Contact: webmaster@CMC-Ocean.org

Center for Plant Conservation

URL: http://www.mobot.org/CPC/welcome.html

Summary: The CPC is a consortium of 28 American botanical gardens and arboreta whose
                mission is to conserve rare plants in the U.S. To meet this end, they are involved
                in plant conservation, research, and education. This site includes information about
                the National Collection of Endangered Plants, which is maintained by the group.

Contact: cpc@mobot.org

Center for Renewable Energy and Sustainable Technology (CREST)

URL: http://crest.org/

Summary: CREST was established in 1993 by the Solar Energy Research & Education
                Foundation to provide educational and informational materials regarding renewable
                energy, energy efficiency, sustainable development, and the environment. The
                Solstice site contains reports, newsletters, slides, and fact sheets pertaining to
                energy-efficient buildings, case studies, sustainable living, and renewable energy.

Contact: www-content@crest.org

Center for Resourceful Building Technology (CRBT)

URL: http://www.montana.com/crbt

Summary: The CRBT is a nonprofit organization created to promote use of environmentally-friendly building materials and technologies. They are the publishers of the book *Guide to Resource Efficient Building Elements*. Their site includes information about research, publications, programs, and some pictures of their projects.

Contact: crbt@montana.com

Center for the Study of Environmental Endocrine Effects

URL: http://www.endocrine.org

Summary: The Web site of The Center for the Study of Environmental Endocrine Effects contains information on research and laws pertaining to the effects that environmental agents may have on the "endocrine functions of humans, wildlife, and ecology." Included here is a paper written by the Center staff that serves as an overview of the scientific knowledge in this area.

Contact: csee@endocrine.org

Central European Environmental Data Request Facility (CEDAR)

URL: http://www.cedar.univie.ac.at

Summary: This facility is administered by the International Society for Environmental Protection. CEDAR's goal is to support and encourage the environmental efforts of Central and Eastern Europe. It is a large repository of materials including professional papers, proceedings, and information on conventions, training projects, and laws and legal information. It contains CEED, the Central and Eastern European Environmental Expert Database, which lists regional experts, their research, and publications. This site also contains the searchable archives of the EIA, economic instruments, environmental accounting, environment valuation, envjobs-l, infoterra, habitat2, and waste discussion groups' messages.

Contact: webmaster@cedar.univie.ac.at

Centre for Agriculture and Environment, The Netherlands

URL: http://www.clm.nl

Summary: This is a non-profit foundation whose focus is on the promotion of "sustainable agriculture with an extended function." It brings farmers and growers together with conservationists and environmentalists. The Centre conducts research and makes recommendations for practitioners and policy-makers. The abstracts of their research reports are available as well as information about the newsletter, *CAPER (Concerted Action on Pesticide Environmental Risk indicators)*. Fourteen European countries are involved in *CAPER*; links to the contact people from each country are available.

Contact: clm@clm.nl

Centre for Alternative Transportation Fuels

URL: http://www.bcr.bc.ca/catf/

Summary: The CATF is operated by BC Research, Inc., in British Columbia. There are searchable citations to technical papers and reports. The quarterly *CATF Review* is also available at this site.

Contact: ainglis@bcr.bc.ca

Centre for Development and Environment

URL: http://www.giub.unibe.ch/cde/

Summary: The CDE is one of the research programs supported by the University of Berne's Department of Geography. They are concerned with "aspects of development and environment in international cooperation." Its main focus is on sustainable use of natural resources. One of their many activities is the creation and maintenance of the WOCAT (World Overview of Conservation Approaches and Technologies) Database. This database contains information about proven and promising soil and water conservation practices.

Contact: ludi@giub.unibe.ch

Cetacean Society International

URL: http://elfnet1a.elfi.com/csihome.html

Summary: CSI is a nonprofit society whose mission is to preserve and protect all cetaceans (whales, dolphins, and porpoises) and the marine environment around the world. They are a "conservation, education, and research organization" based in the U.S. with volunteer representatives in 26 countries. Their site includes action alerts and current issues updates, the *CSI Captivity Flyer,* listing of marine mammal species that can be found in African waters, and issues of their *Whales Alive!* newsletter.

Contact: bshall@snet.net

Chanslor Wetlands Wildlife Project

URL: http://www.sonomawetlands.org/

Summary: This project is dedicated to preserving the wildlife and habitat of the Chanslor Wetlands. The Wetlands covers 250 acres near Bodega Bay in Northern California. The site includes a list of the "sensitive species" of animals and plants in the region.

Contact: friends@sonomawetlands.org

Charles Darwin Research Station

URL: http://www.polaris.net/~jpinson/welcome.html (U.S.)
        http://fcdarwin.org.ec (Ecuador)

Summary: The Charles Darwin Research Station conducts research in the Galapagos Islands and the Galapagos Marine Resources Reserve of Ecuador. It operates under the auspices of the Charles Darwin Foundation, an international nonprofit organization. They also provide educational assistance with their volunteer and scholarship programs. This site contains news and press releases, current research, postings of employment opportunities, and scientific papers.

Contact: webmaster@fcdarwin.org.ec or cdrs@fcdarwin.org.ec

Chemcyclopedia

URL: http://pubs3.acs.org:8899/chemcy98/

Summary: This online database contains searchable company, service, and product information with over 11,000 chemical listings. You may browse through the alphabetical listings or search by product, service, or company. Links have been made to businesses that have Web sites and/or e-mail addresses. Sections of the *Chemcyclopedia* that may be of interest to environmentalists are the company directory and the environmental chemicals and services.

Contact: pubwebmaster@acsinfo.acs.org

Chemical Industry Institute of Toxicology (CIIT)

URL: http://www.ciit.org

Summary: This is a nonprofit institution that performs research to assist in the understanding of and assessment of potential adverse effects of chemicals, pharmaceuticals, and consumer products. Ongoing research involves endocrine research, cancer research, neurotoxicology, and respiratory research. This organization is supported by industrial organizations. The site includes *CIIT Impact*, which are summaries of toxicological research performed at CIIT. The summaries are of good size, and citations to the published articles are also included.

Contact: CIITinfo@ciit.org

Chicago Wilderness

URL: http://www.chiwild.org

Summary: Chicago Wilderness consists of the natural communities (grasslands, woodlands, streams, and wetlands) that exist in the Chicago metropolitan region. The Chicago Wilderness covers more than 200,000 acres. This group was formed by the area and regional governments, research, academia, citizens, and conservation groups. Information at this site pertains to land management, education, organizational activities, and projects and news.

Contact: chiwild@chias.org or sstein@mcs.net or dwachtel@mcs.net

The Chilkat Bald Eagle Preserve

URL: http://www.haines.ak.us

Summary: The Chilkat Bald Eagle Preserve is near Haines, Alaska. It covers 48,000 acres and was established to "protect the world's largest concentration of Bald Eagles and their critical habitat." More than 3,000 eagles are in the region from early October through January. Visitors to this site may listen to the eagle preserve.

Contact: hainesak@wwa.com

China Council for International Cooperation on Environment and Development (CCICED)

URL: http://iisd1.iisd.ca/trade/cciced/default.htm

Summary: Established by the Canadian International Development Agency, this group consists of approximately 50 Chinese and international members. This site includes information regarding their structure, activities, and working groups. Working group reports and papers and the CCICED newsletter are available here.

Chlorine Chemistry Council

URL: http://c3.org

Summary: This group is comprised of chlorine and chlorinated product manufacturers. Affiliated with the Chemical Manufacturers Association (CMA), their purpose is to "achieve policies that promote the continuing, responsible uses of chlorine and chlorine-based products." This site includes a library, newsroom, and a *Glossary of Chlorine Chemistry Terms.*

Contact: info@c3.org

Citation Publishing, Inc.

URL: http://www.citation.com/company.html

Summary: Citation Publishing is an electronic publisher of regulatory environmental, health and safety compliance literature. This site gives information on their CD-ROM publications and restricted Internet access.

Contact: sales@citation.com

City Farmer

URL: http://www.cityfarmer.org/

Summary: Home of *Urban Agriculture Notes*, this Canadian site contains a diverse sampling of issues pertaining to urban agriculture with an international scope. Included are articles on rooftop gardens, composting toilets, rain barrels, and sustainable living.

Contact: cityfarm@unixg.ubc.ca

ClO_2 Water Treatment Resource Center

URL: http://clo2.com

Summary: This site is sponsored by Sterling Pulp Chemicals, Ltd., in Canada with focus on the use of chlorine dioxide for water treatment and disinfection. The site contains news alerts, specific processing information, information on government regulations regarding the use of ClO_2, and full text articles on ClO_2.

Contact: info@clo2.com

CLU-IN (Hazardous Waste Clean-Up Information)

URL: http://www.clu-in.com

Summary: This site is made possible by Environmental Management Support, Inc., under contract with the Technology Innovation Office of the U.S. EPA. It was created to disseminate information on innovative treatment technology to the hazardous waste remediation community. There is a wealth of information here on hazardous waste, remediation technologies, programs, and regulations. Full text of the newsletters, *Bioremediation in the Field* and *Ground Water Currents,* are available.

Contact: Use form at Web site.

Cochrane Ecological Institute/Cochrane Wildlife Reserve

URL: http://www2.cadvision.com/mosquito/cei.htm

Summary: This site contains information regarding the efforts being made to reintroduce the Swift Fox into its natural habitat in Canada. Included is information regarding its background, the research being performed, and breeding and release efforts.

Contact: cei@cadvision.com *or* Patrick Scholefield: scholefp@cadvision.com

Code of Federal Regulations

URL: http://www.access.gpo.gov/nara/cfr/cfr-table-search.html

Summary: This site contains a searchable interface to the CFR. The CFR contains the text of public regulations issued by Federal agencies. This site also includes links to the U.S. Code and the Federal Register.

Contact: gpoaccess@gpo.gov

Colorado Department of Natural Resources

URL: http://www.dnr.state.co.us/index.asp

Summary: Colorado's Department of Natural Resources home page has links to a variety of information on Colorado. Included here is information about the Colorado Environmental Land Based Evaluation & Research Technology (ELBERT) information system. This site includes links to Colorado's parks, wildlife, water, geology, oil and gas, mining and land.

Contact: kathy.kanda@state.co.us

Colorado Department of Public Health and Environment

URL: http://www.state.co.us/gov_dir/cdphe_dir/cdphehom.html

Summary: The mission of this department is to protect and enhance the health and environment of the people of Colorado. Included here are publications of the office, including *Permitting Made Easy,* (a guide to applying for environmental permits in Colorado), a large, topical directory of health and environment topics of resources within the Colorado Department of Public Health and Environment, advisories, regulations, directories, and press releases.

Contact: comments.cdphe@state.co.us

Colorado School of Mines

URL: http://gn.mines.colorado.edu or http://www.mines.edu

Summary: This site contains information about the earth science, energy, and environmental research and activities at the Colorado School of Mines. One of the sites is the International Ground Water Modelling Center (http://www.mines.edu/igwmc/). This site contains information on groundwater modelling software, publications, and events.

Contact: webmaster@mines.edu

Columbia Earth Institute, Columbia University

URL: http://www.earthinstitute.columbia.edu

Summary: The mission and goals set forth by this Institute are both innovative and ambitious. It is a research program that intends a synergy among disciplines. Of interest to this institute are human sciences, biological sciences, knowledge creation, innovation and education. The site includes links to its Biosphere 2 Center in Arizona, the Center for Environmental Research and Conservation, and other research centers.

Contact: petere@ldeo.columbia.edu

Commission for Environmental Cooperation (CEC)
Comision para la Cooperacion Ambiental (CCA)
Commission de Cooperation Environnementale (CCE)

URL: http://www.cec.org

Summary: The CEC was established by Canada, Mexico, and the United States and contains text in French, Spanish, and English. The purpose of this group is to help support the North American Free Trade Agreement by addressing transboundary issues and concerns. Included here is the full text of the North American Agreement on Environmental Cooperation (NAAEC) that the CEC abides by. In addition, other agreements, laws, and treaties are available. The summaries of the environmental laws of the member countries are included here. All areas of environmental laws are covered, including protection of the atmosphere, oceans and coastal areas, and laws regarding mining, land use planning, wildlife conservation, agriculture, forest management, and energy. There is an acronym list of legal and environmental terms used. The site also has their newsletter, *Eco Region,* publications, and reports of the organization.

Contact: Marcos Silva: msilva@ccemtl.org

Committee for the National Institute for the Environment (CNIE)

URL: http://www.cnie.org

Summary: This is a nonprofit organization whose goals are to establish a National Institute for the Environment so that scientific analysis and research pertaining to environmental issues may be facilitated. Their site includes a wealth of services and information. There is a topical directory covering population and environment, global climate change, agriculture, air, biodiversity, energy, forestry, marine, mining, public lands, stratospheric ozone, waste management, water quality, and wetlands. These sections contain information from several sources. Included here also is a nice section on educational resources, which includes a directory of higher education environmental programs.

Contact: cnie@cnie.org

Communications for a Sustainable Future

URL: http://csf.colorado.edu

Summary: This site contains the archives of the many environmental mailing lists that the Communications for a Sustainable Future supports.

Contact: roper@csf.colorado.edu

Compost Resource Page

URL: http://www.oldgrowth.org/compost/

Summary: This award-winning site offers information on all aspects of composting including home composting, vermicomposting, composting toilets, gardening information, and composting products and services.

Contact: bodie@cmc.net

Connecticut Department of Environmental Protection

URL: http://dep.state.ct.us/

Summary: Information about the mission and activities of the various divisions is available here. Divisions are: Natural Resources (fisheries, forestry, wildlife), Water Management, Air Management (air quality control, permitting & enforcement, monitoring & radiation), and Waste Management.

Contact: webmaster@dep.state.ct.us

Conservation Agency

URL: http://bdol.com/tca/tca.htm

Summary: The Conservation Agency was founded in 1980 to help preserve "rare, endandered, and little-known species." There is a bibliography of their peer-reviewed scientific research publications at this site.

Contact: Tca@bdol.com

Conservation International

URL: http://www.conservation.org/

Summary: This is a nonprofit group whose focus is on the protection of our biologically rich areas. They promote biodiversity conservation in tropical rain forests and other endangered ecosystems. The site contains news and information on their projects.

Contact: webmaster@conservation.org

Consortium on Green Design and Manufacturing (CGDM)

URL: http://euler.berkeley.edu/green/cgdm.html

Summary: This is a project operating under the auspices of the University of California, Berkeley and government and industry. The Consortium concentrates on developing environmentally-conscious product design and manufacturing. The CGDM site provides details of the ongoing research at the CGDM facility.

Contact: psheng@euler.me.berkeley.edu

Consultative Group on International Agricultural Research

URL: http://www.cgiar.org

Summary: CGIAR is an association of public and private sector members sponsored by the World Bank, the Food and Agricultural Organization of the United Nations, the United Nations Development Programme, and the United Nations Environment Programme. Their mission is to contribute research that will assist in the promotion of sustainable agriculture for food security in developing countries. The CGIAR site has links to all (16) international agricultural research centers, which include the following:

CIFOR	- Center for International Forestry Research (Indonesia)
ICARDA	- International Center for Agricultural Research in the Dry Areas (Syrian Arab Republic)
ICLARM	- International Center for Living Aquatic Resources Management (Philippines)
ICRAF	- International Centre for Research in Agroforestry (Kenya)
ICRISAT	- International Crops Research Institute for the Semi-Arid Tropics (India)
IFPRI	- International Food Policy Research Institute (Washington, D.C.)
IIMI	- International Irrigation Management Institute (Sri Lanka)
IITA	- International Institute of Tropical Agriculture (Nigeria)
IPGRI	- International Plant Genetic Resources Institute (Italy)
ISNAR	- International Service for National Agricultural Research (The Netherlands)

Contact: dlucca@worldbank.org

Coral Forest

URL: http://www.blacktop.com/coralforest

Summary: This is a nonprofit organization whose focus is on the protection of coral reef ecosystems. The site contains information on activities and events, news reports, facts and maps. Also includes information for K-12 school teachers.

Contact: coral@igc.apc.org

Coral Health and Monitoring Program (CHAMP)

URL: http://coral.aoml.noaa.gov

Summary: CHAMP was established by the Ocean Chemistry Division of the Atlantic Oceanographic and Meteorological Laboratory under the National Oceanic and Atmospheric Administration to provide information and services to aide in improving and sustaining the health of coral reefs worldwide. This site contains a wealth of literature, research, informative abstracts, and data regarding coral health and monitoring. This is a must-see for any serious researcher with interests in coral reefs. The coral-list archives are also located at this site.

Contact: gmoriss@aoml.noaa.gov

Coral Reef Alliance

URL: http://www.coral.org/Home.html

Summary: CORAL is a nonprofit organization created to address the worldwide problems that coral reefs face. They provide information to divers and interested persons and support conservation efforts. This site contains information about the current state of coral reefs around the world and *The Coral Reef NGO Directory*, a directory of groups worldwide involved in coral reef research and conservation efforts.

Contact: CORALmail@aol.com

Cornell Center for the Environment

URL: http://www.cfe.cornell.edu

Summary: This Cornell University site contains information about the research activities at
                The Center. There are many programs and initiatives at the Cornell Center for the
                Environment. Just a few of them are the Cornell Waste Management Institute
                (CWMI), which promotes "energy efficient, environmentally sound solid waste
                management," the Institute for Comparative and Environmental Toxicology
                (ICET), and the Water Resources Institute (WRI). Many of the ongoing programs
                have made their research available here. One of the programs is the Breast Cancer
                and Environmental Risk Factors in New York State. This site also includes the
                Center's newsletters, the *Carrier Pigeon* and *Environmental Updates*. There is a
                listing of links to other Cornell University environmental sites, including some
                selected environmental law materials from the Legal Information Institute of the
                Cornell University Law School, at: http://www.cfe.cornell.edu/cornell.html

Contact: cucfe@cornell.edu

Council for Agricultural Science and Technology (CAST)

URL: http://www.cast-science.org/

Summary: This nonprofit organization was established to perform research on environmental
                and agricultural issues and for the purpose of providing information gained to
                legislators and policy makers so that better decision making may take place. A
                listing of the member societies—including links to them—is included at this site.
                Also included are full text publications, press releases, and testimonies.

Contact: cast@cast-science.org

Council on Environmental Quality (CEQ)

URL: http://ceq.eh.doe.gov or http://www.whitehouse.gov/CEQ/

Summary: The CEQ was established by the U.S. Congress in 1969 when it passed the National
                Environmental Policy Act (NEPA). Within this site is NEPAnet
                (http://ceq.eh.doe.gov/nepa/nepanet.htm.) The NEPAnet site includes the text of
                the NEPA, CEQ regulations, annual reports, decisions, and pointers to other sites
                of environmental laws.

Contact: feedback@whitehouse.gov

Coweeta LTER Site

URL: http://sparc.ecology.uga.edu

Summary: Coweeta is part of the Long-Term Ecological Research group (LTER), which is sponsored by the National Science Foundation's Division of Environmental Biology. The Coweeta site performs research on water, soil, and forest resources within an ecosystem context. Datasets from research performed are available.

Contact: webmaster@sparc.ecology.uga.edu

Crop Protection Institute

URL: http://www.cropro.org

Summary: This is a nonprofit institute comprised of the manufacturers, formulators, and distributors of crop protection products in Canada. They are "dedicated to the development of crop protection and pest control technology that is environmentally sound and beneficial to all Canadians." This site contains a library of press releases, speeches, scientific papers, and a newsletter. There is information on pesticides including food safety, human health, stewardship, and urban use.

Contact: brennerj@cropro.org

Cygnus Group

URL: http://cygnus-group.com

Summary: The Cygnus Group helps companies in the development and implementation of waste-preventing strategies. This site offers information and resources to both businesses and consumers. Included are newsletters, including *The ULS Report* (Use Less Stuff), and reports from Partners for Environmental Progress on packaging and waste reduction.

Contact: info@cygnus-group.com

Danube Information System (DANIS)

URL: http://www.ceit.sk/wwwisis/danis.htm

Summary: DANIS is made available by the Environmental Programme for the Danube River Basin with the assistance of the Centre of Eco-Information and Terminology. It contains documents, treaties, standards, legislation, and information about contact persons from Austria, Bulgaria, Croatia, Czech Republic, Hungary, Moldova, Romania, Slovakia, Slovenia, and Ukraine.

Contact: ceit@internet.sk

Declining Amphibian Populations Task Force (DAPTF)

URL: http://www.open.ac.uk/OU/Academic/Biology/J_Baker/JBtxt.htm

Summary: The DAPTF was established in 1991 by the Species Survivial Commission of the World Conservation Union. It is comprised of biologists and conservationists who are concerned about the decline of amphibian populations. The DAPTF site contains some informational materials about their research. The group's newsletter is *Froglog*.

Contact: DAPTF@open.ac.uk.

Defenders of Wildlife

URL: http://www.defenders.org

Summary: The mission of this organization is to protect all native wild animals and plants in their natural communities. Their focus is on endangered species and the other threats to our natural environment. They promote conservation and protection of ecosystems. This site contains research, state laws pertaining to endangered species, news items, and information on the activities of the Defenders of Wildlife. This site also sponsors the Grassroots Environmental Effectiveness Network (GREEN), which publishes GreenLines and Action Alerts.

Contact: webmaster@defenders.org

Defense Environmental Network & Information eXchange (DENIX)

URL: http://denix.cecer.army.mil/denix/denix.html

Summary: DENIX was established to provide Department of Defense personnel with timely access to environmental, legislative, compliance, restoration, cleanup, safety & occupational health, security, and Department of Defense guidance information. Parts of this site may be accessed by the public. Included here are environmental news briefs, newsletters, speeches, calendar of environmental events, legislation, regulations, policies, a library of environmental information, and a town hall forum.

Contact: http://denix.cecer.army.mil/denix/contact.html
                  (Fill in form at the above address.)

Defense Environmental Restoration Program (DERP)

URL: http://dogbert.ncr.usace.army.mil/military/derp/derp.htm

Summary: DERP is dedicated to correcting environmental damage and reducing the risk to human health from contamination resulting from past Department of Defense activities. Their site includes a searchable state-by-state database of restoration areas and a project information retrieval system.

Contact: Michael.J.Tarpey@mvr.usace.army.mil

Defense Technical Information Center

URL: http://www.dtic.mil

Summary: This information center, which operates under the auspices of the U.S. Department of Defense, contains searchable citations with abstracts to technical reports and research via its *Scientific and Technical Information Network*. The interface allows field searching which makes the databases much more valuable. The DTIC collection includes information relating to a broad range of topics, which include environmental pollution and control, biological weapons and warfare, environmental impacts of military activities, and toxic hazards.

Contact: bcporder@dtic.mil

Delaware Department of Natural Resources and Environmental Control

URL: http://www.dnrec.state.de.us/

Summary: The DNREC site contains information about the activities and resources available from its divisions. Completely searchable, divisions include the Division of Fish and Wildlife, the Division of Parks and Recreation, the Division of Soil and Water Conservation, the Division of Water Resources and the Division of Air and Waste Management.

Contact: wmaster@state.de.us

Department of Defense Environmental Cleanup Home Page

URL: http://www.dtic.mil/envirodod

Summary: This site contains information pertaining to all aspects of environmental cleanup. Included are the Environmental Restoration Small Business site, which was created to disseminate environmental information to members of the small business community who are interested in cleanup activities. Materials available include reports, policies, press releases, planning materials, and conference information.

Contact: jdorsey@dtic.mil

Department of Energy, U.S.

URL: http://www.doe.gov/

Summary: The U.S. Department of Energy has a substantial Web presence. Their Web sites offer an incredible amount of current news, data, research, reports, speeches, and other materials. The offices listed below offer a wealth of information for the environmental researcher.

Alternative Fuels Data Center	http://www.afdc.doe.gov
Biofuels Information Center	http://www.biofuels.doe.gov
Energy Efficiency and Renewable Energy Network	
	http://www.eren.doe.gov
Energy Information Administration	http://www.eia.doe.gov
Environmental Measurements Laboratory	http://www.eml.doe.gov
Office of Civilian Radioactive Waste Management	
	http://www.rw.doe.gov/
Office of Energy Research	http://www.er.doe.gov
Office of Environmental Management	http://www.em.doe.gov/
Office of Environment, Safety and Health	http://tis-hq.eh.doe.gov/
Office of Fossil Energy	http://www.fe.doe.gov

Contact: webmaster@apollo.osti.gov

Department of the Environment, Transport and the Regions (Great Britain)

URL: http://www.detr.gov.uk

Summary: This site provides information regarding the activities, responsibilities, and policies of Great Britain's Department of the Environment, Transport and the Regions. Included are press releases, newsletters, information on research, and links to other environmental sites in Great Britain. For information on their environmental protection efforts, see: http://www.environment.detr.gov.uk. This environmental portion of the site includes information on air quality, water quality, wildlife protection, chemicals in the environment, energy efficiency, environmental assessment, and radioactivity.

Contact: lochcarron@edinburgh.sac.co.uk

Department of the Interior, U.S.

URL: http://www.doi.gov

Summary: The DOI maintains the natural and cultural resources of the United States. Included at this site are press releases and information on natural hazards including floods, earthquakes, hurricanes, volcanoes, radon, fire, and weather. News releases from its bureaus and services are available (Bureau of Indian Affairs, Bureau of Land Management, Bureau of Reclamation, National Park Service, Minerals Management Service, Office of Surface Mining, Fish and Wildlife Service, and Geological Survey.)

Contact: webteam@ios.doi.gov

Desert Research Institute

URL: http://www.dri.edu

Summary: Located in Nevada, this is a nonprofit component of the state's University and Community College System. The Desert Research Institute has several research centers (Atmospheric Sciences Center, Biological Sciences Center, Energy and Environmental Engineering Center, Quaternary Sciences Center, and the Water Resources Center) that support research in the areas of air quality, atmospheric chemistry, climate dynamics, geomorphology, dendroecology, integrated watershed systems, and thirty other areas. This site includes synopses of the research projects, the DRI newsletter, and citations to publications.

Contact: wwwadm@sage.dri.edu

Direct Contact Environmental Toll-Free Directory

URL: http://www.owt.com/dircon/envdir.html

Summary: This is a toll-free telephone directory of more than 7,000 businesses, industries, services, governmental agencies, and nonprofit organizations in the U.S. It is searchable by subject area. Some of the subject areas are environmental consulting, air pollution control, hazardous waste, and energy conservation.

Contact: dcfeedback@owt.com

DiveWeb

URL: http://diveweb.com/

Summary: Sponsored by Doyle Publishing Company, this site contains current reports on diving, oceanography, marine animal behavior, and offshore petroleum news.

Contact: ncree@diveweb.com

The Earth Council

URL: http://www.ecouncil.ac.cr

Summary: This is an international organization whose purpose is to support the Earth Summit agreements. This site, The Earth Network for Sustainable Development, contains papers and speeches of council members, databases of information pertaining to sustainable development activities, and links to sustainable development sites including the Earth Charter.

Contact: earthnet@terra.ecouncil.ac.cr

Earth Day Network

URL: http://www.cfe.cornell.edu/EarthDay/ednethome.html

Summary: This nonprofit network was created to be a vehicle for increased awareness and responsibility through the promotion of Earth Day. This site contains activity reports, speeches, and promotional materials for Earth Day.

Contact: earthday@qualcomm.com

Earth Island (Institute)

URL: http://www.earthisland.org

Summary: Earth Island is provided by the Earth Island Institute, a nonprofit organization whose mission is to assist in the development of conservation, preservation, and restoration projects. Information regarding those projects are available at this site. The database is searchable by keyword.

Contact: Use online form at site or earthisland@earthisland.org

Earthlink

URL: http://www.green-pages.com.au/

Summary: Formerly Green Pages, the focus of this group is to educate people on green products and to support green manufacturing. They have created a directory of primarily Australian businesses that adhere to environmentally friendly manufacturing processes. Included here are links to environmental resources, including the *Earth Garden* publication.

Contact: editor@earthlink.com.au

Earth Observing System Amazon Project (University of Washington)

URL: http://boto.ocean.washington.edu/eos/index.html

Summary: This project, under the auspices of NASA and the River Systems Research Group at the School of Oceanography, has as its purpose the study of the biogeochemistry, hydrology, and sedimentation of the Amazon River and its drainage basin. Includes information on the specific projects, data gathered, and reports. Other projects at this River Systems Research Group site include CAMREX (Carbon in the Amazon River Experiment), AARAM (Andean Amazon Rivers Analysis and Monitoring Project), and the World Rivers Project.

Contact: http://boto.ocean.washington.edu/eos/webmasters.html

Earth Pledge Foundation

URL: http://earthpledge.org

Summary: This nonprofit foundation was created as a result of the Earth Summit in 1992. Contains news publications and a reading room where discussion is centered around books on sustainable development. Also includes information about and reports from the Business Coalition for Sustainable Cities (BCSC), which was created by the Earthpledge Foundation.

Contact: lhoffman@earthpledge.org

Earth Resources Laboratory at MIT

URL: http://www-erl.mit.edu

Summary: This site operates under the Department of Earth, Atmospheric, and Planetary Sciences at MIT. It includes an extensive listing of Earth Resources Laboratory Publications and the research and activities of the Laboratory.

Contact: webmaster@erl.mit.edu

Earth's Resources Observation Systems (EROS) Data Center

URL: http://edcwww.cr.usgs.gov/

Summary: The U.S. Geological Survey's Earth Resources Observation Systems (EROS) Data Center is involved in data collection and distribution. Besides handling data from several series of satellites, they archive more than 8 million photographs taken from airplanes. Their base of earth science information is the world's largest. They maintain the National Satellite Land Remote Sensing Data Archive. The Alaska Field Office is managed by the Science and Applications branch of the USGS EROS Center (http://www-eros-afo.wr.usgs.gov/welcome.html). Remote sensing and GIS research of Alaska and the Arctic region is performed at this location. Information in the form of maps and other images, text, and data are available. The Alaska Ecoregions Mapping Monitoring and Assessment Program's data is stored here. This program is a joint project of the U.S. EPA and the U.S. Geological Survey. Included is information on climate, terrain, soils, vegetation, wildfire, delineation methods, references, and a representative photo for each Alaskan ecoregion. These twenty ecoregions include the Arctic Foothills, Brooks Range, Yukon Flats, Aleutian Islands, and Seward Peninsula.

                  Also included at this site is the Conservation of Arctic Flora and Fauna (CAFF) site.

Contact: webmaster@www-eros-afo.wr.usgs.gov

Earthwatch Institute

URL: http://gaia.earthwatch.org

Summary: Earthwatch is a nonprofit organization whose goal is to initiate and apply scientific field research to raise the understanding of our planet and thereby the quality of life on Earth. Summaries of the findings of research efforts are available. They established the Center for Field Research (CFR), which is responsible for awarding grants for research. This site contains the large yearly grants lists that give the recipients' name, affiliation, position, and research endeavor. Information required for obtaining grants and college credit information is also available at this site.

Contact: info@earthwatch.org

ECN (Environmental Change Network)

URL: http://www.nmw.ac.uk/ecn/index.html

Summary: This U.K. site was created to conduct and disseminate the findings and data of long-term environmental research. Many agencies and organizations are involved in this program and there is a wealth of data available here. Information includes the biannual ECN Newsletter and the core measurements, which are collected.

Contact: ecnccu@ite.ac.uk

Ecologia

URL:	http://ecologia.nier.org/ecologia/
Summary:	Ecologia (ECOlogists Linked for Organizing Grassroots Initiatives and Action) is a U.S.-based, international organization. It was created in 1989 to deliver technical assistance and information to independent environmental organizations. The organization continues to provide these services to local governments and NGOs in Eurasia and the United States. Their site contains information about the organization's programs, activities, and their newsletter. Back issues of the newsletter are available at this site in English. It is also available by subscription in English, Russian, and Lithuanian.
Contact:	ecologia@igc.apc.org

Ecology Action Centre

URL:	http://www.cfn.cs.dal.ca/Environment/EAC/EAC-Home.html
Summary:	This site is part of the Chebucto Community Net in Nova Scotia. Dedicated to conservation and environmental protection, the Ecology Action Centre offers a library of environmental resources, their quarterly newsletter, and information on their research from its committees, which focus on marine, wilderness, and transportation issues. The Chebucto Community Net has been an ongoing source of local and regional environmental information.
Contact:	at420@chebucto.ns.ca

EcoMall

URL:	http://www.ecomall.com
Summary:	The EcoMall is a collection of environmentally conscious companies. Their products range from food and clothing to solar products. Their catalogs include informational materials relating to the environment. In addition to the catalogs of environmentally conscious merchants, there are quotes pertaining to the environment and lists and contacts for environmental activism groups.
Contact:	ecomall@ecomall.com

Econet

URL:	http://www.igc.org/igc/econet/

Summary: Econet is part of the Institute for Global Communications Network. This site contains databases rich in reports, bulletin boards, weekly news releases, congressional actions, congressional voting, and coverage of regional environmental issues. One must be a member for full access to the services of Econet, but a great deal of their information is freely available at this Web site. Subjects in their opening menu cover activism, atmosphere and climate, economics, energy, law, human rights, toxics and wastes, and more than 30 additional topics.

The American Wind Energy Association (http://www.igc.apc.org/awea/) provides information on wind energy technologies at this Econet site. Information includes a catalog of wind energy publications, a calendar of events, news, technical papers, conference information and archives of *Wind Energy Weekly*. Contact: windmail@awea.org

Contact: For information about Econet, send blank message to: econet-info@econet.apc.org

The Ecotourism Society (TES)

URL: http://www.ecotourism.org

Summary: This international nonprofit organization was established in 1990 to foster a link between outdoor travel entrepreneurs and researchers and conservationists. To meet this end, sections of this site are devoted to the professional, the traveler, and the researcher. There is also membership information, a bookstore, and a section on training and education.

Contact: ecomail@ecotourism.org

EcoTradeNet

URL: http://www.ecotradenet.com

Summary: EcoTradeNet was created to help users locate "environmental and clean energy technologies, products, and services and to help environmental and clean energy firms promote their goods and services." There are more than 6,000 companies in the growing database.

Contact: webmaster@ecotradenet.com

Eco-Village Network

URL: http://www.gaia.org/

Summary: This network, sponsored by Gaia Trust and the Global Eco-Village Network (GEN), was created to help in the development of sustainable human settlements and to disseminate information regarding sustainable settlements. They offer materials on ways to live without destroying our environment. Included are links to an Eco-Directory, Eco-Businesses, and Eco-Resources.

Contact: webmaster@gaia.org

Ecovote Online

URL: http://www.ecovote.org/ecovote/

Summary: This site is sponsored by the California League of Conservation Voters. This large and active group supports environmentally responsible candidates for office. Included at their site are league endorsements, action alerts, and an up-to-date listing of California legislation dealing with environmental issues.

Contact: tschilling@ecovote.org

The EcoWeb, University of Virginia

URL: http://ecosys.drdr.virginia.edu

Summary: This highly-rated web site is dedicated to providing information regarding the conservation of the environment, recycling, and environmental protection. It is sponsored by the Office of Recycling and Environmental Information in the Division of Recoverable and Disposable Resources (DRDR). Included at this site are the archives of many of the environmental discussion groups, information on recycling efforts, and additional links to environmental resources.

Contact: www@ecosys.drdr.virginia.edu

EDIE (Environmental Data Interactive Exchange)

URL: http://www.edie.net

Summary: This site is a source of global environmental news and information for the professional with emphasis on Europe. The coverage is comprehensive and independent. Included at the site are full text research articles from environmental journals, a news archive, information on software, and interactive exchange. Visitors must fill out a (free) registration form to gain access.

Contact: Use form at Web site.

Edison Electric Institute

URL: http://www.eei.org/

Summary: Edison Electric Institute is comprised of shareholder-owned electric companies. Its members generate approximately 79% of all of the electricity generated by electric utilities in the U.S. This institute provides information pertaining to "electric utility operations, regulations, sales and revenues, environmental practices, marketing opportunities and other topics."

Contact: Multiple contact addresses. Check Web site.

Edwards Aquifer Research and Data Center (EARDC)

URL: http://www.eardc.swt.edu

Summary: The Edwards Aquifer is an underground reservoir supplying water for 1.5 million people. This site, operating under the auspices of Southwest Texas State University, contains information regarding the Aquifer including its history, hydrogeology, water use, and recharge data. Also included are a simulation model and video clips. There is also a listing of the endangered species of the region and the environmental surroundings.

Contact: ourso@eardc.swt.edu

EE-Link (Environmental Education-Link)

URL: http://www.nceet.snre.umich.edu or http://eelink.net

Summary: This is a program of The National Consortium for Environmental Education, with support from the Environmental Protection Agency. The information at this site is aimed at K12 environmental science educators, students, and professionals. There is a nice variety of software, activities, resources, and facts. Also included is an impressive directory of environmental Web sites. They are the sponsor of the EE-Internet discussion group.

Contact: eeadmin@eelink.umich.edu

Electric Power Research Institute (EPRI)

URL: http://www.epri.com

Summary: This institute was created by U.S. electric utilities to make "the generation, delivery, and use of electricity affordable, efficient, and environmentally sound." The site contains ENERGYSEARCH, which enables users to search for Web sites covering all aspects of energy. The Web sites represent organizations, companies, and government agencies.

Contact: Use addresses at site depending on type of information needed.

Elsevier Science Tables of Contents

URL: http://www.elsevier.nl (Netherlands)
http://www.elsevier.com (U.S.)
http://www.elsevier.co.jp (Japan)

Summary: Elsevier Science publishes some very solid scientific research journals. This table of contents service is a nice way to keep up on research and papers being published by Elsevier in environmental areas. The citations are fully indexed making it possible to use advanced search features to search for keywords in the title, author, journal, date, ISSN, or abstract fields. The searchable abstracts make this service very powerful. Journals include *Agriculture, Ecosystems and Environment, Environmental Impact Assessment Review, Environmental Pollution, Journal of Hazardous Materials, Journal of Contaminant Hydrology, Journal of Environmental Radioactivity,* and many other journals from the natural sciences.

Contact: Contact addresses at site by location and type of information needed.

Endangered Habitats League

URL: http://www.cyberg8t.com/wroberts/ehl/ehlwww.html

Summary: This group has an interest in protecting our endangered and threatened ecosystems. They hold a special interest in the protection of coastal sage scrub. Information includes newsletters, press releases, and calendars.

Contact: Warren S. Roberts: wroberts@cyberg8t.com

Endangered Species Recovery Program

URL: http://arnica.csustan.edu/esrpp/esrpp.htm

Summary: The Endangered Species Recovery Program operates under the auspices of California State University, Stanislaus Foundation. The Program was created to enable cooperative research on the conservation of biodiversity in the region of San Joaquin Valley. Included are area endangered species profiles, press releases, and a comprehensive guide to the mammals of California.

Contact: Daniel F. Williams: dwilliam@koko.csustan.edu

ENDS Environmental Data Services

URL: http://www.ends.co.uk/

Summary: ENDS is a publisher of environmental information in the United Kingdom. This site includes an environmental newsletter, news releases, and a monthly review of environmental developments. Regular registration or visitor registration is required.

Contact: post@ends.co.uk

Energy & Environmental Research Center (EERC)

URL: http://www.eerc.und.nodak.edu/

Summary: The EERC was established as a federal research and development facility in 1951. It has operated at the University of North Dakota since 1983. The EERC is involved in research in advanced energy systems and the prevention and cleanup of environmental pollution. Information from each of the research areas is available at this site. Their informative newsletter and news releases are also available here.

Contact: pmiller@eerc.und.nodak.edu

Energy Ideas Clearinghouse

URL: http://www.energy.wsu.edu/ep/eic

Summary: This site provides information regarding energy conservation for both the residential and commercial sectors. It contains listings of sources of publications and job information. They also make technical software available at this site. Software includes conversion programs, energy cost estimating, life cycle cost analysis, and many others.

Contact: powerline@energy.wsu.edu

Energy Technology Data Exchange

URL: http://www.etde.org/

Summary: This is a program of the International Energy Agency. They collect energy technology research and make it available via their Energy Database. The database covers the subject areas of accelerators and instrumentation, biomedical sciences, chemistry and geology, energy conservation, storage, and use, energy policy and planning, environmental sciences, fission reactor and isotope technology, fossil fuels, general and power engineering, materials, physics, plasma physics and fusion, and renewable energy sources.

Contact: info@etde.org

Enviro-Access

URL: http://www.enviroaccess.ca/eng/index.html

Summary: Enviro-Access is a service provided by a nonprofit group in Canada. Their mission is to assist the smaller "environmental sector organizations" in developing and using new technologies. Offered at this site are many informative fact sheets pertaining to site contamination and restoration, treatment of air and gas, treatment of wastewater and filtrates, waste and residue treatment/recycling, and sludge treatment.

Contact: enviro@enviroaccess.ca

Envirolink Network

URL: http://envirolink.org

Summary: This network consists of directories of environmental information in its Environmental Library and throughout the site. It contains listings of electronic discussions, a directory of environmentally aware companies, electronic journal listings, discussion archives, and listings of environmentally friendly places. This is one of the few environmental sites that cannot be described easily due to its breadth and depth of environmental information.

Contact: support@envirolink.org

ENVIROMINE

URL: http://www.enviromine.com

Summary: This site was established so that persons interested in the environmental issues related to mining activities could stay informed. It is part of the Info-mine Network and is sponsored by Robertson GeoConsulting, Inc. The site currently includes information on many aspects of mining including news, policies, industrial information, technical guidelines and standard procedures, research notes, mine reclamation, and sources of additional information. There is a nice section on "Wetlands for Treatment of Mine Drainage" (http://www.enviromine.com/wetlands/)

Contact: gbaldwin@info-mine.com

Environmental Alliance for Senior Involvement (EASI)

URL: http://www.easi.org

Summary: EASI is interested in the "sustainability of their communities, their nation, and their world." They offer information pertaining to their mission, goals, and projects. Several publications are available at this site.

Contact: easi@easi.org

Environmental and Societal Impacts Group

URL: http://www.dir.ucar.edu/esig/index.html

Summary: ESIG is a part of the National Center for Atmospheric Research located in Boulder, Colorado (http://http.ucar.edu). ESIG is concerned with the weather, climate shifts, and human behavior. Its research covers both the impact of the environment on human behavior and the impact of human behavior on the environment. This site contains information regarding ESIG, its publications, and research. There is a good deal of research on weather, climate, and crops at this site.

Contact: jan@ucar.edu

Environmental Assessment Association

URL: http://iami.org/eaa.html

Summary: The EAA is an organization of professionals who provide environmental inspection services and work with the government sector. Included at this site is a searchable directory of members, the *EAA Environmental News*, and other issues pertaining to environmental inspection such as radon, lead, asbestos, and procedures.

Contact: eaa@iami.org

Environmental Careers Organization

URL: http://www.eco.org

Summary: This nonprofit organization was established to help those interested in working with the environment a means of establishing and developing their careers. Included here are listings of internships, publications, and links to other Internet sites for environmental career searching.

Contact: Visit site for listings of contact addresses.

Environmental Chemicals Data Information Network

URL: http://ulisse.etoit.eudra.org/Ecdin/Ecdin.html

Summary: This database is made possible under auspices of the Commission of European Communities at the Ispra Establishment. It was created "to bring together a wide variety of data on chemicals that are being produced by human activity in such amounts as to be actually or potentially of environmental significance." The search interface to this database allows searching by name, ECDIN, or CAS numbers, or molecular formula. There is a wealth of information including production and use, legislation and rules, occupational health and safety, toxicity, concentrations and fate in the environment, detection methods, and hazards and emergency.

Contact: flavio.argentesi@etoit.eudra.org or valerio.pagliari@etoit.eudra.org

Environmental Compliance Assistance Center

URL: http://www.hazmat.frcc.cccoes.edu/

Summary: This center is a joint venture of industries, Front Range Community College, and the U.S. EPA. This site contains regulations covering the aerospace industry, the automotive industry, aircraft maintenance, printed wiring board manufacturers, heavy equipment, and metal finishers. Sections also cover environmental acts, new products, pollution prevention, waste minimization certification testing, and state contacts.

Contact: webadmin@www.ha zmat.frcc.cccoes.edu

Environmental Contaminants Encyclopedia

URL: http://www.aqd.nps.gov/toxic/index.html

Summary: This database is provided by the National Park Service. It contains comprehensive information on 118 chemicals and chemical combinations. Each entry contains a brief introduction, water, sediment and soil data interpretation, concentrations and toxicity, tissue and food concentrations, and information on bioconcentration, biomagnification, or bioavailability.

Contact: Roy_Irwin@nps.gov

Environmental Data Pages

URL: http://www.techstuff.com

Summary: Environmental Data Pages offers a unique database for environmental engineers, lawyers, and technicians who will find it an invaluable resource for specialized equipment, professional technical software and books. You may locate expert witnesses, consultants, and remediation firms and receive answers to environmental/technical issues in a timely manner. The site also offers a selection of news, interesting commentary, and informative data for environmental professionals from other professionals.

Contact: info@techstuff.com

Environmental Defense Fund

URL: http://www.edf.org

Summary: The EDF offers information on the Endangered Species Act and environmental protection efforts. There is a program that shows how each states' electricity is produced and how much pollution is created in the process. Also included are news and sections on human health, transportation, rainforests, and wildlife. Includes several forums on specific topics such as endangered species and recycling/energy efficiency. Their Chemical Scorecard is available at http://www.scorecard.org. This database contains information on manufacturers' pollution and hazardous chemicals.

Environmental Industry Web Site

URL: http://www.enviroindustry.com

Summary: This is an indexed directory to industries, companies, or organizations that deal in some way with environmental products or services. It is made available by Extended Marketing, Inc. The directory provides both environmental products and services as well as products and services to environmental agencies. These industries are grouped by name and by type of business. Entries may give background and mission of the company or organization, and contact information.

Contact: homepage@extend.com

Environmental Journalism Home Page

URL: http://www.sej.org

Summary: This is sponsored by the Society of Environmental Journalists. Their newsletter, *SEJournal,* is available as well as information and other publications pertaining to their activities. Also included is TipSheet, which alerts journalists of potential environmental stories and sources. TipSheet is a joint product of the Society of Environmental Journalists, the Radio and Television News Directors Foundation, and the National Safety Council's Environmental Health Center.

Contact: sejoffice@aol.com

Environmental Law Information Center

URL: http://www.webcom.com/~staber/welcome.html

Summary: This site was established and is maintained by Steve Taber, a member of the law firm, Ross & Hardies, so that current cases, acts, bills, policies, and aspects of environmental law could be disseminated. This site has a section of recently-decided cases concerning major environmental statutes and a forum for discussion of legal environmental issues.

Contact: Steve Taber: staber@webcom.com

Environmental Measurements Laboratory

URL: http://www.eml.doe.gov

Summary: The Environmental Measurements Laboratory (EML) is in New York and is administered by the Office of Environmental Management of the U.S. Department of Energy's Chicago Operations Office. Several large reports are available for download from this site. They are also available via ftp from ftp://eml.doe.gov/pub/publications. This site also includes a nice bibliography of research dating from 1948 to present.

Contact: webmaster@eml.doe.gov

Environmental News Network

URL: http://www.enn.com/

Summary: ENN offers daily news summaries and full text of articles. Sources include Associated Press, Reuters, Business Wire, Knight-Ridder, and the Federal Register. At the time of this writing, the member fee to access this source is $49.95 per year. Email delivery of the Daily News is $24.95 per year. Free features at this site include selected news articles, ENN Radio audio scripts, Earthwatch Radio broadcasts, and interactive forums.

Contact: mgt@enn.com

Environmental Organization Web Directory

URL: http://www.webdirectory.com/

Summary: Includes listings for hundreds Web sites of organizations, government agencies, educational institutions, and commercial and nonprofit agencies dealing with the environment. Searchable by keyword or by browsing through the 30 subject areas. Also includes a bulletin board system for sharing thoughts and news about the environment.

Contact: http://www.webdirectory.com/writeus.shtml

Environmental Protection Agency, U.S.

URL: http://www.epa.gov/

Summary: The U.S. Environmental Protection Agency has placed a great deal of its information library online. Included are research summaries, fact sheets, software, congressional testimony, summaries of environmental bills, and Federal Register sections dealing with wetlands, toxics, endangered species, air, waste, water, and pesticides. In addition, there is information on research grants and fellowships, ongoing research, and job vacancies. With the variety of information offered at this site, its searchable word index is a great asset. It is a must when performing a search and can be used effectively for finding most terms or topics. It is also a good way to get to know the different types of information that are available at this site. The searchable records of the Comprehensive Environmental Response, Compensation, and Liability Information System (CERCLIS) are at http://www.epa.gov/enviro/html/cerclis/cerclis_query.html. The Envirofacts Warehouse (http://www.epa.gov/enviro/index.html) provides access to data from seven EPA environmental databases including the Toxic Release Inventory System, Superfund Data and Hazardous Waste Data. This site also includes the National Center for Environmental Publications and Information (NCEPI). The NCEPI has placed more than 5,500 available titles here with many of the most popular available online. Web sites within the EPA that have home pages offering their research and publications:

Acid Rain Division - http://www.epa.gov/ardpublc/acidrain/
Office of Air and Radiation - http://www.epa.gov/oar
Office of Pollution Prevention and Toxics - http://www.epa.gov/opptintr/
Office of Research and Development - http://www.epa.gov/ORD
Office of Science and Technology - http://www.epa.gov/OST
Office of Solid Waste and Emergency Response - http://www.epa.gov/oswer
Office of Water - http://www.epa.gov/watrhome
Office of Wetlands, Oceans and Watersheds - http://www.epa.gov/owowwtr1
Stratospheric Ozone Home Page - http://www.epa.gov/ozone/index.html

Contact: http://www.epa.gov/epahome/comments.html

Environmental Research Institute of Michigan (ERIM)

URL: http://www.erim.org/

Summary: This is a private, nonprofit organization performing research and related services for its sponsors. Includes information regarding private sector activities and services for applications of impact assessments, utility planning, observations, data collection, and forms of imaging analysis. They are affiliated with ERIM International, Inc.

Contact: webmaster@erim-int.org

Environmental Resource Center

URL: http://www.ercweb.com

Summary: This is an environmental consulting firm that offers services in hazardous waste management, air emissions, water effluents, toxic substances, pesticides, impact assessment, and compliance auditing. Their site contains resources, software, and regulatory information.

Contact: service@ercweb.com

Environmental Resources Information Network (ERIN)/ Environment Australia Online

URL: http://kaos.erin.gov.au

Summary: This is a project maintained under the auspices of the Australian Federal Department of the Environment, Sport and Territories. ERIN and Australian Environment On-line offer some of the larger and best databases of environmental information available. This site is rich in primary information on wildlife, endangered and threatened species, and biodiversity of Australia. Much of the material is also of international interest. Includes the BioRap database which was designed to be used in appraisal of biodiversity resources. Contains press releases, laws and regulations, newsletters, and conference papers. The Australian Environment Education Network (AEEN) is located at this site.

Contact: http://kaos.erin.gov.au/general/feedback.html

Environmental Resources Management

URL: http://www.erm.com

Summary: This site contains publications, newsletters, and alerts containing information on regulations, employment opportunities, conferences, and events. The ERM weekly update contains state-by-state regulatory information.

Contact: mkt_info@erm.com

Environmental Routenet

URL: http://www.csa.com

Summary: RouteNet was created by Cambridge Scientific Abstracts. It includes daily news and several searchable databases including Cambridge Scientific Abstracts, TOXLINE, Comtex, and LEGI-SLATE. A fee is required for use of most of the databases. However, the Policy and Compliance Forum, which is cosponsored by the Committee for the National Institute for the Environment, and other sections of this site are available to guests. The Forum provides an avenue for the discussion of environmental policy and compliance issues, problems, and practical solutions. A different environmental topic is introduced each month (archives available).

Contact: support@csa.com

Environmental Science and Forestry at SUNY

URL: http://www.esf.edu/

Summary: The State University of New York's College of Environmental Science and Forestry has a Web site that presents a great deal of information on its research activities. Available information includes research from the Adirondack Ecological Center projects, the Willow Biomass for Bioenergy project, and an extensive annotated bibliography of selected publications of the research program at Huntington Wildlife Forest.

Contact: webmaster@esf.edu

Environmental Simulations, Inc.

URL: http://www.groundwatermodels.com

Summary: This company provides groundwater modelling software. Its site includes demonstrations and detailed information regarding its modelling software.

Contact: info@groundwatermodels.com

Environmental Treaties and Resource Indicators (ENTRI)

URL: http://sedac.ciesin.org/pidb/pidb-home.html

Summary: ENTRI, a database of searchable treaties and resource indicators, is provided by the CIESIN organization with the assistance of many other groups. They use nine specific "issue areas" to search the database. Those areas are: 1)land use/land cover change and desertification, 2) global climate change, 3) stratospheric ozone depletion, 4) transboundary air pollution, 5) conservation of biological diversity, 6) deforestation, 7) oceans and their living resources, 8) trade and the environment, and 9) population. Treaties are searchable by date, location, subject area, and governmental unit. This database and its unique search interface has a lot to offer the environmental researcher.

Contact: www.mail@ciesin.org

Environmental Working Group

URL: http://www.ewg.org/

Summary: The Environmental Working Group is a nonprofit organization whose mission is to provide citizens with the environmental information they need to stay healthy and to maintain a healthy environment. This site includes state-by-state information about water quality, wetlands, pesticides, anti-environmental groups, political contributions, and population. It also contains issues of *A CLEAR VIEW*, a publication of EWG's Clearinghouse on Environmental Advocacy and Research.

Contact: info@ewg.org

Environment Canada (The Green Lane)

URL: http://www.doe.ca/

Summary: Environment Canada hosts one of the better environmental sites on the Web. There
                   is a lot of primary, original data here. Where many sites on the Internet give listings
                   with pointers to others' resources, The Green Lane succeeds in its mission to
                   provide information on environmental products and services to its national and
                   international visitors. This site has a tremendous amount of news releases,
                   speeches, databases, reports, fact sheets, and other information and should appeal
                   to a wide audience.

                   The Greenhouse Gas Miser Handbook can be found at: http://www.ns.ec.gc.ca/co2/
                   greenhouse1.html. This handbook is a good, basic introduction of ways to reduce
                   greenhouse gas emissions. It includes a bibliography of reference sources.

                   The Green Lane is comprised of five regions:

                   Atlantic Region   http://www.ns.doe.ca
                     (Nova Scotia, New Brunswick, Prince Edward Island, Newfoundland and
                   Labrador)
                   Quebec   http://www.qc.doe.ca/envcan/indexe.html
                   Ontario   http://www.cciw.ca/green-lane/or-home.html
                   Prairie and Northern   http://www.mb.ec.gc.ca/
                   Pacific and Yukon   http://www.pwc.bc.doe.ca/

                   Each of the above sites may contain geographically relevant weather and climate
                   information, frequently asked questions, publications, and laws and legislation
                   affecting its area.

Contact: http://www.doe.ca/comments_e.html

The Environment Council, U.K.

URL: http://www.greenchannel.com/tec/

Summary: The Environment Council is "an independent charity dedicated to enhancing and
                   protecting Britain's environment through building awareness, dialogue and
                   effective solutions." This site contains the newsletter, *Habitat On-line,* and
                   information pertaining to the environmental activities that the Council is involved
                   in.

Contact: environment.council@ukonline.co.uk

Environment in Asia

URL: http://www.asianenviro.com/

Summary: This site is sponsored by AET, Ltd. (Asia Environmental Trading), a U.K. firm. Its goal is to provide comprehensive information on environmental news, policies, and markets in the Asia-Pacific region including Japan, China, Hong Kong, Taiwan, South Korea, Malaysia, Thailand, the Philippines, Indonesia, Singapore, Vietnam, India, Sri Lanka, Brunei and Cambodia/Laos/Myanmar. The tables of contents of the periodicals, *Asia Environmental Review* and *China Environmental Review*, and ordering information is available.

Contact: aet@asianenviro.com

Enviroene

URL: http://es.epa.gov

Summary: This is one of the Environmental Protection Agency's best sites. It acts as a "single repository for pollution prevention, compliance assurance, and enforcement information." The site includes several databases, handbooks, case studies, statutes, executive orders, and compliance policies and guidelines. Included are the Integrated Solvent Substitution Data System (ISSDS), the National P2 Vendor Database (Vendinfo) and EPA Sector Notebooks with profiles of selected major industrial groups.

Contact: http://es.inel.gov/comments.html

EnviroSources

URL: http://www.envirosources.com

Summary: This is a search engine for environmental, health and safety, civil engineering, and related fields and is focused on the U.S. and parts of Canada. It allows keyword searching, pull-down subject searching, and browsing by type or sponsor of material needed—such as laws, regulations, laboratories, or statistics. Pull-down subjects range from accreditation/certification to wildlife.

Contact: info@envirosources.com

EnviroText

URL: http://tamora.cs.umass.edu/info/envirotext/index.html

Summary: Envirotext is the result of joint efforts of the U.S. Environmental Protection
            Agency, the U.S. Departments of Energy, Interior, Justice, Defense, the U.S. Army
            Corps of Engineers Construction and Engineering Research Laboratory, and the
            University of Illinois. The database contains information on environment, safety,
            and health requirements. Included in the database are the United States Code, most
            of the Code of Federal Regulations, and the Federal Register.

Contact: support@tis.eh.doe.gov

Essential Information

URL: http://essential.org/EI.html

Summary: Essential Information is a nonprofit organization that was founded by Ralph Nader
            in 1982. The goal of this organization is to provide interested citizens the
            information they need to participate and be active in making their communities and
            the general environment more healthy.

Contact: ei@essential.org

European Centre for Nature Conservation

URL: http://www.ecnc.nl/

Summary: The ECNC is an independent foundation that links policy makers and scientists.
            They are dedicated to the conservation of nature and biodiversity in Europe. The
            site is comprised of information about its activities, ecological research and reports,
            and a databases of experts.

Contact: ecnc@ecnc.nl

European Environmental Agency

URL: http://www.eea.dk

Summary: The EEA was established to provide environmental information to the European community. This site includes publications, air pollution tables, information regarding assessments, and databases pertaining to air emission, air quality, inland waters, land cover, marine and coastal environment, nature conservation, and soil. To assist in providing information, the EEA created the European Environmental Information and Observation NETwork (EIONET). This site contains a link to EIONET, which offers additional information regarding the state of the European environment.

Contact: Use form at Website.

European Forest Institute (EFI)

URL: http://www.efi.fi

Summary: EFI is a nongovernmental body that conducts multi-disciplinary forest research. This site contains information about the mission and organization of EFI, a calendar of events, databases, and job prospects. Includes a searchable database of their projects.

Contact: efisec@efi.fi

Everglades Information Network

URL: http://everglades.fiu.edu/index.html

Summary: The EIN is a joint project of the Florida International University Libraries and Everglades National Park. This site offers a digital library of several types of information, including reports, pamphlets, photos, maps, and books pertaining to the Florida Everglades' ecosystem.

Contact: glades@fiu.edu

EXTOXNET (Extension Toxicology Network)

URL: http://ace.orst.edu/info/extoxnet/

Summary: EXTOXNET is a project of the University of California, Davis, Oregon State University, Michigan State University, and Cornell University. Available at this Oregon State University site is searchable literature including pesticide information profiles, toxicology information briefs, factsheets, news regarding toxicology, newsletters, and technical information. Includes a pesticide index of trade names.

Contact: Terry L. Miller millert@ace.orst.edu

Federal Emergency Management Agency (FEMA)

URL: http://www.fema.gov/fema/

Summary: This site provides information pertaining to a variety of emergencies and disasters. Fact sheets on preparation for disasters cover natural disasters including earthquakes, floods, tsunamis, and fires; and technological disasters including nuclear power plant emergencies and radiological accidents. Includes the full text of *A Guide for Disaster Recovery Programs,* which lists programs that may be used for disaster recovery. Also includes the *Emergency Management Guide for Business & Industry*, a full text document for emergency planning, response and recovery for companies of all sizes.

Contact: eipa@fema.gov

Federal Geographic Data Committee

URL: http://fgdc.er.usgs.gov

Summary: The Federal Geographic Data Committee (FGDC) was established by the Office of Management and Budget and is responsible for the "coordinated development, use, sharing, and dissemination of geographic data." This site contains large downloadable files of standards, reports, newsletters, and press releases.

Contact: fgdc@www.fgdc.gov

Federal Remediation Technologies Roundtable

URL: http://www.frtr.gov

Summary: The FRTR is an interagency group seeking to build a more collaborative atmosphere among the federal agencies involved in hazardous waste site remediation. This site contains the *1997 Web Version 3.0 of the Remediation Technologies Screening Matrix and Reference Guide,* which was prepared by reviewing and compiling the collective efforts of several U.S. Government agencies into one compendium document.

Contact: johnette.c.shockley@usace.army.mil

Fedworld Information Network

URL: http://www.fedworld.gov

Summary: Fedworld presents a wealth of governmental information from a variety of sources and is made available by the National Technical Information Service (NTIS), a division of the Department of Commerce. Of interest to environmental researchers would be the searchable reports and studies submitted by governmental agencies. NTIS receives approximately 7,000 reports, studies, and products per month. Also of interest would be the new governmental sites and the subject listing of governmental sites. Includes a searchable database of emission related vehicle information mandated by the Clean Air Act.

Contact: webmaster@fedworld.gov

Finnish Forest Research Institute - METLA

URL: http://www.metla.fi

Summary: The Finnish Forest Research Institute operates under the auspices of the Finnish Ministry of Agriculture and Forestry. The Institute "produces research-based information for decision-makers, forest industries and practical forestry, as well as for the public at large." Information about their research activities and their publications are located here. Several different forest-related databases are available.

Contact: webmaster@www.metla.fi

Fish and Wildlife Information Exchange Homepage

URL: http://fwie.fw.vt.edu

Summary: This site is presented by the Department of Fisheries & Wildlife Sciences at Virginia Tech. It includes information about research projects and activities. The staff at the Fish and Wildlife Information Exchange have been working with several factions in developing a species information database. Part of that database is available here in their Master Species File; and more will be added in the future.

Contact: fwiexchg@vt.edu

Florida Center for Environmental Studies

URL:	http://www.ces.fau.edu
Summary:	The Florida CES is sponsored by Florida Atlantic University and is a joint project of the 15 public and private universities in the state of Florida. This site includes several of their publications and information about their research.
Contact:	webmaster@ces.fau.edu

Florida Cooperative Extension Service

URL:	http://www.wec.ufl.edu/Extension
Summary:	The Florida Cooperative Extension Service is affiliated with the University of Florida. They offer a variety of information about the wildlife of the state. Included are informative quick reference fact sheets and detailed fact sheets on the native species.
Contact:	Use form at Web site.

Florida Department of Environmental Protection

URL:	http://www.dep.state.fl.us
Summary:	The mission of Florida's DEP is to "protect, conserve, and manage Florida's environment and natural resources." Materials and information supporting this mission are located at this site; this includes program information, a calendar of events, information on permits, and rules and regulations. There are several environmental education publications available here. These cover topics such as the environmental effects of the automobile, environmental citizenship, drinking water in Florida, exotic species of Florida, groundwater in Florida, presence of mercury, and the wetlands of Florida. Also includes an environmental glossary.
Contact:	Use form at Web site.

Florida Design Initiative

URL:	http://fcn.state.fl.us/fdi/fdi-home.htm
Summary:	The Florida Design Initiative is composed of professional design associations, state agencies, local governments, utilities, and academic institutions in Florida. It is sponsored by the Department of Community Affairs' Florida Energy Office and by the U.S. Department of Energy. The FDI is located at Florida A & M University. Offered at this site is information on energy-efficient design, applicable programs, materials, and guidelines.
Contact:	fdi@famu.edu

Forest History Society

URL: http://www.lib.duke.edu/forest/

Summary: The Forest History Society is affiliated with Duke University. Their focus is on "the history of interactions between people, forests, and their related resources-timber, water, soil, forage, fish and wildlife, recreation, and scenic or spiritual values." There is an extensive, searchable bibliography of resources pertaining to the history of forests, which includes more than 23,500 citations to books, articles, and dissertations.

Contact: recluce2@acpub.duke.edu

Forest Service Ecosystem Management

URL: http://www.fs.fed.us/land/

Summary: This site contains research publications of the USDA Forest Service. It contains information on fire, timber, forest health, and global forestry. Included are maps, databases, software, research, and many full text publications. One of these is *Description of the Ecoregions of the United States*. This document, compiled by Robert G. Bailey, contains the description of the land surface form, climate, vegetation, soils, and fauna of the ecoregions.

Contact: comments@www.fs.fed.us

Forest Service Employees for Environmental Ethics

URL: http://www.afseee.org/

Summary: This is a nonprofit organization composed of governmental employees, concerned citizens, and present, former, and retired Forest Service Employees who stand behind the tenets of Aldo Leopold in their conservation efforts. They actively monitor Forest Service activities and publish *Inner Voice* and the *FSEEE Activist,* which are available at this location. This site also includes reports, press releases, and forest service documents.

Contact: afseee@afseee.org

Friends of the Earth International

URL: http://www.xs4all.nl/~foeint/

Summary: This organization is comprised of groups from 52 countries around the world. Addresses and telephone numbers are included for the groups; many entries include an email address as well. At this main site, there is information on current FOE activities and events of interest. Links are also included to sites in Australia, Canada, British Isles, Philippines, Scotland, and the U.S. Each country site offers information about their areas. For example, at the England site, there is a "Chemical Release Inventory" for England and Wales; the U.S. site contains the electronic publications, *Dirty Little Secrets* and *The Green Scissors Report*.

Contact: foeint@antennal.nl

The FROGGY Page

URL: http://frog.simplenet.com/froggy/

Summary: Though at first glance this site may appear elementary, it quickly becomes apparent that there is a wealth of basic and scientific information here related to the frog. The site includes sound files, pictures, species information, and links to additional amphibian sites on the Web.

Contact: sandra@shore.net

Gaia Forest Archives

URL: http://forests.org/gaia.html

Summary: Contains information on forests and forest conservation efforts in countries all over the world. Information is in the form of newsletters, news releases, and commentary. The Worldwide Forest/Biodiversity Campaign News is available here and is indexed by country.

Contact: grbarry@students.wisc.edu

Galapagos Coalition

URL: http://www.law.emory.edu/PI/GALAPAGOS/

Summary: The Galapagos Coalition is composed of biologists, other scientists, and lawyers with expertise in environmental and international law. They are concerned with the environmental degradation of the Galapagos Islands. This site contains news and research reports concerning the biodiversity, conservation efforts, laws and political events surrounding the Islands.

Contact: nprocto@emory.edu

GAP (Gap Analysis Program), National

URL: http://www.gap.uidaho.edu/gap

Summary: This program is coordinated by the U.S. Geological Survey's Biological Resources Division. It was created "to provide regional assessments of the conservation status of native vertebrate species and natural land cover types and to facilitate the application of this information to land management activities." GAP is conducted as state-level projects with a cooperative effort among regional, state, and federal agencies, and private groups. There is data and information at this site about each state's inventory, monitoring, and research activities.

Contact: mattw@uidaho.edu

General Accounting Office, U.S.

URL: http://www.gao.gov

Summary: This site is a searchable interface to the Government Accounting Office reports. The full text of the reports may be searched, or fields may be specified. The additional search fields are: title of report, subject terms, report number, and date. The full text is available. This is an excellent way to locate information on hazardous waste, toxic substances, regulatory issues, energy supply, pollution, superfund, and other environmental topics.
                Also available via telnet://swais.access.gpo.gov

Contact: webmaster@www.gao.gov

GENIE Project (Global Environmental Network for Information Exchange in the U.K.)

URL: http://www-genie.lut.ac.uk/

Summary: The GENIE Project is funded by the Economic and Social Research Council (U.K.). Many other members of the U.K. government are involved in this project. The database contains data sets, records of projects and events, and information about organizations. A nice interface allows searching by subject, location, or person. This should be of interest to researchers or scientists.

Contact: genie@lut.ac.uk.

Georgia Department of Natural Resources

URL: http://www.DNR.State.Ga.US

Summary: There is a good deal of information at this site. Of particular interest to
                environmentalists would be the information from the Coastal Resources Division,
                the Environmental Protection Division, the Wildlife Resources Division, and the
                Pollution Prevention Assistance Division (P2AD).

Contact: Use form at Web site.

Germinal Project

URL: http://dgrwww.epfl.ch/GERMINAL/Germinal.html

Summary: Operating under the auspices of the Departement de Genie Rural (Department of
                Rural Engineering) and the Swiss Federal Institute of Technology, GERMINAL
                performs research regarding land use planning and environmental management
                using geographic information systems and a database management system. The
                goal is to develop an integrated, global approach that encompasses all areas of
                environmental management and planning in a conceptual data model. The site
                includes information regarding its research and publications.

Contact: Christophe.Claramunt@dgr.epfl.ch

Global Change Master Directory (GCMD)

URL: http://gcmd.gsfc.nasa.gov

Summary: This directory is a comprehensive source of information about Earth science,
                environmental, biosphere, climate, and global change data holdings made available
                to the scientific community throughout the world. The directory provides many
                search features including specific fields, full text, and boolean. The GCMD is the
                American Coordinating Node of the Committee on Earth Observation Satellites
                International Directory Network (CEOS IDN) and is a component of the Global
                Change Data and Information System (GCDIS).

Contact   gcmduso@gcmd.gsfc.nasa.gov

Global Change Research Information Office

URL: http://gcrio.org

Summary: This United States office provides information about global change research from
                several different agencies and departments. This site includes a searchable catalog
                of abstracts of publications. Many of the publications may be ordered free of
                charge.

Contact: help@gcrio.org

Global Climate Web Site Research

URL: http://climate.gsfc.nasa.gov/

Summary: The Climate and Radiation Branch of Goddard's Laboratory for Atmosphere specializes in research on the Earth's climate with an emphasis on the effects of atmospheric radiation on the water and energy cycles of the Earth. Located at this site are informative reports on projects conducted by the Climate and Radiation Branch researchers. Topics cover aerosols, clouds, modelling, rainfall, and remote sensing.

Contact: robert.cahalan@gsfc.nasa.gov

Global Environmental Options (GEO)

URL: http://www.geonetwork.org

Summary: GEO is a nonprofit corporation that assists its clients in project development, design, planning, and project management. This site contains an enormous number of links to sites regarding sustainability. There are links to over 500 Web sites. Primary information at this site includes a directory of environmental businesses in California.

Contact: geo@geonetwork.org

Global Environment Outlook Project (GEO-1 Report)

URL: http://grid2.cr.usgs.gov/geo1

Summary: The Global Environment Outlook Project covers five areas: the major regional and global environment problems, the major demographic, social, and economic driving forces behind observed problems and trends, future outlook considering our current state, choices we may make toward a better future, and what is currently being done and what can be done in the future to aid in achieving sustainable development. The document at this site is a report of the assessment undertaken by members of the GEP Project. It is an extensive (biennial) review of the state of the world's environment.

Contact: geo@unep.org or grid@grida.no

Global Futures Foundation (GFF)

URL: http://www.quiknet.com/globalff/globalfu.html

Summary: GFF is a nonprofit foundation with interests in sustainable living, recycling, pollution control, and environmentally conscious manufacturing. Contains news and information on activities.

Contact: webmaster@globalff.org

Global Hydrology and Climate Center

URL: http://wwwghcc.msfc.nasa.gov

Summary: The GHCC was established by NASA and is a joint venture of the Marshall Space Flight Center, the Universities Space Research Association, and the Space Science and Technology Alliance of the State of Alabama, which includes several Alabama universities. The focus of the research center is "to understand the Earth's global water cycle, the distribution and variability of atmospheric water, and the impact of human activity as it relates to global climate change." Their research activities are documented at this site.

Contact: webmaster@wwwghcc.msfc.nasa.gov

Global Network of Environment & Technology

URL: http://www.gnet.org/ or http://gnet.together.org

Summary: This network was created by the Global Environment & Technology Foundation whose mission is to "facilitate the cooperative integration of enterprise, technology, and environment into sustainable systems." This site contains information on environment and technology industries, people, and products. This site also contains information on government activities, news summaries, abstracts, press releases, and calendars. Includes TechKnow, an interactive search engine. Use TechKnow to search or browse for innovative remediation technologies or for innovative ozone depleting substance (ODS) management technologies. Users may search by keyword or use specific field searching by contaminant, by affected area, by federal remediation roundtable structure, or by activity.

Contact: gnet@gnet.org

Global Recycling Network, Inc.

URL: http://grn.com

Summary: GRN was created to assist businesses around the world in recycling their resources, surplus manufactured goods, and outdated or used machinery. Their site includes listings for recycling services, recycled products, and legislative and business news. Includes a large, searchable directory of publications from business, government and research sectors. Also includes information on recycling stocks, commodity prices, and an interactive forum.

Contact: grn@grn.com

Global Research Information Database (GRID)

URL: http://www.grida.no/

Summary: The GRID is a network of United Nations Environment Program (UNEP) centers in Brazil, Canada, Denmark, Japan, Kenya, Nepal, Norway, Poland, Switzerland,Thailand, and the U.S. This particular site is located in Arendal, Norway. Located at this site are maps and datasets, the Arctic Environmental Data Directory (http://gaia.grida.no/prog/polar/add), the Arctic Monitoring and Assessment Programme Home Page (http://www.grida.no/prog/polar/amap/), and the Program for the Conservation of Arctic Flora and Fauna (http://www.grida.no/prog/ polar/caff). Also includes nuclear reactors of the world.

Contact: webmaster@grida.no

GLOBE Program

URL: http://www.globe.gov

Summary: The GLOBE Program is comprised of scientists, educators, and students who are interested in gaining a better knowledge of our environment. It is managed through the combined efforts of national and international organizations and under the auspices of the National Oceanographic and Atmospheric Administration. More than 5,000 schools from 70 countries participate in the GLOBE Program.

Government Institutes, Inc.

URL: http://www.govinst.com

Summary: Government Institutes provides government regulatory information and publishes environmental materials. They also conduct training in areas pertaining to the environment and health and safety. This site includes summaries of their print, video, CD-ROM publications, and announcements of courses and seminars.

Contact: giinfo@govinst.com

Great Lakes Fishery Commission

URL: http://www.glfc.org

Summary: The GLFC was established for the purposes of sustaining the productivity of Great
            Lakes fish, to coordinate research efforts, to initiate the control of sea lampreys,
            and to publicize the information gathered. This site contains research reports,
            databases with commercial fishing information, and other databases from research
            activities.

Contact: mgaden@glfc.org

Great Lakes Information Network (GLIN)

URL: http://www.great-lakes.net

Summary: GLIN is a product of several agencies and organizations interested in the binational
            Great Lakes Region, which is the area of the U.S. and Canada surrounding the
            Great Lakes. There is a wealth of information about this region at this site. Included
            is news and information about the natural resources, the ecosystems, legal issues,
            congressional activities, pollution, ecology, and weather.

Contact: Christine Manninen: manninen@glc.org

Greenbelt Alliance

URL: http://www.rahul.net/gba/

Summary: This group was formed to protect the "Greenbelt" of farmlands, watersheds, and
            parks in the nine county, San Francisco Bay Area. This site includes information
            on activities and events, laws, regional maps and mapping, and geographic
            information systems. The publication, *Beyond Sprawl: New Patterns of Growth to
            Fit the New California*, is available here. They administor the GreenInfo Network
            (http://www.greeninfo.org), which contains several maps and related GIS
            information.

Contact: webmaster@greenbelt.org

Green Mountain Institute for Environmental Democracy

URL: http://www.gmied.org

Summary: This organization was founded by the staff of the Northeast Center for Comparative
            Risk. Included at this site are their newsletter, *Synergy,* information about their
            activities, and environmental indicators.

Contact: mwitten@gmied.org

GREEN PAGES

URL: http://eco-web.com

Summary: GREEN PAGES is sponsored by ECO Services International. It is a directory of
                environmental businesses and industries or environmentally-conscious
                technologies. The site contains listings of manufacturers, engineering consultants
                and information services in water and waste water treatment, waste management
                and recycling, cleanup and soil rehabilitation, air and noise pollution control, power
                generation and energy efficiency, and new and renewable energy technologies.

Contact: feedback@eco-web.com

Green Parties of North America

URL: http://www.greens.org

Summary: This site contains information relating to the activities of the various Green Parties
                in North America as well as Taiwan, Australia, New Zealand, and several countries
                in Europe. Contact information is included for each group.

Contact: cls@greens.org

Greenpeace International

URL: http://www.greenpeace.org (Amsterdam)
                http://www.kiss.com.au/greenpeace/ (Australia)
                http://greenpeace.meer.net/ (U.S.)

Summary: This organization is concerned with protecting the natural environment. Their main
                Internet site is at the Amsterdam location with other locations as mirror sites. At
                these sites are listings of current campaigns and activities, searchable text of
                environmental reports and information on Greenpeace International ships. Included
                are links to Greenpeace National organizations of: Argentina, Austria, Australia,
                Belgium, Canada, Czech Republic, Denmark, Germany, Greece, Italy, Japan,
                Luxembourg, Netherlands, New Zealand, Russia, Slovakia, Spain, Sweden,
                Switzerland, the United Kingdom, the United States, and the Mediterranean region.

Contact: webmaster@xs2.greenpeace.org

Green Seal

URL: http://www.greenseal.org

Summary: Green Seal is a nonprofit organization whose focus is on the protection of the environment by promoting green manufacturing. They set environmental standards and award a "Green Seal of Approval" to products that are environmentally friendly. This site contains a database of approved products that may be searched by product, company name, or category of product such as building materials, copy paper, or re-refined engine oil.

Contact: mshor@greenseal.org

GREENTIE (Greenhouse Gas Technology Information Exchange)

URL: http://www.greentie.org

Summary: GREENTIE was created under the auspices of the International Energy Agency and the Organisation for Economic Cooperation and Development to "improve the awareness of, and facilitate the access to, suppliers and experts of 'clean technologies,' particularly technologies that help mitigate the emissions of greenhouse gases." The database covers suppliers of energy, energy end-use products and services, and agriculture and forestry products and services.

Contact: greentie@greentie.org

Green University Initiative

URL: http://www.gwu.edu/~greenu/

Summary: The Green University Initiative is sponsored by The Institute for the Environment at George Washington University. Their mission is to help create a sustainable future. This site includes information regarding their research activities and links to new environmental sites on the Internet.

Contact: greenu@gwis2.circ.gwu.edu

Ground-Water Remediation Technologies Analysis Center

URL: http://www.gwrtac.org

Summary   This center collects and disseminates information on innovative groundwater remediation technologies. This site contains a remediation technology database, a vender information database, technology reports, a calendar, and links to state contacts. GWRTAC is supported by Concurrent Technologies Corporation (CTC), the University of Pittsburgh, and U.S. EPA.

Contact: gwrtac@chmr.org

Habitats - The Growth of a Forest

URL: http://www.nationalgeographic.com/features/97/habitats/index2.html

Summary: Habitats is a National Geographic site containing a pictorial tour of forest growth over an 86-year period in West Virginia.

Contact: editor@nationalgeographic.com

Harbor Branch Oceanographic Institution

URL: http://www.hboi.edu/

Summary: The Harbor Branch Oceanographic Institution is occupied with research and education in the marine biological, chemical, and physical sciences. They are dedicated to protecting the environment through the understanding of the oceans, estuaries, and coastal regions. This site contains information about HBOI, a calendar of events, data on tours HBOI research ship schedules, and material on jobs, internships, and volunteer programs. Ship specifications and images are available in Acrobat .pdf format.

Contact: webmaster@hboi.edu

Harvard Environmental Resources On-Line

URL: http://environment.harvard.edu/

Summary: The Harvard Environmental Resources On-Line site contains information on environmental research and course work at Harvard as well as data on jobs, conferences, an environmental calendar of events for the greater Boston area and links to other environmental centers affiliated with Harvard University. Reference guides on international environmental policy and China's environment are available at this site as well as access to several environmental journals and information on several environmental lists.

Contact: Thomas M. Parris: tparris@fas.harvard.edu

Harvard Forest

URL: http://lternet.lternet.edu/hfr/

Summary: The Harvard Forest site includes information about the forest at Petersham, Massachusetts, educational programs and fellowships, and funding. This site also provides guidelines for researchers, the Harvard Data Catalog (not complete at this time), an overview of the Harvard Forest LTER site, abstracts from the 1998 annual Harvard Forest Ecology Symposium, online datasets and metadata.

Contact: Richard Lent: rlent@fas.harvard.edu

Hawaiian Ecosystems at Risk (HEAR)

URL: http://www.hear.org/

Summary: The goal of HEAR is to provide information to natural resource managers to assist in the fight against invasive alien species into the Hawaiian ecosystems. Information available at this site includes lists of alien flora and fauna invading Hawaii, maps of alien species locations, the Hawaiian Natural Resources Monitoring Database, news releases, the Harmful Non-Indigenous Species Database (HNIS), and other reports on alien species.

Contact: halesci@hawaii.edu

Hawaii Biological Survey

URL: http://www.bishop.hawaii.org/bishop/HBS/hbs1.html

Summary: The HBS site contains data for biologists, entomologists, and environmentalists. Some information presented here pertains to Hawaii's endangered mammals, birds, plants, and reptiles. There are databases, descriptions of publications, and an image library also at this location.

Contact: hbs@bishop.bishop.hawaii.org

Hawaii National Wildlife Refuges/Marine Sanctuaries

URL: http://www.gorp.com/gorp/resource/us_nwr/hi.htm

Summary: This site offers descriptions of a number of national wildlife refuges in Hawaii. Some of the information includes primary wildlife at the refuge, habitat, recreational facilities, educational resources, and data on the location of the sanctuary.

Contact: http://www.gorp.com/gorp/suggbox.htm

Hawaii's Endangered and Threatened Species Page

URL: http://www.bishop.hawaii.org:80/bishop/HBS/endangered/

Summary: This page is a product of the Hawaii Biological Survey whose goal is to inventory all the native and non-native flora and fauna in the Hawaiian Archipelago and maintain a reference collection for use by such agencies as the U.S. Fish and Wildlife Service and the Nature Conservancy of Hawaii. Data found at this site includes lists of threatened and endangered species, an image gallery, several plant and wildlife databases, and a bibliography of HBS publications.

Contact: Neal@bishop.bishop.hawaii.org

Hawk Mountain Sanctuary

URL: http://www.hawkmountain.org/

Summary: Hawk Mountain is a nature preserve in eastern Pennsylvania and the first refuge for birds of prey in the world. This site provides information about the sanctuary's education, research, conservation, and monitoring programs; a calendar of events; membership data; recent happenings; and everything one needs to know about visiting Hawk Mountain.

Contact: webmaster@hawkmountain.org

HawkWatch International

URL: http://www.info-xpress.com/hawkwatch/

Summary: The purpose of HawkWatch is to monitor and protect eagles, hawks, and other birds of prey by inspiring public awareness and commitment to the protection of the ecosystems in which these birds live. This site contains information on how to become a member of HawkWatch, the adopt-a-hawk program, research and education programs at HWI, plus a number of articles on raptor activities and ecological threats to raptors.

Contact: hawkwatch@juno.com

Hazardous Substance Research Centers

URL: http://www.hsrc.org/

Summary: This is a national organization involved in basic and applied research, technology transfer, and training. They are supported by the U.S. EPA, Department of Energy, and Department of Defense, as well as academia, industry, and other state and federal governmental agencies. Included here are newsletters, searchable project abstracts, research reports, and tutorials.

Contact: mark.hodges@gtri.gatech.edu

HazDat - Hazardous Substance Release/Health Effects Database

URL: http://atsdr1.atsdr.cdc.gov:8080/hazdat.html

Summary: The Hazardous Substance Release/Health Effects Database provides access to information on the effects of hazardous substances on humans. The database gives information on emergency events, which include what contaminants were found, where they were found, concentration levels of hazardous materials, what kind of public health threat was involved, what the physical hazards at the site were, and other related information. The database also contains EPA data on the release of hazardous substances.

Contact: Mike Perry: lmp1@cdc.gov

HazWrap

URL: http://www.ornl.gov/HAZWRAP/

Summary: Under the guidance of the DOE, HAZWRAP, the Hazardous Waste Remedial Actions Program works with federal, state, and local U.S. agencies to provide solutions to environmental problems presented by environmental remediation, pollution prevention, and waste minimization. This site contains information on HAZWRAP partnerships, services, and capabilities. The site also includes articles on such topics as land use planning, environmental training and education, hydrogeology, airborne hazards, and environmental biotechnology.

Contact: phillipsad@ornl.gov

Headwaters Forest

URL: http://host.envirolink.org/headwaters/

Summary: Headwaters Forest is the largest, unprotected old growth redwood forest in the world and is the habitat for several endangered species. This site contains information on how Headwaters is threatened by those who want to log it, news updates about the forest and data on what you can do to help save it. Headwaters Forest is now part of the Institute for Global Communications.

Contact: headwaters@enews.org

Headwaters Science Center

URL: http://www.northernnet.com/science/index.html

Summary: Headwaters Science Center in Bemidji, Minnesota is committed to science education and environmental awareness; offering interactive exhibits, an environmental learning center, and a Mississippi River Watch program. Their site provides descriptions of these programs, membership information, workshop data for educators, and a Saturday Science program for children.

Contact: oishsc@northernnet.com

Heartwood

URL: http://www.bloomington.in.us/heartwood/

Summary: Heartwood is an organization of individuals, groups, and businesses dedicated to forest and wildlife conservation and preservation. This site contains forest action alerts, forest protection resources, a "Voices of the Forest" speakers program, volunteer data, and membership materials.

Contact: dscherub@mail.coin.missouri.edu

Hiraiso Solar Terrestrial Research Center

URL: http://hiraiso.crl.go.jp/

Summary: The Hiraiso Solar Terrestrial Research Center site contains a glossary of solar-terrestrial terms, telnet access to their real-time space environment network, geomagnetic observatory data, a solar activity chart, a geomagnetic activity chart, and high energy particle flux data that you can view for any date you enter. This site is accessible in Japanese and English.

Contact: rwc@crl.go.jp

Holland Island Preservation Foundation

URL: http://www.intercom.net/local/holland/

Summary: Holland Island is a barrier island to thousands of acres of wetlands, protecting them from the storms of Chesapeake Bay. This site contains information on the egrets, curlues, oyster catchers, ospreys, mallards, black ducks, geese, swans, gulls, terns, and bald eagles that nest here. There is data here on how you can help preserve this wildlife habitat and wetland area.

Contact: twhite@shore.intercom.net

Horned Lizard Conservation Society (HLCS)

URL: http://www.psy.utexas.edu/psy/brooks/hlcs/index.htm

Summary: The Texas Chapter of the Horned Lizard Conservation Society (HLCS) is devoted to discovering why the Texas Horned Lizard (aka, the horny toad) has declined in number and what can be done to reverse the process. Information at this site includes conference announcements, press releases, images, a bibliography, and membership material.

Contact: Bill Brooks: brooks@psyvax.psy.utexas.edu

Houston Audubon Society

URL: http://www.io.com/~pdhulce/audubon.html

Summary: The Houston chapter of the National Audubon Society strives to use conservation education as a means to implant the value of our natural resources in people. The chapter encourages the protection and preservation of wildlife and its habitat. This site lists officers, membership requirements, services, and volunteer programs of the Society and also has access to the Lone Star Rare Bird Alert and the North American Rare Bird Alert.

Contact: pdhulce@io.com

Howl - The PAWS Wildlife Center

URL: http://www.paws.org/wildlife/index.htm

Summary: This site contains articles on coexisting with wildlife, dealing with wildlife problems, what to do if you find an injured wild animal, and the dangers of feeding wildlife. Howl is sponsored by the Progressive Animal Welfare Society.

Contact: email@paws.org

Hubbard Brook Experimental Forest

URL: http://www.yale.edu/edex/new/index.html

Summary: The Hubbard Brook Experimental Forest (HBEF) and the Hubbard Brook Ecosystem Study (HBES) in New Hampshire is the longest continually operating ecosystem study in the nation. This site contains forest inventory information and forest floor watershed data plus bibliographies and an experimental phytosociological generator.

Contact: None listed.

Hydrographic Survey Data

URL: http://www.ngdc.noaa.gov/mgg/geodas/hyddas.html

Summary: This NOAA site contains information on the uses of hydrographic data, frequently asked questions about hydrographic data, and information on their free bulletin board. The GEODAS searchable database is located at this site.

Contact: cmoore@ngdc.noaa.gov

ICLEI - International Council for Local Environmental Initiatives

URL: http://www.iclei.org/

Summary: ICLEI is an agency based on the idea that local environmental action has global implications and that as city populations increase there is not only a need but an opportunity to get local governments to come up with new ways of reducing and managing the wastes produced by such population growth. This site contains documents describing ICLEI programs and projects, lists of officers and members, excerpts from their latest newsletter, ICLEI policies, a local initiatives clearinghouse, and a calendar of events.

Contact: urbanco2@iclei.org

Idaho Department of Fish and Game

URL: http://www.state.id.us/fishgame/fishgame.html

Summary: The Idaho Department of Fish and Game site contains information on the management of fish hatcheries and wildlife habitats, the conservation of rare animal and plant species, and Idaho wetlands conservation projects, and publications. A report on the Idaho Rare Plant Conference is available, in .pdf format and a searchable aquatic database of water resources in Idaho, Montana, Oregon, and Washington can be accessed at this site.

Contact: idfginfo@idfg.state.id.us

Idaho Wilderness

URL: http://www.wild-eyed.org/whatis.htm

Summary: The Idaho Wilderness site includes information on Idaho's threatened and endangered species, such as grizzlies, wolves, woodland caribou, peregrine falcons, and whooping cranes. This site also contains wild Idaho images, information on how you can help Idaho wildlife, and the complete text of the Wilderness Act.

Contact: msheils@micron.net

IEEE TAB Environment, Health and Safety Committee

URL: http://www.ieee.org/tab/ehshome.html

Summary: The objective of the Institute of Electrical and Electronics Engineers Technical Activities Board is to guarantee that environmental, health and safety considerations are incorporated into electronic products and processes from design and manufacturing to termination. This site is comprised of documents detailing conference activities, upcoming events, articles, the committee charter and information on joining the IEEE Technical Activities Board.

Contact: j.cerone@ieee.org

IFAW - International Fund for Animal Welfare

URL: http://www.easynet.co.uk/ifaw/home.htm

Summary: The mission of the IFAW is to prevent cruelty to animals, to protect animals and
                their habitats, and the abolishment of Canadian and Norwegian offshore seal
                killing. There is a large amount of information here including data on fox and deer
                hunting, the fur trade and the IFAW research vessel, *Song of the Whale*, whose
                objective is the conservation of marine life.

Contact: IFAW@easynet.co.uk

IISDnet - International Institute for Sustainable Development

URL: http://iisd1.iisd.ca/

Summary: IISD is a site that supports the ideal of conserving the world's resources along with
                social and economic development. Available information includes several
                definitions of sustainable development, lists of projects, a sustainable development
                timeline, publications, and global news items.

Contact: info@iisd.ca

Illinois Natural Resources Information Network (INRIN)

URL: http://dnr.state.il.us/

Summary: The INRIN site is maintained by the Illinois Department of Natural Resources and
                includes data on Illinois ecosystems, flora and fauna. Natural resources educational
                material, laws, and programs can be found here, as well as information on minerals,
                energy, environmental quality, and data on the Illinois Conservation Foundation.

Contact: webmaster@dnrmail.state.il.us

Illinois Recycling Association

URL: http://www.ilrecyclingassn.org/

Summary: The Illinois Recycling Association represents citizens on critical waste
                management issues at the state level by promoting waste reduction, recycling, and
                re-use. Information at this site includes state recycling facts, a calendar of events,
                news, and state and county contacts.

Contact: ilrecycle@aol.com

Indiana Department of Natural Resources

URL: http://www.ai.org/dnr/index.html

Summary: The Indiana DNR site contains general DNR information, data on state parks and recreational facilities, Riverwatch and Crawdad committees on water quality information, newsletters, forestry information, the latest DNR news releases, and facts about camping. There is also a pointer to the Indiana Natural Heritage Data Center Homepage here.

Contact: Raju Maharjan: maharjar@dnr.state.in.us

Indonesian Mangrove Foundation

URL: http://www.mangrove-f.org/

Summary: This site provides information about the Indonesian mangrove forests, what they are used for, and how they are managed. Membership data, conference and seminar agendas, and information on books and publications can also be found here.

Contact: webmaster@mangrove-f.org

Information Center for the Environment

URL: http://ice.ucdavis.edu/

Summary: The Information Center for the Environment is a cooperative effort between UC Davis and more than 30 federal, state, local, and international organizations working toward the protection of the environment. This site contains a searchable index, information about the Center and its supporters, as well as data about its programs, which include the California Watershed Projects Inventory and the Natural Resource Projects Inventory.

Contact: info@ice.ucdavis.edu

Inland Seas Education Association

URL: http://www.schoolship.org/

Summary: ISEA is a nonprofit organization whose goal is to furnish a floating classroom where people of all ages can gain first-hand training and experience in the Great Lakes ecosystem. Some topics covered in "A Day Aboard the Schoolship," are weather, water chemistry, plankton, and sediments. This site provides data on the schooner Inland Seas, the Schoolship program for schools, membership in the association and ISEA's shipboard programs.

Contact: isea@traverse.com

Institute for Terrestrial Ecology

URL: http://www.nmw.ac.uk/ite/

Summary: ITE is a research institute that strives to understand the natural environment and terrestrial ecology for the benefit of decision makers in the areas of environmental protection, conservation, and the sustainable use of natural resources. This site contains information on ITE projects, conference announcements, employment opportunities, training programs, publications, and library holdings.

Contact: K.Goodsir@ite.ac.uk

Institute of Freshwater Ecology (IFE)

URL: http://www.ife.ac.uk/

Summary: IFE is dedicated to research on pollution, acid rain, waste management, and climate change and their effects on freshwater ecology. Information at this site includes annual reports, current research projects, a catalog of algae and protozoa strains, library and information services, and aquatic processes topics.

Contact: i.mculloch@ife.ac.uk

International Arid Lands Consortium

URL: http://ag.arizona.edu/OALS/IALC/

Summary: IALC is committed to the support of ecological sustainability in arid and semiarid lands worldwide. This site contains information on IALC current activities, their fellowship program data, an online newsletter, information on conferences and workshops, project summaries, and a directory of arid land researchers.

Contact: Katherine Waser: kwaser@ag.arizona.edu

International Bee Research Association (IBRA)

URL: http://www.cardiff.ac.uk/ibra/index.html

Summary: IBRA is the world information service for bee science and beekeeping, dedicated to promoting beekeeping as a form of sustainable agriculture. This site contains descriptions of publications and journals produced by the Association including *Bee World*, which is free to members of IBRA. There are lists of conferences, meeting announcements, and articles from past meetings also at this site.

Contact: ibra@cardiff.ac.uk

International Canopy Network (ICAN)

URL: http://lternet.edu/ican/

Summary: ICAN supports research, education, and conservation of international forest canopies. This site provides information on joining ICAN, several canopy science bibliographies, access to ICAN's newsletter, and an email bulletin board for the exchange of information on forest canopies.

Contact: canopy@elwha.evergreen.edu

International Center for Living Aquatic Resources Management

URL: http://www.cgiar.org/ICLARM/

Summary: ICLARM is an international research organization concerned with the management of aquatic resources to serve users and consumers in developing countries. Material at this site includes current news about ICLARM, research programs and activities, publications, employment opportunities, information on their library resources, and symposium information.

Contact: iclarm@cgnet.com

International Centre for Gas Technology Information

URL: htp://www.icgti.org/open/

Summary: The International Centre for Gas Technology Information (ICGTI) site is the entry to the GTI Online forum that exists to further the exchange of ideas in the gas industry to promote technological innovation and growth. To use some of the information on this forum you must be a member. Registration is free, but some information is available only to internal ICGTI colleagues.

Contact: icgti@icgti.org

International Coral Reef Initiative

URL: http://www.mbnet.mb.ca/vps/icri/index.html

Summary: ICRI is concerned with the plight of coral reefs and is dedicated to reversing the trend of their extinction. This site contains workshop summaries, calendars of events, and a list of sites containing information on coral reefs.

Contact: swise@igc.apc.org

International Council for the Exploration of the Sea (ICES)

URL: http://www.ices.dk/

Summary: ICES is an intergovernmental agency in Copenhagen, Denmark, that is concerned with marine science. This site provides access to oceanographic and environmental databanks, projects, conferences, and workshops.

Contact: www@ices.dk

International Crane Foundation (ICF)

URL: http://www.baraboo.com/bus/icf/whowhat.htm

Summary: The ICF works to conserve cranes and the wetland and grassland habitats on which they depend by providing experience, knowledge, and inspiration to resolve threats to these ecosystems. This site contains a searchable literature database, education resources, an adopt-a-crane program, information on the many species of cranes, and membership data.

Contact: gordon.icf@baraboo.com

International Energy Agency Solar Heating and Cooling Programme

URL: http://www.iea-shc.org/

Summary: The IEA Solar Heating and Cooling Programme supports the participation of a variety of countries in project research using active and passive solar technology applications. This site includes descriptions of projects, planned workshops, the text of the current newsletter, special activities, research activities, publications, a calendar, and software produced by IEA.

Contact: Mike Donn: mike.donn@vuw.ac.nz

International Geosphere-Biosphere Programme

URL: http://www.igbp.kva.se/

Summary: The self-stated goals of the IGBP are to describe and understand the interactive physical, chemical, and biological processes that regulate the total Earth system, the unique environment that it provides for life, the changes that are occurring in this system, and the manner in which they are influenced by human actions. This site includes information about IGBP, its programs, research partners, publications, meetings, data on how it works, and an acronyms and abbreviations dictionary.

Contact: Will Steffen: will@igbp.kva.se

International Ground Source Heat Pump Association (IGSHPA)

URL: http://www.igshpa.okstate.edu/default.htm

Summary: The IGSHPA is concerned with heating, cooling, and water heating using earth energy. The sources available at this site include conference and seminar announcements, descriptions of projects and programs, descriptions of heat pumps and how they work, brochures, a calendar of events, and information on continuing education programs. You can also find data on IGSHPA members and a more detailed explanation of the Association at this site.

Contact: Robert Jones: jrobert@master.ceat.okstate.edu

International Human Dimensions Programme on Global Environmental Change

URL: http://www.uni-bonn.de/IHDP/index.html

Summary: IHDP is an international, interdisciplinary, nongovernmental social science programme concerned with researching, understanding and analyzing the human dimensions of biodiversity, and its relationship to global environmental change. This site contains a detailed calendar of international environmental meetings and events, project descriptions, publications, and access to the HDGEC mailing list.

Contact: ihdp@uni-bonn.de

International Institute for Industrial Environmental Economics

URL: http://www.lu.se/IIIEE/hp.html

Summary: IIIEE is dedicated to the advancement of sustainable development by performing research on cleaner industrial processes and educating those who will make environmental decisions in the future. This site contains information about IIIEE, its research projects, its journals, and other publications that may be ordered. There is access to the program of an online seminar here, in Swedish and English.

Contact: iiiee@iiiee.lu.se

International Marinelife Alliance

URL: http://www.actwin.com/fish/ima/index.html

Summary: The purpose of the IMA is to conserve the diversity of sea life, protect marine
                        environments, and promote the sustainable use of marine resources. Some of the
                        data available at this site consists of the descriptions of programs such as the
                        International Coastal Cleanup Program and the Destructive Fishing Reform
                        Program. Membership information is also available.

Contact: imaphil@mnl.sequel.net

International Marine Mammal Association

URL: http://www.imma.org/

Summary: IMMA is a nonprofit organization that promotes the conservation of marine
                        mammals and their habitats internationally. This site provides conservation
                        factsheets, marine mammal factsheets, conservation guidelines, news articles, and
                        educational packages and resources.

Contact: ccosgrove@imma.org

International Marine Mammal Project

URL: http://www.earthisland.org/immp/immp.html

Summary: IMMP is dedicated to making oceans safe for marine mammals throughout the
                        world and to promoting international sustainable fishing. This site provides data
                        about eradicating dolphin mortality caused by the international tuna fishing
                        industry, eliminating the use of driftnets, and ending tuna purse-seine fishers from
                        encircling dolphins in their nets. There is an archive of articles from Ocean Alert
                        and the Free Willy News located at this site.

Contact: marinemammal@earthisland.org

International Oceanographic Foundation

URL: http://www.rsmas.miami.edu/iof/

Summary: IOF is a nonprofit organization whose goal is to teach people about the oceans so
                        that they will know how important oceans are to human life. This site offers
                        information on oceanography, shipwrecks, and oil spills. There are pointers to other
                        oceanographic sites and a bibliography of oceanographic hardtop resources.

Contact: dtyrrell@rsmas.miami.edu

International Otter Survival Fund

URL: http://www.smo.uhi.ac.uk/~dobhran/iosf/iosf_home.html

Summary: The IOSF is dedicated to saving otters by protecting their habitats and supporting researchers working to rehabilitate otters worldwide. Two projects have been set up to study otter habitats in India and Russia. Information located at this site includes several issues of the IOSF newsletter, membership data and a link to the Skye Environmental Centre.

Contact: iosf@AOL.com

International Primate Protection League (IPPL)

URL: http://www.ippl.org/

Summary: The IPPL site has information on protecting gorillas and other primates from extinction. The Faq describes actions taken by the IPPL every year from its inception in 1973. Other data includes membership data, images, time-sensitive issues for volunteers, sample articles from their newsletter, which is sent only to members, and an archive of important older articles.

Contact: info@ippl.org

International Research Institute for Climate Prediction

URL: http://iri.ldeo.columbia.edu/

Summary: IRI's goal is to assess and develop climate forecasts, and to foster the application of such climate forecasts to the explicit benefit of society. At this site you will find training and visitor programs, a climate data library, climate monitoring data, forecasts, annual reports, a list of speakers for their lecture series, employment opportunities, and a link to the IRI Ocean Expo 98 site in Portugal.

Contact: help@iri.ldeo.columbia.edu

International Rivers Network

URL: http://www.irn.org/index.html

Summary: IRN is an organization devoted to halting the construction of destructive river development projects worldwide and promoting sound river management to save the river inhabitants. This site contains information on the ecological importance of rivers, IRN's current campaigns, events, other river organizations, a library of river publications, and an online journal.

Contact: irnweb@irn.org

International Satellite Land Surface Climatology Project (ISLSCP)

URL: http://www.cais.com/gewex/islscp.html

Summary: ISLSCP is a United Nations project that uses satellite information to understand how carbon, energy, and water are exchanged between the atmosphere and terrestrial biosphere. Information at this site includes ISLSCP background, activities, and project status plus workshop data and conference announcements.

Contact: Pavel Kabat: kabat@sc.dlo.nl

International Snow Leopard Trust

URL: http://www.serv.net/islt/home2.html

Summary: ISLT is a nonprofit foundation committed to the conservation of the endangered snow leopard and its mountain ecosystem through a balanced approach that considers the needs of people and the environment. This site provides data on snow leopard characteristics, habitat, and prey; information on ISLT programs, publications, and conferences.

Contact: islt@serv.net

International Society for Ecological Modelling (ISEM)

URL: http://ecomod.tamu.edu/~ecomod/isem.html

Summary: ISEM fosters the international exchange of ideas, scientific results, and general knowledge in the area of the application of systems analysis, and simulation in ecology and the management of natural resources. This site contains membership information, conference data, material on workshops, and online issues of ISEM's newsletter, "ECOMOD."

Contact: wolfgang@stat.tamu.edu

International Society for Environmental Ethics

URL: http://www.cep.unt.edu/ISEE.html

Summary: The International Society for Environmental Ethics is concerned with environmental philosophy and ecoethics. This site contains information on membership, several bibliographies of books on environmental ethics, issues of their newsletter from 1990 to the present, and a full description of their syllabus project.

Contact: J. Baird Callicott: callicott@unt.edu

International Society of Arboriculture

URL: http://www.ag.uiuc.edu/%7Eisa/

Summary: ISA is a society created to keep members of the tree care industry up-to-date on tree care issues. Some of the Society's goals are to improve the quality of arboriculture practice, to promote research and increase the knowledge of urban tree care, and to increase public awareness of the benefits of trees and proper tree care. This site includes materials on what arborists do, the benefits of trees, tree care, insect problems, and recognizing tree hazards. There are also journal and newsletter abstracts and articles, a searchable bibliography, conference announcements, press releases, and a calendar of events located at this site.

Contact: isa@isa-arbor.com

International Solar Center

URL: http://emsolar.ee.tu-berlin.de/iscb/home.html

Summary: ISC's aim is to reduce the destructive environmental impact of producing power that contributes to climate change, by creating renewable, efficient energy sources. This site contains information about the Center and its membership and a calendar of solar events. It also has an index of environmental newsletters, bulletin boards, and discussion groups with brief descriptions. There is more information in the German language pages than in the English pages.

Contact: wwwsolar@emsolar.ee.TU-Berlin.DE

International Solar Energy Society

URL:	http://www.ises.org/
Summary:	ISES is the most prominent organization in the field of research and the use of renewable energy. This site contains information on the organization, its members, and its mission. There are also lists of energy congresses, international projects, and environmental news items at this location.
Contact:	hq@ises.org

International Union for the Conservation of Nature

URL:	http://w3.iprolink.ch/iucnlib/
Summary:	IUCN is an international conservation organization that was originally established in France to protect nature. It is now comprised of many government agencies and worldwide environmental groups. This site contains information on many endangered species, international conferences, programs, legislation, forums, and employment opportunities.
Contact:	toby@troberts.demon.co.uk

International Union of Forestry Research Organizations (IUFRO)

URL:	http://www.ncfes.umn.edu/iufro/
Summary:	IUFRO is a nonprofit, nongovernmental international network of forest scientists whose goal is to promote international cooperation in forestry and forest products research. This site contains information on environmental constraints in forestry, sustainable forestry, and silvaculture. There are meeting announcements, newsletters, and other publication data, material on programs and task forces, and information on SylvaVoc, IUFRO's clearinghouse for multilingual forest terminology at this site.
Contact:	iufro@forvie.ac.at

International Wildlife Coalition - (IWC)

URL: http://www.webcom.com/~iwcwww/welcome.html

Summary: The International Wildlife Coalition is an organization that was created to promote the welfare of wildlife, in order to stop the malicious killing and maiming of animals in the wild and the destruction of their habitat. This site contains information on Canadian baby seals, koalas, kangaroos, and other wildlife.

Contact: iwcadopt@capeonramp.com

International Wolf Center

URL: http://www.wolf.org/

Summary: The International Wolf Center focuses on education about wolves and stewardship of wolves. Some of the information at this site includes population recovery, socioeconomics, international expert perspectives, news and events, articles, management programs, and publications.

Contact: wolfinfo@wolf.org

International Year of the Ocean - 1998

URL: http://ioc.unesco.org/iyo/

Summary: The International Year of the Ocean objective is "to focus and reinforce the attention of the public, governments, and decision makers at large on the importance of the oceans and the marine environment as resources for sustainable development." This site provides information on events and exhibits, data on educational materials, IYO News subscription information, access to the IYO discussion forum, and a frequently asked questions section.

Contact: p.pissierssens@unesco.org

Investigating Wind Energy

URL: http://sln.fi.edu/tfi/units/energy/windguide.html

Summary: This site is a unit of the Franklin Institute Science Museum, which describes aspects of wind energy including whether the wind is friend or foe, and the basics for building the best windmills.

Contact: webteam@sln.fi.edu

Iowa Department of Natural Resources

URL: http://www.state.ia.us/government/dnr/index.html

Summary: The Iowa DNR page contains information on forestry, wildlife, energy recycling, and land management programs. Some of the information at this site includes Iowa's Wildlife Diversity Program, which includes the eastern bluebird and river otters, lists of publications, air and water quality programs, and Iowa recycling directories.

Contact: sprocto@max.state.ia.us

Iowa Raptor Foundation

URL: http://www.cedar-rapids.ia.net/raptor/index.html

Summary: The Iowa Raptor Foundation is committed to preserving raptors and their habitats in Iowa. They sponsor programs for rehabilitating injured raptors, monitoring threatened and endangered raptor species, and educating the public about raptors. This site contains information about raptors, material about the foundation and its programs, and data on grant applications for raptor research.

Contact: Steve Atherton: Steve_Atherton@ail.ccs.k12.ia.us

Iowa's Environment

URL: http://www.cgrer.uiowa.edu/iowa_environment/Iowa_environment.html

Summary: This site contains a large collection of information on Iowa's DNR, EPA efforts to protect the environment in Iowa, National Biological Survey activities in Iowa, U.S. Geological Survey water resources data, and Iowa conservation and environmental organizations.

Contact: Jane Frank: jfrank@cgrer.uiowa.edu

Irish Peatland Conservation Council

URL: http://indigo.ie/~ipcc/

Summary: IPCC is dedicated to the conservation of a representative sample of living, intact Irish bogs, and peatlands. Information furnished at this site includes bog and gardening brochures, a frog survey, data on purchasing bogland nature reserves, and material on how to become a member of IPCC.

Contact: ipcc@indigo.ie

Island Wildlife Natural Care Centre

URL: http://www.islandnet.com/~wildlife/

Summary: Island Wildlife Natural Care Centre is a nonprofit organization whose purpose is to rehabilitate and release wildlife and to educate the public about the interaction of man and wild animals. This site includes information about the Centre, current news, case histories, homeopathic treatments for injured wildlife, statistics of treatment, and an image gallery of wildlife species.

Contact: phocid@aol.com

ISO-14000 Information Center

URL: http://www.iso14000.com/

Summary: This site is sponsored by the Environmental Industry Web Site. It provides an ISO 14000 overview, a list of acronyms used for ISO 14000, articles, business opportunities, education and training, organizations, and publications pertaining to this environmental management standard.

Contact: webmaster2@iso14000.com

Izaak Walton League of America

URL: http://www.iwla.org/

Summary: The Izaak Walton League of America is one of the oldest conservation organizations in the United States. Its members are dedicated to protecting America's soil, air, woods, waters, and wildlife. This site contains information on education programs, legislation, membership in the League, employment opportunities, and current events.

Contact: general@iwla.org

Jane Goodall Institute

URL: http://www.gsn.org/gsn/proj/jgi/index.html

Summary: This site contains information on Jane Goodall, her lecture tours, and Institute membership information. There is a brief description of how you can become a chimpanzee guardian included in the membership data. Information on programs for youth and documents about parks and chimpanzee sanctuaries can also be found at this location.

Contact: jgi@gsn.org

Japan Marine Science and Technology Center (JAMSTEC)

URL: http://www.jamstec.go.jp/index-e.html

Summary: JAMSTEC was created to promote marine science and technology in Japan. This
                site contains information on programs such as Deep Sea Research, Exploration
                Systems, Ocean Research and Ocean Observation Technology. Information on the
                history and development of JAMSTEC, its research, and its research vessels is also
                available here.

Contact: www-admin@jamstec.go.jp

Jardin Gaia

URL: http://skynet.ul.ie/~gwh/jg/index.html

Summary: Jardin Gaia is the first official wildlife rescue and rehabilitation center in Costa
                Rica. Information at this site includes projects, animals at the Center, a catalog of
                the birds and animals in the Manuel Antonia National Park, volunteer
                opportunities, and ways you can help.

Contact: wildlife@cariari.ucr.ac.cr

Jefferson Land Trust

URL: http://www.olympus.net/community/saveland/saveland.htm

Summary: The Jefferson Land Trust is a nonprofit organization dedicated to conserving public
                land and protecting our natural ecosystems and wildlife habitats for their own sake
                and for the enjoyment of future generations. This site includes information about
                land trusts, how to participate in acquiring and donating land, conservation
                easements, and current projects.

Contact: saveland@olympus.net

John M. Judy Environmental Education Consortium

URL: http://www.utm.edu/departments/ed/cece/john.html

Summary: The purpose of the John M. Judy Environmental Education Consortium is to
                cultivate and augment conservation education for persons preparing to teach or
                become environmental consultants. This site contains information about the
                Consortium and those who are affiliated with it.

Contact: Maurice Houston Field: mfield@utm.edu

John Muir Trust

URL: http://www.ma.hw.ac.uk/jmt/

Summary: The goal of the John Muir Trust is to protect and restore Britain's remaining wild places for their own sake, for the wildlife that live there, and for future generations to enjoy. Some of the information at this site includes membership in the Trust, policy papers on acquisition of land, land management and human resources, and data on the JMT properties.

Contact: Denis Mollison: denis@ma.hw.ac.uk

Joint Center for Energy Management (JCEM)

URL: http://bechtel.colorado.edu/Research_Groups/Jcem/jcemmain.html

Summary: The JCEM site contains information on energy research, development, and education. Included at this site is information on research activities, abstracts of papers, and menus of energy related course offerings such as thermal analysis of buildings, building computer simulations, solar building design, and building system controls.

Contact: Michael J. Brandemuehl: jceminfo@colorado.edu

Journey North

URL: http://www.learner.org/jnorth/index.html

Summary: Journey North is an educational site containing information on wildlife migration as it is happening. There is a wealth of migratory information on the bald eagle, hummingbirds, loons, manatees, Monarch butterflies, orioles, robins, whooping cranes, and whales.

Contact: info@learner.org

Kansas Environmental Almanac

URL: http://www.idir.net/~chsjones/

Summary: This site contains information on Kansas air quality, surface water quality, land and climate, agriculture, water usage, public and private well contamination, precipitation acidity, solid waste management, contaminant spills, toxic chemical releases, threatened, and endangered species, and energy production and consumption. There are data tables with dates and figures, aquifer maps, and government spending tables, with comparisons to other states at this site.

Contact: Charles Jones: chsjones@idir.net

Kentucky Department of Fish and Wildlife Resources

URL: http://www.state.ky.us/agencies/fw/kdfwr.htm

Summary: As stewards of Kentucky's fish and wildlife resources and their habitats, the Department increases wildlife diversity and promotes its sustainable use. This site contains annual reports, information on fisheries, wildlife, threatened and endangered species, and a calendar of events. Information on the Salato Wildlife Education Center is also located at this site.

Contact: infocenter@mail.state.ky.us

Kentucky Water Resources Research Institute

URL: http://www.uky.edu/WaterResources/

Summary: The Kentucky Water Resources Research Institute at the University of Kentucky is dedicated to research on water resources and water related environmental issues. Information available at this site includes newsletters, research programs, symposium proceedings, and reports on federal water projects in Kentucky.

Contact: sendlei@pop.uky.edu

Kentucky Water Watch

URL: http://www.state.ky.us/nrepc/water/wwhomepg.htm

Summary: The Kentucky Water Watch program is made up of volunteers committed to protecting streams, rivers, lakes, and wetlands. The volunteer projects located at this site are water quality monitoring projects, community education initiatives, and community leadership and action. There are also lists of people and organizations who are involved in the program and links to other Kentucky water related sites located here.

Contact: kywwp@igc.org

Kola Ecogeochemistry

URL: http://dec01.ngu.no/Kola/index.html

Summary: The aims of Kola Ecogeochemistry are to trace atmospheric pollutants and show their effects while forming international partnerships to curb their destructive effects. Materials found at this site include a bibliographical database, regional geochemical maps, a publications list, and information on projects and project partners in Norway, Russia, and Finland.

Contact: patrice.de.caritat@ngu.no tor.finne@ngu.no jo.halleraker@ngu.no

Lake Pontchartrain Basin Foundation

URL: http://www.saveourlake.org/

Summary: The Lake Pontchartrain Basin Foundation is a membership-based citizens' organization dedicated to restoring and preserving the Lake Pontchartrain Basin. This site contains information about Lake Pontchartrain and its ecosystem, its business partners in saving the lake, environmental articles, and volunteer and membership opportunities.

Contact: lpbfeduc@communique.net

Land Conservancy of San Luis Obispo County

URL: http://www.slonet.org/vv/land_con/

Summary: The Land Conservancy of San Luis Obispo County is a grassroots land trust whose goal is the conservation and protection of open space and its resources. This site contains information on land conservancy, an online newsletter, data on farmland and conservation easements, county maps, and material about the San Luis Obispo Creek Task Force.

Contact: land-conservancy@slonet.org

Land Trust Alliance

URL: http://www.lta.org/

Summary: LTA is dedicated to voluntary land conservation for the preservation of natural systems to benefit communities. Information available at this site includes land trust standards and practices, LTA current news, employment opportunities, membership material, and conference announcements.

Contact: Use form at Web site: http://www.lta.org/feedback.html

League of Conservation Voters

URL: http://www.lcv.org/

Summary: LCV holds members of Congress culpable for their actions on environmental issues by publishing a National Environmental Scorecard for each Congressional year. You may check out your Congress members' environmental voting records back to 1993 at this site.

Contact: lcv@lcv.org

Leave No Trace

URL: http://www.lnt.org/

Summary: Leave No Trace is sponsored by the National Outdoor Leadership School. The mission of the Leave No Trace program is to create a nationally recognized educational system that promotes land stewardship, minimum-impact skills, and wilderness ethics. This site contains data about wildland ethics and principles, desert and canyon use, back country horse use, and rock climbing. A schedule of courses and the full text of the current LNT newsletter are also included.

Contact: lnt@nols.edu

LIFE

URL: http://life.csu.edu.au/

Summary: LIFE is an Australian biology and environmental information site. Materials at this site include conference abstracts, biodiversity data, information on ecological organizations, and conference announcements.

Contact: David G. Green: dgreen@csu.edu.au

Lincolnshire Trust

URL: http://www.enterprise.net/wildlife/lincstrust/

Summary: The Lincolnshire Trust is a voluntary, charitable organization that cares for Lincolnshire's wildlife and countryside. It is one of 47 such Trusts in the United Kingdom and is affiliated with the Royal Society for Nature Conservation. This site provides information about the work of the Trust and includes press releases, membership and volunteer data, reports on conservation issues, and fact sheets on such topics as frogs, toads, newts, composting, feeding wild birds, and butterfly gardens.

Contact: lincstrust@cix.compulink.co.uk

Living On Earth

URL: http://www.loe.org/

Summary: Living On Earth is a National Public Radio program that discusses pollution and polluters and offers alternative action. At this site you will find the agenda for the current week, transcripts for weeks back to January 1996, a listing of radio stations carrying the program and transmission times for all fifty states, Washington, D.C., and Guam. There is also information on politics and environment, sustainable agriculture, health and ecology, endangered species, and where to send your story ideas.

Contact: loe@npr.org

Lloyd Center for Environmental Studies

URL: http://www.ultranet.com/~lloydctr/

Summary: The Lloyd Center for Environmental Studies is a nonprofit organization that provides environmental education programs to cultivate public awareness of the ecology underlying southern New England estuaries and watersheds. This site contains information on their exhibits, trails, educational programs, research programs, public outreach programs, and data on becoming a member. Some of the highlights are an interactive "touch tank," a weekly *Plover Update*, and an interactive teaching lab.

Contact: lloydctr@lloydctr.ultranet.com

Louisiana Department of Agriculture & Forestry

URL: http://www.ldaf.state.la.us/

Summary: The Louisiana Department of Agriculture & Forestry is dedicated to the promotion, protection, and advancement of agriculture and forestry. This site contains information on boll weevil eradication, environmental education programs, and data on mite-resistant honeybees.

Contact: Bob Odom: bobodom@ldaf.state.la.us

Louisiana Energy & Environmental Resource & Information Center

URL: http://www.leeric.lsu.edu/

Summary: LEERIC is a cooperative effort of the LSU Center for Coastal, Energy & Environmental Resources, The Louisiana Department of Natural Resources, and the Louisiana Department of Environmental Quality (LDEQ). The mission of LEERIC is to educate the public on environmental and energy related issues to support informed, scientific based planning, and decision-making. This site contains educational materials in the form of programs, curricula and workshops, business information on speakers, exhibits, and presentations.

Contact: bradley@www.leeric.lsu.edu

Lower Rio Grande Ecosystem Initiative

URL: http://www.msc.nbs.gov/lrgrei/lrgrei.html

Summary: This site contains material on the Rio Grande and its natural resources including a bibliography, partners in preserving and protecting those resources, information on the Transboundary Resource Inventory Program, and a description of its general conservation status.

Contact: Chris Henke: Chenke@msc.nbs.gov

LTER (US Long-Term Ecological Research) Network

URL: http://lternet.edu/

Summary: Established by the National Science Foundation, LTER promotes research on long-term ecological phenomena in the United States, supporting synthesis and comparative research. The LTER site provides information about their projects and programs, conferences, a searchable bibliography of all citations used in their research, a list of new LTER publications, and links to other LTER Web servers.

Contact: helper@LTERnet.edu

Macaw Landing Foundation

URL: http://www.cybernw.com/~mlf/index.html

Summary: The Macaw Landing Foundation is dedicated to protecting the endangered macaw, which is threatened by the destruction of its habitat in the rainforest and by capture for the pet industry. This site contains the MLF newsletter, a list of endangered and extinct macaws, bird images, and membership information.

Contact: mlf@cnnw.net

Maine Department of Conservation

URL: http://www.state.me.us/doc/dochome.htm

Summary: The Maine Department of Conservation is a consolidated agency consisting of the Bureau of Parks and Recreation, the Forestry Department, and other agencies. Their goal is to enhance the land and water of Maine. At this site you will find information about parks, public lands, natural areas programs, and regulations on land use. There is also a new Natural Resources Information and Mapping section at this site.

Contact: webmaster_doc@state.me.us

Maine Department of Environmental Protection

URL: http://www.state.me.us/dep/mdephome.htm

Summary: The Maine DEP site contains information about programs involving ozone, lakes, pollution prevention, plus educational materials, maps, regulatory information, and newsletters. There are also factsheets, issue profiles, activity reports, and employment opportunities at this site.

Contact: webmaster_dep@state.me.us

Maine Department of Inland Fisheries & Wildlife

URL: http://www.state.me.us/ifw/homepage.htm

Summary: The Maine Department of Inland Fisheries & Wildlife page contains information on Maine's youth conservation camps, wildlife programs for schools, wildlife programs for educators, the Gray Game Farm and Visitor Center, and Maine's Outdoor Heritage Fund. There is endangered species data here as well as press releases and safety information.

Contact: webmaster_ifw@state.me.us

Mangrove Replenishment Initiative

URL: http://mangrove.org/

Summary: The objective of the Mangrove Replenishment Initiative is to promote biodiversity and alleviate the effects of pollution on the environment. Information found at this site includes Bob Riley's replenishment methodology, tides and waves, planting simulation, and a planting guide. There are many images of the projects at this site.

Contact: riley@mangrove.org

Manomet Center for Conservation Science

URL: http://www.manomet.org/

Summary: Manomet is a nonprofit research center committed to maintaining, restoring, and protecting the diversity and abundance of wild species and natural systems. Manomet consists of the Avian Conservation Division, Marine Fisheries Division, Conservation Forestry Division, and the Wetlands Conservation Division. Each division has its own mission, goals, projects, and programs.

Contact: jmcorven@manomet.org

Marine Biological Association

URL: http://www1.npm.ac.uk/mba/

Summary: MBA promotes scientific research in all aspects of sea life. This site features MBA research programs, educational courses, membership data and objectives, information on biodiversity initiatives, awards, grants, and visitor's programs.

Contact: CDE@wpo.nerc.ac.uk

Marine Conservation Society

URL: http://www.mcsuk.mcmail.com/

Summary: The Marine Conservation Society of the UK is dedicated to bringing issues of concern and threats to both marine wildlife and the wider marine and coastal environment to the attention of the public, media, politicians, and government agencies. This site contains information on becoming a member, descriptions of projects, a marine conservation book list, and press releases from 1996 to the present.

Contact: mcsuk@mcmail.com

Marine Environmental Research Institute

URL: http://downeast.net/nonprof/meri/

Summary: MERI is a nonprofit organization concerned with protecting the health and biodiversity of the international marine environment by tackling such issues as marine pollution, endangered species, and habitat degradation affecting marine life. This site contains MERI research project data, news updates, employment opportunities, and membership information.

Contact: meri@downeast.net

Marine Mammal Center

URL: http://www.tmmc.org/

Summary: The Marine Mammal Center rescues and rehabilitates marine mammals in distress, including seals, sea lions, whales, dolphins, and sea otters. This site includes a bibliography of scientific papers available on request, descriptions of education programs, a list of universities offering marine mammalogy programs, information on many endangered sea mammals, an adopt-a-seal program, and volunteer data.

Contact: com@tmmc.org

Marine Mammal Stranding Center

UL: http://www.mmsc.org/index1.html

Summary: The Marine Mammal Stranding Center rescues stranded marine mammals and sea turtles in the State of New Jersey. This site contains phone numbers to call to report a stranding, information on becoming a member, directions for visiting the Center, a quarterly newsletter and news archive, and marine animal information.

Contact: dolphins@acy.digex.net

Maryland Department of Natural Resources

URL: http://www.dnr.state.md.us/

Summary: The Maryland DNR site offers descriptions and maps of all the state parks, forests, and wildlife management areas in the state and the recreational ventures available there. This site contains information on bays and streams, parks and lands, educational resources, Maryland DNR publications, fisheries, trees and forests, and wildlife.

Contact: mddnr@erols.com

Maryland Forests Association

URL:	http://mdforests.org/
Summary:	The Maryland Forests Association is a nonprofit citizen's group that promotes the preservation of Maryland's natural resources and forest lands. This site contains articles from the column "Maryland Forests," MFA accomplishments, issues and concerns, data on the Sustainable Forestry Initiative, membership and scholarship information, lessons in silviculture, and Maryland forest facts.
Contact:	mfa@hereintown.net

Massachusetts Department of Fisheries, Wildlife and Environmental Law Enforcement

URL:	http://www.state.ma.us/dfwele/
Summary:	The major programs and divisions of this state department are the Division of Fisheries and Wildlife, the Division of Law Enforcement, the Division of Marine Fisheries, and the Riverways Programs. Each division has its own overview, news releases, and other pertinent information.
Contact:	Steve McRae: steve.mcrae@state.ma.us

Matheson Wetlands Preserve

URL:	http://www.netoasis.com/moab/matheson/index.htm
Summary:	Water is the defining element of the Scott M. Matheson Preserve in Moab, Utah. Th ponds and marshy areas support beavers, frogs and river otters, which are animals not often found in the desert. More than 175 species of birds have been seen here and many build nests and raise their young here. This site holds material on the history of the Matheson Preserve, a calendar of events, information on how the Preserve is managed, data on visiting hours and field trips, and promotional information. Naturalist-guided walks are held every Saturday morning, March through October.
Contact:	webmaster@netoasis.com

Mediterranean Oceanic Data Base

URL: http://modb.oce.ulg.ac.be/

Summary: MODB delivers advanced data products for oceanographic research in the
                Mediterranean Sea. Some of those products are a historical hydrographic database,
                seasonal gridded data sets, and a world ocean gridded bathymetry. The datasets are
                available through the World Wide Web or ftp.

Contact: support@modb.oce.ulg.ac.be

Medomak Valley Land Trust

URL: http://www.midcoast.com/~wpl/mvlt/

Summary: MVLT is a private, nonprofit organization dedicated to preserving the natural
                resources of the Medomak River watershed through education, conservation
                easement, and land gifts. This site contains the text of the Natural Resources
                Inventory, the most recent MVLT newsletter, and a calendar of events.

Contact: rsm@midcoast.com

Mendocino County Ecology Web

URL: http://www.pacific.net/~dglaser/ENVIR/envir.html

Summary: This site offers facts about the many environmental groups in Mendocino County,
                current issues in the county, articles from the Mendocino Environmental Center
                newsletter, current events, and a description of the county.

Contact: Dale Glaser: dglaser@pacific.net

Messinger Woods Wildlife Care and Education Center

URL: http://members.aol.com/messngrwds/index.htm

Summary: Messinger Woods is a nonprofit group located in Holland, New York, dedicated
                to achieving excellence in the field of Wildlife Rehabilitation and Education. This
                site includes excerpts from their newsletter, a calendar of events, and a scrapbook
                of wildlife images.

Contact: Messinger_Woods@msn.com

Michigan Department of Environmental Quality

URL: http://www.deq.state.mi.us/

Summary: The MDEQ's mission is to "drive improvements in environmental quality for the protection of public health and natural resources to benefit current and future generations." Their site contains clean air information, their Grant and Loan Catalog, press releases, and a searchable database of reports.

Contact: deq-webmaster@state.mi.us

Michigan Department of Natural Resources

URL: http://www.dnr.state.mi.us/

Summary: The Michigan DNR site contains information on the state environmental agencies, programs, and the governor's executive orders on the environment. Newsletters, future plans, employment opportunities, and pointers to state environmental agency pages can be found here. Michigan environmentalists and others interested in state programs for ecology and conservation will find much of interest at this site.

Contact: dnr-suggestion-box@state.mi.us

Michigan Environmental Science Board

URL: http://www.mesb.org/

Summary: MESB is an advisory board that renders advice to the Governor and state agencies pertaining to issues affecting the protection and management of the state's environment and natural resources. This site contains information about MESB, reports on air quality, fisheries, radioactive waste, the impacts of lead and mercury on the environment, the effect of chlorine on human health, and links to other Michigan environmental sites.

Contact: mesb@state.mi.us

Michigan Forest Association

URL: http://www.spring-board.com/two/mfa/intro.htm

Summary: The MFA is a nonprofit group that represents the interests of Michigan forests and forest owners. They are committed to the prudent use of forest resources. This site contains information about the Association and its sponsors; excerpts from their publication, *Michigan Forests*, and information about several of Michigan State University's forest projects.

Contact: lrudel@i-star.com

Michigan Pulp and Paper Pollution Prevention Program

URL: http://www.deq.state.mi.us/ead/p2sect/p5/

Summary: The Michigan Pulp and Paper Pollution Prevention Program is a coalition of forest product companies in Michigan dedicted to environmental stewardship. This site provides information about the P5 initiative, annual reports, a list of member companies, and an intern project summary.

Contact: Wendy Fitzner: fitznerw@state.mi.us

Michigan United Conservation Clubs

URL: http://www.voyager.net/mucc/

Summary: MUCC is the largest, nonprofit statewide conservation organization in the United States, and is devoted to the protection and enhancement of Michigan's natural resources. This site contains a monthly *Natural Discovery* section, educational resources, the MUCC Conservation Catalog, information on natural resource employment, a calendar of events, descriptions of MUCC's conservation achievements, and MUCC's legislative agenda for the year.

Contact: mucc@mucc.org

Midwest Renewable Energy Association (MREA)

URL: http://www.the-mrea.org/

Summary: The purpose of MREA is to promote renewable energy and energy efficiency by educating the public about appropriate use of natural resources to meet our energy needs. This site provides information on MREA's annual Energy Fair, including pre-fair workshops and free workshops during the fair. Data on the Sun Chaser mobile renewable energy power source is also available at this site.

Contact: mreainfo@wi-net.com

Milton Keynes Wildlife Hospital

URL: http://www-tec.open.ac.uk/staff/robert/robert.html

Summary: The M.K. Wildlife Hospital site contains information on the rescue of wildlife in the United Kingdom. It includes data on the work of the Hospital, information about permanent residents who cannot be released into the wild, documentation on how you can sponsor a permanent resident, and a description of a normal day at the Hospital. Pictures of birds available for sponsorship are included here.

Contact: Robert Seaton: R.W.Seaton@open.ac.uk

Mineral Policy Center

URL: http://www.mineralpolicy.org/index.html

Summary: MPC is a nonprofit organization whose mission is to prevent environmental pollution caused by irresponsible mining and to clean up the pollution caused by mining in the past. This site contains current press releases, data on their internship program, a mining conservation directory, a list of MPC publications, sections on mining law, mine images, mining alerts, and information on joining MPC.

Contact: mpc-us@msn.com.

Minnesota Department of Natural Resources

URL: http://www.dnr.state.mn.us/

Summary: The Minnesota DNR page contains a quantity of information on water quality, wetlands, fisheries, Minnesota's ecological regions, woodlands and wildlife, the Minnesota Natural Heritage Program, scientific and natural areas, Project Wild, education and youth programs, minerals, trails, waterways, and climatology.

Contact: webmaster@dnr.state.mn.us

Minnesotans for An Energy-Efficient Economy (ME3)

URL: http://www.me3.org/

Summary: ME3 is an organization dedicated to improving the quality of life in Minnesota through the use of renewable energy and energy efficiency. Their *Sustainable Minnesota* site contains climate change documents, a newsletter archive, energy information and legislation, membership data, and ME3 project information.

Contact: John Bailey: bailey@ilsr.org

Minnesota Pollution Control Agency

URL: http://www.pca.state.mn.us/

Summary: This site includes a great deal of information on air, water, and waste pollution in Minnesota. It also contains data on regulations and permits, clean-up techniques, prevention, publications, and programs to protect Minnesota's environment. The MPCA site has a calendar of events, information for children, news releases, training opportunities, and conference information.

Contact: webmaster@pca.state.mn.us

Missouri Audubon Council

URL: http://www.audubon.org/chapter/mo/mo

Summary: The purpose of the Missouri Audubon Council is to represent the interests of the 14 chapters of the National Audubon Society on a state level. This site includes the Council's legislative actions, publications, meeting minutes, and educational initiatives.

Contact: davebedan@sockets.net

Missouri Coalition for the Environment

URL: http://www.moenviron.org/index.htm

Summary: The Missouri Coalition for the Environment is a citizens' organization that provides environmental information and education on issues that affect the state of Missouri. This site contains information on their citizen action campaigns, data on the (not so) Wise Use program, a calendar of events, and material on sustainable living.

Contact: moenviron@aol.com

Missouri Department of Conservation

URL: http://www.conservation.state.mo.us/

Summary: The MDC mission is to protect and manage the fish, forest, and wildlife resources of Missouri and to preserve them for the education and enjoyment of the public. This site contains materials on wildlife and endangered species, educational program data, tips for landowners, a calendar of events, a teacher's page, and a conservation atlas for visiting county conservation sites in Missouri.

Contact: internet@mail.conservation.state.mo.us

Missouri Prairie Foundation

URL: http://www.moprairie.org/

Summary: The Missouri Prairie Foundation is a land conservancy that purchases prairie tracts for conservation and preservation. This site contains information on current events, conferences, the threatened greater prairie chicken, public prairies of Missouri, membership data, and the Stilwell Prairie acquisition and history.

Contact: GFreeman@Mail.Coin.Missouri.EDU

Mmarie

URL: http://www.kuleuven.ac.be/mmarie/

Summary: This is a Belgian site dedicated to the application of high performance computing techniques for the modelling of marine ecosystems. Mmarie contains descriptions of projects, bibliographies of researchers, research lists, and links to courses and related events.

Contact: Hugo.Embrechts@cc.kuleuven.ac.be

Monarch Watch

URL: http://www.monarchwatch.org/

Summary: The goals of Monarch Watch are to further science education and advance the conservation of monarch butterflies by interesting as many people as possible in a cooperative study of the monarch's fall migration. There is a lot of information at this site, including membership data, a monarch faq, reports on previous years' migrations, current monarch sightings, monarch life history, and information on the endangerment of the monarch migration.

Contact: monarch@ukans.edu

Montana Natural Resource Information System

URL: http://nris.msl.mt.gov/

Summary: This site contains information from the Montana State Library on the natural resources of Montana including the Montana Natural Heritage Program, which is comprised of data on fish, amphibians, reptiles, birds, and mammals that may be endangered, and plants that are of special concern in Montana. The Montana Water Information System is also part of this site and includes data on surface water, groundwater, water quality, precipitation, snow pack, and water rights.

Contact: http://nris.state.mt.us/comment.html

Montanas Verdes

URL: http://www.xs4all.nl/~monver/

Summary: Montanas Verdes is dedicated to saving the rainforests in the Ecuadorian Andes by socio-economic development. One of their projects is the Toronche Pilot-project, which introduces sustainable and ecological land use systems to farmers in Ecuador. This site has maps of Latin America, Ecuador, and the world, and links to other sites.

Contact: Ing. J.A.M. Schepers: monver@xs4all.nl

Monterey Bay Aquarium-At the CoRE

URL: http://www.mbayaq.org/atc/index.htm

Summary: The At the CoRE segment of the Monterey Bay Aquarium site contains information on conservation projects, field study research programs, and education programs at the aquarium. Some of these studies include the threatened sea otters and other marine mammal projects. There is information on how you can help and membership data located here.

Contact: Use form at site: http://www.mbayaq.org/mail/mail_cmt.htm

Morris Parks and Land Conservancy

URL: http://www.gti.net/mplc/

Summary: Morris Parks and Land Conservancy is a nonprofit organization dedicated to preserving and protecting open land in Morris County, New Jersey. This site contains information on their projects, their environmental scholarship grants, and their newsletter.

Contact: mplc@gti.net

Mote Marine Laboratory

URL: http://www.marinelab.sarasota.fl.us/

Summary: The Mote Marine Laboratory conducts environmental research and rehabilitates marine life to be released back into its habitat. Materials at this site include projects, research, weather news, a red tide update, courses offered, a link to the Mote Marine Aquarium, distance learning programs, fact sheets about marine animals, volunteer data, and membership information.

Contact: Don Hayward: don@marinelab.sarasota.fl.us

Mountain Institute

URL: http://www.mountain.org/

Summary: The Mountain Institute is a nonprofit organization dedicated to the preservation of mountain environment through scientific research. At this site you can learn about their natural resource conservation programs, cultural conservation programs and educational programs. There is data on how you can get involved and also information on children's programs located here.

Contact: summit@mountain.org

Mountain Lion Foundation

URL: http://www.atanda.com/mlf/

Summary: The Mountain Lion Foundation is a nonprofit conservation and education organization committed to safeguarding the mountain lion, its wild habitat, and the wildlife that shares that habitat. In its efforts to preserve the mountain lion, the Foundation works with legislative and conservation groups. This site includes cougar facts, information on how to stop poachers, data on how states voted on wildlife issues, excerpts from *Cougar: The American Lion*, and information on how to join MLF.

Contact: mlf@mountainlion.org

Mr. Solar Home Page

URL: http://www.mrsolar.com/

Summary: The Mr. Solar Home Page gives access to many frequently asked questions and their answers about alternative energy sources. This site also provides specifications for making your own equipment for using alternative energy in your home. French and Spanish language versions of this site are also available.

Contact: Charlie Collins: CharlieCollins@mrsolar.com

Namibia Animal Rehabilitation Research and Education Centre

URL: http://www.apple.com.na/NGO/Narrec/narrec.html

Summary: NARREC is Namibia's only wild animal rehabilitation center. Its focus is on the treatment, care, and rehabilitation of wildlife, with special emphasis on environmental education. This site includes information on NARREC, wildlife rehabilitation, education programs on the local environment, and current projects.

Contact: Joris Koman: joris@narrec.mac.alt.na

Napa County Resource Conservation District

URL: http://www.napanet.net/~rcdstaff/index.html

Summary: The goals of the Napa County RCD are to reduce soil erosion, to enhance wildlife habitats, to protect and augment water quality, and to promote land stewardship and sustainable agriculture. This site contains data on the Napa River Watershed Monitoring Program, the Napa River Watershed Owner's Manual, an Adopt-A-Watershed curriculum program, a computer model of the Napa River, and a map of the Napa River Watershed.

Contact: 102223.2012@compuserve.com

NAPEnet - National Association of Physicians for the Environment

URL: http://www.napenet.org/

Summary: NAPE is an organization of national, state, and local medical societies plus individual doctors who wish to study and handle the effects of pollution on humans. NAPE dispenses information about these effects to patients, other physicians, and the general public and informs them about ways to prevent, reduce, or eliminate these effects. NAPE's theme is "Pollution prevention is disease prevention." This site contains an Environment and Health Directory, conference reports and news releases, UV Index documents, and other educational materials.

Contact: nape@napenet.org

National Agricultural Pest Information System (NAPIS)

URL: http://www.ceris.purdue.edu:80/napis/

Summary: NAPIS is the database for the Cooperative Agricultural Pest Survey and is maintained by the Center for Environmental and Regulatory Information Systems (CERIS). This site contains pest information, the *NAPIS User Guide*, the *CAPS Program Guidebook*, and the *APHIS Environmental Manual*. There is also a list of government certified nurseries.

Contact: Jim Pheasant: pheasant@ceris.purdue.edu

National Arborist Association

URL: http://www.natlarb.com/

Summary: NAA is a trade association of commercial tree care firms that develops safety and
                educational programs, standards of tree care practice, and management information
                for arboriculture firms worldwide. This site provides information on caring for
                trees, data on the Association, product catalogs, press releases, conference data, and
                a calendar of events.

Contact: NAA@natlarb.com

The National Association of Environmental Professionals

URL: http://www.enfo.com/NAEP/

Summary: NAEP is a multi-disciplinary association that works for the advancement of persons
                in the environmental professions. This site contains data on the Association,
                including regional and student chapters, a conference home page, regulatory news,
                a library of articles, a silent auction, and information on joining the NAEP listserv.

Contact: waterman@enfo.com

National Association of State Foresters

URL: http://sso.org/nasf/nasf.html

Summary: State Foresters supply management and protection services on over two-thirds of
                the nation's forests and provide landowners with help managing their forests. This
                site contains information about the Association, including a directory of members,
                the text of NASF newsletters, meeting announcements, and position
                announcements.

Contact: nasf@sso.org

National Audubon Society

URL: http://www.audubon.org/

Summary: The National Audubon Society was founded to stop the senseless slaughter and extinction of birds and other animal and plant species. It is named for John James Audubon and a short biography of his life resides at this site. There is information here on membership, local chapters, conservation campaigns, educational programs, Audubon wildlife sanctuaries, and electronic field trips. You will also find a list of publications and several booklists at this site.

Contact: administrator@audubon.org

National Center for Atmospheric Research

URL: http://www.ncar.ucar.edu/

Summary: NCAR maintains a number of data archives on atmospheric research, including the SCD Research Data Archives, the ATD Data Archives, UNIDATA, and the Defense Meteorological Satellite Program Data Archive. Other information at this site consists of NCAR resources, education and training, programs, publications, facilities, services, and weather related data.

Contact: webmaster@ucar.edu

National Center for Ecological Analysis and Synthesis

URL: http://www.nceas.ucsb.edu/

Summary: The focus of NCEAS is on research about the structure and dynamics of ecological systems for use by researchers and resource managers relative to environmental issues. This site contains information on current events, ecological software, and the text of NCEAS papers and reports.

Contact: webcontact@nceas.ucsb.edu

National Councils for Sustainable Development

URL: http://www.ncsdnetwork.org/

Summary: National Councils for Sustainable Development (NCSD) embraces the ideal of civil societies becoming partners with government in making policies for the implementation of sustainable development. This site contains regional information on sustainable development events, an NCSD database, an NCSD handbook, and several video presentations.

Contact: ncsd@terra.ecouncil.ac.cr

National Drought Mitigation Center

URL: http://enso.unl.edu/ndmc/

Summary: The NDMC helps individuals and institutions prepare for drought and put plans in place to deal with the effects of drought. Information at this site includes U.S. climate and drought monitoring, data on drought impacts, articles on drought history, policy ideas, plans, publications, and a directory of drought contacts.

Contact: ndmc@enso.unl.edu

National Energy Foundation

URL: http://www.xmission.com/~nef/

Summary: The NEF is a nonprofit organization whose purpose is the development of energy-related instructional materials. The Foundation is supported by businesses, government agencies, associations, and the education community. This site includes many posters, lesson plans, and teaching resource kits that are available for purchase.

Contact: mgm@xmission.com

National Estuary Program

URL: http://www.epa.gov/nep/nep.html

Summary: The National Estuary Program site is sponsored by the EPA's Office of Water. At this site there is information on what estuaries are and what their ecological significance is, an overview of the National Estuary Program, summaries of individual NEP programs, a U.S. map of the NEP watersheds, and the NEP online newsletter. There is also a keyword searchable database of all the documents at this site.

Contact: OWOW-web@epamail.epa.gov

National Ground Water Association

URL: http://www.ngwa.org/

Summary: The National Ground Water Association supplies professional and technical leadership in the responsible development and use of ground water resources. This site contains information on groundwater courses and conferences, tables of contents for several ground water journals, membership data, employment opportunities, a ground water faq, charts, tables, reports, and a catalog of books on related subjects.

Contact: ngwa@ngwa.org

National Institute for Environmental Studies

URL: http://www.nies.go.jp/index.html

Summary: NIES was established to conduct research on the major environmental problems in Japan—namely air and water pollution, soil contamination, noise pollution, and ground subsidence. Materials available at this site include research projects, collaborative projects, meeting announcements, contents of reports, a library of environmental documents, and information on NIES databases. These pages are available in English and Japanese.

Contact: www@nies.go.jp

National Institute of Environmental Health Sciences (NIEHS)

URL: http://www.niehs.nih.gov/

Summary: The NIEHS site contains information on their Scientific Programs, Outreach Programs, their Center Program, National Toxicology Program, and their Superfund Basic Research Program. Other material at this site includes grants and contracts, press releases, pamphlets, employment and training, a calendar of events, and issues of their online journal, *Environmental Health Perspectives* from 1994 to the present.

Contact: webcenter@niehs.nih.gov

National Outdoor Leadership School

URL:	http://www.nols.edu/nols.html
Summary:	NOLS is a wilderness-based school that focuses on leadership and outdoor skills. Some of their course offerings include mountaineering, sea kayaking, sailing, river kayaking, rafting, canoeing, backcountry skiing, and dog sledding. This site contains information on their classes, a frequently asked question section, excerpts from their wilderness publications, and some articles by alumni of the school.
Contact:	admissions@nols.edu

National Parks & Conservation Association

URL:	http://www.npca.org/
Summary:	NPCA is a private, nonprofit, citizen organization devoted to protecting, preserving, and enhancing the U.S. National Park System. This site contains NPCA conservation policies, programs, membership information, press releases, the text of subcommittee testimony, information on park watcher networks, and highlights from *National Parks* magazine.
Contact:	npca@npca.org

National Pollutant Release Inventory

URL:	http://www.ec.gc.ca/press/npri_b_e.htm
Summary:	This site contains a Canadian online database of 178 pollutants found in Canada. NPRI furnishes a mapping tool that permits the analysis of the distribution and amounts of pollutants.
Contact:	thegreenlane@ec.gc.ca

National Pollution Prevention Center for Higher Education (NPPC)

URL:	http://www.snre.umich.edu/nppc/
Summary:	NPPC was created by the U.S. EPA to promote sustainable development by educating students, faculty, and professionals about pollution prevention. This site contains materials on research areas, publications and projects, education and curriculum development, faculty training, internships, and conferences.
Contact:	nppc@umich.edu

National Renewable Energy Laboratory (NREL)

URL: http://www.nrel.gov/

Summary: NREL is the leading laboratory for renewable energy and energy efficiency
                research in the U.S. Some of the projects that they work on involve renewable
                energy technology, developing techniques to clean up our water supplies and
                eradicate toxic wastes. This site lists their research projects and programs,
                information about NREL and its partnerships, publications, educational programs,
                and people.

Contact: webmaster@nrel.gov

National Resources Defense Council

URL: http://www.nrdc.org/nrdc/

Summary: The mission of the NRDC is to save the earth and its people, animals, plants, and
                wildlife habitats. This site contains data on joining NRDC, articles on
                environmental topics, such as air and atmosphere, drinking water, energy, forests,
                recycling, global warming, oceans and marine life, population and consumption,
                and waterways and wetlands. Reports, bulletins, an environmental who's who, and
                the email addresses of U.S. state governors is also included.

Contact: nrdcinfo@nrdc.org

National Sea Grant Depository

URL: http://nsgd.gso.uri.edu

Summary: The National Sea Grant Depository (NSGD) was established as an archive of all
                Sea Grant funded documents. The NSGD staff lends its documents to scientists,
                teachers, fishermen, and many other individuals for research. This site contains a
                searchable publications database; a collection of Sea Grant videos (which may be
                borrowed or purchased), and *Sea Grants Abstracts*, a document which describes
                current acquisitions.

Contact: nsgd@gsosun1.gso.uri.edu

National Sea Grant Program

URL: http://h2o.seagrant.wisc.edu/national/national.html

Summary: The National Sea Grant Program is a network of 29 university-based programs involving Great Lakes, coastal, and marine issues. This site contains pointers to the programs in the Great Lakes Region, the Mid-Atlantic Region, the Northeast Region, the Southeast Region, and the Pacific Region and includes information on aquaculture, exotic species, and water quality.

Contact: jacobs@umbi.umd.edu

National Seal Sanctuary

URL: http://www.sealsanctuary.co.uk/

Summary: The National Seal Sanctuary is a rescue, rehabilitation, and release center for seals in the UK. This site contains many seal photographs, information on seal rescues and releases, and a schedule of times that you may visit.

Contact: seals@sealsanctuary.co.uk

National Society for Clean Air

URL: http://www.mistral.co.uk/nsca/

Summary: NCSA is a nonprofit group made up of organizations and individuals who promote clean air through the reduction of air, water, and land pollution. This site provides information about the Society and their work, including their publications and upcoming events.

Contact: info@nsca.org.uk

National Watchable Wildlife Program

URL: http://www.gorp.com/wwldlife/wwhome.htm

Summary: The National Watchable Wildlife Program is a cooperative effort to help meet a growing national interest in wildlife. This site provides information on programs, tips for watching wildlife, conference announcements, and tips for photographing wildlife. There is also access to the Program's newsletter available at this location.

Contact: wwinfo@gwriters.com

National Wildlife Health Center

URL: http://www.emtc.nbs.gov/nwhchome.html

Summary: The National Wildlife Health Center is a Science Center of the Biological Resources Division of the United States Geological Survey located in Madison, Wisconsin and that is committed to measuring the influence of disease on wildlife and to identifying the causes of wildlife losses. The NWHC pages contain information about wildlife disease, mortality data, the text of the Animal Welfare Act, technical publications data, and project material. There is also a calendar of events, conference information, technical publication information, and metadata database information available at this site.

Contact: Kate Cleary: kate_cleary@nbs.gov

National Wildlife Refuge System

URL: http://bluegoose.arw.r9.fws.gov/

Summary: This is a U.S. Fish and Wildlife site where themes of interest related to wildlife and natural resources management reside. This site contains the contents of the National Wildlife Refuge System Improvement Act of 1997, information on wildlife and plants, habitats, and air quality, publications, and pointers to good wildlife sites.

Contact: Sean_Furniss@mail.fws.gov

National Wildlife Rehabilitators Association

URL: http://www.cloudnet.com/~nwra/main.html

Summary: This site contains information on the Association and what they do, conference data, membership material, articles, and information on becoming involved in wildlife rehabilitation.

Contact: NWRA@cloudnet.com

Native Americans and the Environment

URL: http://conbio.rice.edu/nae/

Summary: This site discusses some of the issues facing Native Americans and the environment including but not limited to agriculture, culture and history, development and energy, fishing, forestry, hunting and fur trapping, nuclear and toxic waste, mining, water rights, and dams. Most topics include a very nice bibliography.

Contact: Alex Dark: dark@hevanet.com

Native Forest Council

URL: http://www.efn.org/~savtrees/savtrees.html

Summary: NFC is a nonprofit organization concerned with saving American forests through legislation, by providing information to activists, and by making the public aware of the destruction of our forests due to logging. The NFC site contains information on our remaining native forests, media articles, and information on how you can become a member and help save the forests.

Contact: savtrees@efn.org

Native Forest Network

URL: http://www.nativeforest.org/

Summary: The Native Forest Network is an organization of forest activists, indigenous peoples, conservation biologists, and nongovernmental groups whose purpose is to protect the earth's remaining forests. This site contains action alerts and links to sites of interest to foresters. Still under construction are links to international forestry news and an NFN directory.

Contact: nfnena@sover.net

NATO SACLANT Undersea Research Centre

URL: http://www.saclantc.nato.int/

Summary: NATO's Supreme Allied Commander Atlantic Undersea Research Centre conducts undersea research to assist major NATO commands in their mission. This site provides information about the Centre's research activities, major assets, publications, and recruitment programmes. It provides form searching of the site and a whois server for personnel.

Contact: www@saclantc.nato.int

Natural Energy Laboratory of Hawaii

URL: http://bigisland.com/nelha/

Summary: NELHA manages comprehensive environmental monitoring of seawater. This site describes the participants in this program and the projects in which they are involved. NELHA's goal is to help businesses utilize Hawaii's natural resources. Information available here includes water quality data, NELHA's Seawater Delivery System information, Ocean Thermal Energy Conversion material, and bibliographical information.

Contact: nelha@ILHawaii.net

Natural Environment Research Council

URL: http://www.nerc.ac.uk/

Summary: The goal of NERC is to facilitate applied research and long-term environmental monitoring of earth, marine, and atmospheric systems and to disseminate the gathered information to scientists and the public. Material available at this site includes environmental data resources, press releases, public events, publications, projects, and educational programs.

Contact: webmaster@nerc.ac.uk

Natural Heritage Programs

URL: http://www.abi.org/

Summary: This sites includes a directory of Natural Heritage Programs, a clickable map of areas in the U.S. and Canada explaining the programs and links to the Nature Conservancy (TNC), Association for Biodiversity Information (ABI), and the U.S. National Biological Service (NBS) who are part of this joint effort. Their goal is to collect standardized data on endangered plants, animals, and ecosystems. There is also a page of related job offerings.

Contact: webmaster@www.heritage.tnc.org

Natural Resource Directory

URL: http://www.nrd.com/

Summary: The Natural Resource Directory is a listing of thousands of environmental and
                health businesses and products available in Los Angeles and Orange County,
                California. It is indexed both alphabetically and by subject. The hard copy is
                available free, although there is a charge for postage.

Contact: Phone: (310) 305-8521 or Fax (310) 823-0300

Natural Resources Services

URL: http://www.northcoast.com/~nrs/

Summary: NRS develops active projects and programs to improve the quality and productivity
                of California's North Coast natural resources. This site provides data on watershed
                management, ecosystem management, vegetation management, tree planting,
                fishery enhancement, and soil erosion. Educational and community outreach
                materials may be accessed here, also.

Contact: nrs@rcaa.org

Nature Conservancy

URL: http://www.tnc.org/

Summary: The Nature Conservancy operates the largest private system of nature sanctuaries
                in the world. Some are tiny and some cover thousands of acres, all of which are
                dedicated to preserving wildlife species and habitats. This site contains an
                abundance of information on conservation issues, endangered species profiles, and
                TNC chapter data. There are materials on field trips, a nature chat area, data on
                state and regional programs, a forum for conservation researchers, volunteer data,
                membership data, and a frequently asked question section also located here.

Contact: Use form at site: http://www.tnc.org/involved/nsforms/comment.html

The Nature Conservancy of Texas

URL: http://www.tnc.org/texas/

Summary: This organization works to preserve and protect the natural animal, plant, air, and water resources of Texas. Information at this site includes documents on Texas bioregions including piney woods, plains and prairies, coastal sand plains, and marshes. There is also data here on scientific research and volunteer opportunities, conservation science, preserves that can be visited and a chat section on birding, fishing, hiking, and plants.

Contact: Lynn McBride: txfo@tnc.org

NatureNet

URL: http://naturenet.net/index.html

Summary: NatureNet is a voluntary enterprise in the United Kingdom that provides practical conservation information. Some of the material furnished at this site includes UK countryside laws, environmental education, biodiversity resources, employment opportunities, an "Ask the Ranger" faq, and volunteer information.

Contact: editor@naturenet.net

Nature Saskatchewan

URL: http://www.unibase.com/~naturesk/

Summary: Nature Saskatchewan is a not-for-profit organization whose goal is to preserve the environment, educate the public, and protect natural ecosystems and their diversity. This site provides data on environmental education, research, and conservation, including programs and publications.

Contact: nature.sask@unibase.com

Nebraska Wildlife Resources

URL: http://ngp.ngpc.state.ne.us/menu.map?304,11

Summary: Some of the projects and programs on the Nebraska Game and Parks Wildlife Resources pages include Nebraska wildlife description, wildlife area regulations, Project WILD, The Wetlands Reserve Program, and Operation Game Thief. There are also wildlife status reports and information about wildlife habitats here.

Contact: Marilyn Tabor: mshea@ngpsun.ngpc.state.ne.us

NEMO - Oceanographic Data Server

URL: http://nemo.ucsd.edu/nemo_front.html

Summary: Nemo is a collection of data sets useful for physical oceanographers. Nemo was created for oceanographers at Scripps Institution of Oceanography and was originally available only to them, but they are trying to make the holdings accessible to the general public.

Contact: David Newton: dnewton@ucsd.edu

New England Wild Flower Society

URL: http://www.ultranet.com/~newfs/newfs.html

Summary: NEWFS owns and manages seven New England wild flower sanctuaries that preserve and protect threatened and endangered New England plant species and habitats. This site contains information on educational programs in horticulture and environmental studies offered by the Society for adults, children, and teachers, as well as data on their 45 acre Garden in the Woods, their New England Plant Conservation Program, and Society membership data.

Contact: news@newfs.org

New England Wildlife Center

URL: http://web.mit.edu/morgana/newc/index.html

Summary: The New England Wildlife Center is a nonprofit organization dedicated to promoting positive values, behaviors, and policies toward wildlife and the environment through education, humane research, and wildlife medicine. This site contains information on undergraduate and graduate internships in widlife care, educational programs, and volunteer data.

Contact: 19 Fort Hill Street, Hingham, MA 02043

New Forests Project

URL: http://www.newforestsproject.com/

Summary: NFP is a program to begin reforestation and reduce deforestation in developing
                countries. The program provides farmers, environmentalists, and communities with
                training and materials to begin reforestation projects. Information at this site
                includes projects and programs, data on tree species, a page dedicated to tree
                education, forest ecology and agroforestry, and solar energy material. Membership
                information and a form to receive your own seeds to start a reforestation project
                can also be found at this site.

Contact: icnfp@erols.com

New Hampshire Department of Environmental Sciences (DES)

URL: http://www.state.nh.us/des/descover.htm

Summary: Some of the responsibilities of the New Hampshire DES consist of seeing that the
                water supplies are safe for drinking and the ecology remains balanced, to regulate
                the emissions of air pollutants, to encourage the proper management of municipal
                and industrial waste, and to ensure that there are water resources for future
                generations. This site describes the programs that work to keep New Hampshire
                ecologically sound.

Contact: pip@des.state.nh.us

New Hampshire Fish and Game Department

URL: http://www.wildlife.state.nh.us/

Summary: The New Hampshire Fish and Game Department has been conserving the state's
                wildlife and their habitats for more than a hundred years. This site contains
                up-to-date information on wildlife happenings in the state, data on educational
                programs at various wildlife centers, and a calendar of events.

Contact: info@wildlife.state.nh.us

New Jersey Department of Environmental Protection

URL: http://www.state.nj.us/dep/

Summary: The goals of the NJDEP are clean air, clean water, safe and healthy communities, and healthy ecosystems for its citizens. This site contains the NJDEP strategic plan to accomplish these goals, descriptions of programs, lists of program units and members, news releases, a calendar of events, and conference announcements.

Contact: lpierce@dep.state.nj.us

New Jersey Division of Fish, Game and Wildlife

URL: http://www.state.nj.us/dep/fgw/

Summary: The New Jersey Division of Fish, Game, and Wildlife page includes material on how to join the Wildlife Conservation Corps, data on Budding Naturalist programs on such topics as feeding the birds and endangered species in New Jersey, lists of endangered and threatened species, and general information on the department.

Contact: feedback@state.nj.us

New Mexico Wilderness Alliance

URL: http://www.sdc.org/nmwc/

Summary: NMWA is a nonprofit, volunteer organization dedicated to preserving the New Mexico wilderness. Information available at this site includes several issues of the NMWA newsletter, wilderness alerts, data on how you can help preserve the wilderness, and membership material.

Contact: nmwc@virgo.sdc.org

The New Mexico Wildlife Association

URL: http://www.swcp.com/~sidprice/nmwa.html

Summary: The objective of the New Mexico Wildlife Association is to create and manage a wildlife park called Wildlife West, for the education of the public about New Mexico's wild flora and fauna. Some of the projects discussed at this site are Habitat Walks and educational programs that teach participants about soil erosion, maintaining wildlife habitats, and creating wetlands. Other information includes the goals of the Association and how to become a member.

Contact: wildlife@swcp.com

New York State Association for Reduction, Reuse and Recycling

URL: http://www.recycle.net/recycle/assn/nysarrr/index.html

Summary: The NYSARRR site contains information on waste reduction and recycling across the State of New York. This site includes material on membership, a calendar of events, conference announcements, and a list of the board of directors.

Contact: pokrec@mh.net

New York State Department of Environmental Conservation

URL: http://www.dec.state.ny.us/

Summary: This is a compact site with access to the New York State DEC's organizational functions, organizational history, programs, and services. These include a sportsman education program, DEC's Generic Environmental Impact Statement, and wildlife documentation.

Contact: Phone: (518) 463-5000

NHBS (Natural History Book Service)

URL: http://www.nhbs.co.uk

Summary: The database for this online bookstore contains more than 40,000 titles including field guides, textbooks, monographs, reports, CDs, videos, and cassettes on natural science and environmental subjects. Just a few of the subjects covered are environmental assessment, acid rain, aquatic toxicology, species and habitat conservation, and effects of contaminants. To make this online database more valuable are its searching and browsing features that allow searches within subject, geographic area, author, and title.

Contact: webmaster@nhbs.co.uk

NIREX

URL: http://www.nirex.co.uk/

Summary: NIREX describes itself as "responsible environmental management for radioactive waste" in the United Kingdom. This site contains news releases, a library of downloadable reports, an introduction to radioactive waste disposal, site access reports, and conference announcements.

Contact: response@nirex.co.uk

NOAA (National Oceanic and Atmospheric Administration)

URL: http://www.noaa.gov/

Summary: This site contains national weather forecasts, NOAA statistics, searchable Ocean and Atmospheric databases, a searchable database of people at NOAA, links to NOAA Data Centers such as the National Climatic Data Center and links to other oceanic and atmospheric sites. NOAA also provides access to the massive World Data Center System provided under the assistance of the International Council of Scientific Unions via the National Geophysical Data Center (http://www.ngdc.noaa.gov)

Contact: help@esdim.noaa.gov

North Carolina Coastal Federation

URL: http://www.nccoast.org/

Summary: NCCF is an organization of citizens working together to maintain a healthy coastal environment. Material at this site includes education programs, a calendar of events, NCCF publications, membership data, and volunteer opportunities.

Contact: nccf@nccoast.org

North Carolina Department of Environment and Natural Resources

URL: http://www.ehnr.state.nc.us/EHNR/

Summary: The mission of the North Carolina DENR is "to promote, protect, and conserve the environment, health, and natural resources of North Carolina and its citizens." This site is the link to various EHNR departments, including Division of Water Resources, Division of Environmental Management, Division of Environmental Health, Division of Forest Resources and Division of Marine Fisheries. There is information at this site on environmental education and a calendar of events.

Contact: Bryan Bass: bryan_bass@mail.ehnr.state.nc.us

North Cascades Conservation Council

URL: http://www.halcyon.com/rdpayne/nccc.html

Summary: The NCCC was created to preserve and protect the environmental and scenic value of the Greater North Cascades ecosystem. This site contains information about NCCC's past accomplishments, future goals, current news, and action alerts. There are articles from the Council's newsletter at this site, as well as membership information.

Contact: Marc Bardsley: MARC.BARDSLEY@metrokc.gov

North Dakota Atmospheric Resource Board

URL: http://water.swc.state.nd.us/arb/

Summary: The North Dakota Atmospheric Resource Board conducts quality atmospheric management programs throughout the state of North Dakota. Its programs include a cloud modification project, a rain gauge network, and a precipitation data site that contains historical precipitation reports. Atmospheric photo images and research project news can also be found at this site.

Contact: dlanger@water.swc.state.nd.us

Northeast Alternative Vehicle Consortium (NAVC)

URL: http://www.navc.org/home.html

Summary: NAVC is a nonprofit organization committed to the ideal that research, design, and commercialization of clean-fuel vehicles is essential to the environment. This site provides information on electric vehicle projects, data on events, meeting information, conference participants, and NAVC publications.

Contact: Elizabeth Albritton: albritton@navc.org.

Northeast Sustainable Energy Association (NESEA)

URL: http://www.nesea.org/neshome.htm

Summary: NESEA is a nonprofit organization founded for the purpose of supporting the use of renewable and sustainable energy, the responsible use of non-renewable forms of energy, and to relate the value of these practices to the preservation of the environment. This site contains information on energy conferences and programs.

Contact: nesea@nesea.org

Northern Lights (Nordlicht)

URL: http://www.psychologie.uni-kiel.de/nordlicht/hpeng.htm

Summary: Nordlicht (northern lights) is a campaign to save the earth from global warming by saving energy and limiting vehicle traffic. This site contains the results of an action package, press releases, background articles from energy conferences, and links to other energy saving sites. There is information in English, Spanish, Dutch, Norwegian, and Swedish, but the German language page has the most complete data at this time.

Contact: klima@psychologie.uni-kiel.de

Northern Michigan Wildlife Rehabilitation

URL: http://www.aliens.com/nonproft/nmwr/top.html

Summary: NMWR is a nonprofit, publicly-funded organization that rescues and rehabilitates injured and orphaned wildlife. This site contains data on how to become a member, what to do if you find an injured or orphaned wild animal, what to do if wildlife is becoming a problem around your home, and some newsletter excerpts.

Contact: Deb Hanchett: critter@nmwr.org

Northern Prairie Wildlife Research Center

URL: http://www.npwrc.usgs.gov/index.htm

Summary: The mission of the Northern Prairie Wildlife Research Center is to gather information on the ecological requirements for sustainable wildlife populations, to carry out studies of flora and fauna (including identification of change resulting from habitat loss and modification), and to disseminate this information where it will do the most good. This site embodies data about NPWRC events such as conferences, bird bandings, biological data, and a joint venture directory. There is also a searchable database of articles by NPWRC staff. These are articles on such topics as endangered species, wetland flora, and the effects of weather on ducks.

Contact: npscinfo@usgs.gov

North Island Wildlife Recovery Association

URL: http://www.islandroots.com/wildlife/

Summary: NIWRA keeps the public up-to-date on what's happening with wildlife on Vancouver Island, B.C. The association has learned how to deal with oil spills, wildlife rehabilitation, and short term rehabilitation of bear, wolf, and cougar. Information contained at this site includes wildlife aid and adoption programs, wildlife images, and membership data.

Contact: niwra@nanaimo.ark.com

Nova Scotia Bird Society

URL: http://ccn.cs.dal.ca/Recreation/NS-BirdSoc/nsbsmain.html

Summary: This site contains information about the Society, data on membership, and a faq about wild birds. There is information here about the Migratory Bird Treaty as well as data on upcoming meetings and field trips.

Contact: ip-bird@chebucto.ns.ca

Oceania Project

URL: http://nornet.nor.com.au/users/oceania/index.html

Summary: The Oceania Project is an Australian nonprofit education and research organization that is dedicated to raising awareness about cetacea (whales, dolphins, and porpoises) and the oceans. This site provides up-to-date information about whales and dolphins and data on how you can help with the protection and conservation of cetaceans.

Contact: trish.wally@oceania.org.au

Oceanic

URL: http://diu.cms.udel.edu/

Summary: The Ocean Information Center site contains data on the World Ocean Circulation Experiment, the TOGA Coupled Ocean-Atmosphere Response Experiment (TOGA COARE) data catalog, and information on the cruise schedules of oceanographic research ships, including those of the EPA and NOAA.

Contact: oceanic@diu.cms.udel.edu

Oceanic Planetary Boundary Layer (OPBL) Laboratory

URL: http://www.oc.nps.navy.mil/opbl/

Summary: The purpose of OPBL is to "understand the role of oceanic turbulent boundary layers in modifying physical and biogeochemical properties in the global oceans." This site contains manuscripts, animated simulations, descriptions of the modelling work done at the Laboratory, and animated numerical models.

Contact: Arlene Guest: aguest@nps.navy.mil

Oceanic Resource Foundation

URL: http://www.orf.org/

Summary: The Oceanic Resource Foundation's mission is to support the preservation of marine biological diversity and to provide educational materials to those interested in a healthy marine ecosystem. Material available at this site includes information on the problems and dangers affecting the earth's oceans, present and future Foundation projects, membership and volunteer data, and information on how you can help.

Contact: feedback@orf.org

Ocean Process Analysis Laboratory

URL: http://ekman.sr.unh.edu/OPAL/

Summary: This Laboratory conducts research on the physical, geochemical, and biological systems in the Gulf of Maine, Gulf Stream, North Atlantic, and California Current. This site provides access to several oceanic datasets that may not be used for commercial purposes. These include the Environmental Data IMS, the Research Environmental Data IMS, and the JGOFS Data System.

Contact: Wendell Brown: wsbrown@kelvin.sr.unh.edu

Ocean Voice International

URL: http://www.ovi.ca/

Summary: Ocean Voice International is an organization whose purpose is to conserve marine ecosystems, work for the sustainable use of ocean resources, and promote marine biodiversity. The site contains information about the organization and facts about the ocean and ocean life.

Contact: mcall@superaje.com

Office of Energy Efficiency

URL: http://oee.nrcan.gc.ca/oee_e.cfm

Summary: The goal of the OEE is to ensure the responsible use of natural resources and help
            protect the environment of Canada. This site contains information and publications
            for individuals, businesses, and government on energy efficiency. There is also a
            media room with the latest energy press releases and speeches at this site.

Contact: general.oee@nrcan.gc.ca

Office of Protected Resources

URL: http://kingfish.ssp.nmfs.gov/tmcintyr/prot_res.html

Summary: The Office of Protected Resources coordinates marine species protection,
            conservation, and restoration for the National Marine Fisheries Service. Some of
            its programs are the Endangered Species Program, which includes sea turtles, seals,
            and sea lions; the Protected Resources Program, including marine mammal health
            and protection, Depleted Species information; and Recovered Species information.

Contact: tmcintyr@kingfish.ssp.nmfs.gov

Ohio Department of Natural Resources

URL: http://www.dnr.ohio.gov/

Summary: The Ohio DNR site contains a large quantity of information on wildlife, forestry,
            recycling, natural areas and preserves, soil conservation, and water conservation.
            There are publications, information on programs, calendars of events, maps, and
            downloadable information located at this site.

Contact: Infomail@dnr.state.oh.us

Ohio Environmental Protection Agency

URL: http://www.epa.ohio.gov/

Summary: The Ohio EPA site contains information on air pollution control, groundwater
            pollution, hazardous waste management, and EPA projects such as the Lake Erie
            Lakewide Management Plan (LaMP) and the Low-Level Radioactive Waste
            Program. There is also information about the agency and its divisions at this site.

Ohio Wildlife Center

URL: http://www.ohiowildlifecenter.org/

Summary: The Ohio Wildlife Center is the only wildlife hospital in Ohio that rehabilitates all species of injured and orphaned native wildlife. This site provides information on helping wild infants, what to do about nuisance waterfowl and rabies, as well as membership and volunteer data.

Contact: 2661 Billingsley Road, Worthington, Ohio 43235, 614-793-WILD (9453)

Okefenokee Swamp Natural Education Center

URL: http://www.gravity783.com/joe1.html

Summary: This site contains environmental information about the Okefenokee Swamp in Florida and Georgia. Information here includes a tour of the Nature Garden, data from the Critter Center about mammals, reptiles, and birds and information on how the Okefenokee became a protected area.

Contact: gravity@companet.net

Oklahoma Department of Wildlife Conservation

URL: http://www.state.ok.us/~odwc/

Summary: The ODWC site contains information on wildlife and its conservation in Oklahoma. The main conservation focus is on Project WILD, which concentrates on the importance of wildlife and wildlife habitat. This site also provides access to the Operation Game Thief Hotline.

Contact: pmoore@oklaosf.state.ok.us

Ontario Environment Network

URL: http://www.web.net/~oen/

Summary: The Ontario Environment Network site contains information on Ontario's Environmental Bill of Rights, environmental groups in Ontario, and the text of several action alerts and bulletins.

Contact: oen@web.net

Ontario Ministry of the Environment

URL: http://www.ene.gov.on.ca/

Summary: The Ontario Ministry of the Environment site includes environmental news releases, conference announcements, recent initiative reports, speech texts, a calendar of events, contamination cleanup guidelines, data on the drive clean program, information about the Environmental Bill of Rights, downloadable publications, and an air quality index for selected Ontario cities.

Contact: darrahdo@ene.gov.on.ca

Open University Ecology and Conservation Research Group (ECRG)

URL: http://www.open.ac.uk/OU/Academic/Biology/C_G_Home.htm

Summary: The Open University Ecology and Conservation Research Group areas of study include amphibians, plants, and tropical ecology. Information at this site includes studies of the primrose, butterflies in Trinidad, and farming and environmental management.

Contact: M.E.Dodd@open.ac.uk

Operation WildLife

URL: http://www.owl-online.org/home.htm

Summary: OWL provides professional rehabilitation services for injured and orphaned wild animals, and wildlife education for the citizens of northeast Kansas and northwest Missouri. This site contains a volunteer bulletin board, educational programs for K-12, tips for dealing with wildlife, a community calendar, and membership information.

Contact: OpWildLife@aol.com

Oregon Department of Fish and Wildlife

URL: http://www.dfw.state.or.us/

Summary: The goal of the Oregon DFW is to protect and increase Oregon's fish and wildlife and their habitats. This site contains information on conservation programs and education, including Project WILD, Naturescaping, and WILD school sites. There are also monthly news releases, research reports, access to the Oregon Rivers Information System database, and a nationwide directory of fish and wildlife agencies at this location.

Contact: Randy Henry: Randy.HENRY@state.or.us

Oregon Department of Forestry

URL: http://www.ohwy.com/or/o/odforest.htm

Summary: The Oregon Department of Forestry site contains information on forest practices, state forest management, forest health, and urban forestry. There are a number of publications and newsletters located at this site that require Adobe Acrobat Reader. This reader is a freeware product that is available by anonymous ftp from several sources on the World Wide Web. (See p. 146)

Contact: Brian Ballou: brian.r.ballou@state.or.us

Organization for Tropical Studies

URL: http://cro.ots.ac.cr/en/main.htm

Summary: OTS is a nonprofit consortium of universities and research institutions that provides research and educational information on the sustainable use of natural resources. The information at this site includes research and education programs in Costa Rica, bulletins, membership and volunteer data, a calendar of events, meeting information, a Costa Rican tropical biology bibliography, and *Tropical Biology Magazine* in Spanish.

Contact: wwwots@ns.ots.ac.cr

ORNL (Oak Ridge National Laboratories)

URL: http://www.esd.ornl.gov/LSET.hml

Summary: The Life Sciences and Environmental Technologies Directorate site at ORNL contains information about the Laboratories' research and programs, including some issues of *Environmental Research News* and articles on saving the environment. The mission and goals of the Energy and Environmental Sciences Division are also contained here.

Contact: Forrest Hoffman: webmaster@www.esd.ornl.gov

Orphaned Wildlife Rehabilitation Society

URL: http://www.realm.ca/owl/

Summary: The aim of O.W.L. is to rehabilitate injured and orphaned birds of prey, with precedence given to endangered species, to educate the public on this rehabilitation, and to maintain breeder programs for the purpose of releasing the young to the wild. This site contains information on programs, adoptions, corporate sponsorships, and volunteering at O.W.L.

Contact: owl_rehab@bc.sympatico.ca

Otter Habitat and Wildlife Rehab Center

URL: http://www.microserve.net/~otters/

Summary: The Center was created to provide a safe haven for all types of wildlife living in central Pennsylvania. The facility has expanded to include a large habitat for Pennsylvania River Otters. The site contains a calendar of events, a what's new section, and information on adopting an otter.

Contact: otters@microserve.net

Oxford Forestry Institute

URL: http://ifs.plants.ox.ac.uk/OFI/OFI.HTM

Summary: The Oxford Forestry Institute pursues the exploration, conservation, and utilization of forest genetic resources and the ecological management of forestry resources. This site includes information about the Institute, papers, annual reports, lecture texts, and data on the Tropical Forestry Resource Group and Forestry Research Programme.

Contact: ofi@plants.ox.ac.uk

Ozone Action

URL: http://www.ozone.org/

Summary: Ozone Action is a nonprofit organization dedicated to addressing the problems of ozone depletion and climate change. Information available at this site includes climate change reports and factsheets, reports on international climate change negotiations, ozone depletion articles, events, internships, and data on how you can help.

Contact: ozone_action@ozone.org

Pacific Forestry Center - Canadian Forest Service

URL: http://www.pfc.forestry.ca/

Summary: The PFC site, which belongs to the Canadian Forest Service, contains information about projects and programs such as the Digital Remote Sensing Project at the Petawawa National Forest Institute and the Advanced Forest Technologies Program. There are some documents on the impacts of forestry procedures and landscape management located here, also. Some are in both French and English.

Contact: Webmaster@pfc.cfs.nrcan.gc.ca

Pacific Northwest Pollution Prevention Resource Center

URL: http://pprc.pnl.gov/pprc/

Summary: PPRC is a nonprofit organization formed to discuss hazardous waste management in the region as a means to prevent pollution, thereby producing less to recycle, treat, or dispose of in landfills. This site contains a keyword searchable database of PPRC research projects, technology reviews, the text of the *Pollution Prevention Northwest* newsletter, articles on case studies, access to the Request for Proposal (RFP) Clearinghouse, and a descriptive list of other PPRC publications.

Contact: office@pprc.org

Pacific Rim Consortium in Energy, Combustion, and the Environment

URL: http://www.parcon.uci.edu/

Summary: PARCON's mission is to promote the use of alternative energy to reduce the impact of energy utilization on the environment for the benefit of our biosphere. This site includes descriptions of meetings, study groups, and international conferences, plus PARCON's goals, objectives, and mission.

Palos Verdes Peninsula Land Conservancy

URL: http://www.pvplc.org/

Summary: The Palos Verdes Peninsula Land Conservancy is a nonprofit, nonpolitical organization dedicated to the preservation of the undeveloped land on California's Palos Verdes Peninsula. Material available at this site consists of preservation success stories, project priorities, events, publications, and volunteer opportunities.

Contact: pvplc@aol.com

ParkNet - The National Park Service

URL: http://www.nps.gov/

Summary: The National Park Service protects, preserves, and maintains the natural resources in the U.S. National Parks. This site contains information on air, water, geologic and wildlife resources, many natural resource publications, and data on air quality programs, water quality programs, and wildlife projects.

Contact: webmaster@nps.gov

Patuxent Wildlife Research Center

URL: http://www.pwrc.nbs.gov/

Summary: The objective of PWRC is to excel in wildlife and natural resource science, furnishing the information needed to better manage the nation's biological resources. Information at this site consists of descriptions of current research, data on the effects of ecological processes, and human effects on bioresources, plus reports on wetland management, habitat alteration, restoration ecology, and contaminants.

Contact: director@patuxent.nbs.gov

Penn State University Weather Pages

URL: http://www.ems.psu.edu/wx/

Summary: The PSU Weather Pages offers current onshore and offshore weather monitoring and includes Quick Time Virtual Reality movies of hurricanes, sea-surface temperature, and the topographical earth.

Contact: Bob Hart: hart@ems.psu.edu

Pennsylvania Department of Environmental Protection

URL: http://www.dep.state.pa.us/

Summary: The PADEP site was created to help those who are interested in learning about environmental issues and preventing pollution. This site contains information on air quality, deep mine safety, land recycling and waste management, mining, pollution prevention, recycling, water management, and waste management. Information on employment opportunities and environmental education, as well as new releases and legislation data can also be found at this site.

Contact: webmaster@a1.dep.state.pa.us

Pennsylvania Resources Council

URL: http://prc.org/

Summary: PRC is a nonprofit citizens' action group seeking solutions to environmental problems. This site provides material on recycling, environmental shopping, litter reduction, and environmental living. Educational materials may be accessed here also.

Contact: imperato@prc.org

Peregrine Falcons at the University of Calgary

URL: http://www.ucalgary.ca/~tull/falcon

Summary: This page recounts the sightings of peregrine falcons on the campus of the University of Calgary and gives information on the care and feeding of this endangered species. Data on habitat, breeding, and care of injured birds can also be located at this site as well as photographs and video clips of young falcons feeding.

Contact: Eric Tull: tull@acs.ucalgary.ca

Peregrine Fund

URL: http://www.peregrinefund.org/

Summary: The Peregrine Fund strives to conserve nature by saving birds and their habitats. This site focuses on birds of prey and song birds. Information on how to become a member, the Peregrine Fund mission, and current program data resides here also.

Contact: tpf@peregrinefund.org

Pesticide Action Network North America - PANNA

URL: http://www.panna.org/panna/

Summary: PANNA is a nonprofit citizens organization that supports the use of ecologically sound practices in place of pesticides. PANNA encourages sustainable agriculture, food security, and social justice. This site contains a searchable database of information about pesticides, alternatives, sustainable agriculture, and related topics.

Contact: paninfopubs@panna.org

Pew Center on Global Climate Change

URL: http://www.pewclimate.org/home.html

Summary: The Pew Center on Global Climate Change is dedicated to educating the public on the risks and challenges of climate change and developing solutions to climate change. This site contains current and past press releases, discussion of key issues, and the Center's goals.

Contact: Phone: (703) 516-4146

Pinecrest: An Adventure Living Off The Utility Grid

URL: http://www.public.usit.net/pinecrst/

Summary: The Pinecrest site explores twelve years of living in an eco-friendly environment. There are pictures and descriptions of the author's earth sheltered home, hydroelectric system and well house, as well as a report on the design of the home and its use of solar energy.

Contact: John Q. McMillian: pinecrst@usit.net

Piping Plover Guardian Program

URL: http://cfn.cs.dal.ca/Recreation/FieldNaturalists/guardian.html

Summary: The goal of the Piping Plover Guardian Program is to assist in the conservation and recovery of the endangered Piping Plover in Atlantic Canada. Information at this site includes data on becoming a guardian and what volunteering involves.

Contact: ip-hfn@chebucto.ns.ca

PlanetKeepers

URL: http://www.ecofuture.org/ecofuture/pk/

Summary: PlanetKeepers is a site of projects, ideas, and people dedicated to communications between individuals and groups who are interested in the health and well-being of humans and the environment. There are environmental articles and book excerpts, a rainforest photo-journey, a list of environmental directories, a guide to information resources, and a list of environmental organizations at this site.

Contact: Fred Elbel: fedesign@csn.net

PLANT-IT 2000

URL: http://www.tesser.com/plantit/

Summary: Plant-It 2000 is a nonprofit organization that is committed to properly planting, protecting, and maintaining as many indigenous species of trees as possible in the world. This site contains information on the benefits of urban, forest, and riparian trees; data on where the trees are planted; Plant-it 2000 partnerships; and material on how you can help, both by volunteering and donating funds.

Contact: plantit@tesser.com

Pollution Probe

URL: http://www.pollutionprobe.org

Summary: Pollution Probe is a Canadian charitable organization devoted to research, education, and practical solutions of environmental issues. Information available at this site include an air quality program, conference data, executive summaries on mercury release into the Great Lakes, a calendar of events, membership options, and Pollution Probe publications.

Contact: pprobe@pollutionprobe.org

Potomac Conservancy

URL: http://www.potomac.org/

Summary: The Potomac Conservancy is dedicated to preserving the beauty and natural resources of the Potomac River. This site contains information on environmental threats to the Potomac, news about the Potomac, membership data, volunteer opportunities, and a calendar of events and activities.

Contact: comments@potomac.org

Prairie Ecosystem Study Project

URL: http://www.cprc.uregina.ca/

Summary: PECOS is a community-based study of the agricultural sustainability of a semi-arid grassland ecosystem. The focus of the study is on land use patterns and the structure of rural communities, environmental pesticide exposure and human health, and the health of the land and its biota. Data on these studies is located at this site along with information on the philosophy of the project, data about the location of the project, other studies, and PECOS newsletters.

Contact: Maura Gillis-Cipywnyk: gillism@usask.ca

Preserve the Dunes, Inc.

URL: http://www.daac.com/sosdunes/index.html

Summary: Preserve the Dunes is a nonprofit organization whose purpose is to protect the dunes of Southwestern Michigan from the destruction of sand mining, overdevelopment, and poor use. This site contains meeting minutes, fund raising information, current actions, and aerial photographs of dune mining destruction.

Contact: sosdunes@daac.com

Primate Info Net

URL: http://www.primate.wisc.edu/pin/

Summary: Primate Info Net is a service of the Wisconsin Regional Primate Research Center. This site contains information on primate conservation, conservation legislation, programs, organizations, and primate information services.

Contact: jacobsen@primate.wisc.edu

Princeton University's Center for Energy & Environmental Studies

URL: http://www.princeton.edu:80/~cees/

Summary: Princeton's CEES site offers information on selected publications of staff and faculty, a list of energy and environmental theses from 1979 to the present, a list of relevant reports, and the topics of current seminars. The majority of this site contains very nicely detailed descriptions of related sites with links to them.

Contact: cees@princeton.edu

Project WILD

URL: http://www.projectwild.org/

Summary: Project WILD is a conservation and environmental education program. This site contains activity guides, program information, newsletters, and data on becoming a Project Wild sponsor. Many state DNR programs include Project WILD.

Contact: natpwild@igc.apc.org

Project Wildlife

URL: http://www.projectwildlife.org/

Summary: Project Wildlife is a nonprofit organization that rescues injured and orphaned wildlife, rehabilitates them, and releases them to the wild. This site contains information on the history and current work of the organization and has a number of articles on living with wildlife. Part of their funding comes from their recycling program, which is described here. Membership information, reports from the Board of Directors, and details on volunteering are included at this site.

Contact: P.O. Box 80696, San Diego, CA. 92138-0696

Protected Areas Virtual Library

URL: http://www.wcmc.org.uk/~dynamic/pavl/

Summary: The Protected Areas Virtual Library is a collection of pointers to national protected area sites, international conventions and programmes, and protected area resource center sites.

Contact: Jeremy Harrison: jerry.harrison@wcmc.org.uk

Protected Marine Species

URL: http://www.rtis.com/nat/user/elsberry/marspec.html

Summary: Protected Marine Species is involved with all aspects of biology and wildlife
management. This site contains material on marine mammals and includes
information on what is necessary to become a marine scientist, data on current
projects such as FINSCAN, a glossary of terms or jargon, and biographical
information on marine species researchers.

Contact: welsberr@orca.tamu.edu

Puget Sound Green Pages

URL: http://www.wolfenet.com/~greenway/index.html

Summary: This site contains articles on many topics including energy, forestry, ecology,
climate, water quality, and pollution prevention in the Puget Sound area of
Washington State. There are also calendars of environmental events, data on
government agencies and programs, environmental directories, and lists of
literature and online media at this location.

Contact: greenway@wolfenet.com

Puget Sound On Line

URL: http://www.wa.gov/puget_sound/

Summary: The Puget Sound On Line sight contains information on the health of Puget Sound,
reports, press releases, a bibliography of estuary program reports, a calendar of
events, information on how Puget Sound is being protected, data on the Puget
Sound/Georgia Basin Environmental Initiative, and information on how you can
get involved.

Contact: shindle@psat.wa.gov

Raincoast Conservation Society

URL: http://www.islandnet.com/~ikrcoast/

Summary: The Raincoast Conservation Society is dedicated to the preservation of temperate
rainforests and the wildlife dependent upon them, particularly the grizzly bears of
the coastal rainforest valleys of British Columbia. This site contains information
on government mismanagement of the threatened grizzly bears, Alaskan grizzly
management, how you can help save the grizzlies, and data about their habitat.

Contact: Ian McAllister: ikrcoast@islandnet.com

Rainforest Action Network (RAN)

URL: http://www.ran.org/ran/

Summary: The Rainforest Action Network works to protect tropical rainforests and the people and wildlife that live in them. This site contains information about rainforests and about current projects that are endangering them. There are lists of campaigns to join in fighting those who would destroy the rainforest ecology. RAN includes a children's section and one that has a listing of what you can do to protect the rainforests of the world. Other information at this site tells about the people and animals who inhabit the rainforests.

Contact: rainforest@ran.org

Rainforest Foundation International

URL: http://www.savetherest.org/

Summary: The Rainforest Foundation International goal is to assist the indigenous and traditional rainforest populations in the protection of their environment. This site addresses environmental issues in Central and South America, Asia, and Africa and describes projects in these areas. Information on events, rates of rainforest destruction, and membership in the Foundation can also be found here.

Contact: rffny@rffny.org

Rainforest Workshop

URL: http://kids.osd.wednet.edu/marshall/rainforest_home_page.html

Summary: The Rainforest Workshop is primarily an educational site containing lesson plans and activities aimed at students in middle school and above. It includes reports on endangered species, information on rainforest research at the New York Botanical Gardens, and general data on Peru, Brazil, and Ecuador.

Contact: Virginia Reid: vreid@osd.wednet.edu

Raptor Center at the University of Minnesota

URL: http://www.raptor.cvm.umn.edu/

Summary: The Raptor Center's mission is preserving biological diversity through saving and treating injured birds. Information available at this site includes a census of birds now in treatment, announcements of Center events, including bird releases, data on nests, and general information on birds of prey. There is data on becoming a member and on volunteering and also information on presentations, programs, internships, and job postings.

Contact: raptor@umn.edu

Raptor Rehabilitation of Kentucky

URL: http://www.raptorrehab.org/

Summary: RROK is a volunteer, nonprofit organization that provides aid to sick, injured and orphaned birds of prey. This site contains information on native Kentucky raptors, including the permanent residents of the Raptor Rehab, a section on adopting a raptor, as well as a calendar of events and volunteer information.

Contact: raptors@aye.net

Raptor Resource Project

URL: http://www.salamander.com/~rrp/

Summary: The Raptor Resource Project is a nonprofit group working to restore the midwestern population of Peregrine falcons and other raptors. This site includes information on conservation, species management, and education and research programs. You will also find facts about peregrine falcons, data on attracting falcons, falcon release information, and membership material.

Contact: RRP@salamander.com

Recycled Pulp and Paper Coalition

URL: http://www.recycledpulp.com/

Summary: The Recycled Pulp and Paper Coalition site contains information on recycled bond, laser, envelope, and copier paper. Information at this site include a description of postconsumer recycled paper and where to get it. There is also a questionnaire about your recycled paper needs.

Contact: info@recycledpulp.com

Reef Relief

URL: http://www.reefrelief.org/

Summary: Reef Relief is a nonprofit organization concerned with the protection and preservation of living coral reef ecosystems worldwide. This site provides information on what coral reefs are and what threatens them as well as information on Reef Relief's marine projects, newsletters, action alerts, and an introduction to coral reef ecosystems. There is an index of coral diseases, membership data, conference information, and material on how you can help also located at this site.

Contact: reef@bellsouth.net

RefugeNet

URL: http://www.refugenet.org/

Summary: RefugeNeT acts as an advocate for refuges and refuge dwellers by gathering and disseminating information, providing education, and fostering conservation and stewardship. This site provides wildlife action alerts, a calendar of events, volunteer information, membership information, publication data, and many wildlife images.

Contact: nwra@refugenet.org

Regional Air Quality Council

URL: http://www.raqc.org/

Summary: RAQC's purpose is to develop plans and strategies for improving the air quality in the Denver metro area. This site has data on the causes of dirty air, a glossary of air quality terms, a timeline for improving Denver's air quality, RAQC's trends and projections, a meeting schedule, and a legislative summary.

Contact: staff@raqc.org

Regional Environmental Center for Central and Eastern Europe

URL: http://www.rec.org

Summary: The Regional Environmental Center is a nonprofit, international organization whose main office is in Szentendre, Hungary. REC was established by the United States, the European Commission, and Hungary but now has several other countries as members. This Center promotes cooperation among the many environmental groups in Central and Eastern Europe and helps to develop solutions to environmental problems. This site contains information about the REC's grants, fellowships, and internships, their discussion groups, and their activities. This site also offers several searchable databases and current environmental news and reports.

Contact: webmaster@rec.org

Renewable Energy Association of Central Texas (REACT)

URL: http://www.txses.org/react/

Summary: REACT's goal is to encourage the development of sustainable energy for the future and the conservation of energy sources now. This site describes the Association and its goals and has links to other environmental and energy related sites.

Contact: react@txses.org

Resource Renewal Institute (RRI)

URL: http://www.rri.org/

Summary: RRI advances Green Plans in order to develop a sustainable environment and economy by encouraging people to agree to a long range environmental scheme. This site contains an archive of green plan documents, an environmental atlas, an annotated bibliography of online environmental resources, and a collection of green plans in French and German.

Contact: webmaster@rri.org

Restore America's Estuaries

URL: http://www.estuaries.org/

Summary: Restore America's Estuaries was formed by eight regional estuary protection groups in 1995. Their goals are to protect and maintain these wildlife habitats to sustain a healthy animal, fish, plant, and human population. This site contains information on RAE and its activities, descriptions of regional estuaries and the major threats to them, and data about member groups.

Contact: raecoalition@estuaries.org

RotWeb

URL: http://net.indra.com/~topsoil/Compost_Menu.html

Summary: RotWeb is a home composting site containing information on how to compost, what to compost, what not to compost, places in North America to see a composting demo, a backyard composting report, and data on composting bins and systems.

Contact: topsoil@indra.com.

Royal Forestry Society of England

URL: http://www.rfs.org.uk/

Summary: The RFS is an organization of professional foresters and individuals who care about the conservation and husbandry of trees. Information at this site includes meeting announcements, a lending library, descriptions of activities, literature searches, forestry awards, data archives, and membership material.

Contact: John Morgan: john@woodlander.co.uk

St. Catherines Sea Turtle Conservation Program

URL: http://www2.gasou.edu/cturtle/001welc.html

Summary: The St. Catherines Sea Turtle Conservation Program strives to study the nesting ecology of Georgia's sea turtles, protect the sea turtle habitat, and train teachers in this area of scientific study. This site contains information on sea turtle habitat, threats to the sea turtle, and conservation measures.

Contact: gabishop@gsvms2.cc.gasou.edu

The Salmon Page

URL: http://www.riverdale.k12.or.us/salmon.htm

Summary: The Salmon Page contains information on everything that has to do with salmon including reports on how to save them. Included at this site are conference announcements, calls for papers, information on sustainable fisheries, pointers to news and newsletters, and information on joining the Salmon listserv.

Contact: pnelson@riverdale.k12.or.us

The Salt and the Earth Wetlands Nursery

URL: http://www.thesaltandtheearth.com/

Summary: This site contains information on the history of wetlands, how to protect them, what and when to plant for erosion control, data on the Chesapeake Bay shoreline, and information on the Shoreline Erosion Advisory Service.

Contact: alor@inna.net

San Francisco Estuary Institute

URL: http://www.sfei.org/

Summary: The aim of SFEI is to provide the scientific understanding necessary to manage the complex and biologically rich San Francisco Estuary. This site contains several searchable databases, educational program descriptions, information on wetlands history and monitoring, downloadable documents from the volunteer monitoring program, several ecological atlas sections, and a list of available reports.

Contact: Margaret R. Johnston: johnston@sfei.org

San Gorgonio Volunteer Association

URL: http://www.edgeinternet.com/sgva/

Summary: The SGVA is a volunteer organization dedicated to the protection and preservation of the San Bernardino National Forest (Southern California), including the San Gorgonio Wilderness. This site is a repository of information on flora and fauna, wilderness trails and their conditions, weather, bears, wilderness use regulations, data on how you can help, material on how to join the volunteer ranger program, and articles on low impact wilderness use.

Contact: mgordon324@earthlink.net

Santa Barbara County Air Pollution Control District

URL:	http://www.silcom.com/~apcd/
Summary:	The Santa Barbara County APCD is a local government agency whose object is to protect its citizens from the effects of air pollution. The information at this site includes clean air programs, air quality monitoring, air toxics hot spot documents, public notices, publications, press releases, and data on what you can do to help.
Contact:	apcd@apcd.santa-barbara.ca.us

Sarvey Wildlife Center

URL:	http://www.accessone.com/~briang/sarvey.html
Summary:	The Sarvey Wildlife Center is a nonprofit corporation that provides care and rehabilitation to sick, injured, and orphaned wildlife, including all species of birds, mammals, and reptiles. This site contains wildlife images and information on volunteer opportunities.
Contact:	Kaye Baxter: hihanska@aol.com

Savannah River Site

URL:	http://www.srs.gov/
Summary:	The Savannah River Site is a DOE facility that focuses on several projects including environmental and waste management issues. Some topics of interest to environmentalists at this site are groundwater remediation processes, an outdoor classroom guide for teachers, and South Carolina wetlands conservation recommendations.
Contact:	Use form: http://www.srs.gov/general/srfeed/feedback.htm

Save Our Everglades

URL:	http://www.saveoureverglades.org/
Summary:	This site contains press releases on the Florida Everglades, a downloadable screensaver, information on membership in SOE, and a document on the Anti-Everglades Veto Campaign.
Contact:	c2985554@aol.com

Save Our Seas

URL: http://planet-hawaii.com/sos/

Summary: The goal of SOS is to preserve, protect, and restore the world's oceans to maintain sea life and ensure the future of ocean habitats. This site contains material on protecting the oceans, the International Year of the Ocean (1998), marine life conservation districts in Hawaii, the Coral Reef Pledge, conferences, and newsletters.

Contact: sos@aloha.net

Save the Manatee Club

URL: http://objectlinks.com/manatee/

Summary: The objectives of the SMC are to rescue and rehabilitate manatees, acquire funding for manatee research, foster education and public awareness of the manatee's plight and encourage the public to participate in conservation efforts. This site contains information about the club and its activities, including the Adopt-A-Manatee program, manatee news, manatee facts, and current mortality statistics.

Contact: education@savethemanatee.org

Save-the-Redwoods League

URL: http://www.savetheredwoods.org/

Summary: The Save-the-Redwoods League preserves our nation's redwoods by buying redwood forest land and turning it over to California's Redwood State Parks. Information at this site includes a Coast Redwood bibliography, education resources, publications, programs, an acquisitions summary, and data on joining the League.

Contact: saveredwoods@igc.org

Save the Rhino International

URL: http://www.kingsley.co.za/clients/rhino/images/rhino.htm

Summary: SRI's mission is to save the endangered rhino species. This site contains information on the different types of rhinoceros species and their habitats, data on how you can make a donation, and descriptions of past fund raisers.

Contact: saverhino@kingsley.co.za

Scottish Environment Protection Agency

URL: http://www.sepa.org.uk/

Summary: EPA is responsible for the protection of the land, air, and water in Scotland. This site contains press releases, meeting papers, public consultations, education policy documents and leaflets, bathing water quality data, environmental research data, technical guidance notes, and conference announcements.

Contact: info@sepa.org.uk

Scripps Institution of Oceanography

URL: http://sio.ucsd.edu

Summary: The Scripps Institution of Oceanography at the University of California at San Diego site contains information on ship operations and marine technical support, special programs, library collections, and datasets.

Contact: www@sio.ucsd.edu

SEACC (Southeast Alaska Conservation Council)

URL: http://www.juneau.com/seacc/

Summary: This page is dedicated to saving the Tongass National Forest, which is being threatened by a congressional bill that will gut the Tongass Timber Reform Act. Descriptions of all the natural resources, wildlife, and human habitats that will be destroyed and what you can do about it reside here.

Contact: info@seacc.org

Sea Shepherd Conservation Society

URL: http://www.seashepherd.org

Summary: The Sea Shepherd Conservation Society is committed to the conservation of marine mammals. This site has data on how you can join, how you can help the fight against illegal whaling operations around the world, news, and alerts, and the Society's current campaigns.

Contact: seashepherd@seashepherd.org

Sea Turtle Restoration Project (STRP)

URL: http://www.igc.apc.org/ei/strp/strpindx.html

Summary: The Sea Turtle Restoration Project is dedicated to protecting the endangered sea turtle populations in a way that also considers the needs of the local human community. The STRP site contains downloadable versions of educational and activist kits, articles from their newsletter, updates and press releases, and information on becoming a member.

Contact: seaturtles@earthisland.org

SeaWorld

URL: http://www.seaworld.org/

Summary: The Sea World site contains descriptions of educational programs at several of their locations, including tours, career camp, detailed descriptions of their "A Pledge and a Promise Environmental Awards" to further conservation projects by school groups and other information on whales, sharks, gorillas, and other wildlife.

Contact: shamu@seaworld.org

Second Nature

URL: http://www.2nature.org/

Summary: Second Nature is a nonprofit organization working to help colleges and universities to make environmental sustainability the foundation of learning. Information found at this site includes workshops, employment opportunities, higher education partnerships, education and training, sustainability databases, full-text papers and speeches, and a bulletin board for online networking.

Contact: info@2nature.org

Sefton Coast Life Project

URL: http://www.merseyworld.com/sclife/sclp.html

Summary: The most important goals of the Sefton Coast Life Project are to protect, manage, and enhance the remaining dune habitats of the Sefton Coast in North-Western England, and to maintain or restore such habitats and their component species. This site contains materials on the Project's objectives, research, and programs including species lists, extinct species lists, and the species recovery program. Access is also provided here to data on the Project's newsletters, publications, and events.

Contact: life@scms.u-net.com

Sempervirens Fund

URL: http://www.sempervirens.org/

Summary: The Sempervirens Fund is a not-for-profit land conservancy working to protect redwood forest lands in the Santa Cruz Mountains and to make that land available for public enjoyment. Information at this site includes a how to protect the land section, data on logging as a threat to forests, and facts on how one person can make a difference.

Contact: webmaster@sempervirens.org

Sierra Club Home Page

URL: http://www.sierraclub.org/

Summary: This site contains information about the Sierra Club and how to join it. There are also descriptions of programs, an issue of the Club magazine with ordering instructions, selected articles from the Club newsletter, and other documents. The Sierra Club Mission Statement is also available at this site.

Contact: information@sierraclub.org

Sierra Solar Systems

URL: http://www.sierrasolar.com/

Summary: This is primarily a commercial site for solar energy users. There are a few articles on solar users here and short reviews of books that are sold at this site.

Contact: solarjon@netshel.net

Silva Forest Foundation

URL: http://www.silvafor.org/

Summary: The Silva Forest Foundation (SFF) is a nonprofit organization made up of scientists and activists who work with rural communities to develop diverse forest uses that protect, maintain, and restore forests. The Foundation's goals are to develop and teach the rules of ecologically responsible forest use. This site contains an archive of data on forests and ecology, an illustrated guide of SFF's forest views, information on landscape planning, and a calendar of training courses.

Contact: silvafor@netidea.com

Simple Living Network

URL: http://www.slnet.com/

Summary: The Simple Living Network is a site dedicated to those wanting to learn how to live a more conscious, simple, healthy, and earth-friendly lifestyle. Information at this site includes a database of earth-friendly and deep ecology discussion groups, a resource catalog, data on how you can join, and how you can help.

Contact: slnet@slnet.com

Skies Above Foundation

URL: http://www.islandnet.com/~skies/

Summary: The Skies Above Foundation is a registered Canadian nonprofit foundation dedicated to fostering education on atmospheric issues. This site contains papers on atmospheric issues, conference announcements, publications, and a description of their television documentary.

Contact: skies@islandnet.com

Skogforsk

URL: http://www.skogforsk.se/

Summary: Skogforsk is a forestry institute in Sweden that promotes sustainable and ecologically sound forest management. Its goal is to provide the forestry community with the information to achieve such management. This site furnishes data on conferences, meetings, and papers. Most of the information is in Swedish, although there are some announcements in English.

Contact: skogforsk@skogforsk.se

Skye Environmental Centre

URL: http://www.smo.uhi.ac.uk/~dobhran/Failte.html

Summary: The goals of the Skye Environmental Centre on the Isle of Skye in Scotland are to promote the understanding of the environment of the Hebrides, including the geology, archeology, flora and fauna found there and the conservation of these resources. Information about the Centre and its work can be found at this site, including their newsletter and data on eco-tourism.

Contact: iosf@aol.com

Smithsonian Institution's Conservation and Research Center

URL: http://www.si.edu/crc/

Summary: The Smithsonian's CRC site contains a wealth of information on migratory birds
                and endangered and threatened species. There is also data on environmental
                education and training and their spatial analysis laboratory project at this location.

Contact: Timothy Boucher: tboucher@alala.crc.si.edu

Society for Ecological Restoration

URL: http://nabalu.flas.ufl.edu/ser/SERhome.html

Summary: SER is a professional organization for people researching, practicing, or interested
                in ecological restoration. This site contains information on how to become a
                member, its projects, conference and workshop announcements, employment
                opportunities, and chapter and regional contacts.

Contact: ser@vms2.macc.wisc.edu.

Society of American Foresters

URL: http://www.safnet.org/index.html

Summary: The Society of American Foresters (SAF) is the national scientific and educational
                organization representing the forestry profession in the United States. SAF's
                purpose is to advance the science, education, technology, and practice of forestry
                to ensure the continued health and use of forest ecosystems to benefit the public.
                The SAF site contains data on forestry and ecology legislation, SAF policy,
                Certified Forester Program information, conference announcements, and data on
                meetings and publications.

Contact: safweb@safnet.org

Society of Municipal Arborists

URL: http://www.urban-forestry.com/

Summary: The Society of Municipal Arborists is an organization of professionals devoted to
                planting and maintaining trees in cities. Information at this site includes
                membership data, news, conference announcements, excerpts from SMA's journal,
                and the Urban Forestry Forum, an online discussion forum.

Contact: Phone: 314-862-1711

Society of Wetland Scientists

URL: http://www.sws.org/

Summary: The Society of Wetland Scientists is a nonprofit organization that cultivates high quality wetland research. Some of the SWS goals include fostering education of the public in wetlands conservation, encouraging wetland science as a distinct discipline, and inspiring the knowledgeable management of wetland resources. This site contains information about the SWS, the society's quarterly journal, news and information about the Alaskan, Central, Rocky Mountain, South Central, and Western chapters of the Society, and data on meetings, grants, workshops, and classes.

Contact: Jim Lynch: lynch@sws.org

Solar Cooking Archive

URL: http://www.accessone.com/~sbcn/index.htm

Summary: This site is dedicated to solar cooking and contains lists of cookbooks, some with descriptions, ideas on how to use solar cookery, an image gallery, and slide show, and addresses of solar cooking organizations.

Contact: tsponheim@accessone.com

Solar Energy Network

URL: http://www.solarenergy.net/tsenindx.html

Summary: The Solar Energy Network is dedicated to all aspects of solar energy. This site contains membership information, a history of solar energy, an alternative energy and conservation mall, and articles on how the sun's energy is being harnessed today.

Contact: solarinfo@solarenergy.com

Solar Energy Society of Canada Inc.

URL: http://www.web.apc.org/sustenergy/sesci_english.html

Summary: SESCI is a nonprofit organization that classifies itself as "a voice of conservation and renewable energy in Canada." This site holds several conference announcements, articles on solar vehicles, the table of contents of *The Canadian Renewable Energy Guide*, membership data, and information on their journal, "Sol."

Contact: sesci@sympatico.ca

The Solid Waste Association of North America

URL: http://www.swana.org

Summary: The mission of this organization is to advance "the practice of economically and environmentally sound solid waste management in North America." Their site contains listings of conference papers and research articles arranged by subject including landfill gas, leachate, planning and management, recycling, waste reduction and composting, and waste-to-energy. Most of the papers were written by practicing MSW management professionals. Papers may be ordered at the site. Also includes a member products and services directory.

Contact: technical_services@swana.org

South Carolina Department of Natural Resources

URL: http://water.dnr.state.sc.us/

Summary: This site contains information on the South Carolina regulations for hunting and fishing, rules for watercraft, and *SCDNR News Releases*, which are published each Friday for the coming week. The Southeast Regional Climate Center has weather information such as lighting statistics and global hydrology data. The children's section contains stories, natural resource quizzes, and environmental graphics. There is also a publication list from the SCDNR Water Resources Division at this site.

Contact: webmaster@water.dnr.state.sc.us

South Dakota Parks & Wildlife Foundation

URL: http://www.state.sd.us/gfp/Foundation/foundation.htm

Summary: The South Dakota Parks & Wildlife Foundation is a nonprofit organization that manages contributions of land and money to benefit park development and wildlife preservation. Some of the projects supported by the foundation are Fort Sisseton State Historic Park, Adams Homestead and Nature Preserve, The Outdoor Campus, George S. Mickelson Trail, Conservation Easements, and Land Acquisition for Wildlife Enhancement.

Contact: susane@gfp.state.sd.us

Southeastern Raptor Rehabilitation Center

URL: http://www.vetmed.auburn.edu/raptor/

Summary: The mission of the SERRC is to treat, rehabilitate and release injured and orphaned birds of prey, and to educate the public about the importance of the relationship of raptors to their ecosystems and to humans. At this site you may see pictures and a slide show of the birds at SERRC and find information on their adopt-a-bird program.

Contact: raptor@vetmed.auburn.edu

Southern Africa Environment Page

URL: http://www.ru.ac.za/departments/law/SAenviro/saep.html

Summary: SAEP is a nonprofit organization whose goal is to encourage the development of environmental law and management in partnership with South African government, nongovernment, and educational institutions. This site contains a wealth of information on all aspects of environmental issues. The sections are rated for the extent of their coverage on topics such as biodiversity, nature conservation, marine resource management, environmental education, forestry, and environmental impact assessment.

Contact: saepnft@iafrica.com

Southern Florida Wildlife Rehabilitation Center

URL: http://www.network411.com/coug-3.htm

Summary: The Mission of the Southern Florida Wildlife Rehabilitation Center is to save all
                  wildlife and to educate the public in the care of injured or abused animals. This site
                  contains information on educational programs and data on the rehabilitation of
                  several animals.

Contact: Phone: (305) 247-7302

South West Florida Wildlife Rehabilitation and Conservation Center

URL: http://www.wildlife-rehab-sf.com/

Summary: The South West Florida Wildlife Rehabilitation and Conservation Center is a
                  nonprofit educational wildlife rehabilitation center, dedicated to the care and
                  rehabilitation of native Florida wildlife. This site contains images of wildlife and
                  information on what the center is doing to help them as well as data on what
                  volunteers can do to help.

Contact: 73121.1142@compuserve.com

Southwestern Riparian Expertise Directory

URL: http://ag.arizona.edu/AZWATER/swexpdir/iparian.html

Summary: This directory is a searchable database of Riparian researchers in Arizona,
                  Colorado, Nevada, New Mexico, and Utah. It may be searched by name or area of
                  specialization such as acid drainage, conservation biology, hazardous/toxic
                  materials, or wetlands delineation.

Contact: Barbara Tellman: bjt@ccit.arizona.edu

State and Territorial Air Pollution Program Administrators - STAPPA

URL: http://www.4cleanair.org/

Summary: STAPPA is one of two national associations comprised of air pollution control
                  agencies in the 54 states and territories of the United States whose purpose is to
                  encourage the exchange of information among air pollution control officials and
                  to promote good management of our air resources. This site contains a list of
                  STAPPA publications, a glossary of environmental terms, and government news
                  releases on air quality.

Contact: 4clnair@sso.org

Students for Environmental and Ecological Development (SEED)

URL: http://www.studorg.nwu.edu/seed/SEEDWeb.html

Summary: SEED at Northwestern University advocates concern for the earth through education and action and gives students the opportunity to encounter and interact with the earth's environment by becoming involved in preserving and regenerating it. SEEDweb contains information on SEED and its projects, data on how to join it, and links to their newsgroup and to their listserv.

Contact: Laura Tiefenbruck: tiefenbruck@nwu.edu

Surfrider Foundation USA

URL: http://www.surfrider.org/

Summary: The Surfrider Foundation is a nonprofit environmental organization committed to protecting, preserving, and restoring the earth's oceans and beaches. Information at this site includes membership data, coastal factoids, a list of Surfrider's successful projects to deter ocean pollution, data on their project to raise public awareness about mountain water quality, and a coastal bibliography.

Contact: info@surfrider.org

Sustainable Ecosystems Institute

URL: http://www.sei.org/

Summary: SEI works to find ethical solutions to ecological problems by sustaining natural habitats and the human communities that depend on them. This site contains information on SEI programs, reports and publications, data on getting involved, some issues of their newsletter in .pdf format, and a conservation quiz.

Contact: sei@sei.org

Sustainable Forestry Directory

URL: http://homepages.together.net/~wow/index1.htm

Summary: This site contains a directory of articles, certification organizations, environmental organizations, and environmentally focused foundations pertaining to ecological forestry issues. There is a quantity of information on forestry meetings, workshops, databases, and publications here.

Contact: info@forestworld.com

Sustainable Sources

URL: http://www.greenbuilder.com/

Summary: The purpose of Sustainable Sources is to provide a solutions-based environmental site. This site contains information on green building sources that are available in *The Sustainable Building Sourcebook*. Sections include water, energy, building materials, and solid waste. There is also local information about Texas.

Contact: billc@greenbuilder.com

Taiga Rescue Network

URL: http://www.sll.fi/TRN/

Summary: TRN is an international network of nongovernment organizations, people, and countries working for the protection and sustainable use of the Boreal Forests. This site contains the text of TRN's newsletter, *Taiga-News*, the text of a report on the trade and consumption of boreal wood products, the TRN platform, and information on the Taiga Terminators Campaign.

Contact: taiga@jokkmokk.se

Tallgrass Prairie in Illinois

URL: http://www.inhs.uiuc.edu/~kenr/tallgrass.html

Summary: This site is dedicated to the six prairie subtypes found in Illinois. Information found at this site includes prairie plants, biodiversity in prairies, the restoration of prairies and prairie habitats in Illinois, and ways to landscape with prairie plants.

Contact: Kenneth R. Robertson: krrobert@uiuc.edu

Tall Timbers Research Station

URL: http://www.fsu.edu/~lbrennan/

Summary: Tall Timbers Research Station asserts that sustainable, consumptive uses of wildlife and natural resources are compatible with maintaining natural diversity and therefore protect outstanding examples of natural ecosystems and all their components in their research. This site includes descriptions of research projects on such subjects as ornithology, forestry, and plant ecology, and also contains historical information on the Station plus a calendar of upcoming meetings.

Contact: lbrennan@mailer.fsu.edu

Tarkine: Wilderness for Heritage

URL: http://www.paranoia.com/~real/tarkine

Summary: The Tarkine region in northwest Tasmania is being threatened by logging, fire, mining, road building, and off-road vehicles, among other things. This site is a plea for the creation of the Tarkine Wilderness Rainforest World Heritage Area to protect the native flora and fauna, which are beginning to disappear. This site describes the area, its plants and wildlife and includes a map of the proposed area and an electronic petition that you can send to help make this a protected region.

Contact: real@paranoia.com

Tata Energy Research Institute

URL: http://www.teriin.org/

Summary: The mission of TERI is to find out how to use the world's natural resources in the most advantageous manner for a better world environment. This site contains research activity areas, reports, publications, databases, a calendar of past and future events, educational projects, and climate change data.

Contact: webgroup@teri.res.in

Teaming with Wildlife

URL: http://www.teaming.com/

Summary: Teaming with Wildlife is a coalition of state fish and wildlife agencies and more than 2,000 groups and businesses to provide conservation strategies and environmental educational opportunities for Americans. This site contains details of the Teaming with Wildlife proposal, a state-by-state needs assessment, a list of benefits to conservationists, a press kit, and conference information.

Contact: teaming@sso.org

Terrene Institute

URL:	http://www.terrene.org

Summary: This is a nonprofit organization that "links business with government, academia, and citizens to improve the total human environment embracing us all: our natural world, governmental policies, societal and individual behavior." Their focus is on education and public outreach. Their site contains searchable databases of research pertaining to nonpoint source pollution and watershed information. The final report of the *National Forum on Nonpoint Source Pollution* is available, as well as information about their products and publications.

Contact: terrinst@aol.com

Texas A&M University Oceanography

URL:	http://www-ocean.tamu.edu/welcome.html

Summary: This site gives access to scientific papers in oceanography authored by faculty, staff, and students at Texas A&M and includes documents, maps, and charts of information about the ocean-atmosphere relationship in the Gulf of Mexico. There is also a section entitled "Keeping an Eye on el Niño," which includes a description of the TOPEX/POSEIDON satellite's observations of sea-surface anomalies.

Contact: Rahilla Shatto: rshatto@ocean.tamu.edu

Texas Environmental Center (TEC)

URL:	http://www.tec.org/

Summary: The Texas Environmental Center (TEC) is a nonprofit organization that provides environmental information through modern technologies. Data at this site include the TEC newsletter, *GreenBeat*, the *Texas Environmental Almanac*, and information on the Barton Springs Multimedia Project.

Contact: webweaver@tec.org

Texas Marine Mammal Stranding Network

URL: http://www.tmmsn.org/

Summary: The Texas Marine Mammal Stranding Network is dedicated to understanding and conserving marine mammals. Information at this site includes education and research programs, a calendar of events, stranding statistics from 1987 to the present, press releases, pathology reports, how to report a stranding, membership data, and a museum exhibit.

Contact: tmmsn@tamug.tamu.edu

Texas Natural Resource Conservation Commission (TNRCC)

URL: http://www.tnrcc.state.tx.us/

Summary: The TNRCC site contains environmental and regulatory information including commission agendas, rules and policies, pollution prevention data, air quality information, water resource data, and waste management facts. Other facts found at this site pertain to sampling, monitoring, and recycling.

Contact: ac@tnrcc.state.tx.us

Threatened Species Network

URL: http://203.111.113.50/member/tsn/

Summary: TSN is an organization that seeks to raise the awareness of the public for the need of involvement in the protection and recovery of wildlife in Australia. This site contains information on Australia's threatened species, a calendar of events, media releases and project bulletins, legislation, and information on what you can do to help.

Contact: ntsnnsw@peg.apc.org

Tiempo Climate Cyberlibrary

URL: http://www.cru.uea.ac.uk:80/tiempo/

Summary: This virtual library of climate change and global warming information contains briefing documents, conference reports, data on environmental education, project information, publications, links to world data centers, and climate change news as it happens.

Contact: Mick Kelly: m.kelly@uea.ac.uk

Tiger Information Center

URL: http://www.5tigers.org/index.html

Summary: The Tiger Information Center contains data on the five sub-species of Tiger remaining in Asia. This site is sponsored by the Save the Tiger Fund and includes information on tigers in zoos, conservation, publications, and conferences about tigers.

Contact: j-tilson@mtn.org

Timber Wolf Information Network

URL: http://www.timberwolfinformation.org/

Summary: The Timber Wolf Information Network's goal is to expand the public awareness and acceptance of the wolf and its ecological role in the environment. There is a profusion of wolf information and facts at this site, including several issues of TWIN's newsletter, data on identifying wolf tracks and understanding wolf postures, membership materials, a children's section, and data on a number of wolf related programs.

Contact: webmaster@timberwolfinformation.org

Toxics Release Inventory

URL: http://www.epa.gov/opptintr/tri/

Summary: TRI is published by the U.S. EPA as a valuable source of information about toxic chemicals that are being used, manufactured, transported, or released into the environment. It is used for the notification of the public, businesses, and government agencies who work together to protect our water, land, and air. This site contains information on various ways to access TRI data, a list of TRI chemicals, material about TRI programs, and other national programs.

Contact: oppts@epamail.epa.gov

Tree Canada Foundation

URL: http://www.treecanada.ca/

Summary: The Tree Canada Foundation (TCF) is a nonprofit organization committed to encouraging public awareness, education, and community involvement in the planting and care of urban and rural trees throughout Canada. This site contains information about Canada's trees, a guide to tree planting, data on the benefits of urban trees, the Provincial trees of Canada, and material on climate change. This site may be viewed in English or French.

Contact: tcf@treecanada.ca

Trees for the Future

URL: http://www.treesftf.org/

Summary: Trees for the Future is a not-for-profit action program initiating international environmental projects to establish sustainable programs to alleviate deforestation, climate change, and loss of biodiversity. This site contains material on international tree planting programs, articles on tree planting issues, the latest issue of their newsletter, and information on becoming a member.

Contact: treesftf@erols.com

Tropical Rain Forest in Suriname

URL: http://www.euronet.nl/users/mbleeker/suriname/suri-eng.html

Summary: This is an all in one site about Suriname. The information found here includes the peoples, plants, and animals living in the rainforest as well as the climate and wildlife habitats.

Contact: Marco Bleeker: mbleeker@euronet.nl

The Trouble With Manatees

URL: http://www.xtalwind.net/~cfa/

Summary: This site includes information on manatees from birth to death, manatee anatomy and feeding habits, habitat and water quality issues, manatees and humans, and protection efforts. There are also bibliographical references on manatees and a PBS manatee documentary film offer available here.

Trumbull Land Trust

URL: http://www.geocities.com/RainForest/5496/

Summary: The TLT is a totally volunteer group whose goals are to promote the preservation of natural resources, to acquire lands and preserve them as natural open spaces, and to encourage natural resource education. Information at this site includes TLT news and events and data on land acquisition.

Contact: frankg@geocities.com

The Trust for Public Land (TPL)

URL: http://www.igc.apc.org/tpl/index.html

Summary: TPL is a national organization that conserves land to be used by people as parks and gardens. TPL encourages the government, businesses, and other groups to acquire land for the public to use and enjoy as natural, open spaces. This site gives information on TPL, its programs, how you can join, and how you can help.

Contact: webmaster@tpl.org

Turtle Trax

URL: http://www.turtles.org/overview.htm

Summary: Turtle Trax is a page devoted to the threatened and endangered marine turtles. This site provides information on the causes of sea turtle extinction, what you can do to help, turtle diseases, and why you should care about sea turtles. There are also articles, bibliographies, and images of marine turtles at this site.

Contact: Peter Bennett: honu@turtles.org

Tusk Force

URL: http://dialspace.dial.pipex.com/town/avenue/oc20/

Summary: Tusk Force is dedicated to protecting endangered species. This site contains information on their projects in the UK, Africa, and Asia; news articles; material on adopting a dormouse, chimpanzee, bear, tiger or watervole; and an issue of their newsletter.

Contact: tusk-force@dial.pipex.com

UCLA Center for Clean Technology

URL: http://cct.seas.ucla.edu/

Summary: This site offers information on programs at the Center for Clean Technology, which include pollution prevention programs, combustion and air toxics programs, information on water and wastewater treatment, and data about risk and systems analysis for the control of toxics (RSACT), among others.

Contact: cct@seas.ucla.edu.

UnCover

URL: http://uncweb.carl.org

Summary: This current awareness and document delivery service contains more than 17,000 serial publications. The database is multidisciplinary with a large number of environmental journals indexed. The database is searchable by keyword or author and browsable by journal title. The tables of contents are available for each issue. This is a great place to locate articles from scholarly, technical journals. Includes indexing to *Environmental Action, Environmental Affairs Law Review, Environmental Claims Journal, Environmental Carcinogenesis & Ecotoxicology Reviews, Environmental Contamination and Toxicology, Environmental Engineering, Environmental Impact Assessment Review,* and many others.

Contact: uncover@carl.org

Union of Concerned Scientists

URL: http://www.ucsusa.org/

Summary: UCS strives to foster ideas and answers on such environmental issues as global change, energy, ozone depletion, and population growth. This site provides information about the interrelationship between population growth and the environment, including the debunking of several popular myths. A scientific overview is given on each topic along with a faq and data on government policy.

Contact: ucs@ucsusa.org

United Nations Environment Programme (UNEP)

URL: http://www.unchs.unon.org/

Summary: UNEP sponsors many international treaties and major programs related to environmental issues. This site contains information on the Basel Convention on Transboundary Movements of Hazardous Wastes, the Convention on Biological Diversity, the Convention on Climate Change, the Convention to Combat Desertification, the Convention on International Trade in Endangered Species (CITES), Financial Services Sector and the Environment, and many more.

Contact: eisinfo@unep.ch

University of Florida's Range Science Program

URL: http://www.wec.ufl.edu/range/

Summary: The University of Florida's Range Science program is designed to develop methods of creating economic livestock industries that sustain rangelands and protect wildlife, water, and soil resources. This site contains information about the UF Range Program and goals, a calendar of events, and data on Florida's rangelands, range grasses and range water quality.

Contact: Steve Coates: coates@gnv.ifas.ufl.edu

University of Maine - Department of Wildlife Ecology

URL: http://wlm13.umenfa.maine.edu/w4v1.html

Summary: The U of Maine's site describes the Department's programs, lists faculty and graduate students, describes ongoing research, reports position openings, recounts departmental resources, and gives the dates and topics of their ecology seminar series. Several documents on managing wildlife can be accessed at this site.

Contact: randy@wlm13.umenfa.maine.edu

Urban Forest Ecosystems Institute

URL: http://www.ufei.calpoly.edu/

Summary: UFEI is an organization dedicated to research and the management of urban and remote semi-developed forests. Information available at this site includes conference announcements, employment opportunities, newsletters, forestry grants, upcoming events, and a tree selection guide.

Contact: urbanforestry@urbanfor.cagr.calpoly.edu

USACHPPM Hazardous and Medical Waste Program

URL: http://chppm-meis.apgea.army.mil:80/

Summary: The USACHPPM site contains information papers, hotline reports, fact sheets, and the January 1995 TG-126, Waste Disposal Instructions, along with hazardous waste findings.

Contact: ddavis@chppm-meis.apgea.army.mil

U.S. Army Corps of Engineers - Sacramento District

URL: http://wetland.usace.mil/

Summary: The Sacramento District Regulatory Home Page contains information, documents, and full text reports pertaining to its regulatory activities involving wetlands and wetland research. The USACE regulate certain activities in all waterways and wetlands under Federal law. Included here are an Index of the Nationwide Permits and Conditions, Recognizing Wetlands, and permit applicant information, which is the online version of "US Army Corps of Engineers Regulatory Program Applicant Information." Also contains sections of Title 33 CFR Navigation and Navigable Waters (COE)) and Title 40 CFR - Protection of Environment (EPA).

Contact: Chris Mayo cmayo@spk.usace.army.mil

U.S. Code

URL: http://law.house.gov/usc.htm

Summary: This U.S. House of Representatives site offers a searchable database of the U.S. Code. The U.S. Code contains the text of current public laws enacted by Congress. There are links here to some states that offer their state codes as well. The Code of Federal Regulations concerned with the environment include Title 18: Conservation of Power and Water Resources, Title 30: Mineral Resources, Title 36: Parks, Forests, and Public Property, Title 40: Protection of Environment, and Title 50: Wildlife and Fisheries.

Contact: usc@mail.house.gov

U.S. Code - Title 16 Conservation

URL: http://www.law.cornell.edu/uscode/16/

Summary: All 77 chapters of Title 16 of the United States Code are located at this site. They include information on laws about wetlands, wildlife, cave preservation, fishing, hydroelectric projects, and other related topics.

Contact: lii@lii.law.cornell.edu

USDA Forest Service

URL: http://www.fs.fed.us/

Summary: The USDA Forest Service motto is "caring for the land and serving the people." Some of their goals include encouraging a conservation ethic to support the health, productivity, diversity, the beauty of forests, and safeguarding and managing the National Forests and Grasslands. The extensive information at this site includes the text of major speeches of Forest Service leaders, an organizational directory, descriptions of national forests by state with maps, articles on forests and people, forest management, forest health assessment, international forestry, publications, and descriptions of forestry software and databases.

Contact: rgreensm/wo@fs.fed.us

U.S. FWS Division of Habitat Conservation - National Wetlands Inventory

URL: http://www.nwi.fws.gov/

Summary: This is a very full site containing a lot of wetlands information including databases, NWI digital maps, the online text of *Classification of Wetlands and Deepwater Habitats of the United States Manual*, and *The National List of Plant Species that Occur in Wetlands*.

Contact: gwen@nwi.fws.gov

U.S. Geological Survey Earth and Environmental Science

URL: http://www.usgs.gov/network/science/earth/usgs.html

Summary: This site is an index to all of the USGS servers on the Web including those listed below:

Biological Resources	Mapping Information
Earthquake Information	Marine Geology
Environmental Information	Publications
EROS Data Center (EDC)	USGS Regional Offices and Field Centers
Geologic Information	Volcano Information
Hazards Information	Water Resources Information
Laboratories/Facilities	

Contact: webmaster@www.usgs.gov

Utah Department of Environmental Quality

URL: http://www.eq.state.ut.us/

Summary: The mission of the Utah DEQ is "to safeguard human health and quality of life by protecting and enhancing the environment." This site contains information from the Division of Air Quality, the Air Monitoring Center, and the Division of Drinking Water, which includes data on meetings and seminars, educational resources, and Utah weather information.

Contact: deqinfo@deq.state.ut.us

Utah Department of Wildlife Resources

URL: http://www.nr.state.ut.us/dwr/!homeypg.htm

Summary: Utah's DWR protects a rich diversity of wildlife and its habitats. This site contains information on public meetings concerning wildlife, data and workshop schedules for Project WILD in Utah, the centennial edition of *Wildlife Review*, the current edition of *Wildlife News*, a calendar of events, information on the Utah wetlands program, and data on teaming with wildlife projects.

Contact: DWREditor@aol.com

Utah Public Lands

URL: http://users.aol.com/utahplr/index.htm

Summary: This site provides information on Utah wilderness areas, Utah public lands research, and Utah land management agencies. There is also a public bulletin board with a calendar of events and a newsbrief section.

Contact: rmwarnick@aol.com

Vancouver Island Marmot Pages

URL: http://www.islandnet.com/~marmot/

Summary: This site is dedicated to the Vancouver Island Marmot, which is disappearing from its native habitat and is facing extinction, partly due to bad weather, disease, and predators. This site contains information on the VC marmot, the VC Marmot Recovery Team, a photo gallery, and the adopt-a-marmot program.

Contact: abryant@island.net

Vegan Action

URL: http://www.vegan.org/

Summary: The Vegan Action site contains material on all aspects of veganism including benefits to animals, environmental advantages, and health values. There is information on McVegan, a Vegan Action campaign, data on how to join, and a catalog of earth friendly products at this site.

Contact: info@vegan.org

Vegan Outreach

URL: http://www.veganoutreach.org/mainsite/main.shtml

Summary: This site is dedicated to persuading humans to stop eating animals. At this site you will find information on many reasons for being vegan, including scientific, health, ecological, ethical, medical, theological, sociological, and philosophical arguments. You will also find the organization's newsletter and a vegan bibliography here.

Contact: VeganOutreach@POBoxes.com

Verde River Watershed

URL: http://www.verde.org/

Summary: This site contains information on the Verde River Watershed, the effects of humans on water resources, ideas for instream diversion structures, a searchable database, maps and GIS data, information on the Verde River Association, and data on the Verde River's annual celebration.

Contact: verde@sedona.net

Vermont Agency of Natural Resources

URL: http://www.anr.state.vt.us/

Summary: The Vermont ANR page includes a monthly newsletter, *Reflections on the Environment*, resources for environmental educators, and information on air quality issues, fish and wildlife habitat, recycling, waste management, forestry, water quality, an ANR publications bibliography, plus much more.

Contact: johnd@anrimsgis.anr.state.vt.us

Vermont Land Trust

URL: http://www.vlt.org/

Summary: Vermont Land Trust is a nonprofit land conservation organization. Information at this site includes a faq about the Trust, newsletter excerpts, press releases, land conservation options, forest management plans, and a calendar of events.

Contact: webmaster@vlt.org

Virginia Coast Reserve LTER

URL: http://atlantic.evsc.virginia.edu/

Summary: The Virginia Coast Reserve LTER studies the barrier-island/lagoon/mainland landscape of the Eastern Shore of Virginia and provides data access to ecological researchers. This site provides information on datasets, databases, reports, research summaries, newsletters, and employment opportunities.

Contact: JPorter@lternet.edu

Virginia Department of Forestry

URL: http://stat.vipnet.org/dof/

Summary: The Virginia Department of Forestry site contains information on forest protection, management, and health programs; forest facts; forest resource assessment; meeting announcements; forest fire reports; insect and disease control; urban tree care; and water quality.

Contact: Use form at site: http://state.vipnet.org/cgi-bin/dof/feedback.cgi

Virginia Natural Heritage Program

URL: http://www.state.va.us/~dcr/vaher.html

Summary: Virginia's Natural Heritage Program is "a comprehensive effort to inventory and preserve the animal, plant and natural community resources of the Commonwealth of Virginia." This site provides information on rare plants and animals, invasive alien plants, natural environments, and natural resource preserves.

Contact: Megan Rollins: mgr@dcr.state.va.us

Walk in the Woods

URL: http://www.washingtonforests.com/

Summary: A Walk in the Woods is the Washington Forest Protection Agency's Website. At this site you can learn about the state of Washington's Forests, find out about the wildlife inhabitants, discover information on watersheds, read about forest products, find forest jobs and learn about trees as renewable resources. You can also read about Washington State's forest regulations and keep up with forest issues.

Contact: Washington Forest Protection Association, Evergreen Plaza Bldg.,Suite 608, 711 Capitol Way, Olympia, WA 98501.

Washington State Environmental Resources

URL: http://www.wa.gov/environ.html

Summary: This State of Washington site contains a large quantity of information about the state environmental resources including government resources, water, forestry, pollution, Washington weather, volcanic information, and data on earthquakes.

Contact: HomePageWA@dis.wa.gov

Waste Prevention Association

URL: http://www.rec.hu/poland/wpa/wpa.htm

Summary: WPA is a nongovernmental, nonprofit environmental organization whose goal is to encourage waste reduction at its source, eco-friendly waste management and recycling efforts. There are many articles on renewable energy resources, sustainable agriculture, recycling, composting, and international government waste regulations at this site.

Contact: office@otzo.most.org.pl

Water Environment Web

URL: http://www.wef.org/

Summary: Water Environment Web is the official site of the Water Environment Federation. This site includes information on U.S. regulations and legislation on water issues, conferences, and professional development data, technical discussion groups, and a member association exchange. Water Environment Web also contains biosolid, watershed, and industrial information, publications, and conference news.

Contact: webfeedback@wef.org

Waterfront

URL: http://www.mbnet.mb.ca/wpgwater/

Summary: The Waterfront is the city of Winnipeg's water conservation page. It includes tips on how to save water, lists of programs and activities that the city has used and is currently implementing, and ways that they have involved school children in the project.

Contact: Use form at site: http://www.mbnet.mb.ca/wpgwater/watrtalk.html

Water Management Research Laboratory (WMRL)

URL: http://pwa.ars.usda.gov/fno/wmrl/

Summary: WMRL is a part of the United States Department of Agriculture whose goal is to develop water management procedures that use soil, water, nutrients, and energy resources productively while improving agricultural sustainability in places where water is scarce. The WMRL site contains progress reports, downloadable software and conference information, as well as archives of the TRICKLE-L and SALINITY-L listservs.

Contact: rsoppe@asrr.arsusda.gov

Watershed Management Council

URL: http://watershed.org/wmc/

Summary: The Watershed Management Council is a nonprofit educational organization that promotes the understanding of good watershed management. This site contains conference announcements and calls for papers, membership data, newsletters, a calendar of events, a glossary of terms, and a riparian bibliography.

Contact: Mike Furniss furniss@watershed.org

WATERSHEDSS Water Quality Decision Support System

URL: http://h20sparc.wq.ncsu.edu/

Summary: The goals of WATERSHEDSS are to help watershed managers in making appropriate land management and land treatment choices to accomplish water quality objectives and to control and minimize water pollution sources. This site contains information on how to protect estuary, river, lake, stream, and wetland resources; the searchable NCSU Water Quality Group Annotated Bibliography of Nonpoint Source Literature; articles on water quality and land treatment; data about WATERSHEDSS; and GIS data.

Contact: Deanna Osmond: deanna_osmond@ncsu.edu

WaterWorld

URL: http://www.waterworld.com/

Summary: WaterWorld bills itself as "serving the municipal water/wastewater industry." The site contains excerpts from news articles about the water/wastewater industry, a searchable database of products mentioned on WaterWorld, a classified advertising section, and access to a subscription to *WaterWorld Magazine* with a brief overview of the current issue.

Contact: waterwld@pennwell.com

Weather and Global Monitoring

URL: http://www.csu.edu.au/weather.html

Summary: This Australian site furnishes up-to-date international weather and climate information, including weather map images, and information on hurricanes, typhoons, cyclones, earthquakes, and volcanoes. There is also data on environmental monitoring from space and current weather satellite images at this location.

Contact: pbristow@csu.edu.au

Whale and Dolphin Conservation Society

URL: http://WWW.WDCS.ORG/

Summary: The WDCS campaigns against killing whales and dolphins for profit and performs research to stop pollution. Data at this site includes articles about the war on commercial whaling and the international tuna industry's pursuit of legitimizing dolphin killing. There is also information on projects in 30 countries and on adopt-a-whale or dolphin programs.

Contact: Heather@wdcs.org

Whale Conservation Institute

URL: http://www.whale.org/

Summary: The goal of the Institute is the conservation and protection of whales through research and education. Information at this site includes data on the Right Whale Program, data on the Ecotox Program, benign research techniques, and articles on education programs. There are also research materials from the WCI ketch "Odyssey" at this site.

Contact: kim@whale.org

WhaleNet

URL: http://whale.wheelock.edu/

Summary: WhaleNet concentrates on whale and marine research and education. This site
                contains information on whale sightings, species and behaviors, whale strandings,
                research and tagging programs. Conference data, educational resources,
                bibliographies, and news reports. Faqs can also be found here.

Contact: whalemaster@whale.wheelock.edu

WhaleTimes SeaBed

URL: http://www.whaletimes.org/whahmpg.htm

Summary: This is predominantly an educational site, but there are some interesting facts on
                whales and other marine life here, plus a form to send in questions to Jake the
                Seadog.

Contact: seamail@whaletimes.org

Wild Animal Rescue Foundation of Thailand (WAR)

URL: http://www.siam.net/war/index.html

Summary: The Wild Animal Rescue Foundation of Thailand promotes campaigning against
                and preventing hunting and cruelty to wild animals, the rescue of wild animals, and
                the conservation and balance of nature and the ecological system. This site contains
                information on the endangered gibbons of Thailand and the gibbon rehabilitation
                project, as well as several volunteer opportunities.

Contact: warft@loxinfo.co.th

Wild Bird Rehabilitation Center

URL: http://science.smsu.edu/~danelle/rehab.html

Summary: The goal of the Wild Bird Rehabilitation Center is to provide the best possible care
                for injured, ill, and orphaned wild birds and to release them back into the wild. This
                site includes data on chimney swifts, bird nesting habits, migratory songbirds, their
                adopt-a-bird program, and information on how you can help the Center.

Contact: wildbirdrehab@hotmail.com

Wildlands League

URL: http://web.idirect.com/~wildland/

Summary: The objective of the Wildlands League is to protect Ontario's wild places. This site encompasses information on becoming a League member, data about their endangered spaces campaigns, excerpts from their twice yearly newsletter, bulletins about current issues, and data on becoming a League volunteer.

Contact: wildland@web.net

Wildlands Project

URL: http://www.twp.org/

Summary: The Wildlands Project is an organization of conservation biologists and conservation activists dedicated to developing a wilderness recovery strategy for all of North America. Information at this site includes a calendar of events, data on current projects, an article on the Project's vision, and a request for help.

Contact: information@twp.org

Wildlife at Risk-Canada

URL: http://www-nais.ccrs.nrcan.gc.ca/schoolnet/issues/risk/ewldlfrsk.html

Summary: This site contains the status, description, population and distribution, habitat, general biology, limiting factors, and protection status of wild species in Canada as well as a bibliography for each genus and a glossary of terms.

Wildlife Center of Silicon Valley

URL: http://www.acoates.com/Wildlife.html

Summary: The Wildlife Center of Silicon Valley (WCSV) is an independent, nonprofit organization that furnishes rescue and care services to local injured, sick, and orphaned wildlife. The purpose of this site is to help preserve wildlife as our natural heritage.

Contact: webmaster@acoates.com

Wildlife Preservation Trust International

URL: http://www.columbia.edu/cu/cerc/WPTI/

Summary: WPTI is concerned with saving endangered species with the help of scientists and educators from around the world. Information at this site includes captive breeding, wild animal healthcare, education programs, and membership data.

Contact: wpti@aol.com

Wildlife Rescue Association of B.C.

URL: http://www.vcn.bc.ca/wra/welcome.html

Summary: The WRA, working with volunteer veterinarians and special advisors, is dedicated to caring for orphaned, injured, and pollution-damaged wildlife. This site contains data on volunteering, organizational information, rescuing wildlife, lifesaving facts, and some tips on when to rescue a baby bird.

Contact: wra@vcn.bc.ca

Wildlife Rescue Center of Napa County

URL: http://www.napanet.net/~wrcnc/index.html

Summary: The Wildlife Rescue Center of Napa County is dedicated to the rehabilitation and release of injured Napa County wildlife and to promote the peaceful cohabitation of the County's human and wildlife populations. Information available at this site includes wildlife tips, volunteer opportunities, and membership data.

Contact: wrcnc@napanet.net

Wildlife Society

URL: http://www.wildlife.org/index.html

Summary: The Wildlife Society is an association of wildlife professionals who are committed to educating others in wildlife administration and dedicated to studying all forms of wildlife in their native habitats. This site includes membership information, meeting data, wildlife policies, and information on Society publications.

Contact: tws@wildlife.org

Wildlife Trusts

URL: http://www.wildlifetrust.org.uk/

Summary: The Wildlife Trusts of the UK works with landowners, families, government, and industry to give nature a chance by managing more than 2,000 nature reserves. Here you can find information on becoming a member or volunteer, pointers to other Trusts online, data on joining a club for young conservationists, and information on jobs with the Wildlife Trusts.

Contact: wildlifersnc@cix.compulink.co.uk

WildNet Africa

URL: http://wildnetafrica.co.za/

Summary: The WildNet Africa site contains information on all aspects of African wildlife. There are many articles on environmental issues from *Bushcraft Wildlife Magazine*, diaries of game preserves, a directory of wildlife and nature preserves, a book and video catalog, and wildlife columns.

Contact: basecamp@wildnetafrica.com

Wild Rockies Slate

URL: http://www.wildrockies.org/

Summary: Wild Rockies Slate is the grassroots activist Web site for the wild Rockies bioregion. Information at this site includes oil and gas leasing in the Rockies, the WRS Eco-defense Library, an activist exchange program between U.S. and Central & Eastern European environmentalists, and the truth about salvage logging.

Contact: webmaster@wildrockies.org

WindStar Wildlife Institute

URL: http://www.windstar.org/wildlife/

Summary: In 1986 the Windstar Wildlife Institute was created to provide a model of wildlife habitat creation and preservation for those concerned about the devastating effects of civilization on wildlife habitats. The Institute's site includes information on attracting wildlife, creating habitats, monthly tips, and news. There is also material about classes, a photo gallery, and data on becoming a member and registering your habitat.

Contact: wildlife@windstar.org

Wisconsin Wildlife Federation

URL: http://www.easy-axcess.com/wwf/

Summary: Some of WWF's goals are to develop and disseminate educational programs and information on conservation of natural resources and wildlife, to encourage and improve cooperation in the preservation of natural resources, and the preservation and production of wildlife and their habitats. This site provides data on WWF membership and mission; affiliate organizations; environmental education programs for children, teens, families, and teachers; and information on the Wisconsin Environmental Leadership Directive.

Contact: wwf@easy-axcess.com

Wolf Haven International

URL: http://www.eleport.com/~wnorton/wolf.shtml

Summary: Wolf Haven International is a nonprofit, scientific, and educational organization whose mission is the conservation of wolves and their habitat, the reintroduction of wolves to their historical ranges, and the education of the public about all wildlife. This site includes wolf fact sheets, data on wolf adoption, images, and articles from *Wolftracks Magazine*.

Contact: WolfHvn@AOL.COM

World Business Council for Sustainable Development (WBCSD)

URL: http://www.wbcsd.ch/aboutus.htm#top

Summary: The WBCSD is an international league of businesses dedicated to developing cooperation between businesses and governments concerned with the environment and sustainable development. This site contains regional news, a list of members, and extensive library of speeches on environmental issues, press releases, publications, and information from a panel discussion on eco-efficiency indicators.

Contact: info@wbcsd.ch

World Climate Research Programme

URL: http://www.wmo.ch/web/wcrp/wcrp-home.html

Summary: The objective of the WCRP is to acquire an understanding of the earth's climate system and climate processes to ascertain the extent to which climate can be predicted and the extent of man's influence on climate. Topics studied include global atmosphere, oceans, sea and land ice, and land surface. Information available at this site includes a definition of WCRP, its goals, its objectives, its research activities, and its observational needs.

Contact: w3server@www.wmo.ch

World Conservation Monitoring Centre

URL: http://www.wcmc.org.uk/

Summary: The World Conservation Monitoring Centre is a nonprofit organization that provides information services on the conservation and sustainable use of species and ecosystems. This site furnishes information on national parks, protected areas, endangered species, and biodiversity. Other information available at the WCMC site includes several conservation databases, inernational conventions and program data, and WCMC training program material.

Contact: info@wcmc.org.uk

World Conservation Society

URL: http://www.wcs.org/

Summary: The World Conservation Society, located at the Bronx Zoo, has the goal of saving wildlife and wildlands around the world. This site contains information on its many international programs, parks, and projects. Descriptions of talks and video clips from the Northern California Council lecture series, school, and public education programs, and membership information can also be found at this site.

Contact: feedback@wcs.org

World Energy Efficiency Association (WEEA)

URL: http://www.weea.org/

Summary: WEEA's goals are to help developing countries to obtain information on efficient energy, to provide information on energy programs and technologies, and to encourage international energy efficiency. This site contains WEEA publications, USAID technical reports, a list of international energy efficient organizations, and information on the Association.

Contact: info@weea.org

World Forum for Acoustic Ecology

URL: http://interact.uoregon.edu:80/MediaLit/WFAEHomePage

Summary: The World Forum for Acoustic Ecology is an organization that is dedicated to the study of the ecology of sound. At this site you will find information on the organization and becoming a member, a discussion group, a database of world acoustic sites, documents, articles, and an archive of *Soundscape*, the newsletter of WFAE. Articles on noise pollution and how it affects your life are also located at this site.

Contact: garywf@oregon.uoregon.edu

World Meteorologic Organization

URL: http://www.wmo.ch/

Summary: WMO organizes worldwide scientific research to make weather, pollution, climate change, and ozone layer depletion information available for public, private, and commercial use. Data at this site includes weather information, WMO long-term plans, a catalog of WMO publications, and links to WMO programs.

Contact: gorre-dale_e@gateway.wmo.ch

World Resource Foundation

URL: http://www.wrfound.org.uk/

Summary: WRF is committed to providing an international database of information about sustainable waste management, recycling, composting, energy recovery, and final landfill disposal. Included at this site are waste information sheets, waste-related archives, and the *Journal of the WRF*.

Contact: wrf@wrf.org.uk

World Resources Institute

URL: http://www.wri.org/

Summary: WRI is an independent center for policy research on environmental issues whose goal is to motivate people to live in sustainable ways to protect earth's environment. Material found at this site includes publications, employment opportunities, educational programs, biodiversity conservation programs, climate programs, coastal resources, policy research initiatives, and news releases.

Contact: philip@wri.org

World Society for the Protection of Animals (WSPA)

URL: http://www.kilimanjaro.com/wspa/wspa.htm

Summary: The WSPA is concerned with the protection of animals and respect for animal life worldwide. This site contains articles from their newsletter, data on what they're about, and information on their programs.

Contact: wspa@igc.apc.org

World Wide Fund Global Network

URL: http://www.panda.org/home.htm

Summary: World Wide Fund is an international organization for the conservation and preservation of wildlife. Some of the information at this site includes current conservation news; global action alerts; and data on endangered species, fisheries, oceanography, the greenhouse effect, wetland conservation, and climate change. This site also contains job postings, a tip of the day, a monthly quiz and a survey, plus information on how you can help.

Contact: Use form at site: http://www.panda.org/forms/feedback.htm

World Wide Water

URL: http://pubweb.ucdavis.edu/documents/gws/envissues/george_fink/masterw.htm

Summary: The World Wide Water page is dedicated to helping all who are interested in fresh water as it relates to agriculture and the environment. This page contains a list of pointers to all types of water resources, including local, state, and federal government sites, and ecological and eco-political resources.

Contact: George Fink: gkfink@ucdavis.edu

World Wildlife Fund

URL: http://www.wwf.org/

Summary: The World Wildlife Fund was developed in an effort to maintain the variety of life on our planet. The WWF site contains information about WWF, their programs, policies, and publications.

Contact: Use form at site: http://www.wwf.org/mail/frame_feedback.htm

Wright's PestLaw

URL: http://www.pestlaw.com

Summary: This site, sponsored by a lawyer, provides regulatory information and other resources pertaining to pesticides. There are discussion group archives, a calendar of events, portions of Title 40 of the Code of Federal Regulations, pesticide regulation notices from the Environmental Protection Agency and from the State of California, and links to other pesticide information sites, including a site with an alphabetized listing of Federal Register notices of tolerance (pesticide) petition applications, and applications to register pesticide products containing a new active ingredient.

Contact: James C. Wright: wright@pestlaw.com

Yellow Mountain Institute for Sustainable Living

URL: http://monticello.avenue.gen.va.us/Community/Environ/YellowMtn/

Summary: The Yellow Mountain Institute is a nonprofit organization that facilitates the introduction of sustainable building techniques to make energy efficient housing available throughout the country. This site contains a lot of information on sustainable construction, alternative energy systems, and alternative water systems.

Contact: Lroyse@worldnet.att.net

Yellowstone Grizzly Foundation

URL: http://www.wyoming.com/~ygf/

Summary: The mission of the Yellowstone Grizzly Foundation is to preserve the Yellowstone Grizzly bear and Yellowstone's wild heritage. Information at this site includes grizzly characteristics and behaviors, education programs on grizzly management and conservation, human-bear interaction research programs, publications, and membership material.

Contact: ygf@wyoming.com

Zero Emissions Research Initiative

URL: http://www.zeri.org/

Summary: ZERI's goal is to introduce methods to industry that will make waste products from one process into the input for another product or system, thereby eliminating industrial wastes. This site provides a schedule of international ZERI events, newsletters and status reports, public discussions, and an archive of zero emission documents.

Contact: Gunter Pauli: gunter_pauli@rocketmail.com

Zero Waste America

URL: http://www.ZeroWasteAmerica.com/

Summary: ZWA facilitates the elimination of waste and pollution by educating the public and legislation. Material at this site includes national and international legislation, data on how to lobby on waste issues, examples of bad recycling, incinerators, environmental law news, composting, water treatment, population impact, solar and renewable energy, and many more environmental topics.

Contact: lynnlandes@zerowasteamerica.org

The Zoe Foundation

URL: http://www.awod.com/gallery/probono/zoe/index.html

Summary: The Zoe Foundation is dedicated to saving the endangered big cats. The primary concentration is on the Indochinese tiger and the Tiger Island project. Information on this project and on how you can help is contained at this site along with links to other carnivore preservation sites.

Contact: designer@2zoe.com

Academy of Natural Sciences, 136, 163
  Know Your Environment, 136, 163

Accidents *see* **Disasters**

Acid rain *see* **Atmospheric precipitation**

Acoustics
  NATO SACLANT, 296
  World Forum for Acoustic Ecology, 364

Advanced Forest Technologies Program, 163, 314

Aerospace Medical Association, 107

Africa
  Africa: Environment and Wildlife, 104
  African Environmental Research and
    Consulting Group, 164
  AFWATER (Discussion group), 10
  EcoNews Africa, 119
  Namibia Animal Rehabilitation Research and
    Education Centre, 286
  Southern Africa Environment Page, 337
  WildNet Africa, 361

Agency for Toxic Substances & Disease Registry,
  165, 189

AGRALIN, 165

Agriculture *see also* **Sustainable agriculture**
  AG-IMPACT (Discussion group), 11
  AGLAW-L (Discussion group), 11
  AGRALIN, 165
  AGRIC-L (Discussion group), 11
  Agriculture Network Information Center, 165
  alt.agriculture, 87
  alt.agriculture.misc, 87
  American Farmland Trust, 168
  City Farmer, 198
  COMPOST (Discussion group), 25
  Compost Resource Page, 201
  Consultative Group on International Agricultural
    Research, 202
  Council for Agricultural Science and
    Technology, 204
  ECOL-AGRIC (Discussion group), 31
  Energy Crops Forum, 123
  Farm Aid News & Views, 127
  Global Food Watch, 129
  gov.us.topic.agri.farms, 94
  IRRIGATION-L (Discussion group), 59
  Louisiana Department of Agriculture & Forestry,
    273
  sci.agriculture, 98
  TRICKLE-L (Discussion group), 77

World Wide Water, 365

Agroforestry
  bionet.agroforestry, 90
  New Forests News, 141
  New Forests Project, 141, 301
  Sylvanet (Discussion group), 76

Air & Waste Management Association, 121, 166
  EM Online, 121, 166

Air pollution
  Air Force Center for Environmental Excellence
    (AFCEE), 166
  AIRPOLLUTION-BIOLOGY (Discussion group),
    12
  British Atmospheric Data Center, 180
  Clean Cities Drive Newsletter, 112
  Environmental Protection Agency, 225
  Environment Canada, 118, 229
  Enviroene (EPA), 230
  EPA-TOX (Mailing list), 45
  gov.us.topic.environment.air, 95
  Kola Ecogeochemistry, 270
  Minnesota Pollution Control Agency, 282
  NAPEnet - National Association of Physicians for
    the Environment, 287
  National Institute for Environmental Studies, 291
  National Pollutant Release Inventory, 292
  National Society for Clean Air, 294
  ORNL Review, 143
  Pollution Probe, 318
  Rachel's Environment & Health Weekly, 146
  State and Territorial Air Pollution Program
    Administrators, 338
  UCLA Center for Clean Technology, 347

Alabama
  Department of Environmental Management, 166

Los Alamos National Laboratory, 114

Alaska
  Alaska Ecoregions Mapping, Monitoring, and
    Assessment Program, 212
  Chilkat Bald Eagle Preserve, 197
  Department of Environmental Conservation, 167,
    303
  Earth's Resources Observation Satellite (EROS)
    Data Center, 212
  Southeast Alaska Conservation Council, 330

Albany Research Center, 167

Alfred Wegener Institute for Polar and Marine
  Research, 167

Alternative Agriculture News, 104

Alternative energy *see also* **Geothermal energy, Sustainable energy, Solar energy, Wind energy**
AE (Discussion group), 9
Alternative Fuels Data Center, 208
American Hydrogen Association, 169
California Energy Commission, 183
Centre for Alternative Transportation Fuels, 111, 194
Energies, 123
Hydrogen (Discussion group), 57
novel-fuels (Discussion group), 65
Pacific Rim Consortium in Energy Combustion, and the Environment, 315

Amazon River, 211

American Academy of Environmental Engineers, 168, 174, 179

American Chemical Society, 168

American Council for an Energy-Efficient Economy, 168

American Farmland Trust, 168

American Forests, 169, 296

American Geophysical Union, 133, 169
HydroWire, 133

American Hydrogen Association, 169
Hydrogen & Fuel Cell Letter, 169

American Library Association
GreeNotes, 130

American Rivers, 170

American Society for Environmental History, 56

American Society of Civil Engineers, 173

American Society of Limnology and Oceanography
HydroWire, 133

American Sociology Association, 44

American Solar Energy Society, 170

American Water Works Association, 170

American Wind Energy Association, 214

Ames Laboratory, 171

Amphibians *see* **Reptiles and Amphibians**

Anaerobic Processes
DIGESTION (Discussion group), 28

Animals and animal ecology
alt.animals.whales, 87
CARNIVORE-L (Discussion group), 20
Cetacean Society International, 157, 195
Cochrane Ecological Institute, 198
International Marine Mammal Project, 260
Oceania Project, 307
Tiger Information Center, 344
Timber Wolf Information Network, 344
The Trouble with Manatees, 345
Vancouver Island Marmot Pages, 352
WhaleNet, 358
Whales Alive!, 157, 195
Wolf Haven International, 362
Yellowstone Grizzly Foundation, 367

Animal welfare
Animal Rights, 13-14, 105
AR-NEWS (Discussion group), 13
AR-VIEWS (Discussion group), 14
Bear Watch, 177
Mountain Lion Foundation, 286
Save the Manatee Club, 329
Save the Rhino International, 329
Whale and Dolphin Conservation Society, 357
Whale Conservation Institute, 357
World Society for the Protection of Animals, 365
Zoe Foundation, 367

Apicultural Information and Issues, 105

Appropriate Technology for Community and Environment, 171

Aquaculture
FISHERIES (Discussion group), 48
Makai, 138
National Sea Grant Depository, 293
National Sea Grant Program, 294
sci.bio.fisheries, 99

Aquatic Conservation Network, 8-9

Aquifers *see* **Groundwater**

Architecture *see* **Buildings and architecture**

Arctic and Antarctic regions
Antarctic and South Ocean Coalition, 171
Arctic Environmental Data Directory, 242

Arctic Monitoring and Assessment Programme, 242
Byrd Polar Research Center, 183
Earth's Resources Observation Satellite (EROS) Data Center, 212
Program for the Conservation of Arctic Flora and Fauna, 242

Argonne National Laboratory, 172

Arid lands and desertification
Arid Lands Newsletter, 106
Desert Research Institute, 115, 209
Desert Research Institute Newsletter, 115
IALC Online Newsletter, 133
International Arid Lands Consortium, 133, 256

Arizona
Arizona Geological Survey, 172
Arizona Highways, 106
Arizona Legislative Information System, 172
University of Arizona, Office of Arid Lands Studies
Arid Lands Newsletter, 106
Verde River Watershed, 353

Arkansas
Arkansas Natural Heritage Commission, 173

ASCE Geotechnical Engineering Seepage/ Groundwater Modeling Software, 173

Asia
Appropriate Technology for Community and Environment, 171
Asia Environmental Review, 230
Asia-Pacific Centre for Environmental Law, 173
China Environmental Review, 230
Environment in Asia, 230

Association for Biodiversity Information, 297

Association of Energy Engineers, 174

Association of Environmental and Resource Economists, 10, 72

Association of University Leaders for a Sustainable Future, 174

Atlantic Salmon Federation, 174

Atmospheric Dispersion of Chemicals (Discussion group), 55

Atmospheric precipitation
Acid Rain Division, EPA, 225

National Center for Atmospheric Research, 220, 289
Skies Above Foundation, 333

Atmospheric radiation
Global Climate Web Site Research, 240
UVB Impacts Reporter, 156

Australia
aus.environment.conservation, 90
Australian Cooperative Research Centres, 175
Australian Oceanographic Data Centre, 175
Biodiversity Information Network, 17, 176, 179
Biolinks, 107
Bushlines, 109
Earthlink, 134, 211, 327
Environmental Resources Information Network (ERIN), 226
HYDROLOGY (Discussion group), 58
LIFE, 272
Linkages, 117, 137
Oceania Project, 307
REEL (Discussion group), 71
Threatened Species Network, 343
Weather and Global Monitoring, 357

Baltic Sea Region
BALLERINA-L (Discussion group), 15

Base De Dados Tropical Center, 176
BIODIV-L (Discussion group), 17

Battelle Memorial Institute
Battelle Environmental Systems and Technology Division, 176
Battelle Seattle Research Group, 177

BC Research, Inc., 111, 194

Bear Watch, 177

Bellona Foundation, 178

Biodiversity
Base De Dados Tropical, 17, 176, 179
Biodiversity Information Network, 17, 176, 179
BIODIV-L (Discussion group), 17
Biolinks, 107
Biological Conservation Newsletter, 108
Mangrove Replenishment Initiative, 276
Tropical Biodiversity, 155

Biogas
DIGESTION (Discussion group), 28

Biological conservation
see also **Botanical conservation, Marine conservation, Wildlife and wildlife conservation**
BIODIV-L (Discussion group), 17
Biological Conservation Newsletter, 108
Center for Conservation Biology Network, 188
CONSBIO (Discussion group), 25
Conservation Ecology, 114
Conservation International CONSLINK (Discussion group), 26
CTURTLE (Discussion group), 27
Patuxent Wildlife Research Center, 315
sci.bio.conservation, 98
sci.environment, 100
talk.environment, 102
Turtle Trax, 346
Wildlands Project, 359

Biology
bionet.plants, 90
BIOSPH-L (Discussion group), 18
CONSBIO (Discussion group), 25
CONSLINK (Discussion group), 26
GAP (Gap Analysis Program), 238
Open University Ecology and Conservation Research Group, 311

Biomass energy
BIOENERGY (Discussion group), 17

BioRap Database, 226

Bioregionalism
BIOREGIONAL (Discussion group), 18
Pinecrest: an Adventure..., 317

Bioremediation
Biocatalysis/Biodegradation Database, 230
BIOGROUP (Discussion group), 18
Bioremediation in the Field, 198
Center for Environmental Biotechnology, 189

Biosphere
International Geosphere-Biosphere Programme, 258
International Satellite Land Surface Climatology Project, 262
mabnet_america (Discussion group), 62

Birds
BBLMTAB (Discussion group), 16
Birdband (Discussion group), 19
Birdbanding Laboratory, 180
Birdchat (Discussion group), 19
Birding on the Web, 180
Canadian Ratite Home Page, 186
Chilkat Bald Eagle Preserve, 197
FWS-Shorebirds (Discussion group), 51
Hawk Mountain Sanctuary, 248
HawkWatch International, 248
Holland Island Preservation Foundation, 251
International Crane Foundation, 258
Iowa Raptor Foundation, 266
Journey North, 269
Macaw Landing Foundation, 275
marshbirds (Discussion group), 63
Milton Keynes Wildlife Hospital, 281
National Audubon Society, 14-15, 68, 82, 88, 106, 251, 283, 289
Nova Scotia Bird Society, 307
Orphaned Wildlife Rehabilitation Society, 313
Peregrine Falcons at the University of Calgary, 316
Peregrine Fund, 317
Piping Plover Guardian Program, 318
Raptor Center (Univ. of Minnesota), 323
Raptor Release, 146
Raptor Resource Project, 323
rec.birds, 98
sanctuaries, 96, 192, 247, 267, 289, 298, 300
Smithsonian Institution's Conservation and Research Center, 334
Southeastern Raptor Rehabilitation Center, 337
tweeters (Discussion group), 77
Wild Bird Rehabilitation Center, 358

Bonnell Environmental Consulting, 180

Botanical conservation
Baker Prairie Natural Area, 173
BEN (The Botanical Electronic News), 107
CBCN-L (Discussion group), 20
Center for Plant Conservation, 192
New England Wild Flower Society, 300

Botany
BEN (Botanical Electronic News), 107
Biodiversity Information Network, 17, 176, 179
Biological Conservation Newsletter, 108
bionet.plants, 90
CBCN-L (Discussion group), 20
lichens (Discussion group), 61
PPBC-L (Discussion group), 69

Brazil
Base De Dados Tropical, 17, 176, 179
Biodiversity Information Network, 17, 176, 179

British Columbia
North Island Wildlife Recovery Association, 307
Vancouver Island Marmot Pages, 352
Wildlife Rescue Association of B.C., 360

Brookhaven National Laboratory, 181

Brown Is Green, 181

Buildings and architecture
Advanced Technologies for Commercial Buildings, 164
alt.building.environment, 87
Arcosanti Project, 169
Center for Environmental Design Research, 190
Center for Renewable Energy and Sustainable Technology (CREST), 192
Center for Resourceful Building Technology, 193
e design, 120
Energy Source Builder, 123
EnergyStar (Discussion group), 36
Environmental Building News, 123
ESSA (Discussion group), 46
Florida Design Initiative, 120, 235
GreenClips, 130
Joint Center for Energy Management, 269
Sustainable Sources, 340
Yellow Mountain Institute for Sustainable Living, 366

Bureau of Land Management, 93, 182, 209

Bureau of Reclamation, 182, 209

Business and industry *see also* **Chemical industry**
Best Manufacturing Practice Center of Excellence, 178
BWZ, 109
CADDET (Centre for the Analysis and Dissemination of Demonstrated Energy Technologies), 183
Carnegie Institute of Technology (Carnegie Mellon University), 187
CERES-L (Discussion group), 187
Chemical Industry Institute of Toxicology, 196
Chemistry & Industry, 111, 163
clari.tw.environment.releases, 91
Consortium on Green Design and Manufacturing, 202
Corporate Watch (News), 114
Direct Contact Environmental Toll-Free Directory, 209
Earthlink, 134, 211, 327
ECDM (Discussion group), 30
ECO-FUND (Discussion group), 31
EcoMall, 213
EcoTradeNet, 214
ENVBUS-L (Discussion group), 37
Environmental Data Pages, 222
Environmental Industry Web Site, 223, 267
Environmental Restoration Small Business, 207
Environment Business Magazine, 126
Global Environmental Options, 240

Global Futures Foundation, 241
Global Recycling Network, Inc., 242
GREEN PAGES, 190, 211, 244, 321
Greenpeace Toxic Trade Updates, 131
Green Seal, 245
GREENTIE, 245
GREEN-TRAVEL (Discussion group), 54
IEEE TAB Environment, Health and Safety Committee, 253
industrial-ecology (Discussion group), 58
International Centre for Gas Technology Information, 257
International Institute for Industrial Environmental Economics, 259
ISO (Discussion group), 60
Journal of Industrial Ecology, 136
Michigan Pulp and Paper Pollution Prevention Program, 281
OILGASLAW-L (Discussion group), 66
ONE-L (Discussion group), 66
Pollution Engineering, 145
PRINTECH (Discussion group), 70
QUEST (Discussion group), 70
Sierra Solar Systems, 332
Sustainable Sources, 340
World Business Council for Sustainable Development, 362
Zero Emissions Research Initiative, 367

Byrd Polar Research Center, 183

CADDET (Centre for the Analysis and Dissemination of Demonstrated Energy Technologies), 183

Cahners Business Information, 145

California
ca.environment, 91, 213
California Conservation Corps, 183-184
California Energy Commission, 183
California Environmental Protection Agency, 184
California Environmental Resources Evaluation System (CERES), 184
California League of Conservation Voters, 215
California Resources Agency, 184
California Watersheds Projects Inventory, 255
CA-WATER (Discussion group), 20
ca.water, 91
Center for Clean Technology (UCLA), 347
Center for Conservation Biology (UC Irvine), 188
Chanslor Wetlands Wildlife Project, 195
Consortium on Green Design and Manufacturing, 202
Ecovote, 215
Global Environmental Options, 240
Greenbelt Alliance, 243

Information Center for the Environment (UC Davis), 256
Land Conservancy of San Luis Obispo County, 271
Mendocino County Ecology Web, 279
Napa County Conservation District, 287
Natural Resources Directory, 298
Natural Resources Services, 298
Palos Verdes Peninsula Land Conservancy, 142, 315
San Francisco Estuary Institute, 327
San Gorgonio Volunteer Association, 327
Santa Barbara County Air Pollution Control District, 142, 328
Save-the-Redwoods League, 329
Scripps Institute of Oceanography, 330
Sempervirens Fund, 332
University of California at Berkeley, Boalt Hall School of Law, 118
University of California at Davis, Information Center for the Environment, 255
University of California at Los Angeles, Center for Clean Technology, 347
U.S. Army Corps of Engineers-Sacramento District, 349
WATER-ON-LINE (Discussion group), 349
Wildlife Rescue Center of Napa County, 360
Wright's PestLaw, 366

Cambridge Scientific Abstracts, 227

Campus Green Vote, 29, 190

Canada *see also* **British Columbia, Nova Scotia**
Advanced Forest Technologies Program, 163, 314
Advanced Technologies for Commercial, 164 Buildings, 36, 123, 130, 164, 192, 269
Aquatic Conservation Network, 8-9
Biodiversity Information Network, 17, 176, 179
Canada Centre for Inland Waters, 185
Canadian Botanical Conservation Network (Discussion group), 20
Canadian Chlorine Coordinating Committee, 185
Canadian Coastal Science and Engineering Association, 21
Canadian Council of Ministers of the Environment, 185
Canadian Environmental Assessment Agency, 186
Canadian Global Change Program, 114
Canadian Institute for Environmental Law and Policy, 109, 186
Canadian Institute for Environmental Law and Policy Newsletter, 109
Centre for Alternative Transportation Fuels, 111, 194

China Council, 197
Cochrane Ecological Institute/Wildlife Reserve, 198
Conference on Communication and the Environment, 24
Crop Protection Institute, 205
Delta, 114
Enviro-Access, 219
Environment Canada, 118, 229
GWCAN-L (Discussion group), 55
National Pollutant Release Inventory, 292
National Water Research Institute, 185
Nature Saskatchewan, 299
Ontario Environment Network, 310
Ontario Ministry of the Environment, 311
Outdoor Classroom, 144, 328
Pacific Biosnet (Discussion group), 67
Pacific Forestry Center, 314
Peregrine Falcons at the University of Calgary, 316
Piping Plover Guardian Program, 318
Raincoast Conservation Society, 321
Royal Botanical Gardens, 20
Skies Above Foundation, 333
Solar Energy Society of Canada, Inc., 336
Sustainable Times, 152
Tin Men - The Inquiring Non-Mainstream Environmental News, 203
Tree Canada Foundation, 345
Urban Agriculture Notes, 198
Waterfront, 355
Wildlands League, 359
Wildlife at Risk-Canada, 359

Carbon Dioxide Information Analysis Center (CDIAC), 187

Carnegie Institute of Technology (Carnegie Mellon University), 187

Catalog of Known and Putative Nuclear Explosions, 187

CEDAR *see* **Central European Environmental Request Facility**

Center for Bioenvironmental Research, 188

Center for Conservation Biology, 188

Center for Disease Control
Agency for Toxic Substances & Disease Registry, 165, 189

Center for Environmental and Regulatory Information Systems (CERIS), 287

Center for Environmental Biotechnology, 189

Center for Environmental Design Research (UC Berkeley), 190

Center for Environmental Philosophy, University of North Texas
Environmental Ethics, 124

Center for Exposure Assessment Modeling Software Users, 21

Center for Health Effects of Environmental Contamination, 190

Center for Holistic Resource Management, 51

Center for International Earth Science Information (CIESIN), 191
Human Dimensions of Global Environmental Change (Discussion group), 57

Center for International Environmental Law, 192

Center for Marine Conservation, 23, 192

Center for Plant Conservation, 192

Center for Renewable Energy and Sustainable Technology (CREST), 192

Center for Resourceful Building Technology, 193

Center for the Study of Environmental Endocrine Effects, 193

Central America
ELAN (Discussion group), 35

Central Europe
Bulletin of the Regional Environmental Center, 108
Central European Environmental Data Request Facility, 193
Danube Information System, 205
ENVBUS-L (Discussion group), 37
ENVCEE-L (Discussion group), 38
GREENSEE (Discussion group), 53
Regional Environmental Center for Central and Eastern Europe, 37, 108, 325

Centre for Alternative Transportation Fuels, 111, 194

Cetacea *see* **Animals and animal ecology**

Cetacean Society International, 157, 195
Whales Alive!, 157, 195

Chanslor Wetlands Wildlife Project, 195

Charles Darwin Research Station, 195

Chemcyclopedia, 196

Chemical Manufacturers Association, 197

Chemicals and chemical industry *see also* **Business and industry**
Alliance for Environmental Technology, 167
Chemcyclopedia, 196
Chemical Industry Institute of Toxicology (CIIT), 196
Chemistry & Industry, 111, 163
Chlorine Chemistry Council, 197
Chlorine Monitor, 50, 112
ClO_2 Water Treatment Resource Center, 198
Environmental Chemicals Data Information Network, 221
Environmental Contaminants Encyclopedia, 222
Foodsafety (Discussion group), 50

Chesapeake Bay
Data Base of the Occurrence and Distribution of Pesticides in Chesapeake Bay, 165
Holland Island Preservation Foundation, 251
The Salt and the Earth Wetlands Nursery, 327

Chicago Wilderness, 196

Chilkat Bald Eagle Preserve, 197

Chimpanzees *see* **Jane Goodall Institute**

China Council for International Cooperation on Environment and Development, 197

Chlorine
Canadian Chlorine Coordinating Committee, 185
Chlorine Chemistry Council, 197
Chlorine Monitor, 50, 112
Foodsafety (Discussion group), 50

CIESIN *see* **Center for International Earth Science Information**

Citation Publishing, Inc., 197

Citizen's Clearinghouse for Hazardous Waste (CCHW), 124

Citizens Network for Sustainable Development, 23

City Farmer, 198

Cleanup *see* **Bioremediation** *or* **Environmental contamination and cleanup**

Climate and climatic change
Australian Oceanographic Data Centre, 175
Carbon Dioxide Information Analysis Center,
187
Center for International Climate and
Environmental Research, Oslo, 191
Climate Variations Bulletin, 113
CLIM-ECON, 23
*ECO: The Climate Action Network
Newsletter*, 117
Environmental and Societal Impacts Group,
220
GEWEX News, 128
GHCC Forecast, 128
Global Change Master Directory, 239
Global Change Research Information Office,
239
Global Climate Web Site Research, 240
Global Hydrology and Climate Center, 128,
241
International Research Institute for Climate
Protection, 261
International Satellite Land Surface Climatology
Project, 262
National Center for Atmospheric Research,
220, 289
National Oceanic and Atmospheric
Administration Network, 305
Niño, el, 342
NOAA News, 141
Penn State University Weather Page, 316
Pew Center on Global Climate Change, 317
sci.geo.meteorology, 101
Texas A & M University Oceanography, 342
Tiempo Climate Cyberlibrary, 343
U. S. Geological Survey, 212, 266, 351
Weather and Global Monitoring, 357
World Climate Report, 159
World Climate Research Programme, 128, 363
World Meteorologic Organization, 364

Coastal areas
Australian Oceanographic Data Centre, 175
CCSEA-L (Discussion group), 21
COASTNET (Discussion group), 24
CZM (Discussion group), 27
National Sea Grant Depository, 293
National Sea Grant Program, 294
North Carolina Coastal Federation, 304
Sefton Coast Life Project, 331
Surfrider Foundation USA, 339
Virginia Coast Reserve LTER, 353

Coastal Management Conference, 24

Cochrane Ecological Institute/Wildlife Reserve, 198

Code of Federal Regulations, 48, 93, 199, 231, 349, 366

Collaborative Environments for Conserving Earth
Resources (Discussion group), 21

Colleges and universities
Advanced Technology Environmental Education
Center, 164
Blueprint for a Green Campus, 190
Brown Is Green, 181
Campus Green Pages Directory, 190
Campus Green Vote, 29, 190
ENCON-L (Discussion group), 36
GRNSCH-L (Discussion group), 54
National Pollution Prevention Center for Higher
Education, 292
PRINTECH (Discussion group), 70
SAFETY (Discussion group), 73
Second Nature, 331
Students for Environmental and Ecological
Development, 339

Colorado
BCWATERSHED (Discussion group), 16
Colorado School of Mines, 199
Department of Natural Resources, 207
Department of Public Health and Environment, 199
Regional Air Quality Council, 324

Commerce Business Daily, 91-92

Commission for Environmental Cooperation (CEC)
CECNET (Discussion group), 200
EcoRegion, 119, 212

Committee for the National Institute for the
Environment, 24, 200, 227

Communications for a Sustainable Future, 23, 31, 33,
201

Composts and natural fertilizers
COMPOST (Discussion group), 25
Compost Resource Page, 201
RotWeb, 326

Comprehensive Test Ban Clearinghouse, 26

Conference on Communication and the Environment,
24

Connecticut
Department of Environmental Protection, 201
Yale Working Papers on Solid Waste Policy, 160

Conservation *see* **Biological conservation, Botanical conservation, Natural resources conservation and management, Soil conservation, Water conservation, Wildlife and wildlife conservation**

Conservation Agency, 201

Conservation of Arctic Flora and Fauna (CAFF), 212

Consortium on Green Design and Manufacturing, 202

Contamination *see* **Environmental Contamination and Cleanup**

Convention on International Trade in Endangered Species, 22, 348

Cooperative Agricultural Pest Survey (CAPS), 287

Coral reefs
Coral Forest, 203
Coral Health and Monitoring Program, 203
CORAL-LIST, 26, 203
Coral Reef Alliance, 203
International Coral Reef Initiative, 257
Reef Line, 146
Reef Relief, 146, 324

Cornell Center for the Environment, 204

Costa Rica
Jardin Gaia, 268
Organization for Tropical Studies, 312

Council for Agricultural Science and Technology, 204

Council on Environmental Quality, 204

Coweeta LTER Site, 205

CREST *see* **Center for Renewable Energy and Sustainable Technology**

Cutter Information Corporation, 129

Cygnus Group, 205

Danube Information System, 205

Datasets
British Atmospheric Data Centre, 180
California Environmental Resources Evaluation System (CERES), 184
Center for International Earth Science Information (CIESIN), 191
Coweeta LTER Site, 205
Mediterranean Oceanic Data Base, 279
National Center for Atmospheric Research, 220, 289
National Wildlife Refuge System, 295
Ocean Process Analysis Laboratory, 308
Scripps Institution of Oceanography, 300, 330
Verde River Watershed, 353

Declining Amphibian Populations Task Force, 128, 206
Froglog, 128, 206

Defending the Environmental Agenda, 88

Defense Environmental Network & Information eXchange, 206

Defense Environmental Restoration Program, 207

Defining Environmental Technology, 164

Deforestation
Sylvanet (Discussion group), 76

Delaware
Department of Natural Resources and Environmental Control, 207

Denmark
International Council for the Exploration of the Sea (ICES/CIEM), 258

Department of the Environment, Great Britain, 208

Departments of U. S. Government *see* **United States Government**

Desert Research Institute, 115, 209

Developing countries
DEVEL-L (Discussion group), 27
New Forests Project, 141, 301
World Energy Efficiency Association, 364

Dioxins
DIOXIN-L (Discussion group), 29

Direct Contact Environmental Toll-Free Directory, 209

Disaster preparedness and prevention
Federal Emergency Management Agency (FEMA), 233
Office of Solid Waste and Emergency Response, EPA, 225

Disasters
 Department of the Interior, 93, 97, 209
 Earth Alert, 116

Discovery Channel, 116

Discussion groups
 sending messages to, 7-9
 subscribing to, 7-9

DiveWeb, 210

Drought
 National Drought Mitigation Center, 290

Earth Day
 Earth Day Network, 210

Earth First
 alt.org.earth-first, 88

Earth Island Institute, 116, 210

Earth Observing System Amazon Project, 211

Earth Pledge Foundation, 211

Earth Resources Laboratory (MIT), 211

Earth Ships and Self Sufficient Architecture
 (Discussion group), 46

Earth's Resources Observation Satellite (EROS), 212

Earth Systems, 33

Earth Times Foundation
 Earth Times, 117, 147

Earthwatch, 30, 48, 212, 224

Earthwatch Radio, 48, 224

Eastern Europe, 37-39, 53, 108, 193, 325
 Central European Environmental Data Request
  Facility, 193
 ENVBUS-L (Discussion group), 37
 ENVCEE-L (Discussion group), 38

ECN (Environmental Change Network), 213

Ecologia, 213

Ecological Society of America, 32, 67, 98, 114

Ecologists Linked for Organizing Grassroots Initiatives
 and Action, 213

Ecologue, 24

Ecology Action Centre, 213

Ecology and ecosystems *see also* **Tropical ecosystems**
 ALIENS-L (Discussion group), 12
 BEN (*Botanical Electronic News*), 107
 BIOSPH-L (Discussion group), 18
 Canadian Journal of Forest Research, 110
 COMPSY-L (Discussion group), 25
 Conservation Ecology, 114
 CORAL-LIST (Discussion group), 26
 ECOL-ECON (Discussion group), 31
 ECOLOG-L (Discussion group), 32
 ECOSYS-L (Discussion group), 33
 EE-CAFÉ (Discussion group), 33
 European Forest Institute, 232
 FISH-SCI (Discussion group), 49
 Hawaiian Ecosystems at Risk, 247
 Hubbard Brook Experimental Forest, 252
 LTER (US Long-Term Ecological Research), 274
 National Center for Ecological Analysis and
  Synthesis, 289
 Open University Ecology and Conservation
  Research Group, 311
 plantpop (Discussion group), 67
 Prairie Ecosystem Study Project, 319
 sci.bio.ecology, 98
 Society for Ecological Restoration, 334
 Sustainable Ecosystems Institute, 339
 USIALE-L (Discussion group), 78
 Wildgarden (Discussion group), 83

EcoMall, 213

Econet, 214

Economics, Environmental
 AERE-L (Discussion group), 10
 American Council for an Energy-Efficient
  Economy, 168
 CLIM-ECON (Discussion group), 23
 Dirty Little Secrets, 237
 ECO-FUND (Discussion group), 31
 ECOL-ECON (Discussion group), 31
 EE-CAFÉ (Discussion group), 33
 Environmental Values, 125
 EPA-GRANTS (Discussion group), 45
 Green Scissors Report, 237
 International Institute for Industrial Environmental
  Economics, 259
 REEL (Discussion group), 71
 RESECON (Discussion group), 72

Ecopsychology *see* **Psychology and sociology**

Ecosystems *see* **Ecology and ecosystems**

Ecosystem Theory and Modeling (Discussion group), 33

Ecotourism
Ecotourism Society, 214
GREEN-TRAVEL (Discussion group), 54

Eco-village Network, 215

Ecovote Online, 215

EcoWeb, 215

Ecuador
Charles Darwin Research Station, 195
Montanas Verdes, 285

Education, Environmental
Advanced Technology Environmental Education Center, 164
Association of University Leaders for a Sustainable Future, 174
Bureau of Land Management, 93, 182, 209
Center for Renewable Energy and Sustainable Technology (CREST), 247
Charles Darwin Research Station, 195
Committee for the National Institute for the Environment, 24, 200, 227
Coral Forest, 203
EE-INTERNET (Discussion group), 34
EE-Link, 216
ENVST-L (Discussion group), 44
Florida Department of Environmental Protection, 235
GLIN-EDUCATION (Discussion group), 53
GLOBE Program, 242
Green Teacher, 131
Harbor Branch Oceanographic Institution, 246
Headwaters Science Center, 250
Inland Seas Education Association, 255
John M. Judy Environmental Education Consortium, 268
Leave No Trace, 138, 272
Lloyd Center for Environmental Studies, 272
Louisiana Energy & Environmental Resource & Information Center, 274
Maine Department of Inland Fisheries & Wildlife, 275
National Energy Foundation, 290
National Outdoor Leadership School, 272, 292
New England Wild Flower Society, 300
Outdoor Classroom, 144, 328
Project Wild, 131, 282, 299, 310, 312, 320, 351

Rainforest Workshop, 322
SeaWorld, 331
WhaleTimes SeaBed, 358

Edwards Aquifer Research and Data Center (Southwest Texas State University), 216

EE-Link, 216

EIONET *see* **European Environmental Information and Observation Network**

Electric power
Appropriate Technology for Community and Environment, 171
Edison Electric Institute, 216
Electric Power Research Institute (EPRI), 217
EPRI Journal, 127
Fuel cells, 65, 123, 127
Home Power Magazine, 132

Electric Power Research Institute, 127, 217
EPRI Journal, 127

Electric vehicles *see* **Transportation**

Electronic journals
Distribution, 103

Elsevier Science
Federal Compliance Alert, 48

Emergencies *see* **Disasters** *or* **Disaster preparedness and prevention**

Employment
Biology - Careers and Jobs, 179
clari.tw.environment.cbd, 91
Environmental Careers Organization, 221
ENVJOBS-L (Discussion group), 43
gov.us.topic.gov-jobs.offered.science, 96
The Scientist, 148

Endangered Habitats League, 217

Endangered species
CITES-L (Discussion group), 22
CONSBIO (Discussion group), 25
Conservation Agency, 201
Defenders of Wildlife, 140, 206
EDF Letter, 120
Endangered Species & Wetlands Report, 122
Endangered Species Bulletin, 122
Endangered Species Update, 122
Environmental Defense Fund, 120, 222
EPA-SPECIES (Mailing list), 45
Froglog, 128, 206

Hawaii Biological Survey, 247-248
Hawaii's Endangered and Threatened Species Page, 248
Headwaters Forest, 250
Idaho Wilderness, 253
International Network of Natural Heritage Programs and Conservation, 297
International Snow Leopard Trust, 262
International Union for the Conservation of Nature, 264
Kentucky Department of Fish and Wildlife Resources, 270
Natural Heritage Programs, 297
Nature Conservancy, 248, 297-299
New Jersey Department of Fish, Game and Wildlife, 302
Office of Protected Resources, 309
sci.environment, 100
Sierra - The Sierra Club Magazine, 149
Smithsonian Institution's Conservation and Research Center, 334
Species-Alert (Discussion group), 76
Tusk Force, 346
Wild Animal Rescue Foundation of Thailand, 358
Wildlife Watch, 158

Energy *see also* **Alternative energy, Biomass energy, Geothermal energy, Renewable energy, Solar energy, Sustainable energy, Wind energy**
American Hydrogen Association, 169
Argonne National Laboratory, 172
Association of Energy Engineers, 174
Electric Power Research Institute (EPRI), 217
Energy and Environmental Research Center, 218
Energy Efficiency and Renewable Energy Network, 208
Energy Ideas Clearinghouse, 218
Energy Technology Data Exchange, 219
Global Climate Web Site Research, 240
Initiatives in Environmental Technology Investment, 134
Joint Center for Energy Management, 269
National Energy Foundation, 290
Natural Energy Laboratory of Hawaii, 297
Oak Ridge National Laboratory, 123, 143, 187
Princeton University Center for Energy and Environmental Studies, 320
sci.energy, 99-100
sci.energy.hydrogen, 100
sci.geo.petroleum, 101

Energy conservation
Albany Research Center, 167
CADDET, 109, 183
Center for Renewable Energy and Sustainable Technology (CREST), 192

ENCON-L (Discussion group), 36
Energy Source Builder, 123
EnergyStar (Discussion group), 36
GreenClips, 130
Living Gently Quarterly, 137
Louisiana Energy & Environmental Resource & Information Center, 274
Midwest Renewable Energy Association, 281
Northern Lights (nordlicht), 306
Office of Energy Efficiency, 92, 309
Pinecrest: an Adventure..., 317
Sustainable Minnesota, 151, 282
Tata Energy Research Institute, 341
World Energy Efficiency Association, 364

Energy Conservation Management Issues in Higher Education (Discussion group), 36

Energy Ideas Clearinghouse, 218

Engineering, Environmental
ENVENG-L (Discussion group), 39

Enviro-Access, 219

Envirolink Network, 104, 219

Enviromine, 220

Environmental Alliance for Senior Involvement, 220

Environmental and Societal Impacts Group, 220

Environmental Assessment Association, 220

Environmental auditing and assessment
Canadian Environmental Assessment Agency, 186
EIA (Discussion group), 34
Environmental Assessment Association, 220
Enviroene (EPA), 230
New York State Department of Environmental Conservation, 303

Environmental awareness, 14, 250
EARTHNET (Discussion group), 29
Earthwatch (Discussion group), 29
Planetkeepers, 318
Sense-L (Discussion group), 74
wholesys-l (Discussion group), 82

Environmental Careers Organization, 221

Environmental communication
Conference on Communication and the Environment, 24

Environmental contamination and cleanup
Careerpro (Discussion group), 19
Center for Health Effects of Environmental Contamination, 190
CLU-IN (Hazardous Waste Clean-Up Information), 198
Defense Environmental Restoration Program, 207
Department of Defense Environmental Cleanup Home Page, 207
Energy and Environmental Research Center, 218
Environmental Contaminants Encyclopedia, 222
Federal Remediation Technologies Roundtable, 233
Global Network of Environment & Technology, 241
Ground-Water Remediation Technologies, 245
Analysis Center, 187, 245

Environmental Data Information Management System, 308

Environmental Defense Fund, 120, 222
EDF Letter, 120

Environmental Engineer, 168

Environmental Foundation Bellona, 178

Environmental Gaming Theory (Discussion group), 34

Environmental Health Perspectives, 124, 291

Environmental impact
Bureau of Transportation Statistics, 182
Consequences: The Nature & Implications of Environmental Change, 113
EIA (Discussion group), 34
EPA-IMPACT (Mailing list), 45
Institute of Freshwater Ecology, 256

Environmental Industry Web Site, 223, 267

Environmental Information Distribution List (Discussion group), 40

Environmental Information System Group (Discussion group), 35

Environmental Interactions of Mariculture, (Discussion group), 35

Environmental Issues in Central and Eastern Europe (Discussion group), 38

Environmental Law Information Center, 223

Environmental Law Institute, 36

Environmentally Conscious Design and Manufacturing (Discussion group), 30

Environmental management
Borderlines, 108
EM Online, 121, 166
Germinal Project, 239
Office of Environmental Management (Department of Energy), 208

Environmental Measurements Laboratory, 208, 224

Environmental News Network, 224

Environmental Organization Web Directory, 224

Environmental Research Institute of Michigan (ERIM), 225

Environmental Resources Information Network (ERIN), 226
Linkages, 117, 137

Environmental Resources Management, 226

Environmental Restoration Small Business (U.S. Department of Defense), 207

Environmental RouteNet, 227

Environmental Simulations, 227

Environmental Statistics
Wildnet (Discussion group), 84

Environmental Studies Association of Canada, 105

Environmental Studies Discussion List, 44

Environmental Treaties and Resource Indicators, 228

Environmental Working Group, 112, 228
A Clear View, 112, 228

Environment and Business in Central and Eastern Europe (Discussion group), 37

Environment Canada, 118, 229

Environment Council, U.K., 229

Environment in Latin America (Discussion group), 35

Environment Technology and Society (Discussion group), 44

Enviroene (EPA), 230
   Envirosense Consortium, 127

Envirosense Online, 127

EnviroText, 231

EPA *see* **United States Government--**
Environmental Protection Agency

ESA *see* **Ecological Society of America**

Essential Information, 231

Estuaries *see* **Rivers and estuaries**

Estuarine Research Federation, 133
   HydroWire, 133

Ethics, Environmental
   Animal Rights, 13-14, 105
   AR-NEWS (Discussion group), 13
   AR-VIEWS (Discussion group), 14
   ENVIROETHICS (Discussion group), 40
   Environmental Ethics, 124
   Environmental Values, 125
   Forest Service Employees for Environmental
      Ethics, 236
   Intellectual Property & Biodiversity News, 134
   International Society for Environmental Ethics,
      263
   Terra Nova - Nature and Culture, 152

Europe *see also* **Central Europe, Eastern Europe,**
Denmark, Finland, France, Great Britain,
Ireland, Netherlands, Scotland, Sweden,
United Kingdom, Baltic Sea Region
   The Bulletin of the Regional Environmental
      Center, 108
   ENVBUS-L (Discussion group), 37
   ENVCEE-L (Discussion group), 38
   ENVEVENTS-L (Discussion group), 39
   EUROFISH-L (Discussion group), 47
   European Centre for Nature Conservation, 231
   European Environmental agency, 232
   European Forest Institute, 232
   Regional Environmental Center for Central and
      Eastern Europe, 37, 108, 325

European Environmental Agency, 232

European Environmental Information and
   Observation Network, 232

European Forest Institute, 232

European Ichthyology Conference (Discussion group),
   47

Everglades Information Network, 232

Everglades National Park, 232

EXTOXNET, 232

FAQs, 8

Federal Emergency Management Agency (FEMA), 233

Federal Geographic Data Committee, 233

Federal Register
   Code of Federal Regulations, 48, 93, 199, 231, 349,
      366
   EPA-Federal Register (Mailing list), 45
   Federal Compliance Alert, 48
   gov.us.fed.nara.fed-register.contents, 93

Fedworld Information Network, 234

FEMA *see* **Federal Emergency Management Agency**

Fertilizersnatural *see* **Composts and natural fertilizers**

Finland
   Finnish Biodiversity Information Network, 179
   Finnish Forest Research Institute - METLA, 234
   Finnish Society of Forest Science, 149
   Silva Fennica, 149

Fish
   Atlantic Salmon Federation, 174
   CICHLID-L (Discussion group), 22
   EUROFISH-L (Discussion group), 47
   Fish and Wildlife Information Exchange, 234
   FISHERIES (Discussion group), 48
   FISHFOLK (Discussion group), 49
   FISH-SCI (Discussion group), 49
   FWIM-L (Discussion group), 50
   Great Lakes Fishery Commission marinefish
      (Discussion group), 53
   PONDS-L (Discussion group), 68
   The Salmon Page, 327

Fisheries
   FISHERIES (Discussion group), 48
   Great Lakes Fishery Commission, 243
   Our Living Oceans Annual Report, 143
   PONDS-L (Discussion group), 68
   The Salmon Page, 327
   sci.bio.fisheries, 99
   Tuna Newsletter, 155

Wildnet (Discussion group), 83

Fisheries Social Science Network, 49

Florida
e design, 120
Florida Design Initiative Everglades Information Network, 235
Florida Atlantic University, 235
Florida Center for Environmental Studies, 28, 235
Florida Cooperative Extension Service, 235
Florida Department of Environmental Protection, 235
Florida Design Initiative, 120, 235
Mote Marine Laboratory, 285
Okefenokee Swamp Natural Education Center, 310
Save Our Everglades, 328
Southern Florida Wildlife Rehabilitation Center, 338
South Florida Environmental Reader, 150
South West Florida Wildlife Rehabilitation and Conservation Center, 338
University of Florida, 235
Florida Cooperative Extension Service, 235
Range Science Program, 348

Food
Global Food Watch, 129
gov.us.topic.agri.food, 94

Food Contamination
Environmental Contaminants Encyclopedia, 222
Foodsafe (Discussion group), 49
Foodsafety (Discussion group), 49

Forest conservation
American Forests, 169, 296
Canadian Journal of Forest Research, 110
FOREST (Discussion group), 50
Forest Service Employees for Environmental Ethics, 236
Forest Voice, 127
Gaia Forest Archives, 237
Harvard Forest, 247
Headwaters Forest, 250
Heartwood, 250
International Canopy Network, 257
Maryland Forest Association, 278
Michigan Forests Magazine, 138
Native Forest Council, 127, 296
Native Forest Network, 296
New Forests Project, 141, 301
Oxford Forestry Institute, 313
Raincoast Conservation Society, 321
Save-the-Redwoods League, 329

SEACC (Southeast Alaska Conservation Council), 330
Sempervirens Fund, 332
Silva Forest Foundation, 332
Sylvanet (Discussion group), 76
Taiga Rescue Network, 340
Trees for the Future, 345
USDA Forest Service, 236, 350
Walk in the Woods, 354

Forest history *see* **History, Forest**

Forest management
Forest Service Ecosystem Management, 236
Indonesian Mangrove Foundation, 255
Michigan Forest Association, 138, 280
National Association of State Foresters, 288
Oregon Department of Forestry, 312
Silva Fennica, 149
Skogforsk, 333
Urban Forest Ecosystems Institute, 348

Forestry *see also* **Sustainable Forestry**
Advanced Forestry Technologies Program, 163
American Forests, 169, 296
Environmental Science and Forestry at SUNY, 227
Finnish Forest Research Institute - METLA, 234
FOREST (Discussion group), 50
gov.us.topic.nat-resources.forests, 96
International Union of Forestry Research Organizations, 264
Louisiana Department of Agriculture & Forestry, 273
Oregon Department of Forestry, 312
Royal Forestry Society of England, 326
SAF-news (Discussion group), 74
Society of American Foresters, 74, 334
Sylvanet (Discussion group), 76

Forest Service Ecosystem Management, 236

Forest Service Employees for Environmental Ethics, 236

France
francom.environnement, 92

Franklin Institute Science Museum, 265

Freshwater biology
Canada Centre for Inland Waters, 185
CICHLID-L (Discussion group), 22
FISH-SCI (Discussion group), 49
PONDS-L (Discussion group), 68

Friends of the Earth International, 237

FTP, 2-4

G7 Environment and Natural Resources Management
    Project, 92

Gaia Forest Archives, 237

Galapagos Islands
    Charles Darwin Research Station, 195
    Galapagos Coalition, 237
    Galapagos Marine Resources Reserve, 195

Game theory
    EGT (Discussion group), 34

Gasification
    GASIFICATION (Discussion group), 51

General Accounting Office, U.S., 238

GENIE Project, 238

GEO-1 Report, 240

Geographic attributes
    Forest Service Ecosystem Management, 236
    Geological Survey, U. S., 240, 351
    Penn State University Weather Pages, 316

Geographic information systems
    Center for Environmental Design Research, 190
    Earth's Resources Observation Satellite (EROS), 212
    GEO-COMPUTER-MODELS (Discussion group), 52
    Germinal Project, 239
    Verde River Watershed, 353

Geological Survey, U.S., 240, 351

Geology
    GEO-COMPUTER MODELS (Discussion group), 52
    GEO-ENV (Discussion group), 52
    GEO-GIG (Discussion group), 52

Georgia
    Department of Natural Resources, 239

Geothermal energy
    International Ground Source Heat Pump Association (IGSHPA), 259
    The Source, 150

Germinal Project, 239

GIS *see* **Geographic information systems**

Global Change Master Directory, 239

Global Change Research Information Office, 239

Global Climate Web Site Research, 240

Global Environmental Network for Information
    Exchange in the U.K. *see* **GENIE Project**

Global Environmental Options, 240

Global Environment Outlook Project, 240

Global Futures Foundation, 241

Global Network of Environment Technology, 241

Global Recycling Network, 242

Global Research Information Database (GRID), 242

Global Research Network on Sustainable Development, 55

Global warming
    Center for International Earth Science Information (CIESIN), 191
    Delta, 114
    Global Environmental Change Report, 129

GLOBE Program, 242

Gophers, 3

Government Institutes, Inc., 242

Grasslands
    Prairie (Discussion group), 69
    Tallgrass Prairie in Illinois, 340
    University of Florida's Range Science Program, 348

Grassroots Environmental Effectiveness Network
    (GREEN), 206

Great Britain *see also* **United Kingdom**
    Department of the Environment, 107, 208, 226
    Sefton Coast Life Project, 331

Great Lakes
    Earthwatch Radio, 48, 224
    GLIN-ANNOUNCE, 53
    GLIN-EDUCATION, 53
    Great Lakes Fishery Commission, 243
    Great Lakes Information Network, 53, 243
    Inland Seas Education Association, 255

NACA-GL (Discussion group), 64
National SeaGrant Program, 294

Greenbelt Alliance, 243

Green Design Initiative (Carnegie Mellon University), 187

Green Energy News
Energies, 123

Greenhouse Gas Miser Handbook, 229

Greenhouse Gas Technology Information Exchange, 245

Green Lane *see* **Environment Canada**

GreenLines, 206

Green Pages, 190, 211, 244, 321

Green Parties of North America, 244

Greenpeace International, 131, 244

Greenpeace Toxic Trade Updates, 131

Green Plans, 325

Green University Initiative, 245

GRID *see* **Global Research Information Database**

Groundwater
ASCE Geotechnical Engineering Seepage/ Groundwater Modeling Software, 173
Canadian Groundwater Remediation Project, 185
Colorado School of Mines, 199
Edwards Aquifer Research and Data Center (Southwest Texas State University), Environmental Simulations, Inc., 216
Groundwater Modeling, 227
Groundwater (Discussion group), 54
Groundwater Currents, 199
Ground-Water Remediation Technologies, 245
    Analysis Center, 187, 245
GWCAN-L (Discussion group), 55
GWM-L (Discussion group), 55
National Ground Water Association, 291

GZA GeoEnvironmental, Inc., 171

Harbor Branch Oceanographic Institution, 246

Harvard Environmental Resources On-Line, 246

Harvard Forest, 247

Hawaii
Endangered and Threatened Species Page, 248
Hawaiian Ecosystems at Risk, 247
Hawaiian Natural Resources Monitoring Database, 247
Hawaii Biological Survey, 247-248
Hawaii Sea Grant College Program, 138
National Wildlife Refuges/Marine Sanctuaries, 247
Save Our Seas, 150, 329

Hawk Mountain Sanctuary, 248

HawkWatch International, 248

Hazardous substances
DIOXIN-L (Discussion group), 29
Enviroene (EPA), 230
gov.us.topic.environment.toxics, 95
Hazardous Substance Research Centers, 249
HazDat - Hazardous Substance Release/Health Effects Database, 249
SAFETY (Discussion group), 73
ToxList (Discussion group), 77

Hazardous Waste Remedial Actions Program, 249

Hazardous wastes
Agency for Toxic Substances & Disease Registry, 165, 189
CLU-IN (Hazardous Waste Clean-Up Information) (Discussion group), 198
DIOXIN-L (Discussion group), 29
EPA-WASTE (Mailing list), 45
Essential Information, 231
gov.us.topic.environment.toxics, 95
NIREX, 303
Rachel's Environment & Health Weekly, 146
SAFETY (Discussion group), 73
USACHPPM Hazardous and Medical Waste Program, 349

HazDat (Hazardous Substance Release/Health Effects Database), 249

HazWrap, 249

Headwaters Forest, 250

Headwaters Science Center, 250

Health *see* **Human health**

Hebrides
Skye Environmental Centre, 261, 333

Hiraiso Solar Terrestrial Research Center, 250

History, Environmental
EDF Letter, 120
Environment and History, 125
H-ASEH (Discussion group), 56

History, Forest
Forest History Bibliography, 236

History, Internet, 1-3

Holistic Resource Management (Discussion group), 51

Holland Island Preservation Foundation, 251

Horticulture, 300
PPBC-L (Discussion group), 69
Wildgarden (Discussion group), 83

Houston Audubon Society, 251

Howl--The PAWS Wildlife Center, 251

HTML, 161-162

Hubbard Brook Experiment Forest, 252

Human health
AEROSO-L (Disscussion group), 10
Aviation, Space, and Environmental Medicine, 107
Bioelectromagnetics Society, 179
Carcinogenesis, 110, 347
Center for Bioenvironmental Research, 188
Center for Disease Control, 165, 189
Center for Health Effects of Environmental Contamination, 190
Center for the Study of Environmental Endocrine Effects, 193
Colorado Department of Public Health and Environment, 199
Conscious Choice, 113
Electromagnetics Forum, 120
Environmental Health Monthly, 124
Environmental Health Perspectives, 124, 291
Environmental Working Group, 112, 228
EnviroText, 231
Foodsafety (Discussion group), 50
HazDat (Hazardous Substance Release/ Health Effects Database), 249
HealthE (Discussion group), 56
Inside & Out, 134
NAPEnet (National Association of Physicians for the Environment), 287

National Institute of Environmental Health Sciences, 291
Office of Environment, Safety and Health (DOE), 208
Planetkeepers, 318
Rachel's Environment & Health Weekly, 146
UVB Impacts Reporter, 156
Waste Not, 1560

Hydrogen
sci.energy.hydrogen, 100

Hydrogeology
Edwards Aquifer Research and Data Center (Southwest Texas State University), 216
GWCAN-L (Discussion group), 55

Hydrographic Survey Data, 252

Hydrology
Earth Observing System Amazon Project (University of Washington), 211
Global Hydrology and Climate Center, 128, 241
GWCAN-L (Discussion group), 55
HYDROLOGY (Discussion group), 58
River Network (Discussion group), 72
sci.geo.hydrology, 100
Wthydrology (Discussion group), 84

Hypertext, 3-5

ICAN *see* **International Canopy Network**

ICE *see* **Information Center for the Environment**

Idaho
Department of Fish and Game, 253
Idaho Rare Plant Conference, 253
Idaho Rivers United Newsletter, 133
Idaho Wilderness, 253
Windows to Wildlife, 158

IEA *see* **International Energy Agency**

IEEE TAB Environment, Health and Safety Committee, 253

IGC *see* **Institute for Global Communications**

IISD *see* **International Institute for Sustainable Development**

Illinois
Chicago Wilderness, 196
Illinois Recycling Association, 254
Natural Resources Information Network, 254

Northwestern University, 339
Students for Environmental and Ecological
    Development, 339
Tallgrass Prairie in Illinois, 340

Indiana
Department of Natural Resources, 255
Indiana Natural Heritage Data Center, 255

Indonesia
Indonesian Foundation for the Advancement of
    Biological Science
    Tropical Biodiversity, 155
Indonesian Mangrove Foundation, 255

Indoor air
AEROSO-L (Discussion group), 10
Envirosense Online, 127

Industry *see* **Business and industry**

Information Center for the Environment (University
    of California at Davis), 255

Information, research, and news
Advances in Environmental Research, 104
Alternatives Journal, 105
American Chemical Society, 168
clari.tw.environment, 91
Dateline Los Alamos, 114
Defense Environmental Network & Information
    eXchange, 206
*Earth Action: The Bulletin for Environmental
    Activists*, 116
Earth Alert, 116
Eco-Compass, 118
EDIE (Environmental Data Interactive
    Exchange), 215
Electronic Green Journal, 121
Elsevier Science Tables of Contents, 217
ENVCONFS-L (Discussion group), 38
ENVEVENTS-L (Discussion group), 39
ENVIRO-NEWS (Discussion group), 42
ENVIRONEWS (Discussion group), 42
Environmental Journalism Home Page, 223
Environmental News Network, 224
Environmental Organization Web Directory, 224
Environment Writer, 126
EPA-PRESS (Mailing list), 46
EPA-R2-PRESS (Mailing list), 46
Essential Information, 231
E, The Environmental Magazine, 160
EWIRE (Discussion group), 47
GreenDisk Paperless Environmental Journal,
    130
International Institute for Sustainable
    Development, 115, 117, 151, 254

Natural History Book Service, 303
NetAction Newsletter, 141
Our Environment, 143
The Planet, 116, 144
POPULATION-NEWS (Mailing list), 69
Regional Environmental Center for Central and
    Eastern Europe, 37, 108, 325
The Scientist, 148
UnCover, 347
World Conservation Monitoring Centre, 22, 363

Information technology
EISG (Discussion group), 35
EON (Environment on the Net Discussion group),
    44

Inland Seas Education Association, 255

Insects
APIS (*Apicultural Information and Issues*), 105
BEE-L (Discussion group), 17
International Bee Research Association, 256
Michiganbutterflies (Discussion group), 63
Monarch Watch, 284
sci.bio.entomology.homoptera, 99
sci.bio.entomology.misc, 99

Institute for Agriculture and Trade Policy
Farm Aid News & Views, 127
Global Food Watch, 129
Intellectual Property & Biodiversity News, 134

Institute for Global Communications Network (IGC),
    213

Institute of Electrical and Electronics Engineers, 253

Inter-American Dialog on Water Management, 28

Interdisciplinary Research Network on the Environment
    and Society, 59

**Interhemispheric Institute for Sustainable
    Development**
Earth Negotiations Bulletin, 117

International Arid Lands Consortium, 133, 256
IALC Online Newsletter, 133

International Association of Landscape Ecology
    (Discussion group), 78

International Bee Research Association, 256

International Canopy Network (ICAN), 257

International Centre for Gas Technology Information, 257

International Council for Local Environmental Initiatives, 252

International Council for the Exploration of the Sea, 258

International Energy Agency
Energy Technology Data Exchange, 219
GREENTIE, 245
Solar Heating and Cooling Programme, 258

International environmental relations
Center for International Environmental Law, 192
Commission for Environmental Cooperation, 21, 119, 200
Environmental Treaties and Resource Indicators, 228
Kola Ecogeochemistry, 270
NATO Scientific & Environmental Affairs Newsletter, 140
Regional Environmental Center for Central and Eastern Europe, 37, 108, 325
Wild Rockies Slate, 361
World Energy Efficiency Association, 364

International Fund for Animal Welfare, 254

International Geosphere-Biosphere Programme, 258

International Global Energy and Water Cycle Experiment Project, 128

International Ground Source Heat Pump Association, 150, 259
The Source, 150

International Human Dimensions of Global Change Programme, 57
IHDP Update, 133

International Institute for Industrial Environmental Economics, 259

International Institute for Sustainable Development
China Council, 197
Developing Ideas Digest, 115
Sustainable Developments, 151

International Marinelife Alliance, 260

International Oceanographic Foundation, 260

International Otter Survival Fund, 261

International Primate Protection League, 261

International Rivers Network, 159, 262

International Satellite Land Surface, 262
Climatology Project, 262

International Snow Leopard Trust, 262

International Society for Ecological Modelling, 262

International Society for Environmental Ethics, 263

International Society of Arboriculture, 263
Journal of Arboriculture, 135

International Solar Center, 263

International Solar Energy Society, 264

International Students for Environmental Action (Discussion group), 60

International Tundra Experiment, 60

International Union of Forestry Research Organizations, 264

International Wildlife Coalition, 158, 265
Wildlife Watch, 158

International Wolf Center, 135, 265

Internet searching
Envirosources, 230

Invasive Species Specialist Group (Discussion group), 12

Investigating Wind Energy, 265

Iowa
Department of Natural Resources, 266
Iowa Raptor Foundation, 266
Iowa's Environment, 266
University of Iowa, Center for Health Effects of Environmental Contamination, 245

Ireland
Irish Peatland Conservation Council, 266

Irrigation
gov.us.topic.environment.water, 96
IRRIGATION-L (Discussion group), 59
TRICKLE-L (Discussion group), 77
World Wide Water, 365

Island Press, 118
 Eco-Compass, 118

Island Wildlife Natural Care Centre, 267

ISO- Information Center, 267

Israel
 Natural Center for Mariculture (Discussion group), 63

Jane Goodall Institute, 267

Japan
 Hiraiso Solar Terrestrial Research Center, 250
 Japan Environment Quarterly, 135
 Japan Marine Science and Technology Center, 268
 National Institute for Environmental Studies, 291
 World Climate Research Programme, 128, 363

Jefferson Land Trust, 268

John M. Judy Environmental Education Consortium, 268

John Muir Trust, 269

Joint Center for Energy Management, 269

Journals, Electronic *see* **Electronic journals**

Kansas
 Kansas Environmental Almanac, 269

Kentucky
 Department of Fish and Wildlife Resources, 270
 Kentucky Water Resources Research Institute, 270
 Kentucky Water Watch, 270
 Raptor Rehabilitation of Kentucky, 323

Kola Ecogeochemistry, 270

Lakes and ponds
 GLIN-EDUCATION (Discussion group), 53
 Lake Pontchartrain Basin Foundation, 271
 LAKES-L (Discussion group), 61
 PONDS-L (Discussion group), 68
 sci.geo.rivers+lakes, 101
 Seiche, 148

Land conservation and restoration
 American Farmland Trust, 168

Bureau of Land Management, 93, 182, 209
Germinal Project, 239
gov.us.topic.nat-resources.land, 96
Greenbelt Alliance, 243
Jefferson Land Trust, 268
John Muir Trust, 269
Land Conservancy of San Luis Obispo County, 271
Land Trust Alliance, 271
Lincolnshire Trust, 272
Missouri Prairie Foundation, 283
Palos Verdes Peninsula Land Conservancy, 142, 315
Tenure (Discussion group), 76
Trumbull Land Trust, 346
Trust for Public Land, 346
Utah Public, 352
Vermont Land Trust, 353
Wild Rockies Slate, 361

Land Tenure Center, 76

Latin America
 Charles Darwin Research Station, 195
 ELAN, 35
 Galapagos Coalition, 237
 Galapagos Marine Resources Reserve, 195
 Montanas Verdes, 285

Law and legislation
 Arizona Legislative Information System, 172
 Asia-Pacific Centre for Environmental Law, 173
 Canadian Environmental Assessment Agency, 186
 Canadian Institute for Environmental Law and Policy, 109, 186
 Canadian Institute for Environmental Law & Policy Newsletter, 109
 Center for International Environmental Law, 192
 Central European Environmental Data Request Facility (CEDAR), 193
 Citation Publishing, Inc., 197
 Code of Federal Regulations, 48, 93, 199, 231, 349, 366
 Commission for Environmental Cooperation, 21, 119, 200
 Compliance Online, 113
 Council on Environmental Quality, 204
 Ecology Law Quarterly, 118
 EIA (Discussion group), 34
 ELI-WETLANDS (Discussion group), 36
 Endangered Species & Wetlands Report, 122
 Endangered Species Bulletin, 122
 ENVIROLAWPROFS (Discussion group), 43
 ENVIRONEWS (Discussion group), 42
 Environmental Compliance Assistance Center, 221
 Environmental Resources Information Network (ERIN), 226
 Environmental Resources Management, 226

Environmental Treaties and Resource Indicators, 228

Environment Canada, 118, 229

Enviroene (EPA), 230

EPA-Federal Register (Mailing list), 45

Federal Compliance Alert, 48

Galapagos Coalition, 237

National Association of Environmental Professionals, 288

National Wildlife Refuge System, 295

Native Americans and the Environment, 188, 295

OILGASLAW-L (Discussion group), 66

QUEST (Discussion group), 70

Southern Africa Environment Page, 337

United Nations Environment Programme, 173, 202, 348

U. S. Code, 199, 349-350

U. S. Code (Conservation), 350

U. S. Water News, 155

WALL-List (Discussion group), 79

Water Environment Web, 355

Wright's PestLaw, 366

Zero Waste American, 367

League of Conservation Voters, 137, 215, 271

Leave No Trace
Master Network, 138

Legislation *see* **Law and legislation**

Lincolnshire Trust, 272

Lloyd Center for Environmental Studies, 273

Long-Term Ecological Research Network *see* **LTER**

Long-term trends and forecasting
ECN (Environmental Change Network), 212

LTER (U.S. Long-Term Ecological Research) Network, 274

National Center for Atmospheric Research, 220, 289

Natural Environment Research Council, 297

Virginia Coast Reserve LTER, 353

Louisiana
Department of Agriculture & Forestry, 96, 273

Department of Environmental Quality, 274, 280, 351

Department of Natural Resources, 274

Energy & Environmental Resource & Information Center, 274

Lake Pontchartrain Basin Foundation, 271

LSU Center for Coastal, Energy, and Environmental Resources, 274

Tulane University, 188

Center for Bioenvironmental Research, 188

Xavier University, 188

Center for Bioenvironmental Research, 188

Lower Rio Grande Ecosystem Initiative, 274

LTER (U.S. Long-Term Ecological Research) Network, 274

MAB Biosphere Reserves (Discussion group), 62

Maine
Department of Conservation, 275, 283

Department of Environmental Protection, 201, 235, 275, 302, 316

Department of Inland Fisheries & Wildlife, 275

Medomak Valley Land Trust, 279

University of Maine, 348

Department of Wildlife Ecology, 348

Mangrove Forests, Indonesian, 255

Mangrove Replenishment Initiative, 276

Mangrove Research (Discussion group), 62

Manufacturing *see* **Business and industry**

Maps
Catalog of Online Vegetation and Plant, 188

Distribution Maps, 188

Earth's Resources Observation Satellite (EROS), 212

Global Research Information Database (GRID), 242

Greenbelt Alliance, 243

Maine Department of Environmental Protection, 275

Montanas Verdes, 285

National Estuary Program, 290

Texas A & M University Oceanography, 342

USDA Forest Service, 236, 350

US FWS Division of Habitat Conservation - National Wetlands Inventory, 350

Weather and Global Monitoring, 357

Marine biology
CORAL-LIST (Discussion group), 26

DiveWeb, 210

FISH-ECOLOGY (Discussion group), 49

Marine Biological Association, 276

Protected Marine Species, 321

WhaleTimes SeaBed, 358

Marine conservation
ACN-L (Discussion group), 9

Center for Marine Conservation, 23, 192

CMC-Oceanalert (Discussion group), 23
CTURTLE (Discussion group), 27
gov.us.topic.nat-resources.marine, 96
International Marinelife Alliance, 260
International Marine Mammal Association, 260
Marine Conservation Page, 276
Marine Environmental Research Institute, 277
Monterey Bay Aquarium-At the CoRE, 285
Oceanic Resource Foundation, 308
Ocean Voice International, 148, 308
Office of Protected Resources, 309
St. Catherines Sea Turtle Conservation Program, 326
Save Our Seas, 150, 329
Sea Shepherd Conservation Society, 74, 330
Sea Turtle Restoration Project, 331
SOS Newsletter, 150
Texas Marine Mammal Stranding Network, 343

Marine ecosystems
COASTNET (Discussion group), 24
EIM (Discussion group), 35
International Marinelife Alliance, 260
Ocean Voice International, 148, 308
South Florida Environmental Reader, 150

Marine environments
Alfred Wegener Institute for Polar and Marine Research, 167
EIM (Discussion group), 167
International Council for the Exploration of the Sea, 258
International Year of the Ocean, 265, 329
Japan Marine Science and Technology Center, 268
Makai, 138
Maryland Marine Notes, 138
MEH-L (Discussion group), 63
National Sea Grant Depository, 293
National Sea Grant Program, 294
NATO SACLANT, 296

Maryland
Bird Banding Laboratory, 16, 180
Data Base of the Occurrence and Distribution of Pesticides in Chesapeake Bay, 165
Department of Natural Resources, 277
Holland Island Preservation Foundation, 251
Maryland Forests Association, 278
Maryland Marine Notes, 138
Maryland Sea Grant College, 31, 138
Potomac Conservancy, 319
The Salt and the Earth Wetlands Nursery, 327

Massachusetts
Department of Fisheries, Wildlife and Environmental Law Enforcement, 278

Harvard University, 246
Environmental Resources On-Line, 246
Harvard Forest, 247
Massachusetts Institute of Technology, Department of Earth, Atmospheric and Planetary Sciences, 211
New England Wildlife Center, 300

Mathematical models *see* **Modeling and simulation**

Matheson Wetlands Preserve, 278

Mediterranean Oceanic Data Base, 279

Mediterranean Sea
Mediterranean Oceanic Data Base, 279

Mendocino County Ecology Web, 279

Meteorology
National Center for Atmospheric Research, 220, 289
sci.geo.meteorology, 101

Michigan
Department of Environmental Quality, 280
Department of Natural Resources, 280
Environmental Research Institute of Michigan, 225
Environmental Science Board, 280
GLIN-EDUCATION (Discussion group), 53
Michiganbutterflies (Discussion group), 63
Michigan Forest Association, 280
Michigan Forests Magazine, 138
Michigan United Conservation Clubs, 281
Preserve the Dunes, Inc., 281

Middle East Water list (Discussion group), 63

Midwest Renewable Energy Association, 281

Milton Keynes Wildlife Hospital, 281

Mining
Colorado School of Mines, 199
ENVIROMINE, 220
ENVIROMINE-ISSUES (Discussion group), 40
ENVIROMINE-TECHNICAL (Discussion group), 41
gov.us.topic.nat-resources.minerals, 96
Mineral Policy Center, 282

Minnesota
Department of Natural Resources, 282
Headwaters Science Center, 250
Minnesota DNR, 139, 282
Minnesotans for An Energy-Efficient Economy, 151, 282

Minnesota Pollution Control Agency, 282
Minnesota Sea Grant, 148
Minnesota Volunteer, 139
Pollution Control Agency, 282
SNAP Shots Newsletter, 149
Sustainable Minnesota, 151, 282
University of Minnesota Extension Service, 151

Mississippi River Watch, 250

Missouri
Department of Conservation, 275, 283
Missouri Audubon Council, 283
Missouri Coalition for the Environment, 283
Missouri Prairie Foundation, 283

Mmarie, 284

Modeling and simulation
ASCE Geotechnical Engineering Seepage/ Groundwater Modeling Software, 173
CEAM-USERS (Discussion group), 21
Colorado School of Mines, 199
ECOSYS-L (Discussion group), 33
GEO-COMPUTER MODELS (Discussion group), 52
Groundwater Remediation Project (Canada), 173
GWM-L (Discussion group), 55
International Society for Ecological Modelling, 262
Mmarie, 284
Oceanic Planetary Boundary Layer Laboratory, 308
Wastewater-modelling-digest (Discussion group), 80

Monarch Watch, 284

Monitoring and Environmental Data
Alaska Ecoregions MappingMonitoring and Assessment Program, 212
AMP (Discussion group), 13
Arctic Monitoring and Assessment Programme, 242
Coral Health and Monitoring Program, 203
Weather and Global Monitoring, 357
World Conservation Monitoring Centre, 22, 363

Montana
Montana Natural Resources Information System, 284
Natural Heritage Program, 282, 284, 354
Water Information System, 284
Wild Rockies Slate, 361

Montanas Verdes, 285

Mountain Institute, 243, 286, 366

Mountain Lion Foundation, 286

Mr. Solar Home Page, 286

Muir, John, Exhibit, 269

Namibia
Namibia Animal Rehabilitation Research and Education Centre, 286

Napa County Resource Conservation District, 287

NAPEnet - National Association of Physicians for the Environment, 287

National Agricultural Pest Information System (NAPIS), 287

National Arborist Association, 288

National Association of Campus Activities, 64

National Association of Environmental Professionals, 288

National Association of State Foresters, 288

National Audubon Society
alt.org.audubon, 88
ASN (Discussion group), 14
AUDUBON (Discussion group), 14
Audubon Advisory, 106
AUDUBON-CHAT (Discussion group), 15
AUDUBON-NEWS (Mailing list), 15
POPULATION (Discussion group), 68
WETLAND-NEWS (Discussion group), 82

National Birding Hotline Cooperative, 19

National Center for Atmospheric Research, 220, 289

National Center for Ecological Analysis and Synthesis, 289

National Center for Environmental Publications and Information, 225

National Climatic Data Center, 113, 304
Climate Variations Bulletin, 113

National Collection of Endangered Plants, 192

National Consortium for Environmental Education, 216

National Energy Foundation, 290

National Environmental Policy Act, 204

National Environmental Trust, 141

National Estuary Program, 290

National Forum on Nonpoint Source Pollution, 342

National Geographic Society, 246

National Ground Water Association, 291

National Institute for Environmental Studies, 291

National Institute for the Environment, 24, 130, 200, 227

National Institute of Environmental Health Sciences (NIEHS), 125, 291

National Marine Fisheries Service
Office of Protected Resources, 309
Our Living Oceans Annual Report, 143

National Oceanic and Atmospheric Administration Network (NOAA)
gov.us.fed.doc.noaa.announce, 92
gov.us.topic.nat-resources.marine, 96
Hydrographic Survey Data, 252
NOAA News, 141

National Outdoor Leadership School, 272, 292

National Parks and Conservation Association
National Parks, 139

National Park Service, 209, 222, 315

National Pollutant Release Inventory, 292

National Pollution Prevention Center for Higher Education, 292

National Public Radio
Living on Earth, 273

National Register of Big Trees, 169

National Renewable Energy Laboratory, 293

National Research Council, 110, 125

National Resources Defense Council, 116, 293

National Science Foundation, 2, 93, 113, 274
gov.us.fed.nsf.announce, 93

National Society for Clean Air, 294

National Technical Information Service, 234

National University of Singapore, 173

National Watchable Wildlife, 140, 294
Nature Network, 140

National Wetlands Inventory, U.S., 350

National Wildlife Federation
International Wildlife, 135
National Wildlife, 139

National Wildlife Health Center, 295

National Wildlife Refuge System, 295

Native Americans and the Environment, 188, 295

Native Forest Council, 127, 296
Forest Voice, 127

NATO
NATO SACLANT, 296
NatoSci (Discussion group), 64
NATO Scientific & Environmental Affairs Newsletter, 140

Natural disasters *see* **Disasters**

Natural Energy Laboratory of Hawaii, 297

Natural gas
International Centre for Gas Technology Information, 257

Natural Heritage Programs, 297

Natural resources *see also* by state
Arizona Highways, 106
Department of the Interior, 93, 97, 209
e-Amicus, 115
FOREST (Discussion group), 50
Illinois Natural Resources Information Network, 254
Iowa's Environment, 266
Jefferson Land Trust, 268
Minnesota Volunteer, 139
Montana Natural Resource Information System, 284
National Wildlife Refuge System, 295
Natural Areas Journal, 140
Natural Energy Laboratory of Hawaii, 297

Nebraska Wildlife Resources, 299
New Hampshire Department of Environmental Services, 301
NRLib-L (Discussion group), 65
ONE-L (Discussion group), 66
PONDS-L (Discussion group), 68
Virginia Natural Heritage Program, 354

Natural resources conservation and management
Chicago Wilderness, 196
International Center for Living Aquatic, 202, 257
Resources Management, 22, 92, 202, 226, 257, 295
Manomet Center for Conservation Science, 276
Michigan Environmental Science Board, 280
Michigan United Conservation Clubs, 281
Missouri Department of Conservation, 283
Mountain Institute, 243, 286, 366
Natural Areas Journal, 140
Nature Conservancy, 248, 297-299
Nature Conservancy of Texas, 299
North Cascades Conservation Council, 305
Protected Areas Virtual Library, 320
Reflections on the Environment, 147, 353
RESECON (Discussion group), 72
San Gorgonio Volunteer Association, 327
Tall Timbers Research Station, 340
Tenure (Discussion group), 76

Natural Resources Defense Council, 115

Natural Resources Librarians List, 65

Natural Resources Services, 298

Nature Conservancy, The, 298-299

Nature Conservancy, of Texas, The, 299

Nebraska
Center for Sustainable Agricultural Systems Newsletter, 111
Game and Parks Wildlife, 299
Project WILD, 131, 282, 299, 310, 312, 320, 351
Wetlands Reserve Program, 299
Wildlife Resources, 239, 270, 283, 299, 315, 351

Negative Population Growth, 69

The Neighborhood Works, 154

NEMO - Oceanographic Data Server, 300

Netherlands
AGRALIN (Agricultural Bibliographic Information System of the Netherlands), 165

CADDET (Centre for the Analysis and Dissemination of Demonstrated Energy Technologies), 183
Centre for Agriculture and Environment, 194

Nevada
Desert Research Institute, 115, 209

New England Wild Flower Society, 300

New Forests Project, 141, 301
New Forests News, 141

New Hampshire, 252, 301
Department of Environmental Services, 301
Fish and Game Department, 301
Hubbard Brook Experimental Forest, 252

New Jersey
EPA-R2-PRESS (Mailing list), 46
Marine Mammal Stranding Center, 277
Morris Parks and Land Conservancy, 285
New Jersey Department of Environmental Protection, 302
New Jersey Department of Fish, Game and Wildlife, 302
Princeton University's Center for Energy & Environmental Studies, 320

New Mexico
New Mexico Wilderness Alliance, 302
New Mexico Wildlife Association, 302

News, Environmental *see* **Information, research and news**

Newsgroups--, 2, 4, 85-87, 91, 97, 101

Newsletters
Distribution, 103

New York
Association for Reduction, Reuse and Recycling, 303
Columbia Earth Institute, 191, 200
Cornell Students for the Ethical Treatment of Animals, 105
Cornell University, Center for the Environment, 204
Department of Environmental Conservation, 167, 303
Environmental Science and Forestry at SUNY, 227
ENVIRONMENT-L, 42
EPA-R2-PRESS (Mailing list), 46
Hudson-R (Discussion group), 57
Messinger Woods Wildlife Care and Education Center, 279

New Zealand
REEL (Discussion group), 71

NOAA *see* **National Oceanic and Atmospheric Administration**

Non-Ionizing Radiation
Bioelectromagnetics Society, 179
Electromagnetics Forum, 120

Nonpoint Source Pollution Information (Discussion group), 65

North American Agreement on Environmental Cooperation, 200

North American Bat Conservation Partnership, 176

North American Bird Banding Program, 16, 180

North Atlantic Treaty Organization *see* **NATO**

North Carolina
North Carolina Coastal Federation, 304
North Carolina Department of Environment and Natural Resources, 304
North Carolina Water Quality (Discussion group), 64

North Cascades Conservation Council, 305

North Dakota
North Dakota Atmospheric Resource Board, 305
University of North Dakota, 218
Energy & Environmental Research Center, 218

Northeast Alternative Vehicle Consortium, 305

Northeast Sustainable Energy Association, 305

Northern Michigan Wildlife Rehabilitation, 306

Northern Prairie Wildlife Research Center, 306

Norway
Bellona Foundation, 178
Center for International Climate and Environmental Research, Oslo, 191

Nova Scotia
Bear River Solar Aquatics Wastewater Treatment Facility, 177
Ecology Action Centre, 213
Nova Scotia Bird Society, 307

Nuclear research
Bellona Foundation, 178
Catalog of Known and Putative Nuclear Explosions, 187
Clari.tw.nuclear, 92
CTB-NEWS (Discussion group), 26
gov.us.fed.nrc.announce, 93
gov.us.topic.energy.nuclear, 94

Oak Ridge National Laboratories, 313
Carbon Dioxide Information Analysis Center, 187
Energy Crops Forum, 123
ORNL Review, 143

Oceania Project, 307

Oceanic, 307-308

Oceanic Planetary Boundary Layer Laboratory, 308

Ocean Information Center, 307

Oceanography *see also* **Marine biology, Marine ecosystems, Marine environments**
Australian Oceanographic Data Centre, 175
DiveWeb, 210
Earthwatch Radio, 48, 224
Harbor Branch Oceanographic Institution, 246
HydroWire, 133
International Oceanographic Foundation, 260
Jam (Discussion group), 61
Japan Marine Science and Technology Center, 268
Mediterranean Oceanic Database, 279
National Oceanic and Atmospheric Administration, 92, 96, 141, 203, 304
NATO SACLANT, 296
NEMO (Oceanographic Data Server), 300
Oceanic, 307
Oceanic Planetary Boundary Layer Laboratory, 308
Ocean News, 142

Oceanography
Ocean Process Analysis Laboratory, 308
Our Living Oceans Annual Report, 143
sci.geo.oceanography, 101
Scripps Institution of Oceanography, 300, 330
Sea Wind, 148
Texas A & M University Oceanography, 342

Oceanography Society
Oceanography, 142
TOS Newsletter, 154

Ocean Process Analysis Laboratory, 308

Ocean Voice International, 148, 308
  Sea Wind, 148

Ohio
  Department of Natural Resources, 309
  Ohio Environmental Protection Agency, 309
  Ohio State University, 183
    Byrd Polar Research Center, 183
  Ohio Wildlife Center, 310
  Wildlife Notes, 158
  Wild Ohio, 158

Oil and petroleum
  gov.us.topic.nat-resources.oil-gas, 97
  OILGASLAW-L (Discussion group), 66
  sci.geo.petroleum, 101

Okefenokee Swamp Natural Education Center, 310

Oklahoma
  Department of Wildlife Conservation, 310

OPAL *see* **Ocean Process Analysis Laboratory**

Open University Ecology and Conservation Research Group, 311

Oregon
  Department of Fish and Wildlife, 270, 312
  Department of Forestry, 312, 354
  EXTOXNET, 232
  rrr-oregon-l (Discussion group), 73

Organization and the Natural Environment (Discussion group), 66

ORNL *see* **Oak Ridge National Laboratories**

Orphaned Wildlife Rehabilitation Society, 313

Our Environment, 143

Oxford Forestry Institute, 313

Ozone layer
  Alfred Wegener Institute for Polar and Marine Research, 167
  Delta, 114
  Environmental Treaties and Resource Indicators, 228
  Ozone (Discussion group), 66
  Ozone Action, 314
  Stratospheric Ozone Home Page, EPA, 159
  WMO Antarctic Ozone Bulletins, 159
  World Meteorologic Organization, 364

Pacific Forestry Center (Canada), 314

Pacific Northwest Pollution Prevention Resource Center, 314

Pacific Rim Consortium in Energy, Combustion, and the Environment, 315

Parks and recreation
  California Environmental Resources Evaluation System (CERES), 184
  Colorado Department of Natural Resources, 199
  gov.us.topic.nat-resources.parks, 97
  Greenbelt Alliance, 243
  Indiana Department of Natural Resources, 255
  Jane Goodall Institute, 267
  Maine Department of Conservation, 275
  Maryland Department of Natural Resources, 277
  National Parks, 139
  National Parks & Conservation Association, 139, 292
  Nebraska Wildlife Resources, 299
  ParkNet - The National Park Service, 315
  Trust for Public Land, 346
  World Conservation Monitoring Centre, 22, 363
  Yellowstone Journal, 160

Partners for Environmental Progress, 205

Patuxent Wildlife Research Center, 315

PAWS Wildlife Center, 251

Pennsylvania
  Hawk Mountain Sanctuary, 248
  pa.environment, 97
  Penn State University Weather Pages, 316
  Pennsylvania Department of Environmental Protection, 316
  Resources Council, 316

Peregrine Falcons at the University of Calgary, 316

Peregrine Fund, 317

Pesticide Action Network, 144, 317
  PANUPS (Pesticide Action Network North America), 144

Pesticides
  Crop Protection Institute, 205
  DRIFTERS (Discussion group), 29
  EPA-PEST (Mailing list), 45
  EXTOXNET, 232
  PANUPS (Pesticide Action Network North America), 144
  Pesticide Action Network North America, 144, 317

ToxList (Discussion group), 77
Wright's PestLaw, 366

Pest management
National Agricultural Pest Information System, 287
Predator_Watch (Discussion group), 70
Resistant Pest Management Newsletter, 147
WDAMAGE (Discussion group), 82

Physicians for the Environment *see* **NAPEnet**

Pinecrest: An Adventure Living Off the Utility Grid, 317

Piping Plover Guardian Program, 318

The Planet, 116, 144

PlanetKeepers, 318

PLANT-IT, 318

Politics and government
alt.politics.greens, 89
Campus Green Vote, 29, 190
ECOPOLITICS (Discussion group), 32
Ecovote Online, 215
Green Parties of North America, 244
Journal of Political Ecology JPE, 136
League of Conservation Voters National Environmental Scorecard, 136, 271
Zero Waste America, 367

Pollution *see* **Air pollution, Soil pollution,** *or* **Water pollution**

Pollution Prevention
Michigan Pulp and Paper Pollution Prevention Program, 281
National Pollution Prevention Center for Higher Education, 292
National Society for Clean Air, 294
Office of Pollution Prevention and Toxics, EPA, 225
Pacific Northwest Pollution Prevention Resource Center, 314

Ponds *see* **Lakes and ponds**

Population
Battelle Seattle Research Group, 177
Center for International Earth Science Information (CIESIN), 191
ECOCITIES (Discussion group), 30
Environmental Reviews, 125

Environmental Treaties and Resource Indicators, 228
Global Environment Outlook Project, 240
People and the Planet, 144
POPENV-L (Discussion group), 68
POPULATION (Discussion group), 69
POPULATION-NEWS (Mailing list), 69
Union of Concerned Scientists, 347

Prairie Ecosystem Study Project, 319

Princeton University's Center for Energy & Environmental Studies, 320

Progressive Animal Welfare Society, 251

Project Wild
Habitats Newsletter, 131

Project Wildlife, 145, 320

Protected Areas Virtual Library, 320

Protected Marine Species, 321

Protected Plantscape Biological Control List (Discussion group), 69

Psychology and sociology
Columbia Earth Institute, 191, 200
COMPSY-L (Discussion group), 25
ECOPSYCHOLOGY (Discussion group), 32
Ecopsychology On-line, 119
ENVBEH-L (Discussion group), 37
Environmental and Societal Impacts Group, 220
ENVTECSOC (Discussion group), 44
GENERAL (Discussion group), 51
Human Dimensions of Global Environmental Change (Discussion group), 57
International Human Dimensions Programme on Global Environmental Change, 133, 259
IRNES (Discussion group), 59
Native Americans and the Environment, 188, 295
Terra Nova - Nature & Culture, 152

Puerto Rico
EPA-R-PRESS (Mailing list), 46

Puget Sound Green Pages, 321

Quality, Environment, Safety in Management (Discussion group), 70

Radiation *see* **Atmospheric Radiation, Non-Ionizing Radiation**

Radioactive substances
  NIREX, 303
  Office of Civilian Radioactive Waste
    Management (DOE), 208

Raincoast Conservation Society, 321

Rainforest Action Network, 322

Rainforests *see* **Tropical forests**

Rainforest Workshop, 322

Raptor Center (University of Minnesota), 323
  Raptor Release, 146

Raptors *see* **Birds**

REACT *see* **Renewable Energy Association of
  Central Texas**

Recreation *see* **Parks and recreation**

Recycled Pulp and Paper Coalition, 323

Recycling
  Advanced Recovery, 163
  alt.building.recycle, 88
  Brown is Green, 181
  Bureau of International Recycling, 181
  CERES-L (Discussion group), 21
  ECDM (Discussion group), 30
  EcoWeb, 215
  Global Recycling Network, Inc., 242
  gov.us.topic.environment.waste, 95
  GRNSCH-L (Discussion group), 54
  Illinois Recycling Association, 254
  New York State Association for Reduction,
    Reuse and Recycling, 303
  Recycled Pulp and Paper Coalition, 323
  Recycling World, 146
  rrr-oregon-l (Discussion group), 73
  WASTENOT (Discussion group), 80
  Waste Prevention Association, 355

Reef Relief, 146, 324

**Regional Environmental Center for Central and
  Eastern Europe**
  *The Bulletin of the Regional Environmental
    Center*, 108
  ENVBUS-L (Discussion group), 37
  ENVCEE-L (Discussion group), 38
  ENVEVENTS-L (Discussion group), 39
  Waste Prevention Association, 355

Religious aspects *see* **Ethics, Environmental**

Remediation *see* **Bioremediation or Environmental
  Contamination and Cleanup**

*Remediation Technologies Screening Matrix and
  Reference Guide*, 233

Renewable Energy
  alt.energy.renewable, 88
  Appropriate Technology for Community and
    Environment, 171
  Arbeitsgemeinschaft ERNEUERBARE ENERGIE,
    172
  CADDET (Centre for the Analysis and
    Dissemination of Demonstrated Energy
    Technologies), 183
  Energies, 123
  Energy Efficiency & Renewable Energy
    (Department of Energy), 208
  International Solar Center, 263
  International Solar Energy Society, 264
  Midwest Renewable Energy Association, 281
  National Renewable Energy Laboratory, 293
  x-news (Discussion group), 84

Renewable Energy Association of Central Texas
  (REACT), 325

Renewable resources
  Center for Renewable Energy and Sustainable
    Technology (CREST), 192

Reptiles and Amphibians
  AMP (Discussion group), 13
  Amphibian & Conservation, 105
  AMPHIBIANDECLINE (Discussion group), 13
  Declining Amphibian Populations Task Force, 128,
    206
  The FROGGY Page, 237
  Froglog, 128, 206
  Horned Lizard Conservation Society, 251

Resource and Environmental Economics List
  (Discussion group), 71

Resource Renewal Institute (RRI), 325

Restore America's Estuaries, 326

Rhode Island
  University of Rhode Island, 24
  Coastal Resources Center, 24

Riparian Environments
  Southwestern Riparian Expertise Directory, 338

Rivers and Estuaries
American Rivers, 170
Earth Observing System Amazon Project, 211
Hudson-R (Discussion group), 57
Idaho Rivers United Newsletter, 133
International Rivers Network, 159, 262
Lower Rio Grande Ecosystem Initiative, 274
Mississippi River Watch, 250
National Estuary Program, 290
Potomac Conservancy, 319
Restore America's Estuaries, 326
River Network (Discussion group), 72
San Francisco Estuary Institute, 327
sci.geo.rivers+lakes, 101
Verde River Watershed, 353
World Rivers Review, 159

Rocky Mountains, U.S., 361

Royal Botanical Gardens (Canada), 20

Royal Society of Canada
Delta, 114

RRI *see* **Resource Renewal Institute**

Russia
International Otter Survival Fund, 261

Safety, Environmental
Federal Emergency Management Agency (FEMA), 233
Office of Solid Waste and Emergency, 225
Response, EPA, 225
SAFETY (Discussion group), 73

Salato Wildlife Education Center, 270

The Salmon Page, 327

San Francisco Estuary Institute, 327

San Gorgonio Volunteer Association, 327

Santa Barbara County Air Pollution Control District, 142, 328

Savannah River Site, 328

Save Our Everglades, 328

Save Our Seas, 150, 329

Save the Manatee Club, 329

Save the Rhino International, 329

Science Advisory Board
EPA-SAB (Mailing list), 45

Scotland
scot.environment, 101
Scottish Environment Protection Agency, 330
Skye Environmental Centre, 261, 333

Scripps Institution of Oceanography, 300, 330

SEACC *see* **Southeast Alaska Conservation Council**

Sea Shepherd Conservation Society, 74, 330

SeaWorld, 331

SEEL *see* **Sustainable Earth Electronic Library**

Sefton Coast Life Project, 331

Sempervirens Fund, 332

Sewage
gov.us.topic.environment.water, 96
SEWER-LIST (Discussion group), 75
Wastewater-modelling-digest (Discussion group), 80

Sewage treatment plants
SEWER-LIST (Discussion group), 75

Sierra Club
alt.org.sierra-club, 88
The Planet, 116, 144
Sierra - The Sierra Club Magazine, 149
Sierra Solar Systems, 332

Silva Forest Foundation, 332

Simple Living Network, 149, 333

Skies Above Foundation, 333

Skogforsk, 333

Skye Environmental Centre, 261, 333

Smithsonian Institution
Biological Conservation Newsletter, 108
Conservation and Research Center, 26, 334
CONSLINK (Discussion group), 26

Snow Leopard Trust, International, 262

Society for Ecological Restoration, 334

Society of American Foresters, 74, 334

Society of Chemical Industry, 111
  Chemistry & Industry, 255, 163

Society of Environmental Journalists, 223

Society of Wetland Scientists, 157, 335

Sociology *see* **Psychology and sociology**

Soil conservation, 309
  Centre for Development and Environment, 194
  SOILS-L (Discussion group), 75

Soil pollution
  Bureau of Transportation Statistics, 182
  National Institute for Environmental Studies, 291
  roadsalt (Discussion group), 73

Soils
  AGRIC-L (Discussion group), 11
  Coweeta LTER Site, 205
  IRRIGATION-L (Discussion group), 59
  SOILS-L (Discussion group), 75
  Soil Science Society of America, 75

Solar activity
  Hiraiso Solar Terrestrial Research Center, 250

Solar Cooking Archive, 335

Solar energy
  AE (Discussion group), 9
  alt.solar.photovoltaic, 89
  alt.solar.thermal, 89
  American Solar Energy Society, 170
  Bear River Solar Aquatics Wastewater Treatment
    Facility, 177
  IASEE-L (Discussion group), 58
  IEA Solar Heating and Cooling Programme, 258
  International Solar Center, 263
  International Solar Energy Society, 264
  Mr. Solar Home Page, 286
  sci.energy, 99-100
  Solar Energy Network, 335
  Solar Energy Research & Education Foundation,
    192
  Solar Energy Society of Canada Inc., 336
  solar_utilities (Discussion group), 75

Solar Energy Deployment and Utilization List, 75

Solid Waste
  Office of Solid Waste and Emergency Response,
    EPA, 225
  The Solid Waste Association of North America,
    336
  Yale Working Papers on Solid Waste Policy, 160

South America *see also* **Latin America**
  Base De Dados Tropical, 17, 176, 179
  Charles Darwin Research Station, 195
  Earth Observing System Amazon Project, 211

South Carolina
  Department of Natural Resources, 336
  Savannah River Site, 328

South Dakota
  Parks & Wildlife Foundation, 337

Southeast Alaska Conservation Council, 330

Southeastern Raptor Rehabilitation Center, 337

Southern Africa Environment Page, 337

Southwestern Riparian Expertise Directory, 338

Standards and Codes
  ACRE Project, 175
  Code of Federal Regulations, 48, 93, 199, 231, 349,
    366
  EnviroText, 231
  Federal Geographic Data Committee, 233
  ISO (Discussion group), 60
  ISO- Information Center, 267
  QUEST (Discussion group), 70
  U.S. Army Corps of Engineers-Sacramento District,
    349
  U.S. Code, 199, 349-350
  U.S. Code, Title 16, Conservation, 350

State and Territorial Air Pollution Program
  Administrators, 338

Sterling Pulp Chemicals, Ltd., 198

Students for Environmental and Ecological
  Development, 339

Surfrider Foundation USA, 339

Sustainability
  Environmental Alliance for Senior Involvement,
    220
  Global Environmental Options, 240
  SUSTAINABLE Times, 152

Sustainable agriculture
  AGRIC-L (Discussion group), 11
  Alternative Agriculture News, 104
  alt.sustainable.agriculture, 89
  BEE-L (Discussion group), 348
  Center for Sustainable Agricultural Systems
    Newsletter, 111

Centre for Agriculture and Environment, 194
International Bee Research Association, 256
Montanas Verdes, 285
Napa County Resource Conservation District, 287
Sustainable Agriculture Newsletter, 151
University of Florida's Range Science Program, 348
Water Management Research Laboratory, 356

Sustainable development
alt.society.sustainable, 89
BIOREGIONAL (Discussion group), 18
CITNET-LIST (Discussion group), 23
Developing Ideas Digest, 115
Earth Council, 210
Earth Pledge Foundation, 211
EcoNews Africa, 119
Eco-Village Network, 215
International Institute for Sustainable Development, 115, 117, 151, 254
International Marinelife Alliance, 260
ISEA-L (Discussion group), 60
National Councils for Sustainable Development, 289
Resource Renewal Institute, 325
Sustainable Developments, 151
World Business Council for Sustainable Development, 362

Sustainable Earth Electronic Library, 104

Sustainable energy
BIOENERGY (Discussion group), 17
Center for Renewable Energy and Sustainable Technology (CREST), 192
DIGESTION (Discussion group), 28
GASIFICATION (Discussion group), 51
Northeast Sustainable Energy Association, 305

Sustainable forestry
American Forestry, 169
FOREST (Discussion group), 50
International Union of Forestry Research Organizations, 264
Skogforsk, 333
Sustainable Forestry Directory, 339
Sustainable Minnesota, 151, 282

Sweden
Skogforsk, 333

Switzerland
Swiss Federal Institute of Technology, 239
University of Berne, Centre for Development and Environment, 194

Taiga Rescue Network, 340

Tall Timbers Research Station, 340

Tarkine: Wilderness Heritage, 341

Tasmania
Tarkine: Wilderness for Heritage, 341

Taylor Engineering, *Compliance Online*, 113

TCP/IP, 1-2

Teaming with Wildlife, 139, 341, 351

Tennessee
University of Tennessee, Knoxville, Center for Environmental Biotechnology, 189

Texas
A & M University Oceanography, 342
Environmental Center, 342
GreenBeat!, 129, 342
Horned Lizard Conservation Society, 251
Marine Mammal Stranding Network, 343
Natural Resource Conservation Commission, 343
Renewable Energy Association of Central Texas (REACT), 325
Rice University, Center for Conservation Biology, 188
Texas Water Resources, 153
Texas Water Savers, 153

Thailand
Wild Animal Rescue Foundation of Thailand, 358

Thoreau Institute
Electronic Drummer, 121

Tiger Information Center, 344

Timber Wolf Information Network, 344

Tongass National Forest, 330

Tourism *see* **Ecotourism**

Toxicology
bionet.toxicology, 90
Chemical Industry Institute of Toxicology, 196
EPA-TOX (Mailing list), 45
EPA-TRI (Maling list), 45
EXTOXNET, 232
Toxicology & Ecotoxicology News, 154
Toxics Release Inventory, 344
ToxList (Discussion group), 77
tws-wtwg (Discussion group), 78

Toxics Release Inventory, 344

Transportation
　　Bureau of Transportation Statistics, 182
　　CATF Review, 111, 194
　　Centre for Alternative Transportation Fuels, 111,
　　　　194
　　EV (Electric Vehicle discussion list), 47
　　Green Guide to Cars and Trucks, 168
　　Northeast Alternative Vehicle Consortium, 305

Travel *see* **Ecotourism**

Treaties and Resource Indicators, 228

Tree Canada Foundation, 345

Trees
　　International Society of Arboriculture, 135, 263
　　Journal of Arboriculture, 135
　　National Arborist Association, 288
　　National Register of Big Trees, 169
　　PLANT-IT, 318
　　Society of Municipal Arborists, 334
　　Tree Canada Foundation, 345

Trends: A Compendium of Data on Global Change,
　　186

Tropical Biology Magazine, 312

Tropical ecosystems
　　Mangrove (Discussion group), 62
　　Organization for Tropical Studies, 312
　　RainForest (Discussion group), 71
　　RainForest-M (Discussion group), 71
　　Sylvanet (Discussion group), 76
　　*Worldwide Rainforest/Biodiversity Campaign
　　　　News Internet Archives*, 159

Tropical Forestry Resource Group, 313

Tropical forests
　　International Canopy Network, 257
　　Montanas Verdes, 285
　　RainForest (Discussion group), 71
　　Rainforest Action Network, 322
　　Rainforest Foundation International, 322
　　RainForest-M (Discussion group), 71
　　Sylvanet (Discussion group), 76
　　Tarkine: Wilderness for Heritage, 341
　　Tropical Rain Forest in Surinam, 345

Trumbull Land Trust, 346

Trust for Public Land, 346

Tundras
　　ITEX (Discussion group), 60

UCLA Center for Clean Technology, 347

UNESCO Mabnet Programme (Discussion group), 62

Uniform Resource Locators (URLs), 3

Union of Concerned Scientists, 347

United Kingdom
　　British Atmospheric Data Center, 180
　　Centre for the Analysis and Dissemination of
　　　　Demonstrated Energy Technologies, 109, 183
　　ECN (Environmental Change Network), 212
　　The Environment Council, 229
　　GENIE Project (Global Environmental Network for
　　　　Information Exchange in the U.K.), 238
　　Institute for Terrestrial Ecology, 256
　　Institute of Freshwater Ecology, 256
　　John Muir Trust, 269
　　Lincolnshire Trust, 272
　　Milton Keynes Wildlife Hospital, 281
　　National Seal Sanctuary, 294
　　Natural History Book Service, 303
　　NatureNet, 299
　　Oxford Forestry Institute, 313
　　Recycling World, 146
　　Royal Forestry Society of England, 326
　　scot.environment, 101
　　uk.environment, 52, 102, 125, 229
　　uk.environment.conservation, 102
　　Wildlife Trusts, 361

United Nations
　　Central European Environmental Data Request
　　　　Facility (CEDAR), 193
　　ECO: The Climate Action Network Newsletter, 117
　　CITES-L (Discussion group), 22
　　Earth Negotiations Bulletin, 117
　　Environment Programme (UNEP), 348
　　Global Research Information Database (GRID), 242
　　International Satellite Land Surface Climatology
　　　　Project, 262

United States Government
　　Bureau of Land Management, 93, 182, 209
　　Bureau of Reclamation, 182, 209
　　Department of Agriculture, 49, 94, 96, 273, 356
　　　　Forest Service, 94, 96, 236, 314, 350
　　　　gov.us.fed.usda.announce, 94
　　Department of Commerce, 92, 234
　　　　Fedworld, 234

Department of Defense, 206-207, 249
  Defense Environmental Network & Information Exchange, 206
  Defense Environmental Restoration Program, 207
  Defense Technical Information Center, 207
  Environmental Cleanup Home Page, 207
Department of Energy, 92, 94, 112, 134, 167, 171-172, 181, 208, 235, 249
  Albany Research Center, 167
  Alternative Fuels Data Center, 208
  Ames Laboratory, 171
  Argonne National Laboratory, 172
  Biofuels Information Center, 208
  Energy Efficiency and Renewable Energy, 92, 208
  Energy Information Administration, 92, 208
  Environmental Measurements Laboratory, 208, 224
  gov.us.fed.doe.announce, 92
  gov.us.topic.energy.misc, 94
  Initiatives in Environmental Technology Investment, 134
  Office of Civilian Radioactive Waste Management, 208
  Office of Environmental Management, 208, 224
  Office of Environment, Safety and Health, 208
  Office of Fossil Energy, 92, 208
Department of Public Health, 199
  Agency for Toxic Substances & Disease Registry, 165, 189
  Center for Disease Control, 165, 189
Department of the Interior, 93, 97, 209
  gov.us.fed.doi.announce, 93
  gov.us.topic.nat-resources.oil-gas, 97
  gov.us.topic.nat-resources.parks, 97
Environmental Protection Agency, 36, 45, 91, 93-96, 130, 184, 216, 225, 231, 309, 366
  ENVIRONB-L (Enviro-Newsbrief), 41
  EPA-Federal Register (Mailing list), 45
  EPA-GRANTS (Discussion group), 45
  EPA-PRESS (Mailing list), 46
  EPA-R2-PRESS (Mailing list), 46
  gov.us.fed.epa.announce, 93
  gov.us.topic.environment.air, 95
  gov.us.topic.environment.announce, 95
  gov.us.topic.environment.misc, 95
Federal Energy Regulatory Commission, 93, 95
  gov.us.topic.energy.utilities, 95
Fish & Wildlife Service, 51, 93, 97, 209, 248
  Endangered Species Bulletin, 122
  gov.us.topic.nat-resources.wildlife, 97
General Accounting Office, 238
Geological Survey, 172, 209, 212, 266, 295, 351
Gap Analysis Program, 238

Global Environment Outlook Project, 240
National Biological Service, 297

Universities *see* **Colleges and Universities** *or* by State

Urban Agriculture Notes, 198

Urban areas
  Chicago Wilderness, 196
  City Farmer, 198
  ECOCITIES (Discussion group), 30
  PedNet (Discussion group), 67
  Society of Municipal Arborists, 334
  Terrain: A Journal of the Built & Natural Environments, 152
  TNW Online, 154
  Urban Forest Ecosystems Institute, 348
  URBWLF-L (Discussion group), 78

Urban Wildlife (Discussion group), 78

URLs *see* **Uniform Resource Locators**

USACHPPM Hazardous and Medical Waste Program, 349

U. S. Army Center for Health Promotion and Prevention Medicine *see* **USACHPPM**

U. S. Army Corps of Engineers, Seattle District, 349

U. S. Code, 199, 349-350

U. S. Code, Title 16, Conservation, 350

USDA Forest Service, 236, 350

Usenet Newsgroups *see* **Newsgroups**

US FWS Division of Habitat Conservation - National Wetlands Inventory, 350

U.S. Geological Survey Earth and Environmental Science, 351

Utah
  Center for Water Resources Research, 106
  Department of Environmental Quality, 274, 280, 351
  Department of Wildlife Resources, 351
  Matheson Wetlands Preserve, 278
  Public Lands, 172, 182, 200, 275, 352
  Water Research Laboratory, 106

Vegetarianism
  Vegan Action, 352

Vegan Outreach, 352

Verde River Watershed, 353

Vermont
Agency of Natural Resources, 147, 353
Reflections on the Environment, 147, 353
Vermont Land Trust, 353

Virginia
Holland Island Preservation Foundation, 251
Natural Heritage Program, 282, 284, 354
Potomac Conservancy, 319
University of Virginia, 215
EcoWeb, 215
Virginia Coast Reserve LTER, 353
Virginia Department of Forestry, 354
Virginia Tech, Fish and Wildlife Information
Exchange, 234

Virgin Islands
EPA-Rw-PRESS (Mailing list), 46

Volunteers in Technical Assistance, 27

Wageningen Agricultural University, 165

Walk in the Woods, 354

Walton, Izaak, League of America, 267

Washington
Energy Ideas Clearinghouse, 218
Environmental Resources, 354
North Cascades Conservation Council, 305
Pacific-biosnet (Discussion group), 67
Pacific Northwest Pollution Prevention Research
Center, 314
Puget Sound Green Pages, 321
Puget Sound On Line, 321
Puget Sound Water Quality Action Team, 150
Walk in the Woods, 354

Washington, D.C.
American University, 74
Eco-Sense, 74
George Washington University, 245
Green University Initiative, 245

Waste management
EM Online, 121, 166
gov.us.topic.environment.waste, 95
Pacific Northwest Pollution Prevention Resource
Center, 314
RE-USE (Discussion group), 72
Savannah River Site, 328

sci.environment.waste, 100
Solid Waste Association of North America, 336
WASTE (Discussion group), 79
WASTENOT (Discussion group), 80
World Resource Foundation, 364

Waste minimization
Battelle Seattle Research Group, 177
Cygnus Group, 205
Ecocycle, 118
Illinois Recycling Association, 254
Journal of Industrial Ecology, 136
New York State Association for ReductionRE-USE
(Discussion group), 72
Reuse and Recycling, 100, 303
rrr-oregon-l (Discussion group), 73

Waste Prevention Association, 355
Zero Emissions Research Initiative, 367

Waste Prevention Association, 355

Wastewater
Bear River Solar Aquatics Wastewater Treatment
Facility, 177
Texas On-Site Insights, 153
WaterWorld, 357

WATER-AND-SANITATION-APPLIED-RESEARCH
(Discussion group), 80

Water conservation
Bureau of Reclamation, 182, 209
Centre for Development and Environment, 194
IRRIGATION-L (Discussion group), 59
Living Gently Quarterly, 137
River Network (Discussion group), 72
Sierra - The Sierra Club Magazine, 149
Texas Water Savers, 153
TRICKLE-L (Discussion group), 77
Waterfront, 355
World Wide Water, 365

Water Distribution Systems (Discussion group), 81

Water Environment Federation, 157, 355

Waterfront, 355

Water Management Research Laboratory, 356

Water pollution
International Oceanographic Foundation, 260
Minnesota Pollution Control Agency, 282
National Institute for Environmental Studies, 291
NPSINFO (Discussion group), 65
roadsalt (Discussion group), 73

Terrene Institute, 342
UCLA Center for Clean Technology, 347

Water quality
AFWATER (Discussion group), 10
American Water Works Association, 170
Aquarius, 106
BCWATERSHED (Discussion group), 16
CA-WATER (Discussion group), 20
ca.water, 91
Coweeta LTER Site, 205
DIALOG-AGUA-L (Discussion group), 28
Environmental and Societal Impacts Group, 220
EPA-WATER (Mailing list), 45
Geological Survey, U.S., 351
GLIN-EDUCATION (Discussion group), 53
gov.us.topic.environment.water, 96
Kentucky Water Watch, 270
National SeaGrant Depository, 209
North Carolina Water Quality (Discussion group), 64
Office of Water, EPA, 225
sci.geo.hydrology, 100
Sound Waves, 150
U.S. Water News, 155
WATER-ON-LINE (Discussion group), 81
Water-Quality (Discussion group), 81
WEF Reporter, 157

Water Research Network, 28

Watershed management
Napa County Resource Conservation District, 287
Watershed Management Council, 156, 356
Watershed Management Council Newsletter, 156
WATERSHEDSS Water Quality Decision Support System, 356

Watersheds
BCWATERSHED (Discussion group), 16
California Watersheds Projects Inventory, 255
Office of Wetlands, Oceans, and Watersheds, EPA, 225
River Network (Discussion group), 72
Verde River Watershed, 353

Water treatment, 50, 60, 198, 244, 367
ClO$_2$ Water Treatment Resource Center, 198
DIALOG-AGUA-L (Discussion group), 28
WATER-AND-SANITATION-APPLIED-RESEARCH (Discussion group), 80

WaterWorld, 357

Weather *see* **Climate and Climatic Change**

Weather and Global Monitoring, 357

Web *see* **World Wide Web**

Web browsers *see* **World Wide Web browsers**

West Virginia
Habitats - The Growth of a Forest, 246

Wetlands
Chanslor Wetlands Wildlife Project, 195
ELI-WETLANDS (Discussion group), 36
Endangered Species & Wetlands Report, 122
Holland Island Preservation Foundation, 251
Irish Peatland Conservation Council, 266
Matheson Wetlands Preserve, 278
National Wetlands Inventory, 350
Office of Wetlands, Oceans, and Watersheds, EPA, 225
The Salt and the Earth Wetlands Nursery, 327
San Francisco Estuary Institute, 327
Society of Wetland Scientists, 157, 335
U.S. Army Corps of Engineers-Sacramento District, 349
WETLAND-NEWS (Discussion group), 82
Wetlands - The Journal of the Society of Wetland Scientists, 157

Whale and Dolphin Conservation Society, 357

Whale Conservation Institute, 357

Whale Times SeaBed, 358

Whole Systems (Discussion group), 82

Wilderness Act, 253

Wildlands League, 359

Wildlife and wildlife conservation
alt.wolves, 90
AMPHIBIANDECLINE (Discussion group), 13
AUDUBON (Discussion group), 14
Audubon Advisory, 106
Bat Conservation International, 176
Bear Watch, 177
Chanslor Wetlands Wildlife Project, 195
Chilkat Bald Eagle Preserve, 197
CITES-L (Discussion group), 22
Cochrane Ecological Institute/Wildlife Reserve, 198
Declining Amphibian Populations Task Force, 128, 206
Department of Wildlife Ecology (Univ. of Maine), 348
Florida Cooperative Extension Service, 235

Froglog, 128, 206
Hawaii National Wildlife Refuges/Marine Sanctuaries, 247
Heartwood, 250
Houston Audubon Society, 251
Howl - The PAWS Wildlife Center, 251
International Fund for Animal Welfare, 254
International Otter Survival Fund, 261
International Primate Protection League, 261
International Wildlife, 135
International Wildlife Coalition, 158, 265
International Wolf, 135, 265
International Wolf Center, 135, 265
Milton Keynes Wildlife Hospital, 281
Monarch Watch, 284
Mountain Lion Foundation, 286
National Wildlife, 135
National Wildlife Health Center, 295
Nature Conservancy, 248, 297-299
Nature Network, 140
Nebraska Wildlife Resources, 299
New Hampshire Fish and Game Department, 301
New Mexico Wildlife Association, 302
Northern Prairie Wildlife Research Center, 306
Okefenokee Swamp Natural Education Center, 310
Oklahoma Department of Wildlife Conservation, 310
Oregon Department of Fish and Wildlife, 312
Patuxent Wildlife Research Center, 315
Primate Info Net, 319
Raincoast Conservation Society, 321
RainForest (Discussion group), 71
RainForest-M (Discussion group), 71
rec.animals.wildlife, 97
Tarkine: Wilderness for Heritage, 341
Teaming with Wildlife, 139, 341, 351
tws-wtwg (Discussion group), 78
Utah Department of Wildlife Resources, 351
Wildlands League, 359
Wildlife Center of Silicon Valley, 359
Wildlife Notes, 158
Wildlife Preservation Trust International, 360
Wildlife Society, 50, 78, 360
Wildnet (Discussion group), 83
WildNet Africa, 361
WindStar Wildlife Institute, 361
Wisconsin Wildlife Federation, 362
Wolf Haven International, 362
World Conservation Society, 363
World Society for the Protection of Animals, 365
World Wide Fund Global Network, 365
World Wildlife Fund, 366
Yellowstone Journal, 160

Wildlife appreciation
National Watchable Wildlife Program, 140, 294

Windows to Wildlife, 158

Wildlife Center of Silicon Valley, 359

Wildlife Damage Management (Discussion group), 82

Wildlife management
FWIM-L (Discussion group), 50
Wildnet (Discussion group), 83

Wildlife rehabilitation
International Otter Survival Fund, 261
Island Wildlife Natural Care Center, 267
Jardin Gaia, 268
Marine Mammal Center, 277
Mote Marine Laboratory, 285
Namibia Animal Rehabilitation Research and Education Centre, 286
National Seal Sanctuary, 294
National Wildlife Rehabilitators Association, 295
Northern Michigan Wildlife Rehabilitation, 306
North Island Wildlife Recovery Association, 307
Ohio Wildlife Center, 310
Orphaned Wildlife Rehabilitation Society, 313
Otter Habitat and Wildlife Rehab Center, 313
Project Wildlife, 145, 320
Project Wildlife Newsletters, 145
Raptor Rehabilitation of Kentucky, 323
Sarvey Wildlife Center, 328
Save the Manatee Club, 329
Southeastern Raptor Rehabilitation Center, 337
Southern Florida Wildlife Rehabilitation Center, 338
South West Florida Wildlife Rehabilitation, 338 and Conservation Center, 338
Wild Bird Rehabilitation Center, 358
Wildlife Center of Silicon Valley, 359
Wildlife Health (Discussion group), 83
Wildlife Rehabilitation (Discussion group), 84
Wildlife Rescue Association of B.C., 360

Wildlife Society, 50, 78, 360

WildNet Africa, 361

Wild Rockies Slate, 361

Wind energy
AE (Discussion group), 9
American Wind Energy Association, 214
Investigating Wind Energy, 265
Mr. Solar Home Page, 286
sci.energy, 99-100
Wind Energy Weekly, 214

Wisconsin
    National Wildlife Health Center, 295
    Wildlife Federation, 135, 139, 362

Witness Against Lawless Logging, 79

Wolf Haven International, 362

World Bank, 126, 202
    Environment Bulletin, 126
    Environment Matters, 126
    World Climate Research Programme, 128, 363

World Conservation Monitoring Centre
    CITES-L (Discussion group), 22

World Energy Efficiency Association, 364

World Forum for Acoustic Ecology, 364

World Meteorological Organization, 159

World Ocean Circulation Experiment, 307

World Resource Foundation, 364

World Society for the Protection of Animals, 365

World Wide Fund for Nature, 76

World Wide Fund Global Network, 365

Worldwide Rainforest/Biodiversity Campaign News Internet Archives, 159

World Wide Water, 365

World Wide Web, 1-5, 9, 161, 279, 312

World Wide Web browsers, 4

World Wildlife Fund, 366

Wright's PestLaw, 366

WWW *see* **World Wide Web**

Zoe Foundation, 367

GOVERNMENT INSTITUTES ORDER FORM

4 Research Place, Suite 200 • Rockville, MD 20850-3226 • Tel (301) 921-2323 • Fax (301) 921-0264
Internet: *http://www.govinst.com* • E-mail: *giinfo@govinst.com*

3 EASY WAYS TO ORDER

1. Phone: **(301) 921-2323**
Have your credit card ready when you call.

2. Fax: **(301) 921-0264**
Fax this completed order form with your company purchase order or credit card information.

3. Mail: **Government Institutes**
4 Research Place, Suite 200
Rockville, MD 20850-3226
USA
Mail this completed order form with a check, company purchase order, or credit card information.

PAYMENT OPTIONS

❏ **Check** *(payable to Government Institutes in US dollars)*

❏ **Purchase Order** (this order form must be attached to your company P.O. <u>Note</u>: All International orders must be pre-paid.)

❏ **Credit Card** ❏ VISA ❏ ▭ ❏ ▭

Exp.___/___

Credit Card No. _____

Signature _____
Government Institutes' Federal I.D.# is 52-0994196

CUSTOMER INFORMATION

Ship To: (Please attach your Purchase Order)

Name: _____
GI Account# *(7 digits on mailing label)*: _____
Company/Institution: _____
Address: _____
(please supply street address for UPS shipping)
_____
City: _____ State/Province: _____
Zip/Postal Code: _____ Country: _____
Tel: (   ) _____
Fax: (   ) _____
E-mail Address: _____

Bill To: (if different than ship to address)

Name: _____
Title/Position: _____
Company/Institution: _____
Address: _____
(please supply street address for UPS shipping)
_____
City: _____ State/Province: _____
Zip/Postal Code: _____ Country: _____
Tel: (   ) _____
Fax: (   ) _____
E-mail Address: _____

Qty.	Product Code	Title	Price

❏ **New Edition No Obligation Standing Order Program**
Please enroll me in this program for the products I have ordered. Government Institutes will notify me of new editions by sending me an invoice. I understand that there is no obligation to purchase the product. This invoice is simply my reminder that a new edition has been released.

15 DAY MONEY-BACK GUARANTEE
If you're not completely satisfied with any product, return it undamaged within 15 days for a full and immediate refund on the price of the product.

Subtotal_____
MD Residents add 5% Sales Tax_____
Shipping and Handling (see box below)_____
Total Payment Enclosed_____

Within U.S:	**Outside U.S:**
1-4 products: $6/product	Add $15 for each item (Airmail)
5 or more: $3/product	Add $10 for each item (Surface)

SOURCE CODE: BP01

Government Institutes • 4 Research Place, Suite 200 • Rockville, MD 20850
Internet: http://www.govinst.com • E-mail: giinfo@govinst.com

GOVERNMENT INSTITUTES
MINI-CATALOG

PC #	ENVIRONMENTAL TITLES	Pub Date	Price
585	Book of Lists for Regulated Hazardous Substances, 8th Edition	1997	$79
4088	CFR Chemical Lists on CD ROM, 1997 Edition	1997	$125
4089	Chemical Data for Workplace Sampling & Analysis, Single User	1997	$125
512	Clean Water Handbook, 2nd Edition	1996	$89
581	EH&S Auditing Made Easy	1997	$79
587	E H & S CFR Training Requirements, 3rd Edition	1997	$89
4082	EMMI-Envl Monitoring Methods Index for Windows-Network	1997	$537
4082	EMMI-Envl Monitoring Methods Index for Windows-Single User	1997	$179
525	Environmental Audits, 7th Edition	1996	$79
548	Environmental Engineering and Science: An Introduction	1997	$79
578	Environmental Guide to the Internet, 3rd Edition	1997	$59
560	Environmental Law Handbook, 14th Edition	1997	$79
353	Environmental Regulatory Glossary, 6th Edition	1993	$79
625	Environmental Statutes, 1998 Edition	1998	$69
4098	Environmental Statutes Book/Disk Package, 1998 Edition	1997	$208
4994	Environmental Statutes on Disk for Windows-Network	1997	$405
4994	Environmental Statutes on Disk for Windows-Single User	1997	$139
570	Environmentalism at the Crossroads	1995	$39
536	ESAs Made Easy	1996	$59
515	Industrial Environmental Management: A Practical Approach	1996	$79
4078	IRIS Database-Network	1997	$1,485
4078	IRIS Database-Single User	1997	$495
510	ISO 14000: Understanding Environmental Standards	1996	$69
551	ISO 14001: An Executive Repoert	1996	$55
518	Lead Regulation Handbook	1996	$79
478	Principles of EH&S Management	1995	$69
554	Property Rights: Understanding Government Takings	1997	$79
582	Recycling & Waste Mgmt Guide to the Internet	1997	$49
603	Superfund Manual, 6th Edition	1997	$115
566	TSCA Handbook, 3rd Edition	1997	$95
534	Wetland Mitigation: Mitigation Banking and Other Strategies	1997	$75

PC #	SAFETY AND HEALTH TITLES	Pub Date	Price
547	Construction Safety Handbook	1996	$79
553	Cumulative Trauma Disorders	1997	$59
559	Forklift Safety	1997	$65
539	Fundamentals of Occupational Safety & Health	1996	$49
535	Making Sense of OSHA Compliance	1997	$59
563	Managing Change for Safety and Health Professionals	1997	$59
589	Managing Fatigue in Transportation, *ATA Conference*	1997	$75
4086	OSHA Technical Manual, Electronic Edition	1997	$99
598	Project Mgmt for E H & S Professionals	1997	$59
552	Safety & Health in Agriculture, Forestry and Fisheries	1997	$125
613	Safety & Health on the Internet, 2nd Edition	1998	$49
597	Safety Is A People Business	1997	$49
463	Safety Made Easy	1995	$49
590	Your Company Safety and Health Manual	1997	$79

Electronic Product available on CD-ROM or Floppy Disk

PLEASE CALL OUR CUSTOMER SERVICE DEPARTMENT AT (301) 921-2323 FOR A FREE PUBLICATIONS CATALOG.

Government Institutes
4 Research Place, Suite 200 • Rockville, MD 20850-3226
Tel. (301) 921-2323 • FAX (301) 921-0264
E mail: giinfo@govinst.com • Internet: http://www.govinst.com